1985

Science Year

The World Book Science Annual

A Review of Science and Technology
During the 1984 School Year

World Book, Inc.

a Scott Fetzer company

Chicago London Sydney Toronto

Our 20th Edition

Some 20 years ago, we set out to launch a new publication. Our aim was to provide the owners of *World Book* with current, in-depth information on scientific developments and their importance to society. We knew we were off on an interesting adventure, but we didn't know how exciting it would be. For example, the first (1965) edition picked up the space program "Midway to the Moon" and reported on the first U.S. spacewalk. Over the years, *Science Year* has followed the astronauts to the moon and sophisticated satellites to the far reaches of the solar system. In this, our 20th edition, "Probing the Secrets of Atmospheres" summarizes what scientists have learned about the other planets, and whether life might have developed on them.

Science Year has also documented the growing concern about the environment of our own planet with such special reports as "Poisonless Pesticides" (1967), "The Fate of Our Lakes" (1971), and "Laying Waste in America" (1984). The coverage continues for 1985. "How Science Is Saving Wild Animals" tells of the new role zoos are playing in breeding endangered species.

For the most part, the tools of science have become increasingly complex — and expensive — over the past 20 years. The 1965 *Science Year* reported on the debate over spending $300 million to build an atom smasher, 4 miles in circumference, to search for the basic building blocks of matter. Now scientists are proposing a $1-billion accelerator at least 60 miles in circumference. "The New Atom Smashers" in this edition traces the development of bigger and bigger machines to seek out smaller and smaller particles.

Science Year also focuses on the men and women behind the science headlines. Articles on prominent scientists provide readers with a better understanding of how scientists live and work — and just may spark a young reader's interest in a career in science. Among the notables who have been featured are anthropologist Margaret Mead; Jonas Salk, developer of the first polio vaccine; and Norman Borlaug, winner of the Nobel Peace Prize for developing high-yield varieties of wheat. This edition profiles Ruth Patrick, whose lifelong study of rivers has helped fight water pollution.

Looking back over the past editions of *Science Year* provides a fascinating glimpse of some of the most exciting and significant stories of our times: the first transplant of a human heart; the microelectronics revolution; the discovery of pulsars in outer space; and advances in cancer treatment. Whether this is your first *Science Year* or your 20th, we invite you to come along with us as we continue on this exciting and important journey.   [A. Richard Harmet]

Copyright ©1984
World Book, Inc.
Merchandise Mart Plaza,
Chicago, Illinois 60654
Portions of the material contained in this volume are taken from *The World Book Encyclopedia,* Copyright ©1984 by World Book, Inc.
ISBN 0-7166-0585-6
ISSN 0080-7621
Library of Congress Catalog Number: 65-21776

Printed in the United States of America

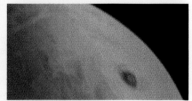

Astronaut Edward H. White II
"Midway to the Moon" (1965)

Close-ups of Mars
"Probing the Secrets of Atmospheres" (1985)

"Poisonless Pesticides" (1967)　　"How Science Is Saving Wild Animals" (1985)　　"Laying Waste in America" (1984)

Science Year profiles
*(clockwise from upper
left):* Norman E. Borlaug,
Margaret Mead, Ruth Patrick,
Jonas Salk

Contents

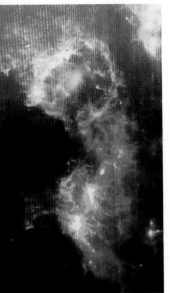

See page 49.

See page 58.

See page 122.

See page 166.

See page 364.

Staff

Publisher
William H. Nault

Editor in Chief
Robert O. Zeleny

Editorial
Executive Editor
A. Richard Harmet

Managing Editor
Wayne Wille

Associate Editor
Darlene R. Stille

Senior Editors
David L. Dreier
Barbara A. Mayes
Jay Myers
Rod Such

Contributing Editors
Sara Dreyfuss
Lynn Gutknecht
Daniel O. Zeff

Research Editor
Irene B. Keller

Index Editor
Claire Bolton

Editorial Assistant
Ethel Matthews

Art
Executive Art Director
William Hammond

Art Director
Roberta Dimmer

Senior Artist
Nikki Conner

Artists
Alice F. Dole
Alexandra Kalantzis

Contributing Artist
Joe W. Gound

Photography Director
John S. Marshall

Senior Photographs Editor
Sandra M. Ozanick

Photographs Editors
Karen M. Koblik
Randi E. Sherman

Research and Services
Director of Research Services
Mary Norton

Director of Educational Services
Susan C. Kilburg

Library Services
Mary Kayaian, Head
Susan O'Donnell

Cartographic Services
H. George Stoll, Head

Product Production
Executive Director
Peter Mollman

Director of Manufacturing
Joseph C. LaCount

Director of Pre-Press
J. J. Stack

Production Control Manager
Barbara Podczerwinski

Assistant Product Manager
Madelyn Krzak

Film Separations Manager
Alfred J. Mozdzen

Film Separations Assistant
Manager
Barbara J. McDonald

Research and Development
Manager
Henry Koval

Editorial Advisory Board

Contributors

Adelman, George, M.S.
Editorial Consultant and Editor
[*Neuroscience*]

Alderman, Michael H., M.D.
Professor of Medicine and Public
Health
Cornell University Medical Center
[*Medicine, Internal;*
Public Health;
Close-Up, Medicine]

Andrews, Peter J., M.S.
Free-Lance Writer, Biochemist
[*Chemistry;*
Choosing the Right Adhesive]

Auerbach, Stanley I., Ph.D.
Director, Environmental
Sciences Division
Oak Ridge National Laboratory
[*Ecology*]

Augee, Michael L., Ph.D.
Senior Lecturer
University of New South Wales
[*Marsupial*]

Beichman, Charles A., Ph.D.
Senior Scientist
Jet Propulsion Laboratory
[*A New View of the Universe*]

Bell, William J., Ph.D.
Professor of Biology
University of Kansas
[*Zoology*]

Belton, Michael J. S., Ph.D.
Astronomer
Kitt Peak National Observatory
[*Astronomy, Solar System*]

Bierman, Howard, B.E.E.
Senior Editor
Electronics Magazine
[*Electronics*]

Black, John H., Ph.D.
Associate Professor of Astronomy
Steward Observatory
University of Arizona
[*Astronomy, Galactic*]

Brett, Carlton E., Ph.D.
Assistant Professor
Department of Geological Sciences
University of Rochester
[*Earth Sciences, Paleontology*]

Coppens, Alan B., Ph.D.
Associate Professor of Physics
Naval Postgraduate School
[*Sound;*
Ultrasound]

Covault, Craig
Space Technology Editor
Aviation Week Magazine
[*Space Exploration;*
Close-Up, Space Exploration]

Cromie, William J., B.S.
Executive Director
Council for the Advancement of
Science Writing
[*Computers That Give Advice*]

Dewey, Russell A., Ph.D.
Assistant Professor of Psychology
Georgia Southern College
[*Psychology*]

Free, John R., B.A.
Senior Editor
Popular Science Magazine
[*Close-Up, Electronics*]

Gates, W. Lawrence, Sc.D.
Professor and Chairman
Department of Atmospheric Sciences
Oregon State University
[*Earth Sciences, Meteorology*]

Goldhaber, Paul, D.D.S.
Dean and Professor of Periodontology
Harvard School of Dental Medicine
[*Medicine, Dentistry*]

Gump, Frank E., M.D.
Professor of Surgery
Columbia University
[*Medicine, Surgery*]

Hartl, Daniel L., Ph.D.
Professor of Genetics
Washington University School of
Medicine
[*Genetics*]

Hester, Thomas R., Ph.D.
Professor of Anthropology and
Director
Center for Archaeological Research
University of Texas, San Antonio
[*Archaeology, New World*]

Higdon, Hal, B.A.
Free-Lance Writer
[*High-Tech Athletes*]

Jennings, Feenan D., B.S.
Director
Sea Grant Program
Texas A&M University
[*Earth Sciences, Oceanography*]

Johnson, Diane W., B.A.
Information Specialist
University of Colorado
[*Camping Out with Computers*]

Jones, William G., A.M.L.S.
Assistant University Librarian
University of Illinois, Chicago Circle
[*Books of Science*]

Kaplan, Marc S., B.A.
Editor
American Technical Society
[*What's New in Telephones*]

Katz, Paul, M.D.
Assistant Professor of Medicine
Georgetown University Medical
Center
[*Immunology*]

Kay, Robert W., Ph.D.
Associate Professor
Cornell University
[*Earth Sciences, Geology*]

King, Lauriston R., Ph.D.
Deputy Director
Sea Grant Program
Texas A&M University
[*Earth Sciences, Oceanography*]

Lamberg, Lynne, M.A.
Free-Lance Medical Journalist
[*The Skin We Live In*]

Lamberg, Stanford, M.D.
Chief of Dermatology
Baltimore City Hospitals and
Associate Professor
Johns Hopkins University
School of Medicine
[*The Skin We Live In*]

March, Robert H., Ph.D.
Professor of Physics
University of Wisconsin
[*The New Atom Smashers;*
Physics, Atoms and Nuclei;
Physics, Particles and Forces]

Maugh, Thomas H., II, Ph.D.
Senior Science Writer
Science Magazine
[*Honoring the Best Teachers*]

Merbs, Charles F., Ph.D.
Professor
Department of Anthropology
Arizona State University
[*Anthropology*]

Merz, Beverly, A.B.
Midwest Bureau Chief
Medical World News
[*Saving Lives with Marrow
Transplants*]

Meyer, B. Robert, M.D.
Chief, Division of Clinical
Pharmacology
North Shore University Hospital
[*Drugs*]

Miller, Lee D., Ph.D.
Curator
Allyn Museum of Entomology/
Florida State Museum
[*Butterfly*]

Murray, Stephen S., Ph.D.
Astrophysicist
Harvard/Smithsonian Center
for Astrophysics
[*Astronomy, Extragalactic*]

Olson, Maynard V., Ph.D.
Assistant Professor
Department of Genetics
Washington University School
of Medicine
[*Molecular Biology*]

Owen, Tobias C., Ph.D.
Professor of Astronomy
State University of New York
[*Probing the Secrets of Atmospheres*]

Patrusky, Ben, B.E.E.
Free-Lance Science Writer
[*The Facts About Bats*]

Pennisi, Elizabeth, M.S.
Free-Lance Science Writer
[*Zoology*]

Piel, E. Joseph, Ph.D.
Chairman
Department of Technology and
Society
State University of New York
[*Selecting a Video Recorder*]

Press, Frank, Ph.D.
President
National Academy of Sciences
[*Closing In on the Math and Science
Gap*]

Salisbury, Frank B., Ph.D.
Professor of Plant Physiology
Plant Science Department
Utah State University
[*Botany*]

Sanders, James V., Ph.D.
Associate Professor of Physics
Naval Postgraduate School
[*Sound;
Ultrasound*]

Schick, Michael, Ph.D.
Professor of Physics
Department of Physics
University of Washington
[*Physics, Condensed Matter*]

Schramm, David N., Ph.D.
Chairman
Astronomy and Astrophysics
Department
University of Chicago
[*The First Second*]

Smith, R. Jeffrey, M.S.
Senior Writer
Science Magazine
[*Close-Up, Archaeology*]

Steinmann, Marion, B.S.
Free-Lance Science Writer
[*Ruth Patrick*]

Sun, Marjorie, B.S.
Staff Writer
Science Magazine
[*Close-Up, Environment*]

Swanton, Donald W., Ph.D.
Chairman
Department of Finance
Roosevelt University
[*Making Money Grow Is a Matter of
Interest*]

Trefil, James, Ph.D.
Professor of Physics
University of Virginia
[*Close-Up, Physics*]

Tringham, Ruth, Ph.D.
Associate Professor of Anthropology
Department of Anthropology
University of California, Berkeley
[*Archaeology, Old World*]

Visich, Marian, Jr., Ph.D.
Associate Dean of Engineering
State University of New York
[*Energy*]

Walter, Eugene J., Jr., B.A.
Editor-in-Chief
Animal Kingdom Magazine
Curator of Publications
New York Zoological Society
[*How Science Is Saving Wild Animals*]

Watson, Patty Jo, Ph.D.
Professor of Anthropology
Washington University
[*Ancient Indians of Mammoth Cave*]

Westman, Walter E., Ph.D.
Professor of Ecosystem Analysis and
Conservation
Department of Geography
University of California, Los Angeles
[*Environment*]

Winston, Judith E., Ph.D.
Assistant Curator
Department of Invertebrates
American Museum of Natural History
[*Life on a Coral Reef*]

Wittwer, Sylvan H., Ph.D.
Director Emeritus
Agricultural Experiment Station
Michigan State University
[*Agriculture*]

Wolinsky, Howard, M.S.
Medical Writer
Chicago *Sun-Times*
[*New Ways to Look Inside the Body*]

Young, Eleanor A., Ph.D.
Associate Professor
Department of Medicine
University of Texas Health
Science Center at San Antonio
[*Nutrition;
Close-Up, Nutrition*]

Zimmerman, David R., A.B.
Free-Lance Writer
[*Sunscreens: Beach Umbrellas in a
Bottle*]

Special Reports

Fourteen Special Reports give in-depth treatment to major advances in science and technology. The subjects were chosen for their current importance and lasting interest.

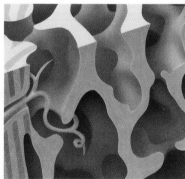

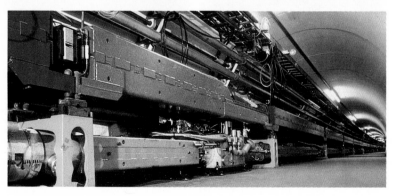

BY JUDITH E. WINSTON

Life on a Coral Reef

The breathtakingly beautiful reefs
created by tiny coral animals are
oases of life in barren tropical seas.

My diving gear smacks the water as I jump from the boat into the calm, warm sea. Settling gently through 25 feet of clear, Caribbean water, I enter a fantastic garden of amazing shapes and dazzling colors, teeming with life. Massive stony spurs and enormous boulders crowd clusters of what appear to be delicate shrubs and bright flowers in shades of rose, green, brown, and gold. A school of tiny blue fish flashes in the filtered sunlight, fleeing a larger fish in hot pursuit. The spines of prickly sea urchins bristle at my approaching shadow. An octopus oozes away into a crevice.

I could spend hours lost in wonder at this undersea splendor. But the main reason I have come here to Rio Bueno, a small bay on the northern coast of Jamaica, is to study the fascinating animals that make up the "shrubs and flowers" that landscape this sunken garden—corals. Over millions of years, these tiny creatures, some no larger than the head of a pin, have constructed huge reefs, undersea structures that rival anything built by human beings.

Early explorers of the Caribbean Sea and the Pacific Ocean dreaded the reefs, which posed a threat to any ship driven against them. These early explorers shared the common belief of the time that coral was a plant. Then, in 1726, Jean André Peyssonnel, a French botanist studying coral off the northern coast of Africa, discovered that the "plant" was actually made up of tiny *invertebrate animals* (animals without a backbone). He also discovered that the menacing reefs were formed from the skeletons of these creatures.

Corals belong to the phylum *Coelenterata* (*sih LEHN tuh rayt uh*), a division of the animal kingdom that also includes jellyfish, hydroids, and sea anemones. Like other coelenterates, coral animals have a cylindrical body with a single internal cavity and an opening at one end. This opening serves as both a mouth and a passage to excrete wastes. Surrounding the mouth are tiny tentacles, from which the coral animal gets its other name, *polyp*, which comes from a Greek word meaning *many-footed*. Most polyps are less than 1 inch in diameter, but some grow to as much as 1 foot.

Coral polyps are *carnivores* (meat-eaters) that generally eat at night. They use their tentacles to capture food. On the tentacles are stinging cells that contain coiled threads coated with a paralyzing chemical. The polyp shoots these threads like darts at tiny fish and the tiny animals that live in the *plankton* (a mass of small, drifting animal and plant life). The threads wrap around the prey or, in the case of some thin-skinned animals, pierce its flesh and stun it. The helpless victim is retrieved by the tentacles, then stuffed into the polyp's mouth.

The mouth leads to a central cavity, which is divided into at least six to eight pockets separated by flaps of tissue. In addition to serving as a stomach, this cavity also contains sex organs that appear temporarily when sexual reproduction takes place.

Nearly all of the 2,500 species of coral can be divided into two groups: soft corals and hard or stony corals, depending on the hardness of their skeleton. Polyps of soft corals have internal skele-

The author:
Judith E. Winston is an assistant curator of invertebrates at the American Museum of Natural History in New York City.

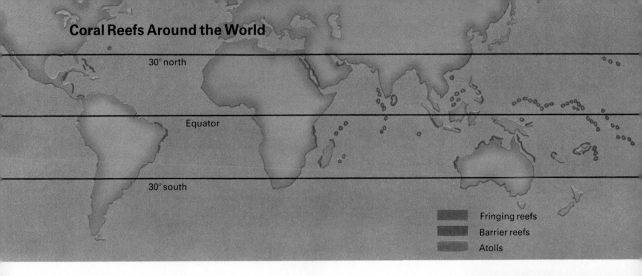

30° north

Equator

30° south

Fringing reefs
Barrier reefs
Atolls

tons made of a flexible, horny material. Polyps of stony corals have a cup-shaped skeleton surrounding the lower half of their body. The skeleton is made of *calcium carbonate* (limestone) manufactured by the polyp from minerals in seawater. The thin layer of tissue covering the skeleton makes the polyp look something like a rubber glove stretched over a teacup. During the day, or when danger threatens, the polyp draws its tentacles and the upper part of its body down against the cup.

A few polyps are solitary creatures. But most live in colonies, made up of identical polyps connected to one another by a sheet of calcium carbonate that they secrete. The colonies grow in an amazing variety of shapes, resembling tree branches, deer antlers, flat plates, mushrooms, mounds, and pillars. Over the years, as the polyps grow and deposit new calcium carbonate, and as polyps die and new polyps grow on the old skeletons, a very large structure may be formed. However, only the outer part of the colony consists of living tissue. The rest is solid limestone.

Where and how corals live

Corals live in nearly all the world's oceans, including the frigid waters of the Arctic Circle, and in both deep and shallow waters. Reef-building corals, however, all of which are stony corals, are very finicky about where they do their building. The water must be warm — with temperatures averaging about 70°F. And it must be fairly shallow — less than about 150 feet deep. As a result, nearly all coral reefs are found within a narrow band around the middle of the earth, extending 30 degrees north and south of the equator.

For *nutrients* (nourishing food), coral polyps depend not only on the animals they snare with their stinging cells, but also on the smaller plant plankton and bacteria that live in the waters around the reef. All reef-building corals, in addition, get nutrients from one-celled algae called *zooxanthellae* (*zoe zan THELL lee*). These algae, which can survive only in clear warm water, live in the polyps' tis-

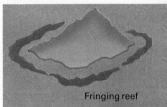

Fringing reef

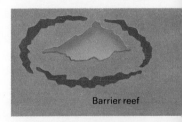

Barrier reef

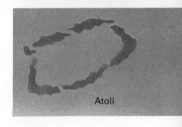

Atoll

Because corals need light and warmth to grow, nearly all coral reefs exist only in a narrow band extending 30 degrees north and south of the equator. Reefs take three basic forms – fringing reefs, barrier reefs, and atolls.

15

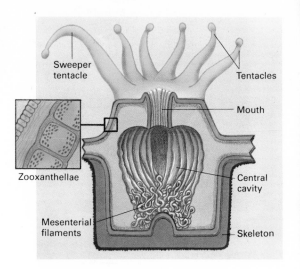

Polyp Parts

Every reef-building coral polyp has a tube-shaped body partly surrounded by a cuplike skeleton, *above*. Algae called zooxanthellae live in the polyp (inset) and supply it with nutrients. The polyp uses its sweeper tentacles and its mesenterial filaments to attack competing coral animals. The polyp's tentacles are used to capture prey, *above right*. They are drawn down against the skeleton, *opposite page,* during the day or when danger threatens.

sues and are remarkable food factories. They produce oxygen, carbohydrates, and *amino acids* (the building blocks of protein) by *photosynthesis*, the process by which plants use sunlight to convert water and carbon dioxide into food. In fact, some corals, especially those with very small polyps, seem to rely on algae for most of their nutrients. In return, the algae get from the coral certain nutrients and a place to live. They are also responsible for the green, blue, or brown color of the corals.

In addition, the algae help the polyps secrete their limestone skeleton, though scientists are not sure how this happens. This energy boost supplied by the algae enables the coral to produce the enormous amount of skeletal material needed to build a reef. Reef-building corals grow at the rate of 2½ to 25 inches a year, depending on the species.

The types of reefs

Coral reefs take three basic forms — *fringing reefs*, *barrier reefs*, and *atolls*. Fringing reefs are submerged coral platforms connected directly to land. Barrier reefs are separated from the land by a deep lagoon and may sit anywhere from a few yards to 150 miles offshore. The world's longest and most famous barrier reef is the Great Barrier Reef of Australia, which stretches more than 1,250 miles along Australia's northeast coast. The third type of coral reef, an atoll, is a doughnut-shaped reef surrounding a shallow lagoon.

For a long time, the reason why there are three types of reefs was an intriguing mystery. Scientists knew that reef-building corals can live only in relatively shallow water and that they need a rocky surface to grow on. Given these conditions, the origin of fringing reefs, which are found close to shore, was fairly easy to understand. However, barrier reefs, which are not connected to land, and atolls,

which are completely surrounded by deep ocean, were another matter. Complicating the mystery was the depth of some reefs, which plummet hundreds or even thousands of feet below the ocean surface, certainly far below coral's 150-foot maximum depth.

In 1842, the British naturalist Charles R. Darwin proposed a solution to the puzzle in his book *The Structure and Distribution of Coral Reefs*. Darwin reasoned that all coral reefs begin as fringing reefs in shallow water surrounding a volcanic island. In some cases, the island begins to sink beneath the ocean surface. However, the coral reef remains and continues to grow as new colonies of coral animals build on top of their ancestors' skeletons. Gradually, as the island sinks farther, the fringing reef becomes a barrier reef. Eventually, the island may disappear beneath the surface altogether, leaving only an atoll. By this time, the foundations of the reef lie far below the 150-foot depth.

Scientists debated Darwin's proposal for more than 100 years. Then, in 1951, a team of geologists drilled more than 4,000 feet into Enewetak, an atoll in the northwest corner of the Marshall Islands in the central Pacific Ocean. Beneath the layers of coral, the scientists discovered a foundation of volcanic rock, confirming Darwin's theory of how reefs come to be.

One of the best and most pleasant ways to understand the world of the coral reef is to explore one underwater. The reef at Rio Bueno, where I do much of my research, is fairly typical of coral reefs found around the world.

Most coral reefs have three sections—a *reef crest*, a *back-reef*, and a *forereef*. The reef crest is the shallowest part of the reef, where the coral growth nearly reaches the surface. Constantly buffeted by ocean waves, the reef crest is a very harsh environment. The crest is also exposed to strong sunlight and to air during very low tides, both of which can kill coral animals. As a result, the reef crest con-

Garden in the Sea

A typical Caribbean reef is
a wondrous sunken garden
landscaped with bright colors
and fantastic shapes. The reef
harbors an amazing variety
of sea creatures, which
live on its surface and in its
many caves (cutaway view).

Inhabitants of the Reef

1. Dictyota
2. Zoanthid
3. Fire coral
4. Crab
5. Elkhorn coral
6. Staghorn coral
7. Sea fan
8. Brain coral
9. Spiny lobster
10. Sea whip
11. Lettuce coral
12. Porites coral
13. Vase sponge
14. Pillar coral
15. Flower coral
16. Feather-duster worm
17. Triton snail
18. Star coral
19. Fireworm
20. Sea anemone
21. Clam
22. Spiny sea urchin
23. Octopus
24. Platy coral
25. Sea horse
26. Ropey sponge
27. Black coral
28. Ellisella
29. Basket star
30. Parrot fish
31. French angelfish
32. Blue chromis
33. Trumpet fish
34. Damselfish
35. Barracuda
36. Clown fish
37. Mantis shrimp
38. Brittle star
39. Squirrelfish
40. Rock-boring sea urchin
41. Dwarf coral
42. Madracis coral
43. Schlerosponge
44. Sponges
45. Nurse shark
46. Stinging hydroid
47. Bryozoans
48. Boring sponge
49. Hydroid
50. Boring clam
51. Peanut worm
52. Sponge tunnels
53. Red foram

10
30
32
31
6
7
7
10
33
34
11
11
10
12
13
11
14
10
16
35
13
15
15
10
16
7
12
36
17
14
10
18
7
7
20
23
24
21
25
26
21
27
28
27
29
27

19

sists mainly of dead coral piled up by storms and rocks coated with *coralline algae* — plants that help cement the reef together by secreting calcium compounds. On the seaward side of the reef crest live the few hardy corals, such as elkhorn coral, that can survive these harsh conditions.

The reef crest may run right to the shoreline, as it does at Rio Bueno. But often, a shallow lagoon separates the reef crest from the shore. This area between the shore and the reef crest is the back-reef. The protected waters of the back-reef have sandy and muddy bottoms and isolated blocks of coral called *patch reefs*. The lagoon may contain meadows of sea grass and beds of algae that harbor many communities of fish and other marine animals.

Extending underwater below the reef crest on the seaward side of the reef is the forereef. A diver descending along the forereef can see the massive coral formations of the crest give way to more delicate forms, creating a fantastic garden. The long purple or gold tendrils of sea whips sway gracefully in the current, and the lacy cross-ribs of sea fans seem to glow in the shafts of sunlight.

These vibrant inhabitants of the forereef grow atop huge spurs made by coral skeletons and called *buttresses*, which protrude from the reef like fingers. Between the buttresses are sandy channels created by the action of waves.

On some reefs, the buttresses give way to sandy terraces populated by mounds of platy corals — corals that look like huge flattened plates — and massive corals, such as brain and star corals, that look like boulders. Gradually, as the terraces slope toward the sea floor, the coral dwindles, then disappears altogether. At Rio Bueno, however, the buttresses end abruptly in a wall that slopes outward for

Stony Corals
The limestone skeletons of stony corals, such as brain coral, *below,* and elkhorn coral, *bottom,* form the framework of a coral reef.

Soft Corals

Such soft corals as sea fans, *left* and *bottom*, add splashes of brilliant color to a reef. A flamingo tongue snail, *below,* a coral predator, is drawn to a sea fan for food, however, not for its beauty.

about 100 feet, then plunges straight down, its base lost in the blue darkness 900 feet below.

Everywhere on a coral reef there is life in motion. Coral reefs harbor thousands of species of sea creatures, ranging from tiny organisms invisible to the naked eye to brilliantly colored fish, starfish, sponges, clams, oysters, and sometimes even sharks and octopuses.

Oasis in an ocean desert

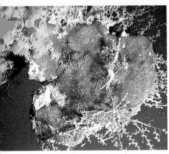

Hidden Communities
A coral reef harbors hidden communities whose members live in the reef's caves and crevices and encrust the undersides of platy coral. Tentacles extended, *top,* dwarf coral searches the waters of a reef cave for food. Dwarf coral, tentacles withdrawn, *above,* and mosslike bryozoans may also grow underneath a platy coral.

The reef's biggest draw is a ready food supply. Most of the tropical seas in which coral reefs grow are sterile ocean "deserts" of very clear water, containing few of the nutrients found in waters farther north or south. Because of this, most of the creatures that live in these waters are found on coral reefs, which are "oases" of productivity and life. Because the waters around a reef are so clear, sunlight can penetrate many feet down, allowing photosynthesis to occur in algae and other plant life. Reefs are actually gigantic food-producing systems created by the *symbiotic* (mutually beneficial) relationships between many of the reef dwellers — plants as well as animals.

Most of the nutrients produced on the reef are a result of the symbiotic relationship between zooxanthellae and coral polyps. However, the coralline algae and sea grasses found on the reef and the excretions of some fish may also enrich reef waters. These nutrients provide food for plankton, which are, in turn, eaten by larger reef dwellers, many of which later become prey themselves.

Most of us tend to think of the coral reef community as being made up of only those plants and animals we can see out in the open while diving or snorkeling. However, reefs also house a hidden or *cryptic* community whose members live in dark caves and crevices within the reef and encrust the undersides of platy corals. The boring and burrowing activities of some cryptic animals, such as feather-duster worms and certain types of sponges, erode and break down the dead coral. This activity makes room for new colonies and opens up caves and crevices so that seawater can circulate around and within the reef, thus recycling reef waste materials. Other cryptic creatures, such as coralline algae, encrust the outer surfaces of dead coral, helping to hold the reef together. In a sense, these cryptic creatures are the reef's maintenance workers.

As we swim around the sunlit peaks of the buttresses, only 25 feet below the surface, we can take pleasure in being one of the biggest "fish" around. But at 80 feet, the bodies of the divers look very small against the vastness of the ocean, and we realize how alien we are in an environment dominated by creatures whose lives are so strikingly different from our own. We are also awed by the tremendous limestone monument constructed by the tiny coral animals as they grow and reproduce.

Coral's versatile reproduction system

Corals reproduce in two ways — by sexual reproduction and by budding. Coral colonies reproduce sexually only when they reach a certain size and age, which varies from species to species. Either female or male sex organs form temporarily on the walls of a polyp's stomach cavity. The polyps that sprout male organs produce sperm, which they release into the sea. Sometimes, the eggs produced by the female polyp are released into the sea and are fertilized there. Most commonly, the sperm swim into the stomach cavities of polyps with female organs and fertilize the eggs produced there. The fertilized eggs develop into larvae with short, whiplike hairs that enable them to swim out of the mother polyp and into the sea.

In the predator-filled sea, the larvae live a risky life at best. Many die or are eaten. Some, however, attach themselves to a rock or a piece of the reef and begin to secrete a limestone skeleton, turning into polyps. Eventually, a new coral colony may grow where the larvae settled.

While sexual reproduction results in the formation of new coral colonies by allowing the polyps to move to new areas on the reef, budding enables existing colonies to grow in size. Budding takes place in two ways, depending on the shape of the colony and where in the colony the polyp is. When a polyp on the outer edge of a colony buds, small knobby growths sprout from its body or the tissue connecting members of a colony. When a polyp in the center of a colony buds, it basically splits and forms two polyps, each with its own skeleton.

The versatile reproduction system of corals is the reason for their

How Corals Reproduce

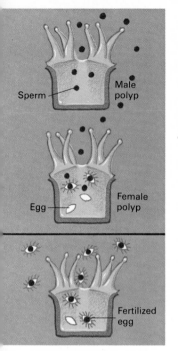

Sperm — Male polyp

Egg — Female polyp

Fertilized egg

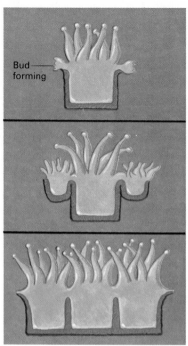

Bud forming

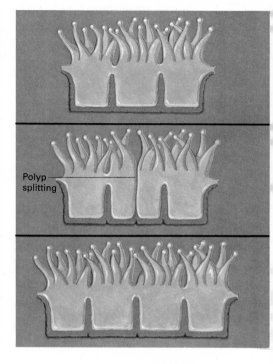

Polyp splitting

Sexual Reproduction

Corals have a versatile reproduction system. During sexual reproduction, *above,* sperm from a male polyp swim into a female polyp's central cavity and fertilize the eggs produced there. The fertilized eggs develop whiplike hairs that propel them out of the female's mouth and into the sea.

Budding

Another form of reproduction – budding – takes place in two ways. Growths may sprout from a polyp, *above, left column,* and develop into new polyps that are identical to the parent. Or a polyp may gradually grow wider, *above, right column,* then split to form two identical polyps.

great longevity. For example, platy coral colonies may live for 500 years, and scientists have found some brain corals that were more than 1,000 years old.

Because coral reef populations tend to live longer than coral reef scientists, long-term studies of corals have limitations — just as long-term studies of forest trees do. Luckily, we have found that some other animals living in the coral reef community are shorter-lived than corals but go through much the same life processes and thus may help us learn about the corals themselves. My work at Rio Bueno has focused on one of these — the *bryozoans,* tiny animals that grow like moss on the undersides of platy corals.

In 1977, marine biologist Jeremy B. C. Jackson of Johns Hopkins University in Baltimore and I hung panels of asbestos cement along the forereef at Rio Bueno. To bryozoan larvae, these panels provided a home as comfortable as platy corals, and so they settled there in large numbers. From time to time, we took the panels back to our laboratory in tanks of seawater. There, we were able to examine the bryozoans under a microscope and map the size and condition of each colony.

Over a three-year period, we discovered a number of interesting things about bryozoans. For example, we found that although many species of bryozoans grew on the panels, most panels were dominated by three species. We also found that no two panels developed in just the same way. Moreover, the colonies' rate of growth was slow. Two of the three dominant species on the panels did not begin to reproduce sexually for at least 1½ years after they settled. We also discovered that the partial death of a colony was common among bryozoans, as it is among corals. That is, colonies frequently lose members — to predators or storms — though the colony itself survives.

The fight for light and life

You might suppose that coral animals — which produce such colorful, beautifully shaped, and often delicate structures — are harmless and peaceful creatures. But because of the algae growing inside them, reef corals must have light. And to get that light, coral animals spend all their lives competing for sunlit space on the reef. They have developed a variety of aggressive ways to get ahead in their world.

Sometimes, fast-growing coral colonies grow up and over slower-growing competitors, shading them so that they die. Sometimes, as marine biologist Judith Lang has reported, coral animals actually eat one another.

Attached to the flaps of tissue in the polyp's stomach cavity are long, deadly strands called *mesenterial filaments*. Lang found that when she placed two coral colonies next to each other, the polyps stuck these filaments out of their stomach cavity and into the bodies of the other colony's polyps. In most encounters of this kind, Lang found that the more aggressive colony won the encounter, digesting the tissue of the losers. Lang also discovered that the most aggressive corals are the slow-growers; the least aggressive, those that grow colonies most rapidly. In this way, the slow-growers can prevent the fast-growers from crowding them out.

Coral animals also compete for space by using *sweeper tentacles*. These deadly weapons are longer than ordinary tentacles and are armed with special stinging cells that damage the competitor's tissues. Some coral species always have sweeper tentacles. However, others develop them only when danger threatens.

Competing colonies, however, are not the only enemies coral animals face. The reef is home to many creatures who find the coral animals delicious prey. Bristle worms, for example, completely engulf the tips of branching corals and digest the polyps down to their skeletons. Some reef fish, such as butterfly fish, nip off individual polyps. Others — including parrot fish, surgeonfish, and damselfish — have jaws specially modified for rasping against or crunching down on coral. These fish eat either the polyp, the algae inside it, or animals that grow on dead coral such as bryozoans or tubeworms.

Coral polyps provide a
delectable meal for many
predators, such as the
parrot fish, *above,*
which rasps the polyp's
skeleton with its
sharp teeth to get
at the tissue inside.
The crown-of-thorns
starfish, *right,* one
of the most fearsome
coral predators, has
devastated many reefs
in the Pacific and Indian
oceans in recent years.

On a quiet morning, this munching can be clearly heard by a nearby diver. Although this grazing activity damages the coral, it also opens bare spots where new coral colonies can settle.

For some of the damselfish, eating coral is only a way to clear a spot for an algae garden, which supplies food for the damselfish. The fish tend these gardens, weeding out unwanted algae, bryozoans, and other organisms that settle there. The feisty damselfish defend their food source against all intruders — including divers, whose unprotected skin they can bite hard enough to draw blood.

One of the best-known coral predators is the crown-of-thorns starfish, which has devastated many reefs in the Pacific and Indian oceans since the 1960's. The starfish are normally found grazing on coral reefs in small numbers. Large numbers of them, however, can severely damage a reef.

The large barren areas of hard coral skeletons they leave behind eventually become covered by soft corals and various types of algae. But the dead coral breaks up into small pieces, on which developing hard coral polyps cannot settle or survive well. Because it is so difficult for reef-building coral to begin growing there again, it may be decades before the reef recovers.

When the crown-of-thorn starfish plagues appeared in the late 1960's, scientists worried that the effects of human activity, such as pollution, might have caused a population explosion among starfish and the resulting devastation. But most researchers now believe that starfish populations explode periodically and then die off, and have been doing so for a very long time. Scientists have found evidence for this theory in the many crown-of-thorns fossils present in different layers of sediments brought up from deep within coral reefs.

Actions of human beings pose a threat to coral reefs. For example, sediment stirred up by dredging can bury coral reefs in mud, blocking out sunlight and killing the algae that provide nutrients for the coral.

Tides, storms, and El Niño

Living creatures are not the only factors that build, destroy, and otherwise alter coral reefs. Natural physical disturbances also play a role in restructuring a reef. For example, on Jamaican reefs, low spring tides, especially during the day, can kill or damage coral and the other organisms that live in the very shallow waters of the reef crest and back-reef. The coral may dry up if exposed to the air or suffer from overexposure to light and heat.

Storms are probably the major physical disturbance affecting reefs to a depth of about 65 feet. During storms of moderate intensity — the kind that occur in reef areas at least every year or two — waves break off or damage some pieces of coral. But most broken or injured coral colonies survive this damage. And, in fact, such storms may benefit the reef by opening up bare patches for colonization by young polyps.

However, severe storms may cause widespread devastation. Marine biologists working at the University of the West Indies' Discovery Bay Marine Laboratory in Jamaica are still studying the effects of Hurricane Allen on the reefs there. The hurricane, which struck

Brightly colored sponges, sea whips, and sea fans crowd the wall of a Caribbean reef – a world both hardy and fragile and one that holds secrets still to be uncovered by the scientists who dive in the sea.

in 1980, was the worst to hit Jamaica in 100 years. Waves 40 feet high broke on the forereef and shattered large blocks of coral or rolled them more than 30 feet down the reef, smashing other corals in their path. On one part of the forereef, large areas of branching elkhorn and staghorn corals were broken into small bits.

Fish and other animals living around the reef suffered, too. The damselfish lost their aggressiveness along with their garden territories and roamed around for several days — before they found new homes on other parts of the reef — too confused and discouraged even to nip at divers.

The scientists have concluded that the effects of Hurricane Allen could last for decades. The reefs at Discovery Bay may eventually recover, but the dominant species of coral on the reefs may change. For example, the devastated elkhorn coral may be replaced by hardier but slower-growing varieties, such as brain corals and star corals, or by faster-growing platy corals.

A new threat to coral reefs — and one that may be potentially catastrophic — appeared in early 1983. Biologist Peter W. Glynn of the Smithsonian Tropical Research Institute in Panama reported that hundreds of thousands of miles of reef corals in the eastern, central, and western Pacific Ocean and in parts of the Caribbean Sea were dead or dying. Glynn and other scientists examined the dying coral and discovered that the polyps had lost their zooxanthellae, the algae that provide nutrients and aid in skeleton-building.

Although the reason for this loss of algae is still unknown, Glynn suspects *El Niño*, an abnormal warm water current that moved across the Pacific Ocean in 1982 and 1983. Although reef-building corals need warm water to grow, water that is too warm can kill the polyps' algae. Glynn believes that the damage in some areas is so extensive that entire reefs may be lost.

The human threat

Coral reefs have also suffered serious damage because of human activity. Sediment seems to create the worst problem. Dredging and filling operations to enlarge and deepen harbors can leave corals buried in mud stirred up from the bottom. Clearing forestland increases the sediment running into rivers and the ocean and thus causes the water to become so muddy near shore that the polyps' algae are cut off from sunlight and the reefs die.

Ironically, fishermen, who depend on the reef's bountiful waters, may cause some of the worst damage by using dynamite to catch fish. The explosions stun or kill most of the fish, which then float to the surface where they can be easily collected. Soon, however, the reef is reduced to rubble and the fish and other marine creatures abandon it because it no longer provides food and shelter.

Industrial and urban development, with their accompanying pollution, are also threatening to coral reefs. Unfortunately, many countries whose reefs are being damaged need the revenue the development provides and lack the resources to control the pollution. Some countries, however, have begun to take action. In 1981, for example, the countries of the Caribbean region agreed to develop management guidelines for their marine resources, including coral reefs.

And so to the scientist's eye, coral reefs are far more than just beautiful underwater gardens. They are complex communities of many different plants and animals, all of whom depend on one another for life. The reef forms a world that is both hardy and fragile—able to repair and maintain itself under most conditions, but often endangered by the actions of nature and human beings. And the reef still holds many secrets that are waiting to be uncovered by the scientists who dive in the sea.

For further reading:

Cousteau, Jacques-Yves, and Diolé, Philippe. *Life and Death in a Coral Sea.* Doubleday, 1971.

Dozier, Thomas A., and Earnest, D. *Life in the Coral Reef.* Time-Life, 1977.

Endean, Robert. *Australia's Great Barrier Reef.* University of Queensland Press, 1983.

Jacobson, Morris K., and Franz, David R. *Wonders of Corals and Coral Reefs.* Dodd, 1979.

Kaplan, Eugene. *A Field Guide to Coral Reefs of the Caribbean and Florida.* Houghton Mifflin, 1982.

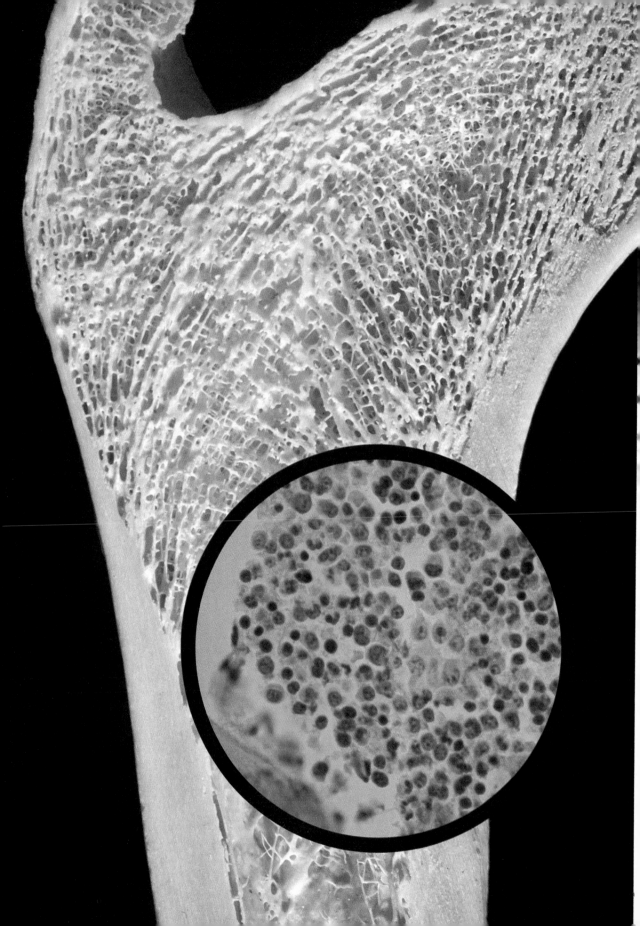

New techniques in bone marrow transplants give
hopelessly ill patients a second chance at life.

Saving Lives with Marrow Transplants

BY BEVERLY MERZ

In the fall of 1980, when Eric was 5 years old, his parents noticed
that he was pale and listless. They thought that Eric might be ane-
mic, so they took him to a physician, hoping that something could
be prescribed to put the color back in Eric's cheeks. But the doctor
told them that Eric's condition was more serious than they had
imagined. Eric had leukemia, a form of cancer in which abnormal
white blood cells grow in an uncontrolled manner at the expense of
other vital blood cells.

The family was devastated. However, Eric's condition was far
from hopeless. He had a type of leukemia that often responds to
treatment. In October 1980, the doctor prescribed *chemotherapy* —
drug treatments that made Eric feel terrible. He was nauseated, and
his hair fell out. Nevertheless, Eric's leukemia was getting better. He
also received radiation treatments to destroy leukemia cells that the
drugs could not reach. Within a few months, all traces of cancer had
disappeared from his blood, and the chemotherapy treatments were
reduced.

By the fall of 1981, Eric was feeling good. When he went to the
doctor for a routine checkup, however, the news was bad. The leukemia was back, and this time Eric's chances for recovery were slim.
Although the chances of a permanent *remission* (disappearance of
cancer cells) are about 60 per cent for patients after the initial treatment for leukemia, the chances of a lasting remission are less than

5 per cent for patients suffering a second episode of the disease. Because Eric's chances of recovery were so poor, his doctor asked his parents for permission to try another procedure — powerful drugs combined with a bone marrow transplant.

Eric's need for a bone marrow transplant stemmed from the fact that nearly all anticancer drugs also injure normal body cells, especially those that, like cancer cells, grow and divide rapidly. Fast-growing cells easily damaged by chemotherapy include bone marrow cells, the blood-forming cells found in the spongy centers of major bones. These cells are so vulnerable to drug damage that the high doses needed to wipe out Eric's leukemia would also destroy his bone marrow. Because no one can live without marrow, he would need a transplant to survive.

Bone marrow is necessary for life because it produces all of the body's blood cells — red cells that carry oxygen, disklike cells called *platelets* that aid clotting, and several types of white cells that play important roles in fighting infection. The marrow itself consists of fat cells, an assortment of immature blood cells, and important blood-forming cells known as *stem cells*. Stem cells can reproduce themselves again and again, and may develop into any type of blood cell — red cells, platelets, or white cells.

Unlike organ transplants, bone marrow transplants do not require a major sacrifice by the donor, such as giving up a kidney. The procedure is somewhat like a blood donation, though slightly riskier and more painful. First, the surgical team gives the marrow donor an anesthestic so that the donor will feel no pain during the removal of the marrow. Then the surgeon inserts a long needle into the donor's hipbone or pelvic bone. When the needle has reached the spongy core in the center of the bone, the physician draws a teaspoon or two of fluid through the needle. The fluid is mostly blood, with some marrow cells. Because up to 8 cups of this fluid are needed for a single transplant, the physician may have to insert the needle as many as 100 times — each time at a different site in the bone. The procedure takes about two hours.

A marrow donor may have some discomfort after the procedure and will probably need a transfusion of red blood cells to replace those removed. But, unlike someone who donates a kidney, the marrow donor's body has not suffered a permanent loss. It readily makes new marrow to replace what has been removed.

Nor is the transplant procedure itself much of an ordeal for the patient who receives it. After the medical team removes the blood and marrow from the donor, they strain it to break up any large particles and add the cells to a fluid containing nutrients to keep the cells alive and a chemical to prevent the blood from clotting. The resulting solution is given to the patient through a needle placed in a vein. To anyone visiting Eric during his marrow transplant, it looked as if he were having a blood transfusion. The transplanted

The author:
Beverly Merz is Midwest bureau chief of *Medical World News.*

Anatomy of a Bone

Bone marrow is found in the spongy tissue at the centers of major bones, where it is protected by the outer compact bone layer and richly supplied with blood by many blood vessels. The marrow itself consists of fat cells, immature blood cells, and vital blood-forming cells called *stem cells*.

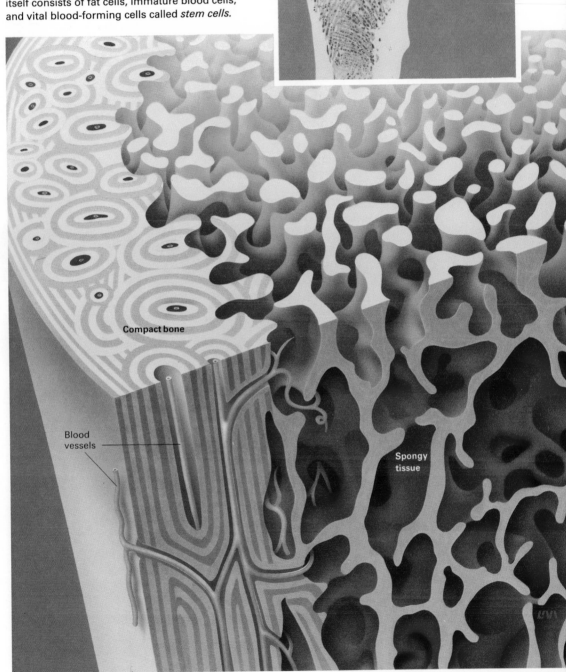

Area of detail

Compact bone

Blood vessels

Spongy tissue

The Bone Marrow Transplant Procedure

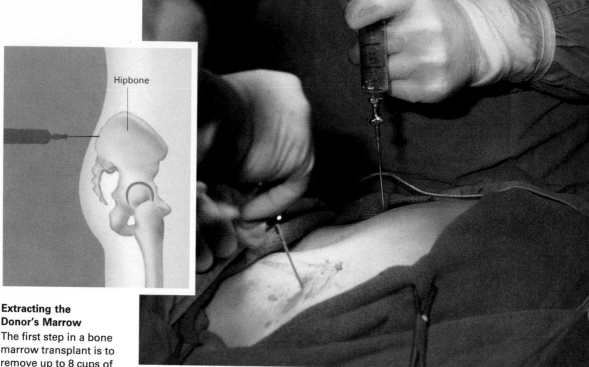

Hipbone

Extracting the Donor's Marrow

The first step in a bone marrow transplant is to remove up to 8 cups of blood and marrow cells from a donor's hipbone. After the donor is anesthetized, a surgeon draws the blood and marrow through a needle, a little at a time.

marrow cells travel through the patient's bloodstream, and some eventually reach the bone marrow, where they grow and reproduce.

If a bone marrow transplant is such a simple procedure, it would seem to be a routine treatment. However, marrow is actually one of the most difficult of all tissues to transplant. If the cells in the donated bone marrow are not identical to the recipient's cells, they may attack and destroy the patient's tissues.

Most of the trouble is caused by a type of white blood cell called a *T lymphocyte* or *T cell*, which is responsible for defending the body from viruses, bacteria, toxic chemicals, and other invading agents. Like other blood cells, T cells originate in the bone marrow as stem cells. They then travel to the thymus, an organ in the chest, where they mature into T cells. (The *T* stands for *thymus derived*.) The mature cells leave the thymus and spread into the bloodstream and tissues. There, the T cells keep watch for foreign molecules that have invaded the body. When the T cells recognize an invader, they signal the body's immune system to attack.

To aid the T cells in determining what is foreign and what belongs to the body, the surface of each body cell is marked with sets of protein molecules known as *HLA antigens*, which act as a cellular "monogram." More than 70 HLA antigens have been identified.

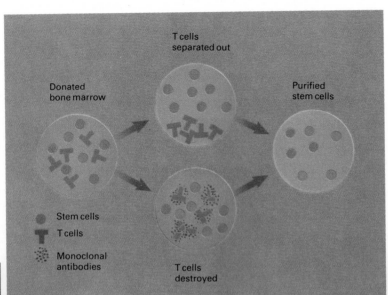

Purifying the Marrow
To prevent the donated marrow from attacking the recipient's body, white blood cells called *T cells* must be removed, leaving only the useful stem cells. In one process, a chemical makes T cells clump together so they can be separated. Another method uses custom molecules called *monoclonal antibodies* to destroy the T cells.

Donated
bone marrow

T cells
separated out

Purified
stem cells

- Stem cells
- T cells
- Monoclonal antibodies

T cells
destroyed

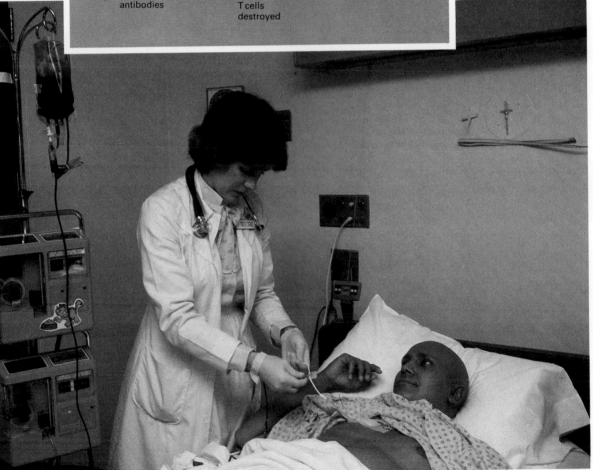

Transplanting the Treated Marrow
A solution containing purified stem cells is transfused into the patient's blood. Some of the cells reach the bones, where they grow and reproduce.

Each person inherits *genes* (the parts of a cell that determine hereditary traits) for two sets of these antigens — one set from each parent. As a result, an enormous number of combinations are possible to make up what is called the HLA type. Identical twins always have the same HLA type, but there is only about a 25 per cent chance that a brother or sister will have the same type. The chances of unrelated persons having the same type are very small.

The greater the number of HLA antigens in common between the donor and recipient, the better the chances for a successful transplant. People receiving organ transplants from a donor with a different HLA type face the danger of having their T cells trigger an attack on the foreign organ, and some bone marrow transplants fail for this reason. But marrow transplant patients face another danger that is even greater. To T cells transplanted directly from a person with a different HLA type, the recipient's entire body looks foreign. Soon the transplanted marrow cells are waging war against every tissue and organ — a condition known as *graft-versus-host disease*. The transplant patient develops a rash, liver problems, and diarrhea, and may die if the condition becomes severe. Even if the donor and recipient have the same HLA type, graft-versus-host disease still frequently occurs because other tissues may not match. With matching HLA types, however, the illness will be mild enough that the patient will have a good chance of surviving it.

Eric had an older brother and a younger sister, but neither shared his HLA type. Sometimes, physicians can match unrelated donors through a registry of HLA-typed donors. But instead of embarking on such a time-consuming search, his doctors decided to try an unusual procedure first investigated in the 1950's and revived in the mid-1970's. Eric would serve as his own marrow donor.

The medical team treating Eric first gave him enough anticancer drugs to cause a remission, so that there were as few leukemia cells as possible in his marrow and other tissues. The doctors then removed about 5 cups of blood and bone marrow from Eric's pelvic bone and destroyed the cancer cells in the marrow with special chemicals. While the removed marrow was being treated, the doctors gave Eric more drugs and a dose of radiation strong enough to kill any cancer cells that remained in his body. The drugs also destroyed whatever marrow cells Eric had left. Because marrow produces the body's disease-fighting cells, when Eric's marrow was killed, his immune system was killed too. For that reason, the doctors treated Eric with antibiotics to ward off infection. They also gave him transfusions of red blood cells to supply oxygen to his organs until his reimplanted bone marrow began producing red cells again.

Finally, Eric's purified marrow was transfused back into his bloodstream. Some of the marrow cells eventually made their way back into the spongy centers of his bones, where they resumed their normal function.

Eric was extremely sick for weeks, not because of the transplant but because of the side effects of the anticancer drugs. But he recovered after five or six weeks and went home from the hospital. By the summer of 1984, he had been free of cancer for more than 2½ years. However, there is always the chance that a few cancer cells remain hidden in his body and might begin to multiply. Although there is no guarantee that Eric's "self-transplant" has cured him of leukemia, most patients who remain cancer-free for that long do not relapse.

Eric and other leukemia patients are not the only ones who have benefited — and may benefit in the future — from these self bone-marrow transplants. The self-transplant technique may also help patients with other cancers, such as *lymphomas* (cancers of the lymphatic organs) and *myelomas* (tumors of the bone marrow). But self-transplants will not work in diseases that arise from basic deficiencies in the bone marrow. Such diseases include sickle cell disease, thalassemia, and aplastic anemia. Sickle cell disease and thalassemia are hereditary disorders in which the marrow produces abnormal red blood cells. In aplastic anemia, the marrow loses its ability to produce red cells and certain other blood cells because of exposure to drugs, poisons, radiation, or other factors. Also in this category are immune deficiency disorders, in which the body's defenses against disease are lowered because the marrow fails to produce certain types of white blood cells. Patients with these diseases must receive transplants from donors whose marrow is normal.

In the past, when treating patients with marrow deficiencies, physicians had to search — often in vain — for a relative or other donor with the same HLA type. This may no longer be necessary. A number of research groups discovered in the early 1970's that a transplant from a donor with a different HLA type would not set off an attack on the recipient's organs if the mature T cells were removed from the donor's marrow before the transplant. The stem cells that were left in the marrow would not turn against the recipient but instead would grow, multiply, and build a new immune system in the patient's body.

Scientists have developed two techniques for removing mature T cells from donated marrow. One method involves adding a substance that makes the T cells clump together so that they can be separated from the rest of the marrow. Two such substances are soybean lectin — a protein derived from soybean plants — and sheep red blood cells. A medical team headed by pediatrician Richard J. O'Reilly at Memorial Sloan-Kettering Cancer Center in New York City uses a combination of both substances in a technique developed by biophysicist Yair Reisner of Israel's Weizmann Institute of Science. O'Reilly and his colleagues have achieved good results transplanting treated marrow into patients with immune deficiencies.

The other method of treating mismatched marrow uses special

proteins called *monoclonal antibodies*, custom-made in the laboratory to hunt down only T cells, leaving all other cells unharmed. Ordinary antibodies are molecules in the immune system that help fight foreign invaders. Scientists make the special monoclonal antibodies by bioengineering techniques. They combine an antibody-producing white blood cell with a cancer cell. Because the cancer cell reproduces rapidly, the new combination cell is used to make large numbers of *clones* — identical offspring — all of which will produce the same antibody.

At Dana-Farber Cancer Institute in Boston, researchers led by internist Ellis L. Reinherz have produced an antibody that acts as a "magic bullet" against T cells, seeking out and destroying them. The Dana-Farber physicians mix donated bone marrow with the antibodies until the T cells in the marrow are destroyed. The valuable stem cells are spared. Researchers are also using similar magic bullets to destroy cancer cells in the marrow of self-donors such as Eric.

The method developed at Dana-Farber made headlines in October 1983, when physicians at Baylor College of Medicine and Texas Children's Hospital in Houston used it to treat the 12-year-old boy known to the world only as David the "Bubble Boy." David was born with severe combined immunodeficiency, a genetic defect that made him unable to fight off even the slightest infection. For people with this condition, even a common cold may prove fatal. Because David's older brother had died from the immune deficiency at the age of 7 months, doctors suspected that David might be born with the condition and placed him in sterile isolation at birth. Except for the last 15 days of his life — and brief excursions into the outside world in 1977 and 1978 in a special astronaut-type suit designed for him at the Lyndon B. Johnson Space Center in Houston — David lived in a series of ever-larger plastic bubbles.

Pediatrician Richard J. O'Reilly of Memorial Sloan-Kettering Cancer Center in New York City holds a press conference introducing children with immune deficiencies who were successfully treated with marrow transplants.

David's doctors believed that a bone marrow transplant might give him a working immune system. But they could not find a donor with a matching HLA type. However, the Dana-Farber technique gave David, his family, and his physicians new hope. Doctors took marrow from David's healthy 15-year-old sister, Katherine, treated it with monoclonal antibodies, and transfused it into David.

At first, the medical team believed that Katherine's marrow cells were taking hold. However, David developed fever, nausea, and diarrhea, symptoms of graft-versus-host disease. In early February 1984, David's doctors released him from his bubble so that they could treat those problems. For the first time, David's mother was able to kiss her son.

Unfortunately, David's condition worsened. Fluid accumulated in his lungs and around his heart. Finally, on February 22, he died. An autopsy showed that David had died not of graft-versus-host disease but of heart failure.

David's bubble was dismantled, and his doctors say that none like it will ever be used again. In the future, children like David will be treated while they are still babies, using marrow transplant techniques based on knowledge gained from David's case and others.

The possibility of processing mismatched marrow to make it usable opens the way for treating patients with a wide range of immune-system disorders. However, mismatched marrow cannot yet be used to treat patients such as Eric, who have functioning immune systems, because their bodies often reject the transplant. Many researchers are working to overcome the rejection problem, but much remains to be done.

Before the bone marrow transplant becomes standard treatment, it must be tried on a broad range of patients to determine if this is indeed the best treatment for each disorder. In addition, there must be enough personnel trained in bone marrow transplant techniques.

The cost of the procedure — ranging from $35,000 to $70,000 — is another consideration. However, some doctors point out that this cost may be less than the expense of several courses of radiation and chemotherapy, or of a lifetime of transfusions or living in a sterile environment.

And the rewards? As one doctor who is a pioneer in the use of bone marrow transplants remarked, "We have had several patients who come to us under a death sentence but now are cured. They come back year after year to visit. The marrow transplant has, in effect, given them a second life."

For further reading:

Bone Marrow Transplantation. American Association of Blood Banks, 1983.
Lax, Eric. *Life and Death on 10 West.* Times Books, 1984.
Margolies, Cynthia P., and McCredie, Kenneth B. *Understanding Leukemia.* Scribner, 1983.
Nourse, Alan Edward. *Your Immune System.* Watts, 1982.

BY CHARLES A. BEICHMAN

A New View of the Universe

A telescope orbiting high above
Earth has provided exciting
discoveries in the infrared.

About 200 of us, scientists and technicians, gathered at dusk to watch the launch. Suddenly, we heard the low, throaty roar of the Delta rocket. It seemed as though evening was transformed to high noon as the exhaust from the rocket lit up the sky. This was the moment we had been waiting for, the culmination of eight years of scientific and technical work. The satellite atop the rocket would soon give us a view of the sky like nothing we had ever seen before.

We were witnessing the Jan. 25, 1983, launch of the *Infrared Astronomical Satellite* (*IRAS*) from Vandenberg Air Force Base near Lompoc, Calif. As a member of the *IRAS* science team, I regarded the launch of the satellite and its infrared telescope as comparable in historical importance to the invention of the first, primitive telescope in 1609 by the Italian astronomer Galileo. Galileo gave us our first close-up glimpse of the heavens. With *IRAS*, astronomers opened wide the infrared "window," the last unexplored window on the universe.

The 2,249-pound *IRAS* went into a perfect 560-mile-high orbit, circling Earth from pole to pole. For five days, scientists checked the satellite's in-orbit performance. Then they ejected the cover that had protected the telescope, and the satellite's exploration of the universe began.

Since Galileo's invention, astronomers have surveyed the sky with optical telescopes, devices that "see" light that is visible to our eyes. However, visible light is only a small portion of a wide range of radiant energies called the *electromagnetic spectrum*. Infrared rays, radio waves, ultraviolet rays, and X rays, along with visible light and gamma rays, are all forms of "light" that make up this spectrum. Beginning in the mid-1950's, astronomers perfected telescopes that could "see" radiant energy in the bands of the spectrum that are invisible to our eyes. This gave the astronomers an entirely new view of the universe. Some stars and galaxies, for example, give off radiant energy that can be observed in all bands of the electromagnetic spectrum.

However, the use of infrared telescopes on Earth has been limited because Earth's atmosphere prevents most infrared radiation from reaching ground-based telescopes. Until *IRAS*, the infrared universe was largely unexplored. But *IRAS*, orbiting above Earth's atmosphere, was able to provide a completely new picture of the heavens. During its brief life, *IRAS* returned a wealth of data. Among the highlights of its findings were these:

■ New comets. *IRAS* detected five new comets, and its findings suggest that these heavenly objects may carry much more dust with them than was previously thought.

■ New star formation. *IRAS* led astronomers to regions in the sky where new stars, like our sun, are being formed. These stars are still hidden by clouds of gas and dust and will not be seen by optical telescopes for hundreds of thousands of years.

■ Other solar systems? If there is life elsewhere in the universe, there must be other solar systems similar to ours. *IRAS* discovered clouds of particles around the star Vega and other stars that suggest the formation of planets and resemble how our solar system must have begun.

■ Unidentified objects. Some astronomers believe these may be among the most distant galaxies in the universe.

But what exactly is the infrared? Why is it important to astronomers? On the electromagnetic spectrum, infrared rays occur at energy levels just below visible light. Although we cannot perceive infrared radiation as light, we can — if it is strong enough — sense infrared energy as heat.

Imagine a steel rod placed in a very hot fire. It glows white-hot with visible light. As it cools off, it stops glowing, but gives off enough heat for us to feel. This is infrared radiation. When it cools down to room temperature, the rod still gives off infrared radiation, but not strongly enough for us to feel. Nevertheless, sensitive detectors can pick up this radiation. Every piece of matter, no matter how low its temperature, gives off some energy in the form of infrared radiation. This is why soldiers can detect enemy tanks or planes at night with infrared sensors.

The author:
Charles A. Beichman is a senior scientist at the Jet Propulsion Laboratory in Pasadena, Calif., and a member of the *IRAS* science team.

Since the 1970's, infrared telescopes on high mountaintops or in high-flying planes, balloons, or rockets have shown that the planets, stars, and galaxies all emit heat, or infrared, radiation. These telescopes revealed that giant clouds of gas and dust within the Milky Way — our own galaxy — contain strong sources of infrared rays. These strong sources are hot young stars many times bigger and brighter than our own sun. As a result of these limited observations, astronomers realized that much more could be learned about how stars form and other aspects of the universe if they could find a way to observe the entire sky in the infrared.

Unfortunately, trying to observe in the infrared from within Earth's atmosphere is like looking for stars in daylight on a cloudy afternoon in an observatory dome with the lights on. The gases in Earth's atmosphere, mainly water vapor, absorb infrared light. Consequently, the infrared rays from distant stars and galaxies travel untold trillions of miles only to be lost in the last few miles of their journey, just before reaching our telescopes. Adding to the problem is the fact that as Earth's atmosphere absorbs infrared radiation, it becomes warm and glows in the infrared, creating a background that swamps weak signals from far out in space. In addition, telescopes — and even the astronomers who operate them — give off infrared radiation that interferes with infrared observations.

IRAS was designed to overcome these problems. *IRAS* went into orbit entirely above Earth's atmosphere so that it escaped interference from atmospheric gases and water vapor. The entire telescope was cooled with liquid helium to −454°F., just 3° above absolute zero, so that the instrument itself gave off almost no heat. With *IRAS*, astronomers had, in a manner of speaking, their first view of the infrared sky on a clear, dark night.

The *IRAS* project began in 1976, under the development and operation of the Netherlands Agency Programs (NIVR), the United States National Aeronautics and Space Administration (NASA), and the United Kingdom's Science and Engineering Research Council (SERC). The United States built the telescope and infrared detectors. The Dutch provided the spacecraft and an auxiliary scientific instrument.

The spacecraft orbited Earth twice each day from pole to pole, staying just over the day-night line. In this way, the satellite could aim its solar panels toward the sun to collect the needed energy to keep operating while aiming its telescope toward the blackness of space. Twice a day until the end of the mission, the satellite radioed back to Earth the stored-up data from the previous 12 hours and received from the ground a new set of commands for what to observe during the next 12 hours. The British provided the ground station, located near Oxford, England.

IRAS proved to be a thousand times more sensitive than any Earth-bound infrared instrument. The heart of *IRAS* was a 22.4-

Exploring with the Electromagnetic Spectrum

Gamma ray telescope

X-ray telescope

Ultraviolet telescope

IRAS

Gamma rays	X rays	Ultraviolet rays	Visible light	Infrared rays	Microwaves	Radio waves

Scientists have explored the universe in all bands of the electromagnetic spectrum, from gamma rays to radio waves, by using satellite or ground-based telescopes. *IRAS,* the latest satellite telescope, surveyed the sky from space in the infrared.

Optical telescope

Microwave telescope

Radio telescope

A nearby spiral galaxy, the Andromeda Nebula, appears as a mass of stars, *left,* in a photograph taken through an optical telescope, which sees as our eyes do with visible light. The patterns of color, *below,* represent the infrared image of Andromeda as it appeared to *IRAS.*

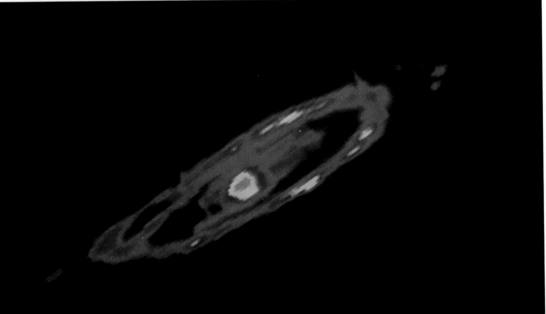

inch telescope with mirrors to collect the infrared light. The *IRAS* telescope was much like an optical telescope except that its mirrors were made of beryllium because this metal distorts much less than glass when cooled to almost absolute zero. When infrared rays from a distant star hit the telescope's large primary mirror, they were reflected onto a small secondary mirror, which focused the rays.

For their observations, astronomers divided the sky into 360 degrees, the same number of degrees as in a circle. The *IRAS* telescope was able to bring into focus an image of a half-degree section of the sky, a field of view about the size of the full moon. *IRAS* built up its picture of the entire 360 degrees of sky by taking one half-degree scan after another, moving a quarter-degree to one side after each scan.

Attached to the back of the primary mirror were 62 infrared detectors and other equipment that converted the infrared rays into electric signals to be sent down to Earth. The detectors were specially designed for use in space. Each consisted of a small piece of carefully prepared silicon or germanium — the materials used to make the transistors found in computers and television sets. When infrared energy was absorbed by the detector, an electron in the silicon or germanium was given enough energy to move through an electronic circuit. The strength of the current was proportional to the amount of infrared radiation hitting the detector. The photo-current was amplified, just as the weak electric signal from a phonograph needle is strengthened by a stereo amplifier. The signals from each of the 62 detectors were recorded on a tape recorder on board the spacecraft for later transmission to the ground station in England.

Another kind of detector measured the visible light from well-known bright stars. Knowing the exact instant at which the image of a star passed over one of these visible-light detectors enabled the *IRAS* project scientists to determine precisely where the telescope was pointing.

The entire telescope was placed inside an aluminum cylinder with hollow double walls. This cylinder was itself placed inside a kind of giant thermos bottle that prevented heat from the outside world from reaching the instrument. Just before the launch, the hollow walls of the aluminum cylinder were filled with 185 gallons of liquid helium. The liquid helium slowly boiled away, keeping the instrument cold despite the sunlight warming the spacecraft. The *IRAS* mission ended on Nov. 22, 1983, when the supply of liquid helium ran out.

One of the first results of *IRAS* was the April 25, 1983, discovery of a comet that came within 2.9 million miles of Earth. Discovered independently by *IRAS* and by Japanese and British amateur astronomers, Comet *IRAS*-Araki-Alcock — named for its discoverers — approached closer to Earth than any comet had since 1770.

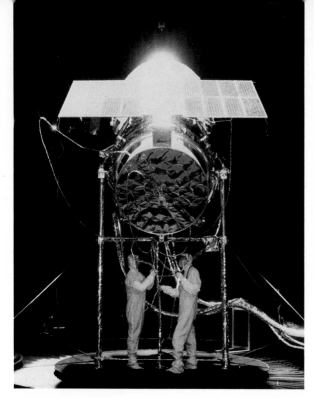

A **Delta rocket** lifted *IRAS* into orbit at dusk on Jan. 25, 1983, *below right*. The dusk launch allowed *IRAS* to orbit continuously over the day-night line, *above*, so that the solar collectors always pointed toward the sun and the telescope toward black sky.

IRAS and Its Telescope

Technicians prepare *IRAS* for final testing, *above.* Solar collectors powered the satellite, *right,* by converting sunlight into electricity. A sunshade shielded the telescope, which was cooled by liquid helium. Mirrors focused starlight onto the focal plane's infrared detectors, while the horizon sensor helped *IRAS* maintain the correct orbit.

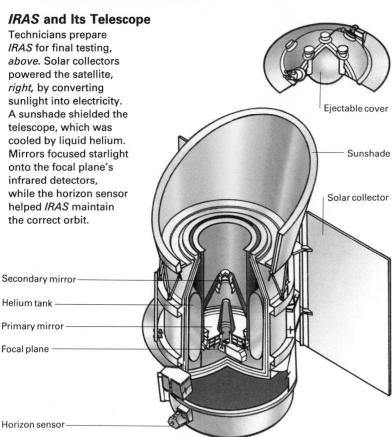

Ejectable cover

Sunshade

Solar collector

Secondary mirror

Helium tank

Primary mirror

Focal plane

Horizon sensor

Data from this rare close-up view of a comet may allow scientists to get a better understanding of what comets are made of. Because comets are thought to be the oldest objects in the solar system, this knowledge could shed light on what the early solar system was like. Also, because comets come from the outermost region of the solar system, the *IRAS* observations of this comet are likely to tell scientists a great deal about this region.

IRAS found a long tail of dust particles stretching 250,000 miles behind the comet, leading to the important finding that comets contain much more dust and are much more complex than was previously thought. Many amateur astronomers spend a lifetime scanning the skies with optical telescopes, hoping to find even one comet. *IRAS* proved to be a prolific comet-hunter, finding five faint new comets between April and July 1983.

A major goal of *IRAS* was to gather information on how stars are formed. *IRAS* was uniquely suited to this task because new stars, embedded within clouds of gas and dust, are invisible to optical telescopes but give off strong infrared radiation. Floating in the space between existing stars, these clouds come in all sizes and are made up of hydrogen gas molecules plus tiny amounts of dust and com-

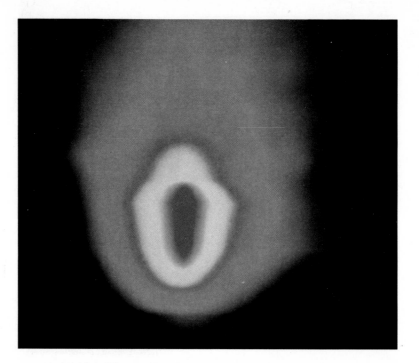

IRAS discovered Comet *IRAS*-Araki-Alcock, *right,* which came within 2.9 million miles of Earth, the closest approach of any comet since 1770. The infrared image shows the comet's dusty tail (blue) trailing 250,000 miles behind the bright nucleus (red).

Opposite page: A false-color image of the Orion constellation produced from *IRAS* data reveals areas where stars are being born. The large red region represents cool dust. The bright spots represent gas heated by large numbers of bright young stars.

plex organic molecules. Some clouds may contain enough matter to make anywhere from a few suns to a few million suns.

Stars begin to form when small clumps within a cloud come together through the force of gravity or, possibly, because of external pressure from nearby exploding stars. As the clump contracts, more gas falls into the center so that it becomes more dense. This dense core is the first stage of a star. As the forming star's gravity pulls more material from the surrounding cloud, the star becomes denser and hotter. Eventually, the temperature and density become great enough to start nuclear reactions. The new star, still deep within the cloud of gas and dust, is invisible to optical telescopes. But the starlight heats the surrounding dust, which then radiates infrared energy that infrared telescopes can detect. The intense heat from the new star's surface produces a stellar wind that will eventually blow away the surrounding gas and dust. After a few hundred thousand years the star will become visible to the naked eye or to an optical telescope.

Scientists do not know exactly what triggers the processes that lead to star formation. *IRAS,* however, provided scientists with their first overview of a region in the sky where massive stars are being formed — the Great Nebula of Orion in the constellation Orion, which can be seen in the winter sky of the Northern Hemisphere. Massive stars are some 30 to 50 times bigger than our sun and nearly a million times brighter. But they are not nearly as numerous as stars like our sun.

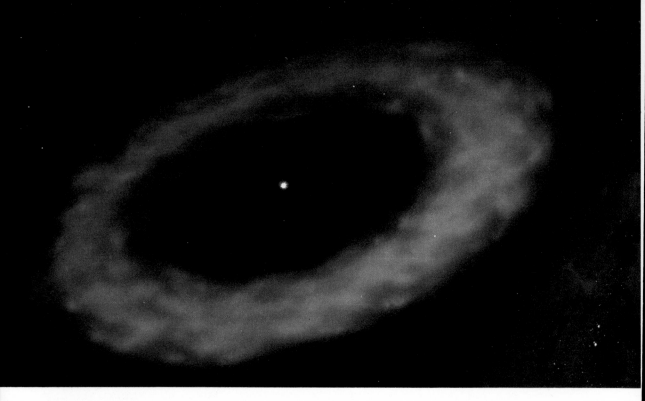

A ring of particles discovered by *IRAS* in orbit around the star Vega appears as a faint, circular cloud in this artist's conception. The ring may be evidence of planets forming around Vega. *IRAS* found similar clouds of particles around other stars.

Massive stars form so quickly and give off so much more energy, compared with smaller stars, that a much more violent and energetic process must be at work in their formation. Scientists hope that the *IRAS* data will provide new insights into the early stages of the formation of these massive stars.

IRAS will also tell scientists for the first time a great deal about the formation of smaller stars, like our sun. Before *IRAS*, this glimpse into the birth of a small star was impossible because of its faintness. Ground-based infrared telescopes could detect only the giant superstars. The Earth-orbiting *IRAS*, however, could detect a small star in its parental cloud at a distance of 2,000 *light-years*. (A light-year is the distance light will travel in one year, or about 6 trillion miles.) In fact, *IRAS* found dozens of small stars like our sun forming in small interstellar clouds. Observing the formation of these nearby small stars allows astronomers to study star birth in its simplest possible form.

One of the most important scientific and philosophical questions astronomers ask is whether life exists elsewhere in the universe. The answer to that question depends on many things, including whether there are planets around any other stars. At present, we know of only one star with planets — our sun. However, one of the most exciting results from *IRAS* is data that could imply the existence of planets, or at least the building blocks of planets, in orbit around certain nearby stars.

This important discovery was actually made almost by accident.

As part of a program to verify the operation of the telescope, *IRAS* astronomers studied six bright stars that they thought they understood well. Five of them had infrared profiles that were just as the astronomers expected. The exception was Vega, the third-brightest star in the summer sky of the Northern Hemisphere, which gave off 10 times more infrared radiation than expected.

The simplest interpretation of this infrared excess is that there is a large cloud of particles in orbit around Vega that gives off strong infrared radiation. The size of the cloud is about 85 *astronomical units*. (One astronomical unit or AU is the distance from Earth to the sun, about 93 million miles.) By comparison, the distance from the sun to the outermost planets is about 40 AU. This orbiting material is most likely to be matter left over from the formation of the star. Vega is roughly 2½ times bigger and 50 times brighter than our sun. Astronomers are not certain how old Vega is, but it is probably around 1 billion years old, much younger than our 4.6-billion-year-old sun.

The *IRAS* data imply that the particles around Vega must be larger than buckshot — much larger than the dust grains typically found in interstellar space. But for now we can only guess at the maximum size and the number of particles. Enough matter could exist to make up anywhere from a few thousand asteroids to a few dozen planets.

The surprising discovery of this shell of matter around Vega points out the importance of an all-sky survey with the orbiting infrared telescope. Until *IRAS*, no one had any reason to suspect anything unusual about Vega. With *IRAS*, they not only discovered a shell around Vega but also found shells around other stars, including Fomalhaut, a bright star in the southern sky. Since many astronomers believe that the planets of our solar system emerged from a similar shell, study of the *IRAS* data may provide clues to explain how our planetary system formed. See PROBING THE SECRETS OF ATMOSPHERES.

The *IRAS* telescope also made important findings about galaxies — huge systems of stars, gas, and dust. Before *IRAS*, only a handful of galaxies had been observed in the infrared. But *IRAS* detected some 20,000 galaxies.

Galaxies come in two main types, *spiral galaxies* and *elliptical galaxies*. Spiral galaxies, such as our Milky Way, are shaped like huge pinwheels with spiral arms swirling around a central bulge. Elliptical galaxies vary in shape from round to oval and have no arms. Scientists believe elliptical galaxies are collections of old stars and that few new stars are born in this type of galaxy.

Some scientists had predicted that spiral galaxies would give off some of their energy in the infrared, because these galaxies are thought to be regions of star formation. *IRAS* confirmed this prediction, but its findings also raised further questions. Now, scientists also want to know what it is that makes some spiral galaxies extremely active star-forming regions.

IRAS discovered a great range of infrared activity within spiral galaxies. At one extreme is the Andromeda galaxy, a spiral galaxy that gives off only a small percentage of its total energy output in the infrared. Since Andromeda is a relatively weak source of infrared radiation, astronomers concluded that few new stars are being formed there. At the other extreme are galaxies that give off as much as 95 per cent of their total energy as infrared radiation. Such galaxies show up only faintly on photographs made with visible light but stand out brightly when observed by *IRAS*. In many of these galaxies, scientists think, hundreds of massive stars form each year. The strength of the infrared radiation from our own galaxy falls somewhere in-between, showing roughly equal amounts of energy in the infrared and the visible parts of the spectrum. This implies that about one new star forms each year in the Milky Way.

IRAS also discovered several hundred mysterious objects that show up clearly in the infrared but are either very faint or totally invisible on optical photographs of the sky. Since their discovery, these unidentified *IRAS* objects have been the focus of intense study by astronomers using giant optical and radio telescopes aimed at the regions of the sky where the infrared objects were found. Optical telescopes equipped with sensitive cameras, such as the 200-inch telescope at the Palomar Observatory in southern California, have found faint galaxylike images in some cases.

IRAS produced this infrared image of the entire sky. The bright horizontal line is our galaxy, the Milky Way. The center of the Galaxy is at the center of the picture. *IRAS* completed its survey of the northern and southern skies on Nov. 22, 1983, after nearly 10 months in orbit.

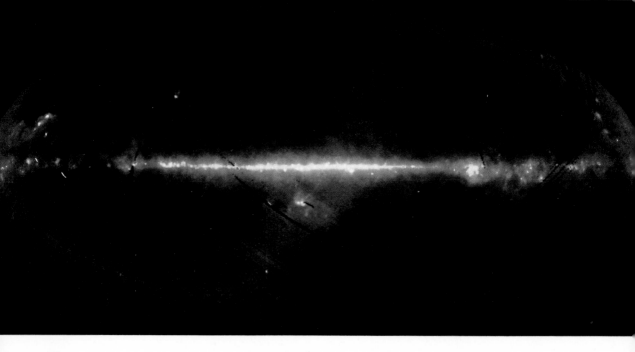

Scientists have advanced several ideas in an effort to explain these mysterious objects. A detailed study shows that some of these objects are, indeed, very distant galaxies.

Some astronomers think that others of these objects could be stars only a few hundred light-years away that are enshrouded within cold, dense cocoons of gas and dust. One or two of the infrared objects could even be inside our own solar system. Astronomers have long suspected the existence of a 10th planet. The orbits of the two outermost planets, Pluto and Neptune, appear to be slightly disturbed, leading astronomers to suspect the gravitational influence of a planet or planets in addition to the nine now known. The search for the 10th planet has not yet turned up any convincing candidates, but astronomers are looking carefully at the *IRAS* data. Another possibility is that *IRAS* may have uncovered a new class of previously unknown objects.

Finally, *IRAS* turned an inquiring gaze at *quasars* — the brightest and most distant objects in the universe, giving off as much energy as a thousand normal galaxies. Many astronomers think that quasars are areas at the centers of galaxies and that they may release their enormous amounts of energy as a result of matter being drawn into a *black hole*. (A black hole is a collapsed star with a gravitational force so great that not even light can escape.) If quasars are, in fact, at the centers of galaxies, then the analysis of *IRAS* data may help determine how they acquired so much energy.

The data-gathering phase of the *IRAS* mission has ended. The satellite will orbit Earth for millions of years, a useless piece of space debris. But scientists will long be occupied in studying the 250,000 infrared sources that *IRAS* surveyed, looking for new and unsuspected properties of the heavens. So in a very real sense the most exciting part of the *IRAS* mission — understanding the scientific results — is just beginning.

For further reading:

Allen, David. *Infrared: The New Astronomy*. Wiley, 1975.

Neugebauer, Gerry, et al. "Early Results from the Infrared Astronomical Satellite," *Science*, April 6, 1984.

Overbye, Dennis. "The Secret Universe of IRAS," *Discover*, January 1984.

Sterrenburg, Frithjof. "IRAS: Mission Invisible," *Astronomy*, April 1983.

Waldrop, M. Mitchell. "The Infrared Astronomy Satellite," *Science*, July 1, 1983.

Scientists have acquired a wealth of information about the habits — and helpfulness — of these amazing mammals.

The Facts About Bats

BY BEN PATRUSKY

Can you guess what cashews, avocados, bananas, dates, cloves, and figs have in common? If you guessed that they're all tropical products, you would be right. But they have something else in common, too — bats. As strange as it may seem, these tropical foods might never have made it to your local supermarket without the help of bats. By scattering seeds and pollinating flowers, bats that feed on fruit and nectar have played a major role in the evolution and survival of many tropical plants. Other products that might never have existed without bats include balsa wood, used in crafts; chicle latex, used in chewing gum; kapok filler, used in life preservers and surgical bandages; and even tequila, a Mexican liquor. In Southeast Asia, a single species of nectar-eating bat helps boost the economy by pollinating durian trees. Regional sales of the spiny fruit of these trees total more than $110 million a year.

And the helpful contributions of bats do not

end there. There is growing scientific evidence that tropical rain forests, among the world's most precious resources, depend heavily on fruit- and nectar-eating bats for their survival. In developing countries, bat droppings, known as *guano*, are an important source of fertilizer. Last but not least, bats are the only major predators of night-flying insects, including the pesky mosquito.

Nevertheless, few people recognize bats for the beneficial animals that they are. In fact, these greatly misunderstood creatures have long been surrounded by fears, myths, and mistaken ideas. Contrary to widespread belief, for example, bats are not blind. All species can see, and many have extraordinary vision. Nor do bats get tangled in people's hair. They actually tend to be quite shy and try to avoid contact with humans. One of the oldest superstitions about bats is that they are all vampires. But there is only one common species of blood-drinking bat, and it clearly prefers cattle and horses to people. Still another common misconception is that bats are dirty. On the contrary, they are meticulously clean. Like many other mammals, bats spend much of their time grooming themselves.

An especially frightening myth, which persists even among some health officials, is that bats often carry rabies. Scientific studies indicate that this is just not true. Less than one-half of 1 per cent of all bats contract the disease, and even rabid bats rarely become aggressive. In the United States, there have been only 10 reported human deaths caused by rabies from bats over the past 40 years. In the same time period, more than 130 people died of rabies from dogs and cats. Statistically, you are far more likely to be hit by lightning than to get rabies from a bat.

Myths aside, bats remain intriguing creatures simply because of their unusual characteristics and life styles. Bats are the only mammals that can fly, and their ability to maneuver in the air rivals that of birds. The bones of a bat's wings are essentially the same as those in human arms and hands. The fingers of a bat, however, are elongated and joined by a membrane of flexible skin that extends to the side of the body. This wing structure accounts for the bats' scientific name, *Chiroptera*, from a Greek word meaning *hand-wing*. Depending on the species, the wing membrane may also be connected to the legs or tail.

The author:
Ben Patrusky is a free-lance science writer and a media consultant to several scientific institutions.

There are nearly 1,000 kinds of bats, representing about one-fourth of all mammal species. Most bats make their home in the tropics, but species are found in every part of the world except the most extreme polar regions. About 40 kinds of bats live in the United States and Canada. Thirteen species are found in the British Isles. Bats range in size from the flying foxes of the tropics, which have wingspans of up to 6 feet and can weigh more than 2 pounds, to the tiny Kitti's hog-nosed bat of Southeast Asia. The hog-nosed bat, about the size of a large bumblebee and weighing less than a penny, is the world's smallest mammal.

Bats come in a variety of sizes from the flying fox of the tropics, *above,* which weighs up to 2 pounds and has a wingspan of up to 6 feet, to the tiny Kitti's hog-nosed bat of Southeast Asia, *left,* about the size of a large bumblebee.

All bats are *nocturnal* — that is, they are active mostly at night. By day, they rest in hideaway roosts, chiefly caves, trees, and buildings. But bats also take shelter in culverts, crevices in cliff faces, animal burrows, termite and bird nests, bamboo stalks, and even unfurled banana leaves. Bats usually hang upside down while roosting. This position enables many bats to huddle close together for warmth and also makes for a fast launch into flight.

Bats live a long time, usually far longer than any other mammals of comparable size. Species found in areas with a temperate climate, such as the brown bats of North America, live 20 years or more. Tropical bats are thought to have somewhat shorter life spans. Scientists believe that the bat's nocturnal life style helps account for its long life. The night air is largely free of predators that attack bats, and flying in the dark protects the thin wings of bats from the damaging, dehydrating effects of sunlight. Another factor that may contribute to a longer life is the ability of many bats to *thermoregulate* — that is, to drop their body temperatures to that of the surrounding

Wrinkled-faced bat

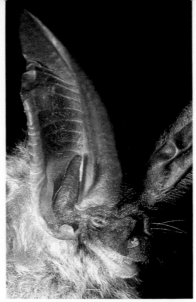

Western big-eared bat

Northern spear-nosed bat

Leaf-chinned bat

Sword-nosed bat

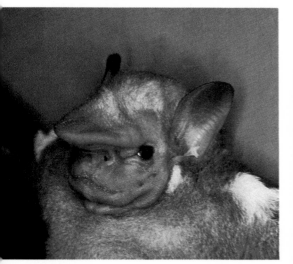

Hooded bat

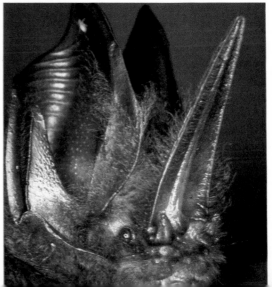

air when at rest. The lower temperatures serve to cut down on body wear and tear. Some species of temperate-zone bats, the brown bat among them, carry thermoregulation one step further. During the winter, they go into hibernation. The bodies of hibernating bats remain at significantly reduced temperatures for months at a time.

To master the night skies, most bats depend more on their hearing than on their vision. In the 1940's, Donald R. Griffin, then a graduate student in biology at Harvard University in Boston, discovered a natural *sonar* system in bats. (The word *sonar* comes from the words *so*und *n*avigation *a*nd *r*anging.) Bats that use sonar emit high-frequency sounds almost continually while in flight. By interpreting the echoes produced when the sounds bounce off objects, a bat can locate prey and navigate safely around obstacles even on the darkest night. Griffin named this amazing ability to "see" with sound *echolocation*. Only the flying foxes of Africa, Asia, and Australia do not echolocate. Instead, they rely on their extremely good vision to guide them in the dark.

Echolocating bats generate their sonar signals by vibrating membranes in the larynx, or voice organ. Depending on the species, these signals are emitted either through the nose or the mouth. Bat faces feature a variety of bizarre adaptations—ranging from folds, flaps, and slits to spearlike projections on noses—that help the bats to magnify and direct the sounds. The huge, funnellike, and intricately folded ears of some bats help them to better hear the returning echoes. A bat's sensitive ears can pick out the echoes of its own sonar signals even among thousands of other echolocating bats.

The sound waves emitted by echolocating bats generally have frequencies ranging from 25 to 75 kilohertz (kHz), far above the 20- to 20,000-hertz range of human hearing. (Frequency is measured in *hertz*, the number of wave cycles or vibrations per second. One kilohertz equals 1,000 hertz.) Different species of bats have different levels of sonar ability. A bat that lives in a relatively obstacle-free desert, for example, requires less precise sonar than one that lives in a dense forest. Bats that use echolocation only for navigation purposes usually produce less intense signals than bats that also echolocate to detect and capture prey. Even among bats that hunt by means of echolocation, sonar abilities vary depending on whether the bat nabs its prey in midair, plucks it from a leaf, or scoops it from a pond.

Most bats produce a combination of the two basic kinds of sonar signals—*constant frequency* (CF) and *frequency modulated* (FM). A CF signal consists essentially of a single tone. An FM signal is a varying tone that sweeps through a band of many frequencies. When a hunting bat is on the lookout for a target, it generally searches with CF signals. But for pinpointing and capturing prey, FM is usually better. The broader range of frequencies provides the bat with more information about the size, shape, texture, motion, distance,

Fascinating bat faces, *opposite page,* reflect the incredible diversity of features found among bat species. The unusual facial folds, bizarre nasal structures, and large ears enable bats to better emit and receive the sound signals of *echolocation,* the natural sonar system that many bats use to navigate and hunt at night.

Hunting with Sound

In the darkness, a bat uses echolocation to scan for prey, *below*. Echoes from the constant stream of sonar signals it emits guide it to an insect. As the bat closes in on its intended victim, it sends out its sonar pulses at an increasingly faster rate, as shown in the graph, *bottom*. After catching and eating its prey, the bat again sends out its search signals.

and speed of the prey. In fact, a bat using FM signals can determine just about everything but the color of its target.

The timing of the sonar signals is also important. For example, the insect-eating Mexican free-tailed bat emits very short CF pulses at the rate of about 30 per second while scanning for prey. When it detects an insect, it switches to the broader band of FM signals and sends these out at a faster and faster rate as it gets closer and closer to its target. By the time the Mexican free-tailed bat is ready to pounce, it is sending out its sonar signals so fast — about 300 pulses per second — that its transmission is almost a continuous buzz. The time between the first contact with the prey and the kill is often less than one second. After eating its prey, the bat starts the search again, repeating the hunting pattern until it has consumed its nightly fill of insects.

Most of the world's bats — about 70 per cent of all bat species —

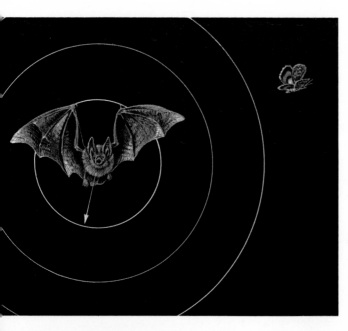

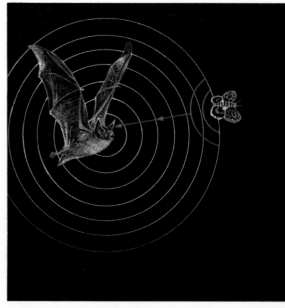

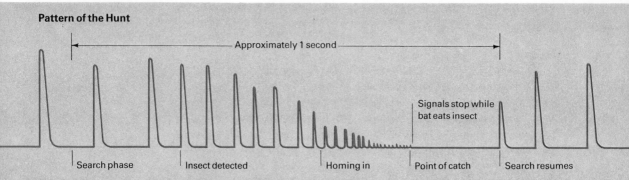

Pattern of the Hunt

Approximately 1 second

Signals stop while bat eats insect

Search phase   Insect detected   Homing in   Point of catch   Search resumes

feed on insects. Almost all bats that live in the United States, Canada, and the British Isles are insect-eaters. The bats consume their prey in huge amounts. One gray bat from the Eastern United States may devour more than 3,000 insects in a single night's outing. Large colonies of bats, as a whole, consume countless billions of insects.

Fruit- and nectar-eating bats make up the second largest group. Fruit-eating bats are now recognized as the most important seed-dispersing mammals in tropical regions. Many of these bats eat and digest their meals while in flight, excreting the seeds as they move. Scientists refer to these droppings as "seed rain." Some seeds even seem to require the chemical action of a bat's digestive juices before they *germinate* (begin to grow). Nectar-eating bats, and some fruit-eating bats that also visit night-blooming flowers, serve as very effective pollinating agents, carrying pollen on their fur or whiskers from one flower to another. Although many of the plant products that once depended on the pollinating and seed-dispersing abilities of bats are now cultivated on plantations, bats are still of major importance in maintaining the wild strains of these plants. These wild strains could prove vital to the development of more productive or disease-resistant plant varieties.

Evidence that fruit-eating bats play a crucial role in the survival of tropical rain forests comes from Donald W. Thomas, a zoologist at Carleton University in Ottawa, Canada, who recently completed a four-year study of fruit bats in West Africa. Thomas found that the bats account for as much as 95 per cent of the seed rain responsible for preserving forests in that area. In fact, he discovered that a single species — the straw-colored *Eidolon helvum* — disperses the seeds of about 200 different kinds of trees and shrubs during its migration across thousands of miles of West Africa. The bats have extremely rapid digestion — no more than 15 minutes from eating to excretion — which means that the animals are scattering seeds almost continuously while on the wing. Moreover, *Eidolon* appears to be the exclusive seeding agent for the *iroko*, a timber tree similar to red mahogany. The iroko harvest brings in about $100 million annually to West African nations.

Scientists have just begun to document the impact of Central and South American fruit bats on tropical vegetation in that region, but early indications are that the impact is considerable. Theodore H. Fleming, a biologist at the University of Miami in Florida, discovered recently that one species, *Carollia*, commonly feeds on the fruit of extremely fast-growing plants. By dropping these seeds on forest regions that have been depleted of plant life by floods, fires, lumbering, or other disturbances, the bat helps to speed up the growth of new vegetation. Moreover, in studies conducted in western Costa Rica, Fleming found the *Carollia* bat to be a major disperser of the seeds of at least 10 to 15 per cent of all local tree and shrub species.

Unlike bats that feed on insects, fruit, and nectar, vampire bats

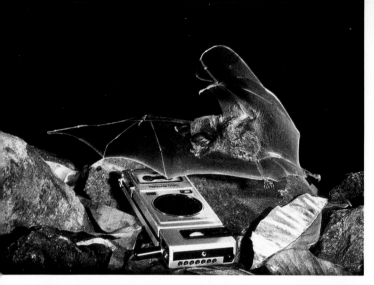

Displaying its remarkable hunting ability, a fringe-lipped bat scoops a frog from a jungle pond, *right.* A recording of a frog's mating call, planted by scientists, attracts a fringe-lipped bat, *above,* showing that it relies on mating calls to locate its prey. The bats also use the calls to distinguish between edible and poisonous species of frogs.

A Niceforo's forest bat makes a meal of a katydid while hanging comfortably from a vine, *left.* Some bats, like the forest bat, specialize in plucking large insects from the ground, rocks, trees, and bushes.

After a Wahlberg's fruit bat discovers a cluster of berries, *far left,* it stuffs its cheek pouches full of the fruit, *left.* The bat uses the pouches to carry its food while in flight. Such fruit bats play a major role in dispersing the seeds of thousands of tropical plants.

are not widespread. There are only three species, and all are found in the tropics of Central and South America. Only one of these species is widespread enough to be considered a serious pest. Contrary to its name, a vampire bat does not actually suck blood from its victims, chiefly cattle and horses. Rather, it makes a small incision in the animal's hide with its razor-sharp teeth and laps up the blood that oozes from the wound. The bat's saliva contains an anticlotting agent that keeps the victim's blood flowing as long as the bat continues to drink. The nose of a vampire bat is equipped with a heat-sensing apparatus that enables the bat to find sites on its prey where blood vessels are close to the surface.

Other bats — about 13 per cent of all species — are flesh-eaters that feed on small fish, rodents, birds, possums, or other bats. Recently, another staple was discovered on the bat menu. Working in the jungles of Panama, Merlin D. Tuttle, curator of mammals at the Milwaukee Public Museum, found that the fringe-lipped bat, originally thought to be an insect-eater, feeds mostly on frogs. Tuttle reported that he first saw a fringe-lipped bat eating a frog one night in 1974, at a pond in a Panamanian forest. But he was puzzled by something. He noticed that there were many species of frogs at the pond, some of which were highly poisonous. The frog-eating bat, however, sought out only the edible frogs, even though they bore a remarkable likeness to their poisonous relatives. How were the bats able to make the distinction in the dark? Tuttle speculated that the bats listened to the mating calls of the male frogs. Since each species of frog has its own call, the bats would be able to distinguish between the edible and the poisonous varieties.

In 1979, Tuttle returned to Panama to test his theory, with the help of Michael J. Ryan, a frog behaviorist then from Cornell University in Ithaca, N.Y. The researchers experimented with captured frog-eating bats in an outdoor flight cage near a jungle pond. They set up speakers inside the cage and played cassette recordings of many different frog calls. Frog-eating bats flew to the speakers only in response to the cries of the edible species. Tuttle and Ryan later determined that the bats depended entirely on frog calls to identify their prey. If the edible frogs were silent, the bats ignored them, even when the frogs were just inches away.

The social behavior of bats may depend, at least in part, on their feeding habits. Bats roost in colonies that vary in size from a few individuals to millions of members. The very large colonies are found primarily in temperate zones. These bats probably roost together in great numbers, chiefly to stay warm. But colony size is directly related to the available food supply among tropical bats, according to Jack W. Bradbury, an ecologist and animal behaviorist at the University of California, San Diego. He reached this conclusion after long-term studies on several closely related bat species in Trinidad and Costa Rica and observations of African bats.

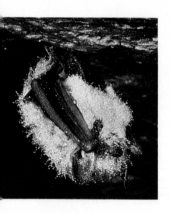

Beads of moisture condense on the body of a hibernating Eastern pipistrelle bat. During hibernation, a bat's metabolism slows greatly, and its body temperature may approach freezing.

Bats live in a variety of places. A group of Lyle's flying foxes make their home in a tree in Thailand, *above*. At dusk, a large colony of wrinkled-lipped bats emerge from their cave in Thailand, *left*. Two tiny disk-winged bats use suction cups on their wings and feet to climb out of their slippery shelter in an unfurled banana leaf in Panama, *below*.

Bradbury believes that the more food available—and the more consistently stable the food supply—the larger the bat colony is likely to be. He cites as examples the greater white-lined bat and its close relative, the lesser white-lined bat, both found in Central America. The greater white-lined bat is nearly twice as big as the lesser white-lined bat and thus can fly over a larger area. The bigger bat roams long distances from one roosting site to another in search of large populations of insects. Since these insects can feed many bats, colonies of the greater white-lined bat have hundreds of members. In contrast, lesser white-lined bats feed in the same small area all year. Their more limited foraging grounds provide only enough food for small groups of bats. As a result, lesser white-lined bats roost together in groups of six or less.

The mating styles of tropical bats also seem to be affected by their foraging habits. In some species of tropical bats that range over long distances in search of food, the females band together for life in a small harem, with one male serving as the sexual partner of all the females. In other species, the females regularly switch harems. For example, a greater white-lined female bat often joins a harem at one roost, mates with the male of that harem, and then goes on to join another harem when the colony moves to another roost. In this species, Bradbury explains, the males control the feeding grounds. Each male gives only the females that mate with him access to the foraging area he controls. Under the circumstances, the females try to ally themselves with males that have staked out the most favorable feeding sites. However, a male with a choice territory at one roost will often be the last to leave when the time comes for the colony to move on to another roost. As a latecomer, he is likely to find the members of his harem involved in new sexual alliances with males that have claimed the best foraging areas at the new roost.

Many temperate-zone bats that hibernate go through a frenzied, helter-skelter mating period in the fall, just before they begin their annual migrations to caves where they will spend the winter. During the mating period, the males of these species mate with as many females as possible. The females store the males' sperm in their bodies during the winter. Pregnancy begins only after they awaken from their winter's sleep and migrate to spring roosting sites. Baby bats, or pups, are born in the late spring or early summer.

Most bats bear just one pup at a time. Tropical bats stay sexually active all year long, and these females may give birth to one pup twice a year. In many species, pregnant females leave their usual colony and move together to special nursery roosts, where they give birth and rear their young. Pups are born with well-developed claws for clinging to the roost or to their mothers. In some species, the females carry their young with them when they go foraging at night. But most leave them behind in the roost. Because there can be millions of baby bats in a single nursery roost, scientists have long

As a greater short-nosed fruit bat feeds on a banana plant, its snout gets coated with pollen. Although bananas are grown commercially without the help of bats, the animals pollinate wild strains of the banana plant. These strains could someday prove vital in developing improved varieties for cultivation.

assumed that mothers returning to the roost after foraging feed the pups on a first-come, first-served basis, whether the pups are their own or not. But a study conducted in 1983 by Gary F. McCracken, a zoologist at the University of Tennessee in Knoxville, indicates that this is not true. By observing Mexican free-tailed bats in a nursery cave in Texas, McCracken found that most of the time, females managed to locate and feed their own young.

Perhaps the most stunning discovery about bat behavior has emerged from studies conducted between 1978 and 1983 in Costa Rica by Gerald S. Wilkinson, then a graduate student in animal behavior at the University of California, San Diego. His investigation centered on *Desmodus rotundus*, the scientific name for the most common of the three species of vampire bat. The bat, which measures about 4 inches from nose to tail, roosts in caves and tree hollows. For many nights, Wilkinson perched in a tree near a hollow that served as the roost of bats that he had banded for identification purposes. He found that females of the roost tended to form small, tightly knit clusters that stayed together for years and maybe even for a lifetime. Each of the clusters consisted of several adult females and their offspring, perhaps 20 bats in all. Some adults in each group were close relatives. But each cluster also contained two or more unrelated adults and their young.

Wilkinson's patient observations led to the discovery that adult females returning from a feeding run would share their meals through regurgitation with other females in the cluster who, for one reason or another, were unable to find food. That, in itself, was a significant finding, says Wilkinson, now at the University of Colorado in Boulder. It would seem that the females could not afford to give up any of their vital food supply because vampire bats have the longest pregnancy of any bat and nurse their young for seven months. Such lavish parental care requires a lot of energy. Nevertheless, the females do share with hungry neighbors, whose plight is serious. The bats die after only two days without food.

But the fact that the vampire bats share their food was only half the surprise. What really startled Wilkinson and other scientists was the observation that the bats shared not only with relatives but also with nonrelated members of the cluster. Accepted scientific theory held that any sharing between animals — other than human beings — occurred only between kin. To be sure that vampire bats shared with nonrelatives, Wilkinson decided to repeat his studies in the lab-

Bats face a number of threats to their existence. This young Thai poacher, for example, is removing bats from a trapping net. He will sell the large fruit bats to local restaurants, where bat meat is a popular item. He will simply kill and throw away smaller insect-eating species, which are of little value to him.

oratory with captive bats. The laboratory group included eight non-related females—four nonrelated bats from one cluster and four from another. Wilkinson chose nonrelated bats from two different clusters to determine if membership in the cluster, rather than a kin relationship, was the determining factor in the sharing behavior. Each night, Wilkinson randomly pulled one bat from the group and deprived it of food. The next morning, he put the unfed bat back in with the rest and watched what happened. Invariably, the starved bat was fed, but only by members of its own cluster.

As scientists continue to make amazing discoveries about bats and their life styles, they are also finding that bats are of great value to medical science. Research on echolocation in bats, for instance, has already led to the development of navigational aids for the blind. The thinness and transparency of bat wings makes the animals very useful in the investigation of new drugs. Under the proper light, blood vessels in the wings become quite visible, enabling scientists to easily see if the experimental drugs have any dilating or constricting effects on the vessels. Studies have also been launched to discover how temperate-zone female bats manage to store sperm for months at a time while they hibernate. Scientists hope that understanding how bats extend sperm life may help to overcome some human fertility problems. Research on the bat's brain, which is highly specialized for handling echolocation, may yield clues about how information is processed in the human brain.

Unfortunately, as the list of the helpful contributions of bats continues to grow, so do the threats to the existence of these creatures. Worldwide, bat populations are declining rapidly. Each year, large bat colonies die out because their habitats are disturbed or destroyed. In Africa and Asia, bats are being hunted in ever-increasing numbers for human food and for use in folk medicines and potions. Fruit-eating bats, which feed chiefly on the fruits of native forests, are often killed by farmers who mistakenly believe that the bats seriously damage their crops. And the myths about bats persist so strongly that millions of the animals are exterminated each year simply because people are afraid of them. Some species of bats are already extinct, and many more are endangered. Until more people come to recognize the value of bats and the need to protect them, the future of these important animals remains uncertain.

For further reading:

Fenton, M. Brock. *Just Bats*. University of Toronto Press, 1983.
Mohr, Charles E. *The World of the Bat*. Harper, 1976.
Tuttle, Merlin D. "The Amazing Frog-Eating Bat," *National Geographic*, January 1982.

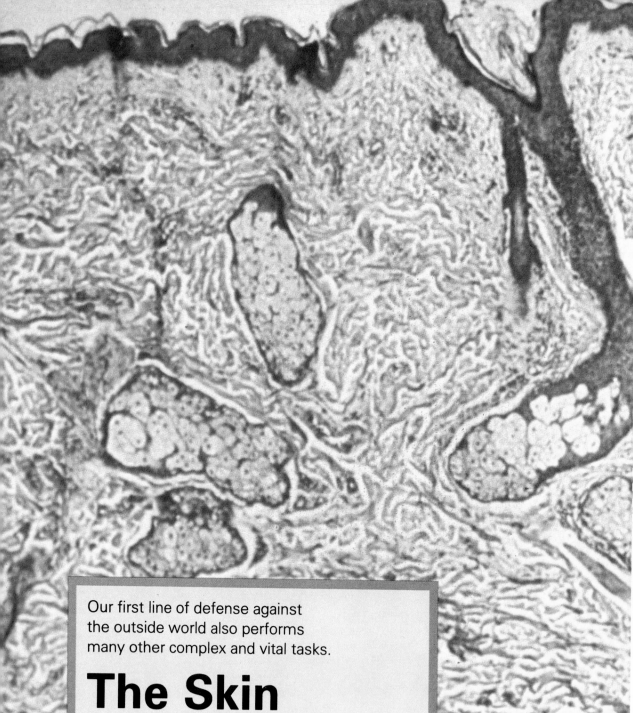

Our first line of defense against
the outside world also performs
many other complex and vital tasks.

The Skin
We Live In

BY LYNNE LAMBERG AND STANFORD LAMBERG

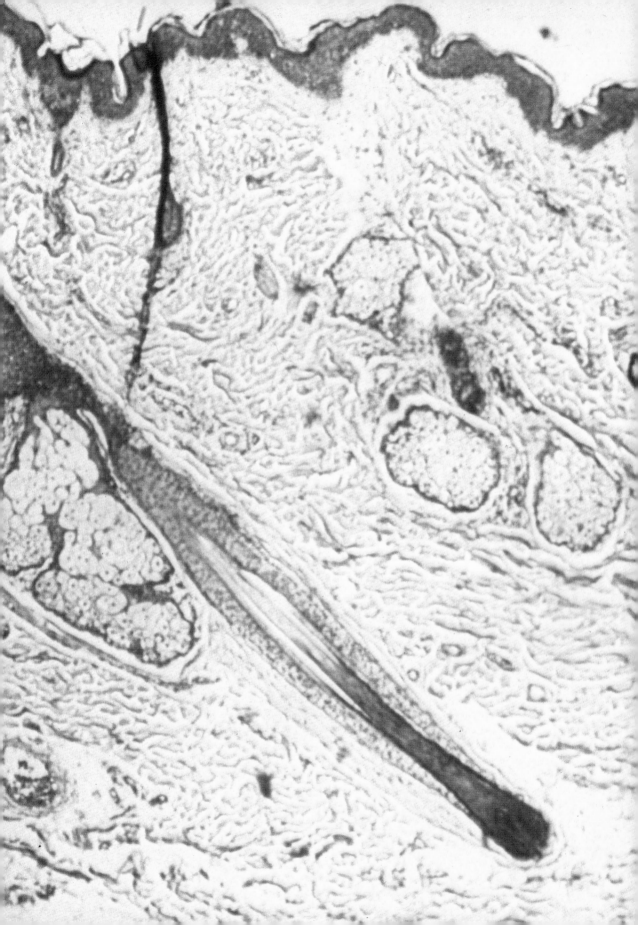

The authors:
Lynne Lamberg is a
free-lance medical
writer. Stanford Lamberg
is chief of dermatology
at the Baltimore City
Hospital and associate
professor of dermatology
at the Johns Hopkins
University School of
Medicine in Baltimore.

Five-year-old Sasha must be treated like a delicate porcelain doll — her skin erupts with painful blisters if her mother hugs her or when she wears scratchy clothing or new shoes. Sixteen-year-old Bob says it never fails — the night before a big date, blemishes start popping out on his chin and forehead. Frank's hands are constantly cracked and frequently bleed — he's a successful mechanic, but he's wondering if he should try another line of work.

These people suffer from different disorders that all originate in a common site — the skin. Sasha has *epidermolysis bullosa*, a rare inherited skin disease for which there is no known cure. Bob, on the other hand, is a perfectly normal teen-ager. His problem is that his anxiety about his social life is literally "breaking out" on his face. In Frank's case, the culprit is the chemicals he uses in his job.

Skin is often regarded as simply a container for bones, muscles, blood, and vital organs. But the skin actually performs many complex tasks. For example, it acts as a barrier that keeps vital body fluids in. Skin is also our first line of defense against the outside world. It provides a nearly impenetrable barrier to dirt, most chemicals, and microorganisms that could cause disease or illness. In fact, dense colonies of bacteria and other microbes, many of them disease-causing, ordinarily live on our skin. As long as the skin remains unbroken, they pose little threat. Skin is also waterproof. Even if you soak in a pool for hours on a hot summer day, your skin will absorb only a small amount of water.

Skin helps you to "know" the outside world. Sense receptors in the skin detect the sweep of a feather, the prick of a pin, the heat of a car seat in summer, the cold of a freezer case at the supermarket. Other receptors act as a pressure gauge that tells you how gently to pat a baby and how firmly to grasp a Frisbee.

Skin stretches when you reach for something on the top shelf of your closet and then quickly contracts to its normal size. It expands as you grow and shrinks if you lose weight. It also mends itself when torn, punctured, or burned and continues to do so for as long as you live.

Skin helps keep your internal body temperature constant. When the air temperature is cold, the blood vessels near the surface of the skin narrow, keeping your body heat in. When the air is hot, glands in the skin release sweat, and the evaporation of the sweat cools you.

Skin manufactures vitamin D, which you need for healthy teeth and bones. It helps shield you from the sun's damaging rays. And, finally, your skin also contains your own personal lifetime identification code — the fingerprints that distinguish you from every other person, living or dead.

To help it perform its many tasks, the skin is packed with specialized cells. Depending on where it is located, one square inch of skin may contain as many as 20 blood vessels, 650 sweat glands, 100 oil glands, 65 hairs and muscles, and 1,300 nerve endings, including 78 sense receptors for heat, 13 for cold, and 160 for pressure. Considering the variety of all these tasks, it may come as no surprise to learn that the skin is the body's largest organ. Skin accounts for about 15 per cent of an adult's weight.

The skin often acts as an indicator of our emotions. That is because of its rich supply of blood vessels and sweat glands, which are controlled by the same part of the central nervous system that regulates heartbeat, breathing, and other "automatic" bodily functions. When you are frightened or angry or otherwise under stress, your blood vessels may expand and cause you to blush, or constrict and cause you to grow pale. In addition, the output of your sweat glands may increase, and tiny muscles called *arrector pili* muscles may cause your hair follicles to stand up, giving you "goose flesh."

We may insist that beauty is more than skin deep, but few of us are able to avoid making judgments about other people based on our perception of the way they look. And in school, on the job, or in social situations, most of us aim to "put our best face forward." Such factors explain why skin disorders often arouse considerable anxiety as well as physical discomfort. In fact, people with disfiguring skin diseases often suffer from low self-esteem.

Many skin disorders are minor and disappear by themselves without treatment. But others are lifelong conditions that may be disabling or even life-threatening. Frequently, a skin disorder is only the most obvious of a group of symptoms reflecting a more serious illness. Severe itching, for example, may signal the presence of liver or kidney disease as well as certain types of cancer.

Because the skin is so accessible, researchers can easily take samples of it for use in the laboratory to study the way other parts of the body work. For example, skin is a ready source of connective tissue cells, which provide structural support throughout the body, and epithelial cells, which line all of the body's openings. Both these types of skin cells can serve as models for understanding the growth and functioning of cells elsewhere in the body.

Skin layers, skin colors

Structurally, the skin has three distinct layers — *epidermis*, *dermis*, and *subcutaneous tissue* — each with specific functions. The outermost layer — the one that you see — is the epidermis. Although the epidermis is 10 to 30 cell layers deep, it is no thicker than a page of this book. Its outer edge, the *horny layer*, is usually not much thicker than the ink on the page. The cells of the epidermis normally replace themselves about once a month, making them some of the most active cells in the body.

New cells form in the *basal layer*, the innermost part of the epidermis, and then migrate outward. On their way to the surface, they manufacture *keratin*, a waterproof protein that makes the skin tough. Keratin is also the chief component of hair and nails. Eventually, however, the cells lose moisture, die, and are painlessly shed. In the winter, if your skin is chapped, you often can see cells of the horny layer flaking off. The epidermis also contains pocketlike in-

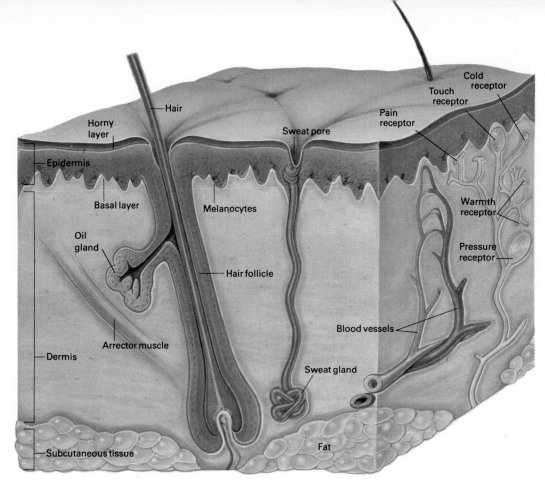

Hair

Horny
layer

Epidermis

Basal layer

Oil
gland

Melanocytes

Hair follicle

Sweat pore

Pain
receptor

Touch
receptor

Cold
receptor

Warmth
receptor

Pressure
receptor

Arrector muscle

Dermis

Sweat gland

Blood vessels

Subcutaneous tissue

Fat

Inside Your Skin

Skin consists of three
layers – epidermis,
dermis, and
subcutaneous tissue.
Skin also contains
hair, sweat and
oil glands, blood
vessels, and many nerve
endings, including
sense receptors for
heat, cold, and touch.

dentations from which hair grows, and pores through which sweat
and oil come to the surface.

The second layer — the dermis — is sturdier and 15 to 40 times
thicker than the epidermis. The depth of the skin, epidermis plus
dermis, may vary considerably. The skin of your eyelids is not much
thicker than this page. But the skin on the soles of your feet may be
¼ inch deep. The dermis provides structural support for the epidermis and makes it possible for skin to stretch and contract easily.
(Leather belts and shoes are made of animal dermis, treated with
chemicals to keep it soft and pliable.) The dermis also contains
nerve endings, muscle, sweat and oil glands, and blood vessels that
nourish both the dermis and the epidermis. And it is the dermis
that gives its name to the medical specialists who treat disorders of
the skin — *dermatologists*.

Beneath the epidermis and dermis is subcutaneous tissue, composed primarily of fat. This layer acts as a cushion to absorb shocks
and protect internal organs from injury and as insulation to help
conserve body heat. This tissue is quite thick in such places as your
buttocks and thighs, but it is absent from other areas of your body,
such as shins and eyelids.

Skin color is the result of a brownish pigment called *melanin*, which protects the skin by absorbing harmful ultraviolet rays from the sun. Melanin is produced by cells known as *melanocytes*, millions of which exist in the epidermis. People of all skin colors actually have about the same number of these cells. The wide range in human skin tones — from white and yellow to various shades of brown to black — results from hereditary differences in the amount of melanin produced by each of these cells and in the size of the melanin particles. Thus, the more melanin the cells produce and the larger the particles, the darker a person's skin will be. Actually, melanin production varies in the skin of even a single individual. Your skin is not the same color and texture everywhere. A section of skin taken from one spot on your body to cover a burn or other injury elsewhere will not blend perfectly with its new surroundings.

Skin color and the sun

Although people of all colors live throughout the world now, our skin color reflects our ancient ancestors' geographic origins. The earliest human ancestors, who lived in Africa near the equator — the place on Earth nearest to the sun — probably had dark skin. The skin of early human beings who moved northward out of Africa, however, became lighter.

In northern climates, dark skin is a hazard, because it does not permit the absorption of enough sunlight to stimulate the production of vitamin D. Before the development of dietary vitamin supplements, such as fortified milk and bread, people with dark skin living in the far north often developed weak curved bones and other symptoms of vitamin D deficiency, a disorder known as *rickets*. On the other hand, in tropical climates, light skin is a drawback. There, people with light skin develop more wrinkles and are more likely to suffer sun-linked skin cancers than are people with dark skin. In the Science You Can Use section, see SUNSCREENS: BEACH UMBRELLAS IN A BOTTLE.

Skin is one of the most obvious indicators of the changes that

Among the many sense receptors in the skin are touch receptors, *below left* (greatly magnified), which detect where we are touched and the texture of the object touching us. A pressure receptor, *below* (also greatly magnified), is among the largest sense receptors in the body.

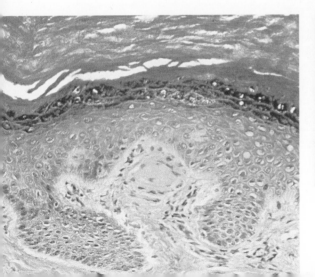

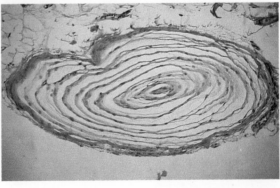

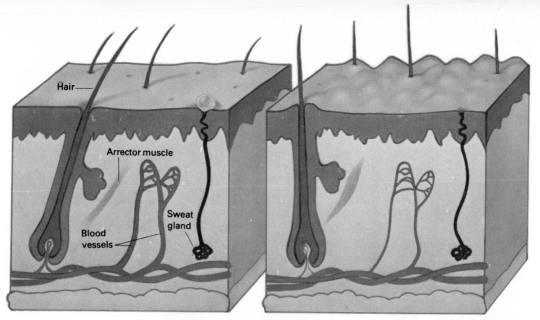

Hair

Arrector muscle

Sweat gland

Blood vessels

Regulating Temperature

Skin helps keep your internal body temperature constant. When the air temperature is hot, the blood vessels in the skin expand, *above* (left), releasing heat. The sweat glands also release sweat, which cools the skin by evaporation. When the air temperature is cold, the blood vessels narrow, *above* (right), keeping body heat in. Tiny muscles in the skin also contract, causing hair to stand up and creating "goose flesh." Sweat clings to the inside of a sweat pore, *right* (shown greatly magnified).

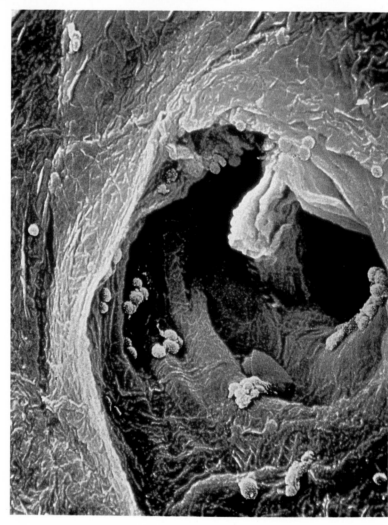

occur as we age. The skin of a newborn baby or a young child is soft, smooth, unlined, and generally free of moles, pigmented spots, and other blemishes. During adolescence, however, the oil glands enlarge, and nearly everyone develops acne and experiences changes in skin color and texture.

At about age 40 in women and somewhat later in men, the oil glands start to slow their rate of secretion. As a result, skin becomes drier. But it actually is water, not oil, that gives skin its plump, smooth look. Oil slows the evaporation of water from the skin and so indirectly maintains the water content. A dry piece of skin that is submerged in oil will remain stiff and brittle. But skin submerged in water will become soft and flexible again.

As we age, the connective tissue in the dermis that provides a framework for the skin loses some of its elasticity, and so the skin sags. The rate of cell renewal — the movement of new cells up through the epidermis — also slows.

But the skin changes that most people regard as inevitable signs of aging — wrinkles, dark spots, small growths — are, in fact, mainly the result of sun exposure. The effects of ultraviolet light are prominently etched on the faces of people who have spent many hours in the sun. Skin that has always been shielded from the sun by clothing remains much smoother and has far fewer wrinkles.

Updates on three common skin diseases

Skin is prone to a number of diseases. In fact, scientists have identified more than 1,500 different conditions that can afflict the skin. According to the American Academy of Dermatology, at any one time, nearly one-third of all Americans probably have at least one skin condition that should be treated by a physician. About 2 million Americans feel that their skin problem severely limits their social life, performance at work, or other activities. Here are the latest findings about three common skin problems.

■ **Acne.** While nearly every adolescent suffers some degree of

People of all skin colors have about the same number of pigment cells in their skin. However, in black skin, *below left,* the cells produce larger and greater numbers of pigment particles than are produced in white skin, *below right.*

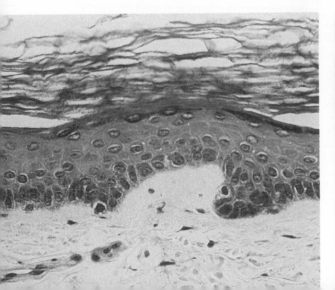
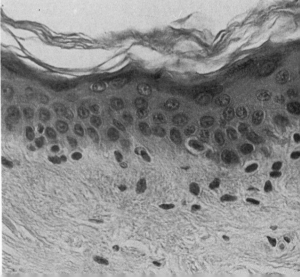

Sun: Our Essential Enemy

Your skin and the sun have a curious relationship. Sun is essential for good health. Without it, the skin could not manufacture vitamin D, needed for strong teeth and bones. However, the sun can also be the skin's worst enemy. Fortunately, nearly all people have a built-in protective mechanism — tanning.

Although many people use the word *healthy* to describe a tan, tanned skin is actually damaged skin — skin injured by too much sunlight. Tanning is a two-step process. Within a few hours after you are exposed to sunlight, the brown pigment in your skin — melanin — starts to darken. Melanin protects the skin by absorbing the ultraviolet radiation in the sun's rays. In addition, ultraviolet light stimulates cells called melanocytes into making more melanin.

Gradually, over a period of about two weeks, this extra melanin works its way up to the skin surface, further darkening the skin. If you spend less time in the sun, the melanocyte-factories slow down and the extra melanin eventually will be sloughed off with dead skin cells. In other words, your tan will fade.

If you get too much sun, however, your skin will burn. Sunburned skin turns red because the blood vessels near the surface of the skin expand in response to the injury. A sunburn can seriously damage your skin. If you could examine sunburned skin cells under a microscope about nine hours after exposure, you would find that some of the cells had shriveled into dark spots.

Over time, too much exposure to the sun, especially for lighter-skinned people, weakens the connective tissue that keeps the skin firm. This results in fine wrinkling that gives the skin a leatherlike appearance.

Wrinkling, however, may be the least of the problems sun worshipers face. Sometimes, ultraviolet light causes skin cells to grow much faster than normal or to grow erratically, producing unsightly growths. The cells may also become *malignant* (cancerous).

Scientists are not sure how sunlight causes cancer. One theory is that the ultraviolet light causes the *deoxyribonucleic acid* (DNA) in the skin cells to break. DNA is the cell's blueprint, telling it how to function and reproduce. When a DNA molecule is damaged, special chemicals in the body rush to repair it. However, the chemicals may not perform their repairs perfectly, and the result may be abnormal DNA molecules. These abnormal molecules may trigger the development of cancer by allowing the cells to reproduce wildly.

In 1979, scientists at several universities and at the National Cancer Institute's Research Center in Frederick, Md., reported that sunlight itself suppresses the body's *immune* (defense) system, making it less able to fight cancers and, thus, enabling cancers to grow more easily.

Skin cancer caused by sun damage may not become apparent for 20, 30, or more years. As a result, most skin cancers appear in older adults. According to the American Cancer Society, about 400,000 people in the United States develop skin cancer each year. Cancers of the skin account for about one-third of all cases of cancer, making them the most common form of cancer. Although light-skinned people are particularly susceptible, black people also develop skin cancer, though far less frequently. Fortunately, more than 95 per cent of skin can-

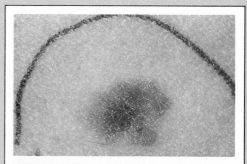

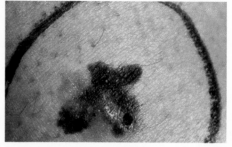

Irregular color and shape, *top,* are warning signs that a mole is likely to become cancerous. Darkly pigmented areas, *above,* indicate a mole has become cancerous.

cers are cured, the highest cure rate for all cancers.

One particularly deadly type of skin cancer — malignant melanoma — arises in the melanocytes. Melanomas develop in about 12,000 persons in the United States every year and account for about 5,000 deaths. The number of melanoma cases occurring in America has doubled since the 1960's. Some skin specialists believe this rise is due to increased sun exposure, mainly because people now wear fewer and lighter clothes and spend more time in the sun.

Often, the first sign of melanoma is a color change in a mole or birthmark. Moles are actually clusters of melanocytes. Some become brown or black, while others become red, white, or blue, or even lose their coloring. Other warning signs include moles that change in size — a sudden increase is of special concern — or moles that change shape, become scaly or flaky, or begin to ooze or bleed. Such moles may also become softer or harder or may become tender, painful, or itchy. In addition, the skin around the mole may change. For example, it may become red or swollen. Any of these danger signs should be reported to a doctor immediately.

If diagnosed early enough, melanomas can often be cured by surgery alone. If surgery is not successful, chemotherapy and radiation treatments may be used. However, if the melanoma is not treated early, it often spreads to the lymph nodes — glands that filter harmful organisms from the lymphatic system. As a result, the nodes must also be removed. Even then, the disease often recurs.

In September 1983, researchers at Emory University in Atlanta, Ga., reported that a vaccine may help reduce the likelihood of melanoma recurring in patients whose melanoma had spread to the lymph nodes. Microbiologist William Cassel and surgeon Douglas Murray, who developed the vaccine, compared two groups of melanoma patients who had their lymph nodes removed. One group received the vaccine; the other did not. After three years, 88 per cent of the patients who received the vaccine were still in good health, compared with only 5 per cent of the group who had only surgery. A further study of the vaccine is in progress at other medical centers.

Scientists also have been able to identify persons who are particularly susceptible to developing melanomas. One group of persons with a higher than average risk are people who were born with moles or whose moles appeared in infancy. This group comprises about 1 per cent of all children. A panel of health experts, convened in 1983 by the National Institutes of Health in Bethesda, Md., urged such people to get regular medical examinations. However, the experts felt that there are insufficient data at present to recommend removing all such moles to prevent their becoming cancerous.

Researchers at the National Cancer Institute and the University of Pennsylvania have also found that perhaps 10 per cent of all people with melanomas are members of families with an inherited tendency to develop the disease. These people frequently have 100 or more moles by the time they reach adulthood, compared with an average of only 25 for most people. Unlike most people, they also continue to get new moles even after age 35. Identifying vulnerable families will allow doctors to watch family members carefully and treat them early, if they do develop the disease. Further, family members can take steps to prevent skin cancer by avoiding too much sun exposure and always using sunscreens, lotions that screen out damaging ultraviolet rays.

Actually, that is good advice for everyone — even children. If you do spend time at the beach in the summer, when sunlight is most intense, or on ski slopes in winter at high altitudes, where there is less atmosphere to filter ultraviolet rays, you should avoid the sun between 10 A.M. and 2 P.M. During this period of the day, the sun's rays are strongest. Hats provide some protection, as does such clothing as ski masks and long-sleeved shirts. But the most effective precaution you can take is to use sunscreens year-round.

Sunscreens, products you apply directly to your skin, contain chemicals that allow you to be in the sun for a longer period without burning. The products differ in their water resistance, so if you are perspiring heavily or swimming, you should reapply your sunscreen. Over-applications are not harmful. In the Science You Can Use section, see SUNSCREENS: BEACH UMBRELLAS IN A BOTTLE.

By taking a few simple precautions — limiting sun exposure and using sunscreens — you can take advantage of the benefits the sun provides while minimizing the hazards. [L. L. and S. L.]

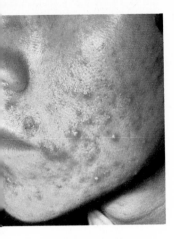

Acne and Psoriasis
Two common skin diseases result from a build-up of substances normally produced by the skin. Severe acne, *above,* occurs when excess oil blocks the pores and bacteria breed in the backed-up oil. Psoriasis results from a build-up of skin cells. A microscopic view of normal skin, *below,* shows a thin, even top layer. The skin of a psoriasis sufferer, *below right,* has a thick top layer because skin cells reproduce and reach the surface at a faster-than-normal rate.

acne — a disorder of the oil glands — about 5 per cent develop *cystic acne*, a severe form of the disease that is likely to leave the skin permanently pitted and scarred. A new drug, a synthetic derivative of vitamin A called *13-cis retinoic acid* (also known as *isotretinoin*), often brings dramatic and long-lasting clearing of the skin. The drug was approved by the Food and Drug Administration (FDA) in 1982 for use in the United States after testing by researchers at the National Institutes of Health in Washington, D.C., and several university medical centers. Unfortunately, the drug has a number of potentially serious side effects, including birth defects.

■ **Psoriasis.** In this inflammatory skin disease, which affects about 4 million Americans, new skin cells reach the surface of the epidermis every three or four days — about seven times faster than normal. The cells collect in thick red patches covered with silvery-white scales, most commonly on the elbows, knees, lower back, or scalp. The aim of treatment is to remove the patches and slow down the rate of cell growth. Effective drugs that can be applied directly to the skin have been available for some time, but they are smelly and messy and often stain or burn the skin. Researchers are investigating ways to eliminate some of these drawbacks. For example, one of these drugs, *anthralin*, is being tried in higher concentrations to reduce the time the drug must remain on the skin. Researchers in the United States are also investigating *etretinate*, a form of vitamin A that European researchers have found to be effective.

In 1982, the FDA approved a psoriasis therapy called *Psoralen Ultraviolet A* (PUVA) treatment, which had been used experimentally since 1974. In this therapy, psoriasis patients swallow a drug called *psoralen*. Two hours after taking psoralen, the psoriasis patients are exposed to ultraviolet light for several minutes. The psoralen makes the skin particularly receptive to the ultraviolet light, which is effective at clearing the skin.

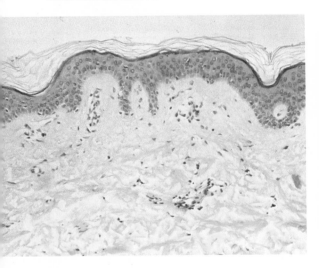

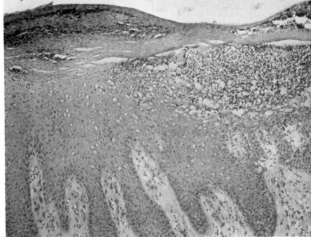

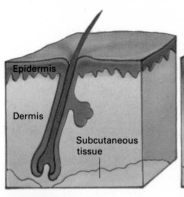
First-degree burn

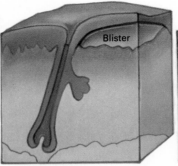
Second-degree burn

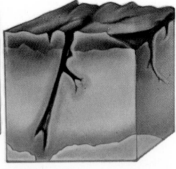
Third-degree burn

Epidermis

Dermis

Subcutaneous tissue

Blister

Burns and Their Repair

A first-degree burn damages only the epidermis. A second-degree burn destroys the epidermis and the top layers of the dermis – perhaps causing blisters to form – but leaves the skin's cell-producing layers intact. A third-degree burn destroys all layers of the skin, causing such severe damage that the skin cannot repair itself. To replace destroyed skin, surgeons may use an artificial skin, *right,* that stimulates the production of new skin. A burn wound repaired with artificial skin, *below right,* shows less scarring than would a burn wound that was covered with a conventional skin graft.

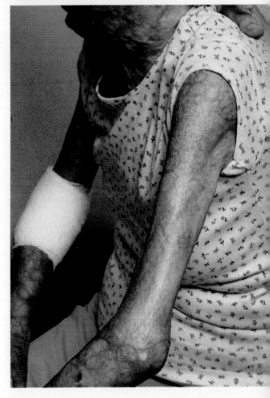

Nearly 75 per cent of patients undergoing PUVA treatment get rid of almost all their psoriasis. However, the therapy is recommended only when other psoriasis treatments fail, because it causes a greater risk of skin cancer among psoriasis patients who have already had skin cancer or whose skin was exposed to radiation therapy before beginning PUVA treatments. For other patients, the risk seems small.

■ **Baldness.** The most common cause of baldness in men is an inherited tendency for it. Over the centuries, numerous compounds and chemicals have been proposed as remedies. In fact, cures for baldness may be the most fertile field for quacks and medical con men. The truth is, no drug has yet been found that stimulates hair growth on bald scalps.

One new line of research, however, seems promising. About 15 years ago, researchers found that many people who were taking *minoxidil,* a drug used in the treatment of high blood pressure, began sprouting hair in such unlikely places as the lips, forehead, and bridge of the nose.

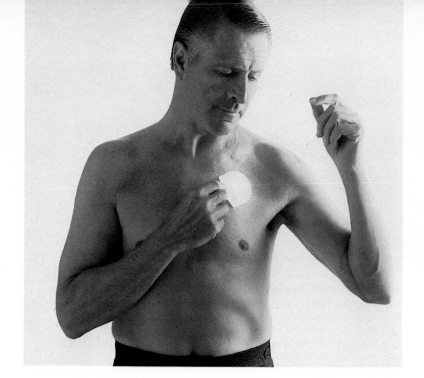

A transdermal patch, which is stuck onto the skin like a Band-Aid, delivers medication – such as nitroglycerine for heart patients – directly to the bloodstream through the skin.

Other researchers heard of the drug's strange effects and reasoned that if the drug was applied directly to the scalp, it might help grow hair on bald heads. Minoxidil's manufacturer, the Upjohn Company of Kalamazoo, Mich., is sponsoring a study of the drug's usefulness for treating baldness at 21 medical centers in the United States.

New ways to treat burns

Skin performs so many vital functions that serious injuries to this vital organ, especially burns, may be life-threatening. If you get a minor burn, your skin repairs itself fairly easily. Skin cells migrate into the wound from the surrounding area and produce a new covering. Some burns, however, are so deep or so extensive that the skin cannot repair itself. This allows vital body fluids to escape and opens the door to infections that could be fatal. Each year, about 10,000 Americans die of burn injuries.

The large number of deaths from burns has made the search for skin replacements particularly urgent. Currently, skin from animals and corpses is used as a temporary wound covering for burn victims. Unfortunately, such skin cannot be used as a permanent replacement because the body soon rejects it as foreign matter. The only material the body will accept is a graft of skin from somewhere else on the same body. However, undamaged skin on a seriously burned person may be in short supply.

Artificial skin developed in 1981 by a research team headed by surgeon John F. Burke of Massachusetts General Hospitals and physical chemist Ioannis V. Yannas of the Massachusetts Institute of

Technology, both in Boston, already has proven helpful to more than 50 severely burned people. Among them was a 3-year-old girl who had burns over more than 90 per cent of her body.

The artificial skin is constructed in two layers that act somewhat like the epidermis and dermis. The protective outer layer is made of plastic. The inner layer is made from shark cartilage and from cow *collagen* — an important type of connective tissue. This layer, which gradually decomposes, serves as a supporting surface to which new nerve fibers, blood vessels, and connective tissue can attach themselves. Skin cells from the edge of the burn wound migrate into this inner layer, attach themselves, and begin to produce new skin cells. Once the new dermis has grown firmly into place, the plastic outer layer of artificial skin is peeled away and replaced by a graft of a very thin layer of undamaged skin taken from another area of the person's body. Because the artificial skin stimulates the growth of dermal skin, surgeons can use a much thinner graft than they could without the artificial skin. In addition, because the graft is so thin, the area from which the graft is taken heals quickly and so the same area can be used repeatedly. Researchers report that burn wounds closed with the artificial skin show less scarring than conventional skin grafts.

An improved version of the artificial skin has proven successful with guinea pigs and will soon be used on people on an experimental basis. This artificial skin is "seeded" with a small number of immature cells from the epidermis and dermis of the patient's own skin. The cells reproduce themselves, forming layers of both dermal and epidermal skin, thus eliminating the need for any grafting.

Another exciting area of skin research has been fueled by the discovery that the skin can be used as a fast way to get certain medications into the bloodstream. These medications are combined with "carrier" chemicals that can easily penetrate the skin in so-called *transdermal* (through the skin) patches, which are stuck onto the skin like Band-Aids. So far, transdermal patches have been developed for some heart medications, motion-sickness drugs, and drugs that lower the blood pressure.

The role the skin plays as either a barrier or a gateway demonstrates the complexity of the remarkable organ that many of us take for granted. Nothing yet developed in this high-technology age even comes close to providing all of the comforts we ordinarily can count on in this wonderful "house" that we live in.

For further reading:

Elgin, Kathleen. *The Human Body: The Skin*. Watts, 1970.
Hare, Patrick J. *The Skin*. St. Martin's, 1966.
Showers, Paul. *Your Skin and Mine*. Crowell, 1965.
Zizmor, Jonathan. *The Doctor's Do-It-Yourself Guide to Clearer Skin*. Lippincott, 1980.

The merger of particle physics and cosmology is leading to an understanding of how the universe probably began — and how it may end.

The First Second

BY DAVID N. SCHRAMM

The creation of the universe and everything in it, most scientists think, began some 15 billion years ago in a brilliant eruption of energy called the *big bang*. According to this theory, every particle that makes up our bodies or the distant stars, all the vast expanses of space between the galaxies — everything that is or ever can be — had its origin in that instant, when even time began.

As it exploded into existence, the universe was dazzlingly bright and inconceivably hot. At every point in its rapidly expanding space, newly forming atomic particles smashed into one another with energies trillions of times higher than any that exist today. The universe was so dense that space and time were churned into countless tiny black holes, which constantly burst and re-formed like a boiling foam. All of this occurred within the merest fraction of a second. From this beginning, the familiar, orderly universe we now live in evolved.

Although the moment of creation might seem to be an event that is beyond our knowing, scientists believe the birth of the universe was governed by the laws of nature. Thus, while we may never be able to say for sure *why* the universe came into being, *how* it did so is a question that science should be able to answer. Since the early 1970's, in fact, there has been a tremendous increase in our understanding of the origin and evolution of the universe. This has come about through the close interaction of two fields of study — *cosmology* and *particle physics*. Cosmology is the study of the very large — the overall structure of the universe, the galaxies and their motions, and the nature of space. Particle physics is the study of the very small — the tiny particles that combine to make atoms and the forces that act between those particles.

The tracks made by a shower of subatomic particles inside a particle accelerator, *opposite page,* are set against a backdrop of distant galaxies. The study of matter on its smallest and largest scales is yielding clues to the origin of the universe.

The author:
David N. Schramm is chairman of the Astronomy and Astrophysics Department at the University of Chicago.

Through most of the 1900's, these two fields developed separately, with scientists in one field paying little attention to what scientists in the other were doing. Modern cosmology got its start in the 1920's, when an American astronomer, Edwin P. Hubble, proved that the universe is much, much bigger than anyone had imagined. Until then, astronomers' observations had been limited by relatively small telescopes, and they had assumed that our Milky Way galaxy was the entire universe. Using a new, 100-inch telescope, Hubble showed that certain hazy patches of light in the heavens are other galaxies of stars, not *nebulae* (gas clouds) within the Milky Way, as was previously thought. The reason they are so faint, he explained, is that they are at immense distances from us.

In 1929, Hubble, following up on the work of another American astronomer, Vesto M. Slipher, announced a second important discovery: The galaxies are moving away from one another. So not only is the universe big, it is getting bigger all the time. Scientists developed two alternative explanations for that finding. One theory held that matter is continuously being created in the space between the galaxies. As the galaxies move farther apart, new galaxies form between them, so that the universe has always existed basically as we see it now and always will. This is called the *steady state theory*. However, it did not fit the growing evidence from observations and calculations, and by the early 1970's, it had lost out to its rival, the big bang theory.

According to the big bang theory, the galaxies are rushing away from one another because they once were part of a dense mass that blew apart—a *primordial fireball*, as many astronomers call it. This theory predicted that the radiation produced by that gigantic explosion, though scattered through the vast reaches of the expanding universe, should still exist as microwaves. In 1965, engineers at Bell Telephone Laboratories, while testing a satellite-tracking antenna, discovered just this sort of radiation coming from all parts of the sky. This microwave radiation—the *cosmic background radiation*—was convincing evidence in support of the big bang.

Popular versions of the big bang theory have sometimes envisioned the universe beginning as a giant "egg" of subatomic particles that somehow exploded. However, this picture is misleading. Cosmologists speak of the first moments of creation as a "decompression" of matter and energy that had been squeezed into an almost infinitely dense state.

It is important, however, to realize that this compacted mass did not burst forth into a vacuum that had been standing empty until that time. Space, too, was created by the big bang and continues to be created as the universe expands. In fact, it is the overall expansion of space that is moving the galaxies ever farther apart. Picture the universe as a rising loaf of bread dough and the galaxies as raisins within it. As the loaf gets bigger, the raisins become farther apart. But the raisins themselves do not move through the dough; they are simply carried along by the dough as it expands. Of course, analogies can be taken just so far. A loaf of bread has edges and a center, while the universe has neither.

After learning that the universe is expanding, cosmologists began to debate whether the universe is *open* (infinite) and will expand forever until it is nothing but cold gas and cinders — "the big chill" — or whether it is *closed* (of limited size) and will eventually contract back to its original density — "the big crunch." Whether the universe is open or closed depends on how much matter it contains. If the big bang had created too little matter, it all would quickly have flown apart into infinity, and galaxies would not have formed. But, if too much matter had been created, the universe would have come to a speedy end through gravitational collapse. That is, the mutual gravitational attraction of all the particles of matter would have reversed the expansion of the universe, and the big crunch would have occurred very soon after creation. The universe seems to be almost exactly at the *critical density* — it is walking a tightwire between being open and being closed. This finding created a major problem with the big bang theory. The theory could not explain why the universe is still here, expanding at a nice steady pace, after a period of 15 billion years.

Several other questions were raised by the big bang theory. Among them were: Where did matter come from, and why is the universe so amazingly uniform, or smooth? On the relatively small scale of human beings, matter appears to be in clumps. It forms into planets, stars, and galaxies. However, if we could step back from the universe, we would see matter filling nearly every part of it, much as the air in a dusty room is filled with dust particles.

Astronomers also found that the cosmic background radiation was almost exactly the same in every direction they looked. The big bang theory had predicted the radiation but not that it would be so unvarying throughout the universe. By the 1970's, it had become clear that the theory would have to be added to before it would give a complete explanation for the birth of the universe.

While cosmologists puzzled over these questions, physicists were discovering how matter is put together. Scientists knew by the early 1900's that there are 92 naturally occurring elements (others have since been made artificially). They also knew that each element consists of individual atoms, and that an atom consists of a small nucleus surrounded by orbiting electrons. In 1932, they discovered that the nucleus consists of both protons and neutrons. For a while, scientists thought that atoms contained just protons, neutrons, and electrons. However, as they began to probe the nucleus with *particle accelerators* — large machines that boost subatomic particles to enormous speeds — they discovered that matter can be broken down into hundreds of other kinds of particles. There seemed to be no end to

Glossary

Black hole: An extremely dense object in space from which not even light can escape.

Bubble universe: A universe that formed within the superuniverse during the period of inflation.

Electromagnetic force: The force that holds electrons in orbit around an atom's nucleus.

Electron: A fundamental particle that orbits the nucleus of an atom.

Fundamental particle: A basic building block of matter that does not consist of smaller units.

Grand Unified Theory: A theory in physics that unites three of the basic forces of nature but excludes gravity.

Gravity: The force that operates between large objects, such as stars and planets.

Inflation: A tremendous, almost instantaneous, increase in the size of the superuniverse.

Lepton: A class of fundamental particles that includes electrons and neutrinos.

Neutrino: A fundamental particle produced by the disintegration of unstable atomic nuclei or subatomic particles.

Neutron: A subatomic particle found in the nucleus of most atoms.

Nucleus: The central part of an atom, composed of protons and neutrons.

Proton: A subatomic particle found in the nucleus of an atom.

Quark: A fundamental particle found in neutrons and protons.

Super Grand Unified Theory: A theory that unifies gravity with the other three forces of nature.

Superuniverse: The entire universe, containing our bubble universe and many other bubble universes.

Weak force: The force that is responsible for some types of radioactive decay.

A Cosmic Chronology

Scientists think the universe developed from a state of almost infinite density some 15 billion years ago. Time zero—that first instant of creation, when all four forces of nature were unified—is a mystery because the universe was in a state that physics cannot describe. However, a moment later, at 10^{-43} second, gravity became a separate force. That may have been the first step in a chain of events that led to the universe we know today. Some of these events—the period of inflation, the separation of the other forces, and the creation of subatomic particles—occurred within just a fraction of a second. The unfolding drama then began to move at a slower pace. After three minutes, simple atomic nuclei formed. Not much happened for the next 100,000 years, and then nuclei and electrons combined to make atoms. After 100 million years, stars and galaxies formed, and the universe began to take its present shape.

Time zero
All forces
are unified.

10^{-43} second
Gravity becomes
a separate force.

3 minutes
Simple atomic nuclei form.

100,000 years
Complete atoms form.

100 million years
Stars and galaxies form.

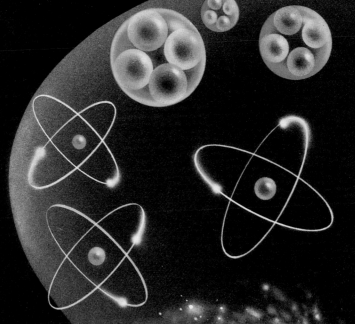

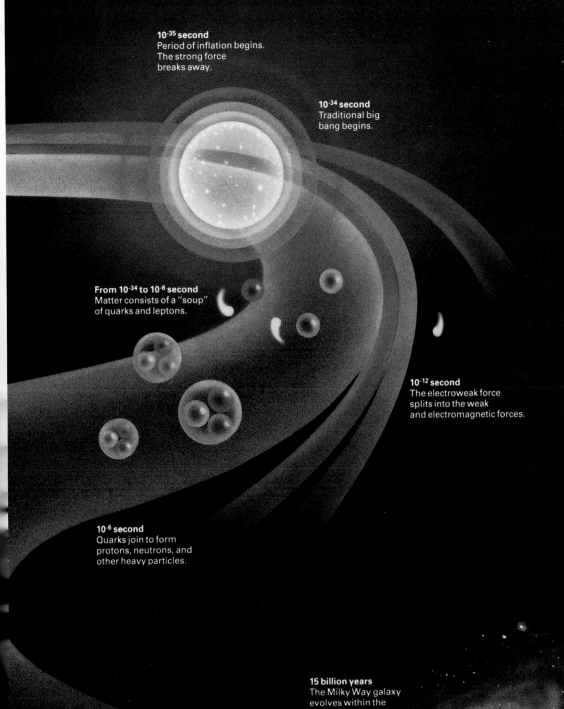

10⁻³⁵ second

10^{-35} second
Period of inflation begins.
The strong force
breaks away.

10^{-34} second
Traditional big
bang begins.

From 10^{-34} to 10^{-6} second
Matter consists of a "soup"
of quarks and leptons.

10^{-12} second
The electroweak force
splits into the weak
and electromagnetic forces.

10^{-6} second
Quarks join to form
protons, neutrons, and
other heavy particles.

15 billion years
The Milky Way galaxy
evolves within the
expanding universe.

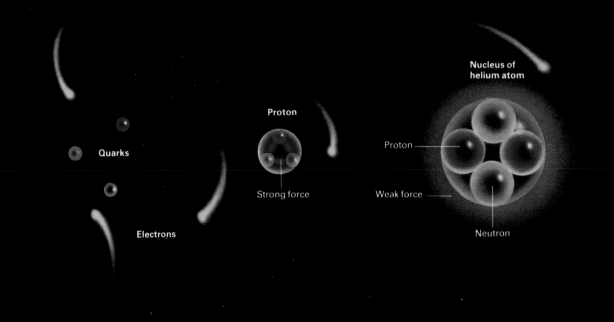

Quarks

Electrons

Proton

Strong force

Nucleus of
helium atom

Proton

Weak force

Neutron

Particles and Forces

All matter is composed
of fundamental particles,
mainly quarks and
electrons. Quarks
come together to make
up protons and neutrons.
These in turn join to
make up atomic nuclei.
An atom consists of
electrons orbiting a
nucleus. Matter is
governed by four
fundamental forces. The
strong force binds
quarks into protons and
neutrons and holds the
nucleus together. The
weak force is responsible
for radioactive decay.
The electromagnetic
force holds electrons in
orbit around the nucleus.
Gravity is very feeble
at the atomic level.

the "elementary" particles that could be created. See THE NEW
ATOM SMASHERS.

In the 1960's and 1970's, physicists worked out a new explanation
for the structure of matter that imposed order on this chaos of particles. They theorized that all heavier particles, including neutrons
and protons, are composed of still smaller fundamental particles.
These "building blocks" were named *quarks* by Nobel Prize-winning
physicist Murray Gell-Mann, who proposed the theory in 1964,
along with physicist George Zweig. Another family of fundamental
particles consists of *leptons*, or lightweight particles. The most familiar of these is the electron.

But discovering the basic building blocks of matter was only half
the battle. Physicists also had to learn what holds those building
blocks together. Over the years, they have found that four basic
forces govern the universe. Two of these forces are familiar to us in
our everyday lives: *gravity* and the *electromagnetic force*. Gravity is the
force that holds galaxies together and keeps our feet firmly planted
on the earth. The electromagnetic force is the force that holds electrons in orbit around the nucleus. It also makes possible light, chemical reactions, and electric power, not to mention radios and video
games.

Two other basic forces rule the atomic nucleus and are called the
weak force and the *strong force*. The weak force is responsible for the
radioactive decay of nuclei. The strong force is the "glue" that binds
three quarks together to form a neutron or proton, and it also holds
the nucleus together. The weak and strong forces make themselves
felt only across tiny distances within the nucleus.

At the present temperature of our universe, the four forces are
separate and have vastly different strengths. The strong force—

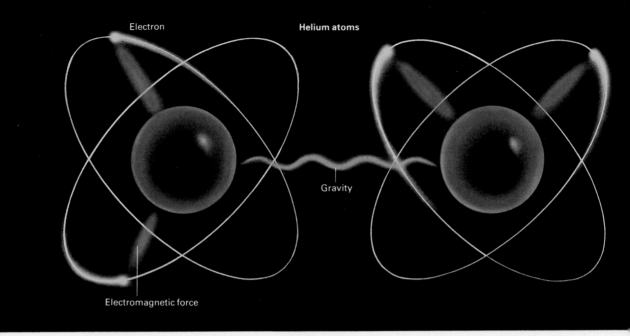

Electron

Helium atoms

Gravity

Electromagnetic force

which, as its name implies, is the most powerful of the forces — is 10^{39} (1 followed by 39 zeros) times stronger than gravity, which is the feeblest force. The effect of gravity increases as mass increases. The gravitational attraction of one atom for another is almost non-existent, but the gravitational force between the earth and the sun is very strong.

Although the four forces are so dissimilar, scientists wondered if they were somehow parts of a single unified force. The first step indicating this might be so came in the late 1960's, when two American physicists — Steven Weinberg and Sheldon L. Glashow — and Pakistani physicist Abdus Salam developed a theory of how the electromagnetic and weak forces could be merged. They predicted that when particles possess an energy of 100 billion electron volts (GeV), the two forces become a single "electroweak" force. (One electron volt is approximately the energy of an electron moving through a flashlight battery.) The three physicists won the 1979 Nobel Prize for physics for their work, and experiments in 1982 and 1983 with the powerful particle accelerator at the European Organization for Nuclear Research (CERN) in Geneva, Switzerland, proved the theory correct.

The next step was to combine the strong force with the electroweak force, and after that to bring gravity into the club. In the past few years, physicists have succeeded in developing so-called *Grand Unified Theories* (GUT's) that unify the strong and electroweak forces, and they hope to create a Super Grand Unified Theory that includes gravity. The problem with GUT and Super-GUT theories is that, unlike the electroweak theory, many of their predictions cannot be tested with particle accelerators. For example, GUT's predict that the strong force will merge with the electroweak force at about

10^{14} GeV, and scientists believe that gravity blends with the other forces at about 10^{19} GeV. These enormous energies are far beyond the capabilities of any conceivable machine. The largest accelerator now being planned, the Superconducting Super Collider (SSC), would have a maximum energy of about 2×10^4 GeV (20,000 GeV), and the accelerator ring would be 60 miles or more in circumference. Physicists estimate that in order to achieve an energy of 10^{19} GeV, a linear particle accelerator would have to stretch from the earth to the center of the Milky Way, a distance of about 200,000 trillion miles.

However, there was one time and place where energy levels *were* that high, and higher — the big bang. Particle physicists therefore turned their attention to a subject that had formerly concerned only cosmologists — the birth of the universe. The physicists hoped that if they could describe how matter, energy, and space interacted during that period, they would be able to make predictions about the nature of matter in today's universe. If those predictions were upheld by certain experiments, the physicists' theories about unified forces would be validated. For example, GUT's predict that protons eventually disintegrate. A number of experiments have been underway for several years to confirm proton decay, but so far those studies have been inconclusive.

This merger of particle physics and cosmology has benefited both disciplines. Physicists have gained new insights into matter and energy, and cosmologists have been able at last to obtain plausible answers to some of the questions raised by the big bang theory. Together, scientists in these two fields have helped to reconstruct the history of the universe beginning with the very first moments of creation.

So let us turn our thoughts back to the beginning of time and see how events may have unfolded. Actually, we cannot return quite all the way to time zero, because for the first 10^{-43} second the universe was in a state that our laws of physics cannot describe. The time span 10^{-43} second is a fraction of a second — written as a decimal point followed by 42 zeros and the numeral 1 — that is a million trillion times shorter than the length of time it takes light to cross a single proton. During that unimaginably small amount of time, as the universe began to decompress from almost infinite density, space was a jumbled foam of tiny black holes that formed, exploded, and re-formed instantaneously. All four forces of nature were merged into one unified master force.

At 10^{-43} second, gravity broke away and became a separate force. Then, at 10^{-35} second, something astonishing may have happened. Many physicists now believe that the universe underwent a gigantic expansion at that instant, becoming billions of billions of times larger than it had been. This sudden, mind-boggling event, called the period of inflation, lasted an incredibly short time — until about

10^{-34} second. At the end of that brief period, the universe had become a superuniverse containing many smaller "bubble" universes. One of these bubbles was the universe we live in, separated forever from all the other bubble universes. Each of the bubbles then continued to expand, but at a much slower rate.

If this theory is correct, matter and energy throughout our bubble must have developed into galaxies. But the universe of galaxies that we now see through our telescopes — called by astronomers the *observable universe* — developed from just a baseball-sized volume of matter and energy within the bubble universe. The other galaxies that formed in the bubble are beyond the range of our telescopes. Thus, the observable universe is just a tiny part of the entire universe within our bubble.

We now date the start of the traditional big bang at the end of the inflationary period. When the period of inflation ended at about 10^{-34} second, the grand unified era — when the strong, weak, and electromagnetic forces were one — also ended. The strong force had become separate from the electroweak force. An instant later, at 10^{-12} second, when the energy level within our bubble universe had fallen to about 100 GeV, the electroweak force split into the weak force and the electromagnetic force. There were now four distinct forces.

During this time, the only matter in our universe was a "soup" of quarks and leptons. Because the universe was still tremendously hot, none of these particles could yet join together. However, at 10^{-6} second, the strong force began pulling quarks together to create protons, neutrons, and other heavy particles. When 3 minutes had passed and the universe had cooled to a temperature not far above that of exploding hydrogen bombs, protons and neutrons joined to make simple atomic nuclei.

Not much happened for the next 100,000 years. The universe grew increasingly larger and cooler, but it was still a dazzling fireball of nuclei and leptons. Finally, when the temperature had fallen to less than 20,000°F., electrons were moving about slowly enough to be captured by nuclei and form complete atoms. Almost all of these atoms were hydrogen or helium.

As the universe continued to expand, cool, and evolve, its brightness slowly faded. The huge clouds of hydrogen and helium broke up into many individual — though still immense — pockets of gas, and these contracted by gravitational attraction into rotating islands. By the time the universe was 100 million years old, countless galaxies had formed, each glowing with the combined radiance of billions of stars. The universe that we know today had begun to exist.

Since then, our universe has continued to evolve. The galaxies move apart, stars die, and other stars are born. Our sun was born about 4.6 billion years ago and is probably a typical star of the Milky Way galaxy. However, to the physicists and cosmologists who are

According to the theory
of the inflationary
universe, *opposite page,*
the universe emerged
from a state of almost
infinite density and
then, an instant later,
expanded to gigantic
size. Within this
huge superuniverse,
smaller bubble universes
formed. One of these
bubbles evolved into
the universe in which
we now live.

trying to learn how matter, energy, and space first came into being, all of the most important events in the history of the universe occurred during the first second of creation. In the past few years, they have been paying a great deal of attention to the inflationary universe theory. This theory, proposed in 1980 by American physicist Alan H. Guth and later modified by others in the field, is the refinement of the big bang theory that cosmologists had been waiting for.

Unbelievable as the idea of inflation may seem, the theory is firmly grounded in physics and mathematics. We think the energy that powered this tremendous outward push of space was produced when the universe underwent a *phase transition* (a change of matter or energy from one state to another). An example of a phase transition in our everyday world is water turning to ice, or ice to water. In the case of the universe, the phase transition was the change from grand unification to the separation of the strong and electroweak forces at 10^{-35} second. This transition was accompanied by alterations in the very nature of space itself.

The space of our present universe is called a *true vacuum* because it contains no stores of energy that can be converted to matter. However, during the grand unified era, space was in a state that physicists call a *false vacuum* — it contained a great amount of trapped energy that was waiting to be freed. When the temperature fell to the point where the strong force could break away and become a separate force, the false vacuum became unstable. Its great store of energy then propelled the infant universe — or rather, the superuniverse — into inflation. Bubble universes formed almost instantly when their space changed from false vacuum to true vacuum. The space within the bubbles then settled down to a more moderate expansion. The space outside the bubbles continued to inflate rapidly, though physicists are not sure for how long. Some physicists think that the remaining false vacuum is still inflating today, creating ever more space between the bubbles. Other physicists say inflation may just have "run out of steam" and stopped throughout the superuniverse.

To understand the concept of inflation, it is important to realize that nothing in space was actually moving. It is just that every region in space suddenly got larger. In this respect, inflation is similar to the regular expansion of our universe — and the rising loaf of raisin bread — only much, much faster.

You might wonder why the superuniverse, which was so terribly hot before inflation began, was not instantly cooled by its sudden increase in size. In fact, inflation did cool space. But as a region of the false vacuum became a bubble of true vacuum and the inflationary period ended, the energy that had been fueling inflation was converted into a firestorm of subatomic particles at a temperature almost as high as that before inflation began. We, in our bubble

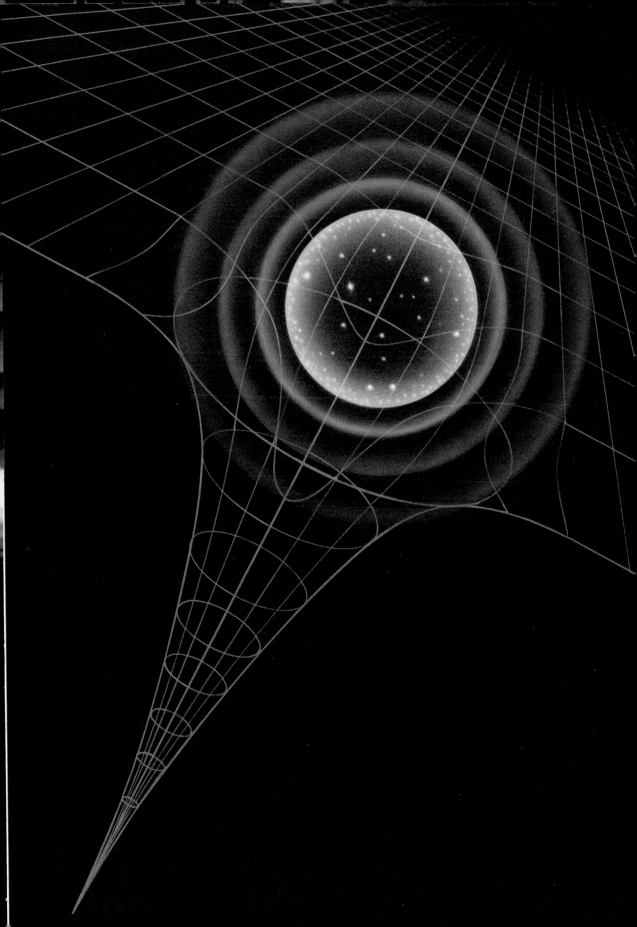

universe, look back on this moment of transition as the beginning of the classical big bang.

Inflation is still just a theory, but many physicists and cosmologists think that it did indeed occur, since it explains several current features of our universe. For example, it answers the question of why the cosmic background radiation is the same throughout the universe. In the standard big bang theory, the initial eruption of matter and energy was so chaotic that it would have been impossible for every part of the universe to contain the same amount of energy. Inflation smooths things out. Because the region of space that would become our universe was incredibly tiny, all parts of that region would have possessed an equal distribution of energy. This uniformity of energy is now spread throughout the universe. Likewise, matter was evenly dispersed through space, enabling galaxies to form in all parts of the universe.

Inflation also explains why our universe is so finely balanced between being open or closed. A universe that is exactly at the critical density is said to be *flat*, just as a small area on the surface of a balloon seems flat if the balloon is inflated to great size. Cosmic inflation works the same way. If an extremely tiny region of space is inflated to a tremendous volume, that space will appear increasingly flat. Thus, inflation not only accounts for the apparent flatness of space, it predicts it. If the inflationary theory is correct, our bubble universe contains just enough matter to be infinite and to expand forever, slowing down but never quite stopping. The same would hold true for all the other bubbles. (It may seem impossible for there to be many bubble universes and for each of them to be infinite and embedded in an infinite superuniverse. However, infinities within infinities are common in mathematics, and physicists think they can also exist in reality.) So although it seems a distasteful future, the big chill may well be the destiny of our bubble universe — and of all the others as well.

The prediction that our universe is at the critical density is still just that, a prediction. It is now up to astronomers to show that the universe contains just enough matter to expand forever. So far, all of the universe's known matter in the form of quarks and electrons adds up to, at most, 15 per cent of the amount needed. That leaves 85 per cent of the matter unaccounted for. Physicists call this the "problem of the missing mass." We think the missing 85 per cent must be in the form of *dark matter* — mass that is not incorporated into stars. One possible candidate for the missing mass is a lepton known as the *neutrino*. This bizarre little particle is a lot like an electron except that it has no electric charge and is constantly moving at or near the speed of light. The universe contains about 10 billion times as many neutrinos as heavy particles, so if neutrinos have even a tiny amount of mass, they could make up the "matter deficit."

The search for the missing mass is just one of several research projects that physicists, cosmologists, and astronomers will be concentrating on in the next few years. Physicists will continue to work with particle accelerators in search of new subatomic particles. One of these—the Higgs particle (named after British physicist Peter Higgs)—is associated with the false vacuum. Confirming the existence of the Higgs particle would help to validate the theory of inflation. To find the Higgs particle, physicists will need a new generation of particle accelerators with much higher energies. They are now developing design plans for the Superconducting Super Collider and looking throughout the United States for a possible site for the huge machine.

Astronomers, for their part, are looking forward to the development of several new instruments that will enhance their ability to observe the heavens. Toward the end of the 1980's, the space telescope—the first optical telescope ever to view the skies from above the earth's atmosphere—will be put into orbit. This telescope should help to resolve questions about the expansion of the universe. Also in the late 1980's, a satellite known as the *Cosmic Background Explorer* will be orbited to look for variations in the background microwave radiation. The information gathered by the satellite should help us to determine how galaxies formed out of the smooth distribution of matter and energy that existed in the very early universe. Finally, in the early 1990's, a satellite called the *Advanced X-Ray Astronomy Facility* will be placed into orbit to search for giant X-ray sources far away in space, including in other galaxies. This satellite, too, will help us to learn about the formation of galaxies and the origin of the universe.

These research projects, together with the ongoing work of the theorists, will continue to enlarge our understanding of the universe—its birth, its structure, and its underlying unity. The more we discover about the universe, the more we will no doubt be forced to conclude that the earth and humanity are but a trivial part of the whole. Indeed, as the inflationary theory suggests, ours may be just one of many universes.

However, there is an alternative point of view—that, perhaps, the only universe that counts is one that produces beings capable of contemplating themselves and their cosmos. If so, then it may be that our place in the universe is not so insignificant, after all.

For further reading:

Abell, George O. *Drama of the Universe*. Holt, Rinehart and Winston, 1978.
Guth, Alan H., and Steinhardt, Paul J. "The Inflationary Universe," *Scientific American*, May 1984.
Overbye, Dennis. "The Universe According to Guth." *Discover*, June 1983.
Trefil, James S. *The Moment of Creation: Big Bang Physics from Before the First Millisecond to the Present Universe*. Scribner, 1983.
Weinberg, Steven. *The First Three Minutes: A Modern View of the Origin of the Universe*. Basic Books, 1976.

BY ROBERT H. MARCH

The New Atom Smashers

Gigantic machines that accelerate beams
of tiny particles to tremendous speeds help
scientists explore the world inside the atom.

Thirty miles west of Chicago, buried deep in the Illinois prairie, is a 4-mile tunnel to nowhere. It was dug to house a working monument to human curiosity — the world's most powerful "microscope," a vast array of sophisticated hardware called the *Tevatron*. This machine was designed to give scientists a glimpse of things as small as one 10-quadrillionth of a millimeter, 10,000 times smaller than the nucleus of an atom.

The Tevatron is located at Fermi National Accelerator Laboratory (Fermilab) near Batavia, Ill. It is the latest in a long line of *particle accelerators*, popularly known as "atom smashers" ever since the first ones were built in the early 1930's. Its ancestors fit comfortably on a laboratory workbench. The Tevatron and other modern accelerators sprawl across hundreds of acres. Particle accelerators helped usher in the atomic age by allowing physicists to examine what atoms are made of. And the bigger the accelerator, the more clearly the physicists can "see."

It may seem peculiar that as science zeroes in on tinier and tinier objects, the machines it uses get bigger and bigger. This is because in order to see something, you must illuminate it with waves that are as small as or smaller than the object under study. In the sub-atomic world, all particles are also waves, and the more energy a particle has, the shorter is its wavelength. To reach high energies takes enormous machines, such as the Tevatron. Energies are measured in terms of *electron volts* (eV). Visible light has an energy of about 3eV. The Tevatron can produce 1 trillion eV, or TeV.

Optical microscopes, which use relatively low-energy beams of visible light, were developed in the 1600's. They enable us to see objects much smaller than the naked eye can see. Because they use beams of visible light, this limits how "small" they can see to one 10-thousandth of a millimeter. With them, we can see such tiny objects as bacteria and blood cells.

The next step toward seeing even tinier objects took place in 1931, when German scientists developed the *electron microscope*. These microscopes produce beams of electrons at energies of thousands or millions of eV, and they enable scientists to see objects as tiny as one one-millionth of a millimeter. With electron microscopes, we can see viruses and large molecules. The most powerful electron microscopes can even show the location of atoms in molecules.

Particle accelerators, which date from the early 1930's, can see inside the atom itself. As these machines have grown bigger and more powerful, they have enabled us to "see" more and more details of the atom. The first accelerators could see an atomic nucleus, which is a few one-trillionths of a millimeter across. As they have grown larger, accelerators have revealed the very parts of which the nucleus is made — protons and neutrons. The largest machines even "see" inside these protons and neutrons, revealing that they consist of tiny objects called *quarks*. These machines can boost beams of electrons, protons, or even whole nuclei to energies of up to hundreds of billions of eV.

Although these mighty machines are built to serve as microscopes, they do not allow researchers to "see" in the usual sense of the word. The low energy levels in ordinary light beams do not seriously disturb the things we look at with microscopes. But this is not the case with beams produced in atom smashers.

Beams in the billion-electron-volt (GeV) or TeV range tear a nucleus apart. To complicate matters further, they actually have enough energy to create new particles by converting energy to mass. When two particles meet head-on in an accelerator, hundreds of particles may emerge. The particles are tracked by complex equipment such as sensitive electronic detectors, which send signals to computers. These computers eventually construct a printout of

The author:
Robert H. March is a professor of physics at the University of Wisconsin and the author of the Special Report CATCHING NATURE'S VANISHING ACT in the 1983 edition of *Science Year.*

data — a visual picture of what happened. Sometimes the results of collisions are recorded in *bubble chambers*, containers of liquid under pressure. As the particles shoot through this liquid, they leave tracks in the form of tiny bubbles, which the physicists photograph for later study.

These experiments provide answers to such simple questions as: How many parts do the particles have? How are they arranged? How big are they, and how heavy? How tightly are they held together? How were the particles moving before the collision? How do they respond to outside forces? Any one experiment can provide only partial answers to a few of these questions. It has taken thousands of experiments involving millions of particle collisions to build up our modern view of the subatomic world.

Although there are several different types of accelerators, all of them basically work the same way. Electrically charged particles, usually protons or electrons, are accelerated to high speeds. The particles must travel in a vacuum, because collisions with air molecules would quickly rob them of energy and slow them down. Accelerators use electricity as the "engine" to power the particles; magnetism provides the "steering" that holds them on course.

As any driver knows, a car must travel a certain minimum distance to reach a high speed. If the road has curves, the car cannot turn as sharply at a high speed as at a low one. This is why a powerful accelerator must be so large. It must provide a long enough track for the particles to reach high speeds, and wide, gentle curves for the particles to turn in.

The first accelerators were built in the early 1930's, and most of the basic designs had been invented by the late 1940's. Since then, accelerators have mainly grown larger and more refined.

The simplest accelerators use a steady electric field to accelerate subatomic particles. This field is created by charging a metal sphere to a very high voltage. The most powerful of these accelerators are based on a design invented by physicist Robert J. Van de Graaff at Princeton University in Princeton, N.J., in 1931 and are called *Van de Graaff generators*. The sphere is mounted at one end of a long pipe. When the voltage becomes large enough, a beam of particles accelerates straight down the pipe and strikes a target.

Hundreds of Van de Graaff generators have been built, more than all other types of accelerators combined. They accelerate electrons, protons, and other particles and are used to study the forces that hold atomic nuclei together. But they are limited to about 10 million electron volts (MeV). Beyond this voltage, a generator's electrical insulators would break down, preventing the sphere from holding its charge.

In order to build accelerators that would boost particles to higher energies, researchers had to by-pass this limitation. They did so by using alternating electric fields, generated by the powerful vacuum

Glossary

Collider: A particle accelerator in which two beams of particles collide with each other.

Cyclotron: A circular accelerator that steers particles entering at its center in a spiral path.

Electric field: The space in which an electric charge exerts its powers of attraction and repulsion.

Electron: A negatively charged particle that orbits an atom's nucleus.

Electron volt (eV): The basic unit of beam energy in particle accelerators. Physicists use the following abbreviations to express beam energy:
  MeV: 1 million eV
  GeV: 1 billion eV
  TeV: 1 trillion eV

Linac: A particle accelerator built in a straight line.

Magnetic field: The space in which a magnet exerts its powers of attraction and repulsion.

Nucleus: The particle or cluster of particles in the center of an atom.

Proton: A positively charged particle in an atom's nucleus.

Superconductor: A material that conducts electric current with no resistance.

Synchrotron: An accelerator that steers particles in a nearly circular path.

Synchrotron radiation: Energy radiated by particles in a synchrotron.

tubes used in radio, television, and radar transmitters. Instead of one steady push, an alternating field delivers a series of small pushes, first in one direction and then in the other.

Through half its cycle, however, the field would push in the wrong direction, slowing the particle beam down, unless accelerator designers took steps to prevent this from happening. One simple way to do so is to shield the beam from the electric field when it reverses direction. This is the principle used in the proton *linear accelerator*, or *linac*. The beam passes through a series of *drift tubes* — open-ended metal cylinders separated by gaps. In the cylinders, there is no electric field. So, the particles coast through the cylinders when the alternating field is pushing the "wrong way." In the gaps between cylinders, the electric field pushes the particles forward.

A linac that accelerates electrons operates on a different principle. The machine quickly accelerates electrons to nearly the speed of light. After that, the electrons simply ride an electromagnetic wave the length of the linac like a surfer riding an ocean wave. No drift tubes are necessary.

The 2-mile linac at the Stanford Linear Accelerator Center (SLAC) in Palo Alto, Calif., is now the world's largest linac. It accel-

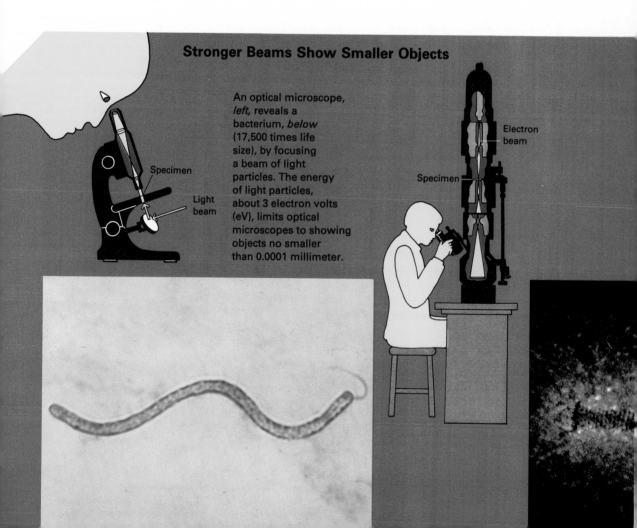

Stronger Beams Show Smaller Objects

An optical microscope, *left,* reveals a bacterium, *below* (17,500 times life size), by focusing a beam of light particles. The energy of light particles, about 3 electron volts (eV), limits optical microscopes to showing objects no smaller than 0.0001 millimeter.

Specimen

Light beam

Electron beam

Specimen

erates electrons to 33 GeV and is being upgraded to 50 GeV.

Electrons in this linac begin their journey when an electric current surges through a wire, tearing 10 billion electrons out of their orbits around atomic nuclei. The electrons streak into the 2-mile-long accelerator tube at an energy of 100,000 eV. A powerful electromagnetic force inside the accelerator boosts the electrons to nearly the speed of light, which is about 186,000 miles per second. Magnetic fields created by magnets outside the accelerator "steer" the electrons and prevent them from striking anything inside the tube.

At the end of the linac, the electrons are split into several beams and directed to their targets. One common target is a sausage-shaped bottle of liquid hydrogen a few inches in diameter and nearly 1 foot long. Most of the beam passes through the hydrogen, but some of the electrons collide with hydrogen nuclei, which consist of single protons. Electronic tubes register information about these collisions and pass it on to a computer. Off in another room, scientists examine a computer printout of the results to "see," for example, how electric charge is concentrated inside protons. Experiments run on this machine produced the first solid evidence that there are particles inside protons and neutrons. Scientists now be-

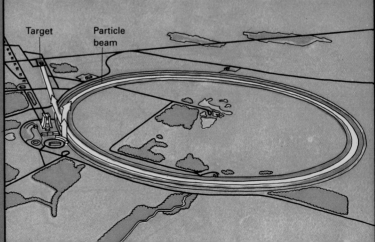

An electron microscope, *left,* shows a virus, *below* (270,000 times life size), by focusing a beam of electrons. Electron microscopes produce beams at energies of thousands or millions of eV, revealing objects as small as one one-millionth of a millimeter.

An accelerator, *below,* smashes a 1-trillion-eV beam of subatomic particles into a target to provide a "view" of objects as small as one ten-quadrillionth of a millimeter. Particles created by the collision leave tracks in a bubble chamber, *left,* enabling researchers to "see" those objects.

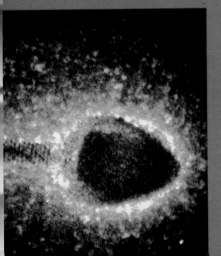

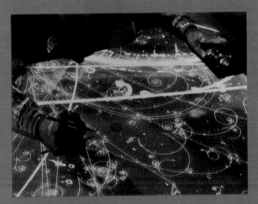

Target   Particle beam

How Particle Accelerators Grew

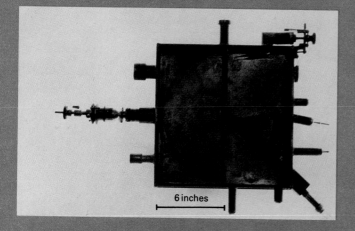

6 inches

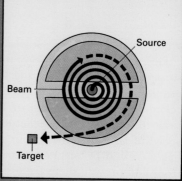

The first cyclotron, *left,* built in the early 1930's, fit in an area of about 1 square foot. Particles entered this machine at the center, *above,* gathered speed as they spiraled outward, then struck a target located outside the cyclotron.

One of the first Van de Graaff generators, *right,* invented in the mid-1930's, accelerated a beam of particles down from a bulblike chamber about 6½ feet high to a target at the end of a tube, *far right.*

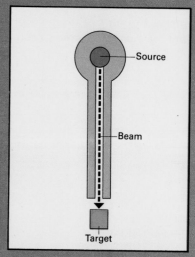

lieve these quarks — as they came to be called — are basic building blocks of matter.

Before linear accelerators were developed, other physicists were working on another design, a circular machine — the *cyclotron,* invented in 1931 by Ernest O. Lawrence at the University of California in Berkeley. Cyclotrons accelerate a range of particles, from simple protons to heavy nuclei. An electrical charge removes protons, for example, from hydrogen gas at the center of the cyclotron and sends them speeding around a vacuum chamber located between the poles of an electromagnet. An electric field in the gap between electrodes in the vacuum chamber accelerates the protons, while the

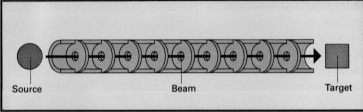

Source　　　　　　　　Beam　　　　　　　　Target

Particle accelerators had become gigantic by 1968, when a
2-mile-long machine was built at Stanford Linear Accelerator
Center in Palo Alto, Calif., *top*. This accelerator boosts
beams of electrons to energies of up to 33 billion eV as
they speed toward a target at the end of the line, *above*.

electromagnet guides them along a circular path that grows in diameter as the protons speed up. Each time the protons pass the
accelerating gap, they receive a jolt of energy that boosts them to an
even higher speed. The protons spiral out until they reach the edge
of the magnetic field. There, other electrodes guide the particles out
of the cyclotron and aim them at a target.

The first working cyclotron had magnet poles 10 inches in diameter. It pushed protons to 1.25 MeV. In the 1930's, Lawrence built
larger machines. They were used during World War II to develop
methods of purifying uranium for use in nuclear weapons. After
the war, Lawrence completed a 184-inch cyclotron that reached 720

MeV. Scientists used this machine to conduct the first systematic study of *unstable particles*, which decay to form other particles.

With this machine, the cyclotron had reached its limit. Smaller versions are still being built. and used to study the structures of atomic nuclei. But to build ever-larger magnets for more powerful cyclotrons would be too expensive. Fortunately, a better approach was discovered in 1945 by Edwin M. McMillan at Lawrence's laboratory, and, independently, by Vladimir I. Veksler in the Soviet Union. It is called the *synchrotron*.

In a synchrotron, the accelerated particles —protons or electrons— do not spiral outward. Instead, they follow a "race track" course, consisting of alternating turns and straight sections. The particles are steered through the turns by electromagnets that are just big enough to enclose the pipe containing the particle beam. Only in these small areas is a magnetic field required. At one or more of the straight sections, the particles pass through a small linac that gives them an electric boost. As they gain speed, the magnetic field must grow stronger in order to hold them on course, and the electrical frequency must be "retuned" to match their higher speeds.

Since the 1950's, the world's mightiest accelerators have all been proton synchrotrons. Only 15 have been built, 7 in the United States and 8 in other countries. No two are alike.

The energy a synchrotron can reach is limited by the strength of the magnetic field its magnets can produce. In all synchrotrons prior to the Tevatron, the field was generated by copper and iron electromagnets, which consume vast amounts of electric power and are very expensive to operate.

The building of the Tevatron was a major advance in proton synchrotrons because the Tevatron uses *superconducting* magnets. The machine's 1,054 magnets are powered by coils made from an alloy of the metals niobium and titanium that at very low temperatures offers absolutely no resistance to the flow of electricity. Once started, a current can flow forever. Moreover, the superconducting magnets can generate fields more than twice as strong as a copper-coil magnet.

But superconductors work only at temperatures

An Atom Smasher of Tomorrow

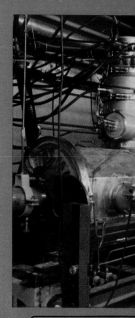

The Tevatron at Fermi National Accelerator Laboratory is now a single-beam machine but will become a proton-antiproton collider in 1985. The electric power unit in its 4-mile ring, *right,* will deliver about 1 million watts to accelerate particles along the inside of a pipe that runs through the center of the unit.

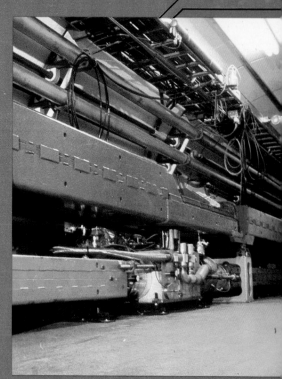

Conventional magnets, *above* (in red and blue housings), will steer particles at lower speeds around the Tevatron ring. Very fast particles will be steered by superconducting magnets (in yellow housing).

Magnets

Detector

Electric power unit

When the Tevatron becomes a collider, two beams of particles – each boosted to an energy of 1 trillion eV – will race in opposite directions around the track of the accelerator, *above,* and collide head-on. A huge detector, like that at *left,* at the point where the beams meet will detect the shower of new particles created by the collision. Powerful computers connected to the detector will produce electronic data about the collision and use it to construct a picture of the particle shower, *below.* Physicists will be able to analyze the picture for clues to the ultimate nature of matter.

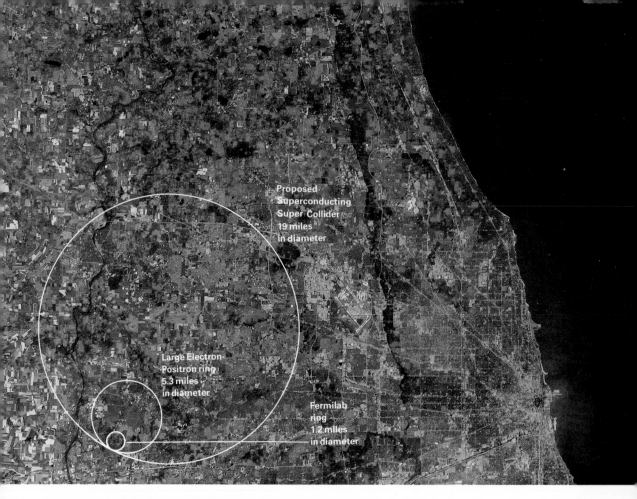

Proposed
Superconducting
Super Collider
19 miles
in diameter

Large Electron-
Positron ring
5.3 miles
in diameter

Fermilab
ring
1.2 miles
in diameter

A picture of the Chicago
area taken by a *Landsat*
satellite reveals the
1.2-mile diameter of
the Tevatron accelerator
ring as a small dot west
of the city. Superimposed
circles show the size
of the Large Electron-
Positron (LEP) ring,
begun in 1983 in Europe,
and the Superconducting
Super Collider proposed
for the United States.

near absolute zero, −459.7°F. To keep them cold, the coils are
bathed in liquid helium, which has a temperature of −451.5°F. The
refrigerators that chill the helium consume some power, but it is a
small fraction of what ordinary electromagnets would require.

The Tevatron is the world leader in beam energy. Each batch of
protons it accelerates travels nearly a million "laps," equivalent to
almost 4 million miles, in 20 seconds. Protons leave the Tevatron
moving at 99.99995 per cent of the speed of light.

Synchrotrons that accelerate electrons have a special set of problems. Electrons swinging through the turns of an electron synchrotron radiate energy out from their path, much like a car's wheel
slinging off mud. This energy is lost to the machine.

To cut down the energy loss, the magnetic fields that steer the
particles in electron synchrotrons are deliberately kept weak. Because of this, the turns cannot be sharp, and an electron synchrotron thus must be much larger than a proton synchrotron of the
same energy level.

To be an effective "microscope," an accelerator must not only
push particles to high energy but also deliver that energy to nuclei
or other particles in a target. Unfortunately, a high-energy acceler-

The World's Most Powerful Particle Accelerators

Accelerator	Laboratory	Location	Began operating	Energy* per beam	Accelerated particles
Tevatron†	Fermi National Accelerator Laboratory (Fermilab)	Batavia, Ill.	1983	1 TeV	protons
Fermilab synchrotron	Fermi National Accelerator Laboratory (Fermilab)	Batavia, Ill.	1972	450 GeV	protons
Super Proton Synchrotron	European Organization for Nuclear Research (CERN)	Geneva, Switzerland	1976	400 GeV	protons
SPS collider‡	European Organization for Nuclear Research (CERN)	Geneva, Switzerland	1981	320 GeV	protons and antiprotons§
Serpukhov	Institute for High Energy Physics	Serpukhov, Soviet Union	1968	70 GeV	protons
SLAC linear accelerator	Stanford Linear Accelerator Center (SLAC)	Palo Alto, Calif.	1968	33 GeV	electrons
Intersecting Storage Rings	European Organization for Nuclear Research (CERN)	Geneva, Switzerland	1971	33 GeV	protons§
PETRA	German Electron-Synchrotron Laboratory	Hamburg, West Germany	1978	18 GeV	electrons and positrons§
PEP	Stanford Linear Accelerator Center (SLAC)	Palo Alto, Calif.	1980	15 GeV	electrons and positrons§

*One TeV equals 1 trillion electron volts. One GeV equals 1 billion electron volts.
†Uses Fermilab synchrotron as beam source. Scheduled to become colliding-beam machine in 1985.
‡Super Proton Synchrotron run as colliding-beam machine.
§Colliding-beam machine.

ator can use only a small fraction of its beam energy to smash a target if the target is stationary. This is so because particles become heavier as they approach the speed of light and because a heavy moving object can transfer very little of its energy to a light, stationary one. Think of a particle in a high-energy beam as your fist and a particle in a stationary target as a toy balloon fastened on a string. No matter how hard you hit the balloon with your fist, the balloon just bounces back and forth, and the motion of your fist is hardly slowed at all. This is because very little energy is transferred from your fist to the balloon.

The same is true for accelerator beams directed at stationary targets. And the more powerful the beam, the lower the percentage of energy transferred. For example, protons from the Tevatron beam transfer less than 5 per cent of their energy to protons in the target.

Now, imagine yourself and a friend smashing your fists together as hard as you can. It would be a painful experience for both of you because all the energy in both fists would be transferred during the impact. What is true of energy in fists is true of energy in particles.

In a head-on collision of particles, the full energy of each particle can be brought to bear on the other. To make use of this fact, accelerator builders in the 1970's turned to machines that accelerate two beams in opposite directions and collide the beams with each other. Some colliding-beam techniques use two separate beams of particles, with equal mass and opposite electric charge, in one synchrotron. Others use beams from two connected synchrotrons.

Developing colliding-beam machines was no mean feat, because the particles in the beams are so far apart. If this subatomic world were scaled up so that a proton in the Tevatron beam were the size of a marble, the average distance between protons would be nearly 1 million miles. Two beams, each containing hundreds of billions of particles, can pass right through each other with little chance of even a single head-on collision.

To overcome this problem, physicists store the beams in the accelerator for hours or even days. As these particles whirl around the track, they meet one another hundreds of thousands of times each second. Thus, the odds of a collision improve tremendously.

The first twin-beam collider, the Intersecting Storage Rings (ISR) at the laboratory of the European Organization for Nuclear Research (CERN) in Geneva, Switzerland, went into operation in 1971. ISR produced two 31-GeV proton beams. This machine was the first to provide physical evidence of a collision between two quarks.

In 1972, electron-positron rings went into service at several laboratories in the United States and Europe. This kind of ring collides a beam of electrons with a beam of positrons. A positron is a positively charged counterpart of an electron. Electron-positron rings produced the first direct evidence for the existence of *gluons*, particles that hold quarks together in protons and neutrons.

Every large accelerator built since 1972 has been designed to function as a colliding-beam machine. The most impressive of these is CERN's proton-antiproton collider, with 320 GeV in each beam, which went into operation in 1981. The supreme challenge faced by its designers was simply to get enough antiprotons to make a beam. Since these negatively charged counterparts of protons are a form of antimatter, they are not available from any natural source. They must be produced in particle collisions in a smaller synchrotron, and patiently accumulated over many hours in a beam storage ring. Experiments run on the CERN machine verified that the *electromagnetic force*, which is responsible for electricity and magnetism, and the *weak force*, which helps transform particles from one kind to another, are both aspects of the same fundamental force.

The Tevatron, now a single-beam machine, will become a proton-antiproton collider in 1985. Some time thereafter, it may be eclipsed by a 3-TeV collider now under construction in the Soviet Union. These machines will produce particles more rapidly than does the CERN collider. And because of their higher energies, they will give scientists a clearer "look" at the particles that make up protons and neutrons as well as the forces that hold them together.

Perhaps the most ambitious project, from the point of view of sheer size, is CERN's Large Electron-Positron (LEP) ring, for which a 16-mile-long tunnel is now being dug. Since LEP will be an electron synchrotron, these huge dimensions are necessary to counteract synchrotron radiation, not to reach a new high in energy. LEP is designed for 70-GeV beams. Researchers will use this ring for detailed studies of the *Z particle*, which "carries" the weak force, and to search for new kinds of quarks.

Accelerator designers at Stanford believe that the next leap in electron accelerators should be a different design — a *single-pass* collider. They plan to take electron and positron beams from their 2-mile linac and bend each through a half turn to meet face to face.

This design does not have the enormous advantage of having each beam pass through the other many times. To make up for this, the Stanford designers must drastically reduce the diameters of the beams by packing the particles closer together. This improves the odds for collisions. Currently, physicists can produce millimeter-sized beam diameters. They must squeeze this to micrometers. (A micrometer is only one one-thousandth of a millimeter.)

Design studies are now underway in the United States for a 20-TeV circular Superconducting Super Collider. Even with superconducting magnets, it would have to be at least 60 miles in circumference and would cost more than $1 billion.

The benefits of such a machine are difficult to foresee, but the history of the smaller machines gives us clues about what it may have in store for us. Particle accelerators have provided both scientific and practical benefits. Scientifically, they have shown us what matter is made of — from whole atoms to protons and neutrons to the apparently indivisible quarks. They have also revealed the forces operating inside the atomic nucleus. In addition, accelerators have given scientists insights into how matter may have been created at the beginning of time. See THE FIRST SECOND.

Their practical benefits include advances in medical research and treatment — for example, destroying tumors with particle beams and producing radioactive tracers to probe the human body without surgery. What accelerators have helped scientists learn about the atomic nucleus has been used in the development of nuclear power plants, and accelerators are at the forefront of the new technology of superconductivity. Design engineers already are applying this technology to the development of superspeed trains, and to finding more efficient ways to store and transport electrical power.

Where may research from larger and more powerful accelerators lead? Perhaps the best answer is the one given by Benjamin Franklin more than two centuries ago in France, while witnessing the first flight made by a human being — a flight in a hot-air balloon. A skeptical bystander asked, "Of what use is it?" Franklin replied, "What is the use of a newborn child?"

BY HAL HIGDON

High-Tech Athletes

The use of computers, high-speed cameras, and other devices of modern technology is helping athletes reach new levels of performance.

Archer Tricia Green deftly raises her bow, pulls its string taut, and squints through her sight until the arrow points straight at the target. Then, *snap!* Forty-five pounds of pressure coiled into the bow propels the arrow toward the target to pierce the bull's-eye.

Olympic archery coach John Williams nods in appreciation of a well-executed shot. But Williams cannot immediately rush over and congratulate his athlete. Tricia Green is in Ohio. Williams is analyzing the shot on a television device more than 1,000 miles away at the Olympic Training Center of the United States Olympic Committee (USOC) in Colorado Springs, Colo.

Williams watched Green's performance on a TV monitor. Through a technique called split-screen broadcasting, one half of the screen showed Green looking through the sight on her bow. The target with the arrow striking it appeared on the other half of the screen. By analyzing the aiming patterns of his archer — how she tracked the bull's-eye before releasing the arrow — and where the arrow struck the target, Williams can advise Green on how to improve her performance.

The TV device is only one of many new technological aids available to the coach and his archers. When Williams meets with an archer he can use a *beam-splitter*, which is a partially reflecting mirror that fits on the bow. Standing beside the archer, Williams uses the beam-splitter to see the target exactly as the archer sees it through the sight. The coach studies how archers sight and when they release the arrow. Inexperienced archers try to put the sight exactly on target, wavering back and forth until they fix on the bull's-eye. Then they let the arrow go. Tests show they should release the arrow the instant it centers on the bull's-eye. When the target is 90 meters away — one of the standard distances — a sighting movement of 1 millimeter can result in a 90-millimeter displacement. In other words, each minor error at the bow is magnified 90 times at impact.

High-speed motion-picture filming is still another technological aid. High-speed filming shows that an arrow does not fly "straight as an arrow." Instead, it "snakes" its way toward the target, wavering in flight. The degree of snaking depends on how smoothly the archer releases the string. Less snaking means a more accurate shot. Analyzing close-up films of the finger-release action can help an archer achieve a smooth release.

Split-screen television, beam-splitting, and high-speed filming are examples of how today's high technology, particularly in applying the principles of *biomechanics*, helps athletes improve their performance. Biomechanics — with reference to the human body — refers to the effects of forces on the skeleton and the muscular system.

Today's sport scientists work with a vast range of sophisticated equipment and analytical techniques to discover how athletes perform. In addition to the high-speed filming and other devices already mentioned, they use such sensitive devices as force plates, computers that create stick figures of athletes in action, wind tunnels to test both equipment and techniques, and a blend of high technology and psychology called imaging. Armed with the knowledge gained from all this, the scientists and coaches hope to teach American athletes how to perform more efficiently: to jump higher, to skate faster, to lift heavier weights, and to perform with more consistency.

The application of technology to athletics began in the 1960's. At that time, such colleges as Pennsylvania State University developed the first graduate program in the United States in the area of sports biomechanics. Gideon B. Ariel, a former Israeli Olympic shot-putter studying at the University of Massachusetts, became interested about that same time in using computer science to find ways to improve athletic performance. Ariel developed the first commercial

The author:
Hal Higdon is a long-distance runner and senior writer for *The Runner* magazine.

biomechanics laboratory. Among the laboratory's projects was the design of running shoes that could better absorb the shock of the foot striking the track.

This interest in high technology in sports was partly encouraged by the success of Eastern European nations in international competition. Since the 1960's, scientists and coaches in such countries as the Soviet Union and East Germany have shown that they are well organized at developing improved techniques and getting that information to their athletes. The success of the Eastern Europeans helped stimulate the United States to upgrade its selection and training of athletes. Traditionally, the United States has relied on enough gifted athletes surfacing every four years to ensure a large number of victories in Olympic competition. But today's administrators of U.S. sports programs found that system, however successful in the past, is outdated. Natural talent is no longer enough; it now must be combined with sophisticated training methods to produce better athletic performance.

During the 1970's, the USOC made a strong commitment to using science as a means of improving American athletic performance. In 1977, the USOC moved its headquarters from New York City to Colorado Springs, where Gideon Ariel helped develop the USOC's biomechanics laboratory. In 1978, the USOC established its Olympic Training Center (OTC), where athletes in more than 20 Olympic sports go for training and coaching. In 1981, the USOC opened a Sports Medicine Division, including a new Department of Biome-

An archer practices on a force plate, which measures tiny changes in foot pressure. Information from the force plate is fed into a computer. By analyzing data from the computer, the archer and her coach can identify and correct problems in balance and foot position to improve her accuracy.

chanics and Computer Services now under the direction of Charles J. Dillman. In 1983, some 5,000 athletes trained at Colorado Springs. High tech finally has come to American Olympic sports.

The OTC is located in a quiet residential neighborhood a short distance from downtown Colorado Springs. It resembles a college campus with clusters of buildings and sports facilities. These include dormitories where athletes sleep, a track where they can run, and an all-purpose gymnasium for practicing sports as diverse as gymnastics and team handball. If facilities are not available for a specific sport, such as swimming, athletes travel to the nearby U.S. Air Force Academy. The heart of the OTC campus consists of buildings devoted to science. There, athletes come to be studied as well as to study their sport, using the latest equipment and techniques.

At the OTC, scientists apply the most recent high technology to provide coaches with valuable information for improving an athlete's performance. Dillman describes the relationship between scientist and coach: "Coaches can pick out only large errors in form by eye. A lot of what we do in biomechanics magnifies what the coach can see. We use high-speed photography and electronic methods to measure forces that you can't see when an athlete performs. We focus on small factors, such as the position of an arm, the angle of a hip. These factors seem small, but in terms of performance, they are very important.

"Now this field is expanding to where we can offer advice. We can pick out an athlete's weaknesses. We try to help the athlete understand the mechanics of his or her own body and how it relates

High-speed photography helps athletes analyze each element of their form. The sequence of a figure-skating jump from take-off to landing can be studied by the skater and a coach to find errors of technique that would be impossible to see with the naked eye.

to maximum performance in a given sport. The next question is, how does the coach correct the weaknesses? Then, how do the athletes make that correction in competition?"

The *force plate* is one of the most important high-technology tools available to athletes. A force plate is a square slab of metal on which athletes stand while practicing their event. Highly sensitive electronic devices called *sensors* are wired to its underside. The sensors can detect tiny changes in pressure on the plate itself. The sensors also provide data on whether a foot moves vertically, forward, sideways, or twists. The force plate can assist an athlete in an event where proper balance and footwork are vital. For example, weight lifters use force plates in analyzing how their body shifts as they lift a heavy weight. The force plate sensors register pressure from the weight lifters' feet. Computers determine how much force is applied to the plate, where, and for how long. In analyzing data from force plate tests, scientists learned that as successful lifters raise a barbell off the ground, they move back on their heels. As they complete the lift, they move forward onto the balls of their feet. This sequence of motions results in better balance, which is extremely important in lifting. A weight lifter and his coach examining an analysis of his force plate test can learn how well he lifted. Was his right foot too far forward or too far back? Did he lose his balance at a critical point in the lift? Should he position his body differently to improve the leverage he exerts on the barbell?

Coaches also use the force plate to determine stability in shooting. How much does body sway affect accuracy when someone fires a

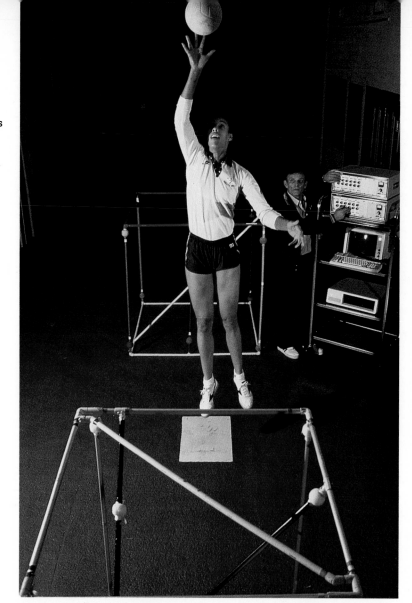

A volleyball player jumps on a force plate to measure the impact with which various parts of the athlete's feet strike a surface. In the background, her coach operates the testing equipment. From the data, the player and the coach can learn how to improve the efficiency of her jump in order to hit the volleyball more effectively.

rifle or releases an arrow? Through repeated experiments, scientists discovered that the top shooters and archers are extremely stable. "Like rocks," says Dillman. "They have almost no movement. So if you want to improve your shooting, you have to work first on your stability." This is an example of a fact coaches always felt to be true in shooting and archery. Now they have high-tech proof.

Computerized film analysis is another valuable high-technology aid. Scientists program computers to project stick-figure images on a screen. They do this by first filming or videotaping an athlete's performance, often with several cameras and from different angles.

If the filming is done in the lab, scientists tape black dots to key points on an athlete's body, usually at the joints — the elbows, wrists, hips, knees, and ankles. This procedure aids the researchers in precisely determining the point that a specific joint occupies in space.

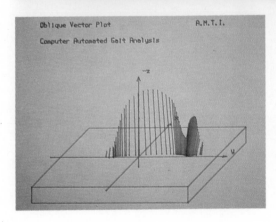

As a discus thrower, *above left,* practices her form on two force plates, her coach, *left,* gets immediate data on her performance from a computer set up in the back of a van. Using graphs generated by the computer, *below,* the coach later can do a more detailed analysis of the athlete's balance and footwork.

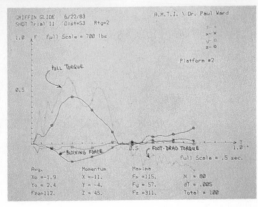

Oblique Vector Plot   A.M.T.I.

Computer Automated Gait Analysis

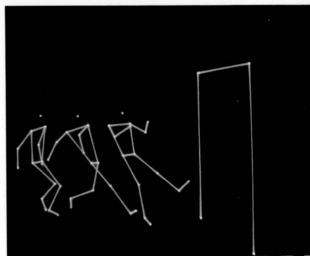

After a performance has been filmed, the researchers view the film or videotape of the athlete, using stop-action motion. The film "freezes" a frame of the athlete in action on a screen, as though in a still picture. Using a magnetic pen, the scientists mark dots on the screen where the athlete's joints appear. The computer instantly translates these marks into computer-language numbers and connects the dots to form a stick figure. Then the scientist goes on to the next frame of the film. The athlete's joints will have moved up, down, or sideways from their positions in the first frame. The new positions are marked with dots, and the computer again stores the information. Eventually, after enough frames are marked, scientists have a complete stick-figure record of the athlete in action and can analyze, for example, how and where the elbow moves.

Stick figures are actually simplified pictures of how the athlete moves in space. This analytical technique makes it easier for athletes to visualize their movements. Using stick figures, the coach can show the athlete the angle of feet and arms to the trunk of the body. This is particularly important in running and jumping and similar sports that involve rapid pumping of arms and elbows.

"Stick figures more vividly represent body positions than the body itself," says Dillman. "You can see the angles better. Plus you can concentrate on specific parts, eliminating from the screen other parts that might confuse you." A track coach might concentrate, for example, on the hip movements of a runner or hurdler, screening out trunk, arms, and legs. "During one recent training camp session at the OTC," says Nancy L. Greer, a research assistant, "we had weight lifters sitting there for hours watching and comparing stick figures of their performances."

Computers can generate both two-dimensional and three-dimensional figures using data taken from cameras that photograph from

Analysis of animated stick figures can detect flaws in an athlete's technique. Using film of a high-jumper, a scientist "freezes" frames on a screen, *opposite page,* and uses a magnetic pen to mark dots where the athlete's joints appear. A computer converts the marks into stick figures. By studying the stick figures, *below,* the coach can examine each key body movement.

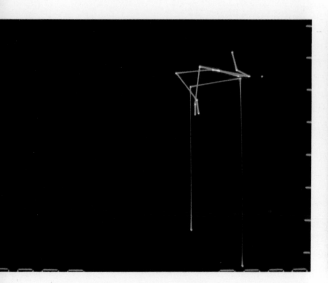

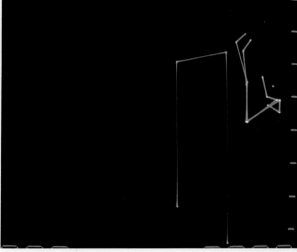

ARVIN/CALSPAN
ADVANCED TECHNOLOGY CENTER

Sports equipment and techniques are tested in wind tunnels to find ways of reducing drag that cuts down on speed. A sledder on a luge, *above,* undergoes wind tunnel tests of his luge, helmet, and suit. A jumper, *opposite page,* suspended from the ceiling of a wind tunnel, watches a TV screen to check the position of his head and hands and the angles of his skis, while devices measure the wind resistance.

various angles — side, front, or from above. "Very rarely does the human move totally in one plane," Dillman says. "Most human movement is three-dimensional, so it's actually a more accurate way of seeing what is happening in three planes."

Three-dimensional analysis of figure skating, for example, permits coaches to determine the best way for their athletes to do various jumps. Where should the free leg be before a jump? What is the appropriate speed for a double toe loop versus a waltz jump? What should the position of the body be on take-off?

In the past, a coach might have answered these questions by having the skater make hundreds of jumps, taking off at different speeds and with the arms and legs in different positions. But this procedure takes a great deal of time, and mistakes made during the learning process can cause injuries. The computer permits a coach working with a sports scientist to simulate the effects of changes in body positions, projecting the results onto the screen as animated stick figures.

High-tech methods of analyzing player movement patterns have been successfully used in team sports such as ice hockey. Scientists at the OTC used high-speed cameras placed above three different areas of the rink to analyze how hockey players skated. They learned that hockey was a game of quick bursts, one- or two-second accelerations followed by periods of rest. Researchers fed the data from the cameras into computers, which produced a graphic display of stick figures that showed hockey players could accelerate fastest

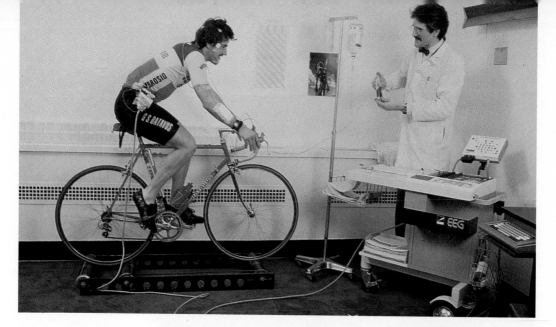

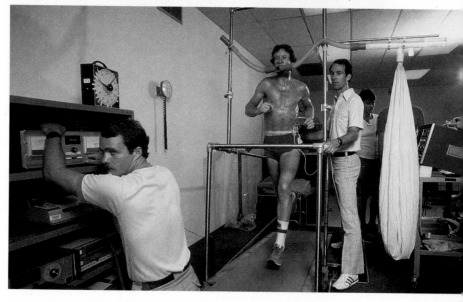

Treadmill tests are used to measure an athlete's heart rate, blood pressure, and other bodily functions during physical activity. The cyclist, *top,* is tested at various times of the day to evaluate how his performance varies. The runner, *right,* wears a mask that collects the gases he breathes out for analysis to determine how efficiently his lungs are working.

by starting from a flexed-leg position. Using this technique, a player can increase his range of movement by 3 feet during a two-second acceleration. That distance may spell the difference between getting to the puck or having an opponent get there first.

Scientists are using *wind tunnels* to test equipment and performance techniques. For example, downhill skiers benefit from wind-tunnel tests done in Buffalo, N.Y., in a wind tunnel loaned to the U.S. ski team by Calspan Corporation. The tunnel, capable of generating winds up to 70 miles per hour, normally is used to measure the effect of winds on buildings. Calspan scientist Michael Holden positioned skiers, fully clad in race clothing with ski poles, in the tunnel. Instruments that measure wind speed and air pressure pro-

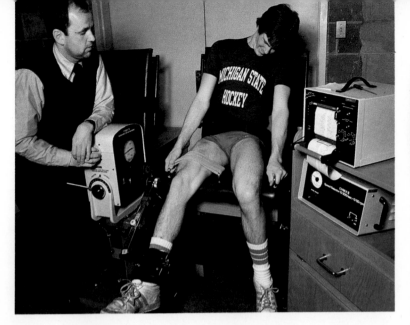

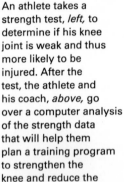

An athlete takes a strength test, *left,* to determine if his knee joint is weak and thus more likely to be injured. After the test, the athlete and his coach, *above,* go over a computer analysis of the strength data that will help them plan a training program to strengthen the knee and reduce the possibility of injury.

vided instant feedback of the effects of the wind on various body positions and on the skier's helmet, gloves, and other equipment and clothing. Video cameras allowed the skiers to monitor their body positions. The research showed that the skiers encountered the least wind resistance in a deep "tuck" position with the upper body parallel to the ground. The researchers concluded that by holding this position longer, the skiers would go faster. Wind tunnel tests also showed that ski jumpers, who do not use poles, create less wind resistance if they hold their hands behind their backs.

In their desire to improve performance, sports scientists have even merged high technology with psychology to produce a training technique called *imaging.* Using this technique, athletes imagine themselves performing in their particular sport, such as throwing a discus or executing a complicated dive. They watch films and videotapes of world champions performing in their particular sport. By imagining the champion's technique over and over, athletes can teach their bodies to consistently perform in the same way.

Weight lifters have been among the beneficiaries of imaging. Each member of the United States weight-lifting team owns a personal video cassette containing films of his lifts taken at various meets and in training. As additional meets are filmed, the athletes add new cassettes to their collection. With his library of cassettes, the weight lifter can compare his lift style against previously filmed lifts of his own or compare himself to other lifters — other members of his team, or world champions filmed during competition.

Unquestionably, high technology will continue to make major contributions to the improvement of athletic performance. But it is still only one of many elements needed to produce a championship talent. Technological aids have to be combined with natural ability, good coaching, and — perhaps most important of all — the athlete's own desire to excel.

Why — apparently — did only our planet, Earth, evolve an atmosphere that is capable of supporting life?

Probing the Secrets of Atmospheres

BY TOBIAS C. OWEN

Of the nine known planets that orbit the sun, one is dramatically different from the other eight. While some appear gray and others red or orange, only one is blue with shifting swirls of white. Only Earth has oceans of blue liquid water and clouds of white water vapor. And it appears that only Earth has life on it.

Earth owes its uniqueness in great part to its *atmosphere*, the envelope of gases that surrounds the planet and which we perceive as our blue sky. Earth's atmosphere keeps the surface temperature moderate, so that the oceans neither freeze nor boil away. It protects us from harmful solar rays, and it provides the very air we breathe.

The other planets also have atmospheres, but scientists knew little about them until the 1960's. Since then, space probes have revealed a great deal about the atmospheres on other planets. By studying the data, planetary scientists hope to learn how atmospheres evolved, why apparently only Earth has an atmosphere capable of supporting life, and perhaps how atmospheres that could support life might form around planets of other stars.

The atmospheres of the other planets in our solar system are very different from that of Earth. Earth's atmosphere contains about 78 per cent nitrogen, 21 per cent oxygen, and tiny amounts of carbon dioxide and other gases. In contrast, the atmospheres of Venus and Mars are composed mainly of carbon dioxide — 96.5 per cent for Venus and 98 per cent for Mars — with small amounts of nitrogen, oxygen, and other gases. Mercury has almost no atmosphere.

The atmospheres of Jupiter and Saturn are mainly hydrogen and helium. The same may be true of Uranus and Neptune. Pluto, the outermost planet, appears to have some methane, but scientists do not know yet what other gases its atmosphere contains. Space probes have not yet visited Uranus, Neptune, or Pluto, and they are difficult to observe from Earth since they are so far away.

For over 300 years — since the time of the Italian astronomer Galileo — planetary astronomers had to rely solely on their Earth-based telescopes for all their knowledge about the planets. Over the years, they devised many instruments and techniques to help them collect more details. One of the most important was *spectroscopy*, a method of detecting what chemical elements are in an object by analyzing light coming from the object. With spectroscopy, they were able to determine some of the gases in some of the planetary atmospheres.

Since the 1960's, however, a wealth of new data has emerged, thanks to space exploration. Spacecraft traveling to the planets have taken photographs, recorded such information as temperature, and sometimes sent probes into a planet's atmosphere to take direct measurements. By the mid-1980's, 19 major space missions from the Soviet Union and the United States returned important information from five planets.

Some of this new data radically changed our understanding of planetary atmospheres. For example, ground-based observations had shown scientists that the atmospheres of Mars and Venus contain some carbon dioxide, but they could not tell how much. It took space probes to reveal that the atmospheres of these planets are almost entirely carbon dioxide.

Space exploration has added so much to our knowledge about atmospheric conditions on Mercury, Mars, Venus, Jupiter, and Saturn that the challenge to planetary scientists no longer lies in discovering what those atmospheres are like but in understanding how they got that way. Scientists want to know how the planets evolved — how their atmospheres were produced and how they changed.

Most scientists believe that about 4½ billion years ago our sun and its planets formed out of a huge cloud of gas and dust called the *solar nebula*. The original size of this cloud was probably 100,000 times greater than the present distance from Earth to the sun,

The author:
Tobias C. Owen is professor of astronomy at the State University of New York in Stony Brook, N.Y.

which is about 93 million miles. As the cloud caved in on itself due to gravity, most of the dust and gas went to make up the sun. But some of it began rotating around the sun in the shape of a disk and probably began to form increasingly larger solid bodies.

What happened next is still a mystery. But it seems apparent that the planets closest to the sun — the *inner planets* of Mercury, Venus, Earth, and Mars — formed differently from those farthest from the sun — the *outer planets* of Jupiter, Saturn, Uranus, and Neptune. The inner planets are small and rocky compared with the larger outer planets, which are composed mainly of gases and ice. The outermost planet, Pluto, is considered a special case and is not classified as an outer planet because scientists know so little about it.

Scientists have proposed three basic theories to explain how planetary atmospheres began. The oldest theory, dating back to the 1800's, holds that the planets captured their atmospheres from the original cloud of gases out of which the solar system was formed. According to this theory, the planets' gravitational forces simply pulled the gases from the original cloud. This process produced what is called a *primary*, or original, atmosphere.

The second theory, which became popular in the 1950's, contends that the dust grains in the original cloud of gas and dust contained small amounts of *volatile compounds*. Volatiles are substances that turn easily into gases. These volatiles were trapped in the planets' rocky material, but when they were heated to high temperatures, they were released as gases. Scientists call this process *degassing*, the release of a gas. A volcanic eruption — in which huge amounts of steam and hot gases are released from the molten rock in the interior of the planet — is an example of degassing. Degassing produces what scientists call a *secondary* atmosphere.

The third theory, which developed in the mid-1970's, holds that some atmospheres were created by a combination of the first two processes. A planet may first capture its gases from the original cloud of gas and dust, but later release other gases into the planet's atmosphere from its own rocky or icy material.

Finally, scientists have proposed a number of variations on each of these theories. The *comet-asteroid hypothesis*, which was proposed in the 1960's, holds that the inner planets obtained their atmospheres mainly as a result of collisions with comets and asteroids during their early histories. Scientists think these early forms of comets and asteroids were rich in the volatile compounds that form atmospheres. These volatiles were released as the comets and asteroids collided with the planet.

It is extremely difficult to test theories about events that took place 4½ billion years ago. To make matters worse, a lot has happened since then. The gases that make up atmospheres change with time. Some gases escape from the planet, and others interact with the planet's surface or with each other to form new gases.

Profile of the Planets

Mercury
36 million miles*

Venus
67.2 million miles*

Earth
92.9 million miles*

The Sun. *Diameter,*
865,000 miles.
Temperature, 10,000° F.
Chief gases, hydrogen
and helium.

Mars
141.7 million miles*

The Inner Planets

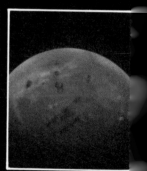

Mercury. *Diameter,* 3,031
miles. *Temperature
range,* −315° to 648° F.
Chief gases, almost no

Venus. *Diameter,* about
7,520 miles. *Temperature,*
850° F. *Chief gases,*
carbon dioxide and

Earth. *Diameter,* about
8,000 miles. *Temperature
range,* −126.9° to 136° F.
Chief gases, nitrogen and

Mars. *Diameter,*
about 4,200 miles.
Temperature range,
−191° to −24° F.

The Outer Planets

Jupiter. *Diameter,* about 88,700 miles. *Temperature,* − 236° F. *Chief gases,* hydrogen and helium.

Saturn. *Diameter,* about 74,600 miles. *Temperature,* − 285° F. *Chief gases,* hydrogen and helium.

Uranus. *Diameter,* about 31,570 miles. *Temperature,* − 357° F. *Chief gases,* hydrogen and, possibly, helium.

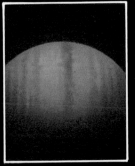

Neptune. *Diameter,* about 30,200 miles. *Temperature,* − 360° F. *Chief gases,* hydrogen, maybe helium.

Pluto. *Diameter,* about 1,900 miles. *Temperature,* about − 300° F. *Chief gases,* methane and as yet unknown gases.

Jupiter
483.7 million miles*

Saturn
885.2 million miles*

Uranus
1.7 billion miles*

*Mean distance from sun

Neptune
2.7 billion miles*

Pluto
3.6 billion miles*

Gases can leave a planet by flying off into space like rockets. This occurs when gas molecules travel fast enough to escape the gravitational pull of the planet. The bigger the planet, the stronger is its gravitational field, and thus the faster the molecules must travel to escape. On Earth, any substance—whether a gas molecule or a rocket—must travel at 25,000 miles per hour to get into space. However, it is very easy to escape the pull of gravity on tiny Phobos, a moon of Mars that is just 12½ miles in diameter. There the necessary escape speed is just 40 miles per hour.

How fast molecules travel depends on how heavy they are and how hot the atmosphere is. The warmer the atmosphere, the greater the average speed of the gas molecules. And lighter gas molecules will travel faster than heavy gas molecules. For example, hydrogen is 16 times lighter than oxygen, and helium is 4 times lighter than oxygen. Lighter gases such as hydrogen and helium will therefore have a better chance than oxygen of escaping from a planet's gravity. (Of course, when hydrogen combines with other gases, as it does with oxygen to form water, it becomes heavier.)

The ability of gases to escape explains the basic difference between the atmospheres of the outer planets and three of the inner planets—Venus, Earth, and Mars. Hydrogen and helium have escaped from the warmer atmospheres of Venus, Earth, and Mars. However, hydrogen and helium still dominate the atmospheres of the colder, larger outer planets.

The gases that do not escape from an atmosphere may undergo changes. Cosmic rays and ultraviolet light from the sun break molecules apart. Fragments of molecules can then combine to form new kinds of gases. An important chemical reaction occurred on Earth, for example, when hydrogen atoms combined with oxygen atoms to form water vapor. This water vapor eventually became Earth's oceans. Other chemical reactions also occur between the atmosphere and a planet's surface. For example, when carbon dioxide in the air interacts with water on Earth's surface, a chemical change takes place that breaks down carbon dioxide to form a weak acid known as carbonic acid.

Knowing that all these dramatic changes can occur, how do we reconstruct what actually happened in the evolution of a planetary atmosphere? Fortunately, science has clues for this kind of detective work that can lead us back to original conditions.

For one thing, we know what the starting conditions were. We know that the sun's present atmosphere—mainly hydrogen and helium—resembles its original condition because its great mass will not allow any gases to escape. So hydrogen and helium must have been the main gases in the original solar nebula. Still other important clues can be found in studies of a special type of gases, called the heavy *noble gases* because they refuse to combine with other elements and form compounds.

The heavy noble gases are *neon, argon, krypton,* and *xenon* (from Greek words for *new, lazy, hidden,* and *strange*). The noble gases are too heavy to escape into space. Once they become part of a planetary atmosphere, they stay there, unchanged.

These stable gases provide the means for determining whether a planet has a primary atmosphere, captured from the original solar nebula, or a secondary atmosphere, produced from gases released from its own rocky or icy material. A primary atmosphere that has simply been captured from the solar nebula should be similar to the sun's atmosphere, and the percentage of the noble gases should be about the same. If the percentages are not the same, then the planet must have a secondary atmosphere. For example, far too little of the noble gas neon exists in Earth's atmosphere, compared with the amount found in the sun's atmosphere, for Earth to have a primary atmosphere. Therefore, scientists conclude that Earth has a secondary atmosphere.

Before the era of space probes, most scientists believed that two planets in our solar system — Jupiter and Saturn — had primary atmospheres. However, the *Voyager* spacecraft explorations of the late 1970's raised a number of questions that cast doubt on this theory. The spacecraft sent back information on the amounts of lighter and heavier gases in the atmospheres of Jupiter and Saturn. Analysis showed that these are not in the same proportions as found on the sun. If these planets had primary atmospheres, the light-to-heavy gas ratio would be the same as it is on the sun. Instead, on Jupiter, heavier gases are more abundant, indicating that some degassing must have taken place. As a result, the best explanation now for how Jupiter and Saturn developed their atmospheres may be the third theory — that is, a combination of capturing gases from the original nebula and degassing.

Jupiter and Saturn have many more secrets yet to reveal. Among the most exciting is the possibility that Earth's original atmosphere was much like the one found today on Jupiter or on Titan, a satellite of Saturn. The chemical reactions taking place now on Jupiter or on Titan may resemble those that occurred on the early Earth.

How Did Atmospheres Form?

The ***primary atmosphere*** **theory** says that as a planet formed, it captured its atmosphere from the original solar nebula, a cloud of dust and gas, *below*.

The ***secondary atmosphere*** **theory** holds that a planet could obtain its atmosphere from degassing, such as when a volcano releases gases from the planet's interior, *below*.

A third theory argues that asteroids and comets colliding with a planet, *below,* released gases trapped in their ice and rock to form the planet's atmosphere.

Titan offers the most intriguing possibilities. Astronomer Gerard P. Kuiper, considered the father of modern planetary astronomy, discovered an atmosphere on Titan in 1944. This was a significant finding since Titan is the only satellite of an outer planet to have a substantial atmosphere. Scientists became aware of Titan's great importance because of a fortunate decision in the planning of the *Voyager 1* orbit. Planners of the space mission faced the dilemma of deciding whether *Voyager 1* should journey on to visit the more distant planets of Uranus and Neptune after passing Saturn in 1980 or whether it should detour and make a closer pass by Titan. Luckily, enough was known about Titan to justify such a detour.

On Titan, *Voyager 1* uncovered a variety of organic molecules that may be like the forerunners of life on Earth. Moreover, the atmosphere on Titan resembles Earth's atmosphere more than those of Jupiter or Saturn. Nitrogen dominates Titan's atmosphere, as it does Earth's.

By analyzing data from *Voyager 1*, scientists learned that the atmosphere on Titan is not a modified version of a captured primary atmosphere like Saturn's or Jupiter's. If Titan had a primary atmosphere, it would contain about 66 per cent neon and 33 per cent nitrogen. Instead, *Voyager 1* found less than 1 per cent neon, which is a strong argument for Titan having a secondary atmosphere. Thus, planetary scientists have added Titan to Venus, Earth, and Mars for their study and comparison of secondary atmospheres.

Jupiter's colorful clouds, *below,* were photographed by the *Voyager 1* spacecraft as it passed the planet in 1979. The planet's Great Red Spot – probably swirling masses of gas – can be seen clearly near the bottom of the picture. Data from *Voyager* flights have led many scientists to believe the giant planet's atmosphere was formed by a dual process of capturing gases from the solar nebula and degassing.

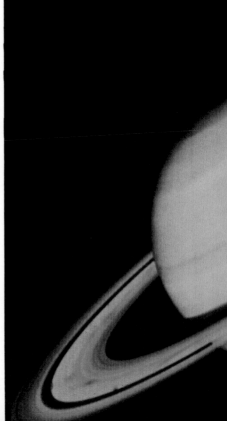

Scientists believe that Venus, Earth, and Mars have secondary atmospheres produced primarily by degassing from the rocky material that makes up the planets themselves. Studies of Earth and ground-based observations and space probes of Venus and Mars have shown scientists that these planets could not have primary atmospheres because they have such a small percentage of noble gases in their atmospheres. Therefore, they must have evolved their own atmospheres without capturing gases from the original solar nebula. For example, chemist Edward Anders of the University of Chicago and I analyzed findings from the 1976 *Viking* spacecraft mission to Mars. This analysis confirmed that the percentage of the noble gas neon found in the Martian atmosphere was too small, compared with the percentage found in the sun's atmosphere, for Mars to have captured its atmosphere from the solar nebula.

The most intriguing aspect of the comparative studies of Earth, Venus, and Mars is the possibility that all three of these planets had similar atmospheres during their primitive beginnings. For instance, we now know that Earth has degassed a huge amount of carbon dioxide, almost as much as scientists have found in the atmosphere of Venus.

The clues to this discovery came from the study of rocks. In the early 1950's, William W. Rubey, a geologist with the U.S. Geological Survey, recognized that the presence of *calcium carbonate* (limestone) on Earth meant that during the course of its history, Earth's atmos-

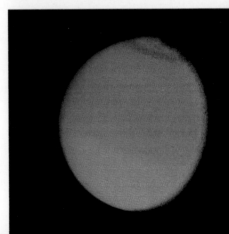

The planet Saturn, *left,* and its largest satellite, Titan, *below,* are studies in atmospheric contrasts. Titan is the only moon in the outer solar system that has a substantial atmosphere, but its atmosphere is very different from that of Saturn, which is mostly helium and hydrogen. Titan's atmosphere is dominated by nitrogen, which is also the chief gas in Earth's atmosphere.

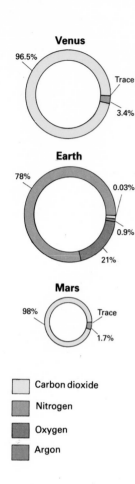

Venus

96.5%
Trace
3.4%

Earth

78%
0.03%
0.9%
21%

Mars

98%
Trace
1.7%

☐ Carbon dioxide

☐ Nitrogen

☐ Oxygen

☐ Argon

Crucial Differences

The gases that make up Earth's atmosphere are very different from those that make up the atmospheres of its neighbors, Mars and Venus, *left.* Venus' clouds of sulfuric acid and an atmosphere rich in carbon dioxide, *above,* prevent heat from escaping into space, making Venus the hottest planet in the solar system. Blue oceans of liquid water on Earth, *right,* helped alter its atmosphere and moderate its temperature, making the planet hospitable to life. A thin atmosphere on Mars, *far right,* created subfreezing temperatures that caused the white icecap of frozen carbon dioxide at the planet's south pole.

phere must have contained a large amount of carbon dioxide. The carbon dioxide was removed by interactions between the atmosphere and the oceans. Water on Earth's surface dissolved carbon dioxide in the air to form carbonic acid. This acid combined with calcium in water to form calcium carbonate. In turn, marine organisms such as clams, sea urchins, and oysters made shells from this dissolved carbon dioxide. Their fossilized remains produced large deposits of limestone. Also, limestone was deposited along shorelines as water there evaporated. Coral reefs in the tropics and the famous white cliffs of Dover in England are examples of large limestone deposits. Rubey realized that in order for such vast amounts of limestone to form, Earth's atmosphere must have had vast amounts of carbon dioxide at one time. Later, scientists found that the amount of carbon dioxide in Venus' atmosphere is about the same as that locked up in limestone on Earth. Less than 1 per cent of Earth's atmosphere is carbon dioxide, but an estimated 4,000 times that amount is trapped in the rocks. If all the trapped carbon dioxide from Earth's rocks were released, Earth's atmosphere would resemble that of Venus. Also in the 1960's, I suggested the similarity

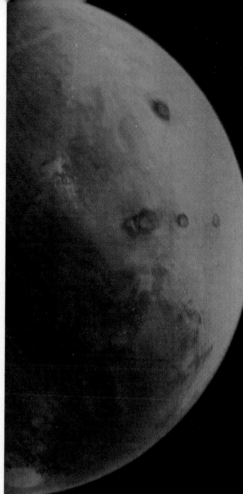

between the present level of carbon dioxide in the atmosphere of Mars and the level of carbon dioxide that must have once existed in Earth's atmosphere.

Still another striking similarity in the histories of Venus, Earth, and Mars is the tantalizing evidence that water, which allowed life to develop on Earth, once existed on Mars and Venus also. There are features on Mars's surface that resemble ancient riverbeds. Today, Mars probably contains a large store of water beneath its surface in permanently frozen ground. If its climate were warmer, that underground water would melt and form seas, lakes, and rivers.

Scientists had long speculated that water once existed on Venus, too, but evidence of Venus' early history of water activity was not discovered until 1978 when the *Pioneer Venus* spacecraft sent probes into the Venusian atmosphere. Three years later, physicist John H. Hoffman of the University of Texas in Dallas and atmospheric scientist Thomas M. Donahue of the University of Michigan in Ann Arbor examined the data from this probe. They discovered a huge amount of deuterium, a naturally occurring but relatively rare *isotope* of hydrogen. Isotopes are forms of the same element that have

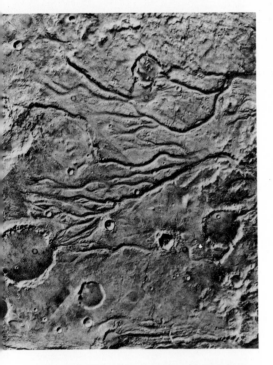

Deep gullies on Mars, *top,* photographed by the *Viking 1* orbiter in 1976, could be ancient riverbeds. The *Viking 1* lander found a rugged, dry terrain of sand dunes, rocks, and boulders, *above.* If surface water once existed on Mars, it now may be trapped in the form of underground ice.

different atomic weights. For example, the nucleus of an ordinary hydrogen atom has one particle—a single proton. The nucleus of a deuterium atom has two particles—one proton and one neutron. This makes deuterium twice as heavy as ordinary hydrogen. Therefore, it will have a more difficult time escaping from an atmosphere.

When scientists discovered huge amounts of deuterium in Venus' atmosphere, they reasoned that there must have once been enormous quantities of hydrogen in Venus' atmosphere. They reasoned further that this missing hydrogen had at one time combined with oxygen to form water. Therefore, the discovery of large amounts of deuterium implied that Venus perhaps once had rivers, oceans, and a moderate climate like Earth. Scientists then had to ask: What could have happened to the water on Venus?

The fate of Venus' water was first suggested in the late 1960's by planetary scientists Andrew Ingersoll of the California Institute of Technology in Pasadena and Catherine de Bergh and S. Ichtiaque Rasool of the National Aeronautics and Space Administration's Institute for Space Studies in New York City. They proposed a *runaway greenhouse* theory. This theory is based on the *greenhouse effect* that can be observed in Earth's atmosphere. Rays from the sun easily penetrate Earth's atmosphere. Most of the warming rays are radiated back into space. But certain gases in Earth's atmosphere—such as carbon dioxide and water vapor—trap some of the rays. This phenomenon is much like that caused by the glass in a greenhouse. It allows sunlight in but prevents heat from escaping.

Carbon dioxide and water vapor make up only a tiny percentage of Earth's total atmosphere, so most of the heat escapes from Earth. However, on Venus, carbon dioxide makes up 96.5 per cent of the atmosphere. Even though little sunlight can get through Venus' dense clouds to the planet's surface, the small amount of heat radiation that does get reflected from its surface is completely trapped by carbon dioxide, water vapor, and clouds of sulfuric acid. Therefore, de Bergh, Ingersoll, and Rasool proposed that as Venus' surface temperature got hotter, its water started evaporating, leading to more water vapor in the air. This, in turn, increased the trapping of heat radiation, leading to even hotter surface temperatures and more evaporation — the runaway greenhouse. As Venus' surface temperatures got hotter and hotter, its water literally boiled away.

The discovery of water on Venus lends new support to the theory that Venus, Earth, and Mars obtained a large share of their atmospheric gases from collisions with comets and asteroids. For years, some scientists reasoned that Venus had no water because it came into being too close to the sun and was therefore too hot for water to form. If this was so, then perhaps comets and asteroids colliding with the planet after Venus cooled delivered the water as a volatile compound in their dust and gas.

Since Venus, Earth, and Mars began with such similar gases, why are their atmospheres so different today? What happened to enable life to evolve on Earth but apparently not on Venus or Mars? One answer appears to lie in Earth's distance from the sun, which created a moderate climate allowing liquid water to exist on the planet's surface. The liquid water removed carbon dioxide from Earth's early atmosphere, preventing the occurrence of a runaway greenhouse like that which apparently took place on Venus. The resulting moderate temperatures set the conditions for life to evolve out of water. Later, as plant life evolved on Earth, it gave off oxygen into the atmosphere creating the air that animals need.

Although distance from the sun was the decisive factor in the evolution of Earth's atmosphere, with Mars the determining factor was size. Because of its smaller size and weaker gravitational pull, Mars lost most of its atmospheric gases. Its carbon dioxide atmosphere simply became too thin to produce much of a greenhouse effect. So, instead of developing a moderate climate, Mars became too cold, and the water beneath its surface froze.

Scientists wonder whether life began on Venus before its water evaporated or on Mars before it went into its deep freeze. But as yet no one knows. Liquid water on Mars seems to have frozen about 3½ billion years ago. Thus, the first billion years of history on Mars and Earth must have been most similar. Interestingly, the oldest-known evidence of life on Earth bears this same date — 3½ billion years. If life could evolve in the first billion years of our planet's history, something similar may have happened on Mars. Life may have originated there too but then died out.

What we have learned about the planets and their atmospheres allows us to be more hopeful that life might exist elsewhere in the universe. Even in our own solar system, we see chemistry occurring now on Titan and Jupiter that may resemble the chemistry that led to life on Earth. In all the immensity of space, around some distant star, life may be evolving on other planets with atmospheres that also feature gases uniquely suited to sustain life.

BY PATTY JO WATSON

Ancient Indians of Mammoth Cave

In Kentucky's Mammoth Cave system, scientists are discovering details about the lives of people who lived in and mined the caves 4,000 years ago.

With sure-footed confidence, the man made his way through the dark, silent corridors of the cave. The torch he carried in his right hand cast only a small pool of orange light into the surrounding blackness, but it was enough. He had been this way many times, as had his ancestors for a hundred generations before him. For much of the 45 years of his life, the man had lived with his family inside the mouth of this immense cave. On some days, he was a hunter; on others, a warrior. But today, he was a miner, on his way to gather valuable mineral crystals from the walls deep inside the cave.

At last, the man saw what he had come for: a sparkling deposit of gypsum crystals growing on a rockface several feet above his head. He climbed onto a ledge that gave him closer access to the crystals and wedged his torch into the sand. Then he began to scrape at the crystals with a limestone rock, catching the crumbling fragments in a woven fiber bag. The man did not notice the large boulder that was balanced delicately above him, held in place by a small column of rock that he now began to strike with his stone tool to dislodge the gypsum that encrusted it.

The man never returned from that routine trip into the winding cave. Perhaps his family and friends went in to look for him the next day. Perhaps they passed the ledge where he had been working without seeing his crushed body beneath the fallen rock. Or maybe they found him and decided to leave him where he lay. Whatever happened, the man's body remained on that lonely shelf of rock for nearly 2,000 years until his mummified remains were discovered in 1935 by guides in what is now called Mammoth Cave.

The ancient miner, nicknamed "Lost John," was not the first human being whose naturally preserved body was found in the maze of passages that make up the Mammoth Cave system in west-central Kentucky. In 1875, three amateur explorers found the body of a young boy, later dubbed "Little Al," who may have been ceremonially buried inside a large, mineral-rich cave known today as Salts Cave. Other such "mummies" were also found during the 1800's, including the remains of several people who had been wrapped carefully in deerskins and buried with their earthly possessions.

These discoveries stimulated the interest of archaeologists, who began to visit the caves in the late 1800's. In 1916, Nels C. Nelson, an archaeologist with the American Museum of Natural History in New York City, undertook an extensive investigation of the area, digging in the mouth of Mammoth Cave and along the nearby Green River. By that time, countless artifacts left by the prehistoric cave dwellers had been carried away by the growing numbers of explorers and tourists who tramped through the caves. Still, it was another 40 years before archaeologists began systematically excavating the cave floors.

My own interest in the Mammoth Cave system and its prehistory began in the early 1950's when, as a graduate student in archaeology at the University of Chicago, I married philosopher and geologist Richard Watson. Red, as everyone calls him, had been an avid caver since his undergraduate days in college. We were married in July 1955, and the day after the wedding, he took me exploring in Crystal Cave. I was hooked. But it was not until several years later that I began to do systematic archaeological research in the caves. First, I earned my Ph.D. degree, and then I had a baby daughter, Anna. In 1963, I made my first actual research expedition to the Mammoth Cave area. Since then, I have managed to get to the caves six or eight times a year, working mostly in Salts Cave.

My research on the Kentucky cave dwellers is closely related in some ways to my graduate studies. While I was working toward my Ph.D. degree, I participated in the excavation of an early farming culture that thrived in northern Iraq from about 10,000 to 7000 B.C. The establishment of farming, which enables people to stay in one

The author:
Patty Jo Watson
is professor
of anthropology
at Washington
University
in St. Louis, Mo.

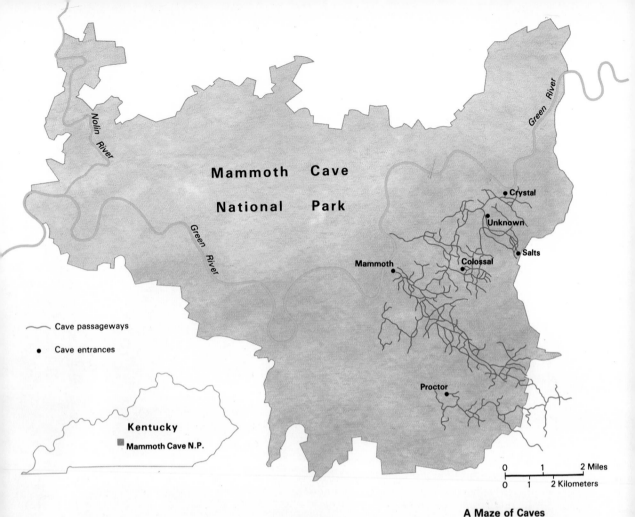

Cave passageways

• Cave entrances

Mammoth Cave National Park

Crystal

Unknown

Salts

Mammoth

Colossal

Proctor

Kentucky
■ Mammoth Cave N.P.

| 0 | 1 | 2 Miles |
| 0 | 1 | 2 Kilometers |

A Maze of Caves
Mammoth Cave National Park, located in west-central Kentucky, contains a vast network of caves, including Mammoth Cave and Salts Cave, where the author has done most of her work.

place rather than having to move periodically from one place to another to obtain food, is a necessary step toward civilization. When I began to investigate the Mammoth Cave culture, I discovered that the prehistoric residents of the caves were at the same stage of economic development as the Near Eastern society, though at a much later time in history. For more than 20 years now, my colleagues and I have been piecing together a picture of the beginning of plant cultivation among the Kentucky cave dwellers. Along the way, we have also learned a great deal about their way of life.

By studying the debris of their daily lives, we have learned that these long-forgotten people were American Indians of the period that archaeologists call Late Archaic-Early Woodland. This period lasted from about 4,000 years ago to 2,500 years ago. Like other Indians in the Americas, the Mammoth Cave inhabitants were descended from Ice Age hunters who migrated to this continent from Asia at least 20,000 years ago by way of a now-vanished land bridge. They came in pursuit of game, especially the great herds of mammoths and mastodons. About 10,000 years ago, however, the last of those huge elephantlike animals became extinct, and the Indians developed new patterns of living.

By 4,000 years ago, many Indians, including those living in the forests east of the Mississippi River, were learning to cultivate plants to supplement their diet of small game, fish, berries, and nuts. Since agriculture enables a more settled existence than hunting and gathering, many Indian groups took up permanent or semipermanent residence in various parts of the continent. They built simple huts with thatched roofs or took shelter where they could find it. In the Green River uplands of Kentucky, the Indians made their homes in natural rock shelters and in the entrances to the many caves that honeycomb the forested limestone hills.

Some of these caves are located in Mammoth Cave National Park, founded in 1941. The Mammoth Cave system is the longest network of caves in the world, with almost 300 miles of interconnected passageways. In addition to Mammoth and Salts caves, the system includes Colossal Cave, Unknown Cave, Crystal Cave, and Proctor Cave, among others. The Kentucky caves are among thousands that have formed within a region of massive underground limestone beds stretching from southern Indiana to northern Alabama and Georgia. In this large area, water from rain and melting snow runs into the earth through hundreds of thousands of *sinkholes*, or natural drains. The water flows underground, slowly dissolving the limestone and, over millions of years, forming the caves.

The water that creates a cave eventually emerges from the ground through springs that feed into a nearby river. In the case of the Mammoth Cave system, the neighboring waterway is the Green River, a major tributary of the Ohio River. As a cave forms, the water carves ever deeper into the rock, and the water level within the cave drops. This means that the higher passages become dry and cease to change, except when part of a ceiling or wall collapses under its own weight. The Mammoth Cave system contains four major levels of passages, the highest (and thus the oldest) of which was formed as long as a million years ago. The conditions that made these upper corridors appealing to the Indians as a place to live — protection from wind and rain and

"Lost John," *above,* an Indian whose naturally mummified body was found in Mammoth Cave in 1935, was killed in a prehistoric mining accident. An Indian's footprint, *below,* is one of many preserved in the mud and dust of the cave floors.

To test the cave-exploring techniques of the ancient Indians, archaeologists climb barefoot through Salts Cave, lighting their way with primitive torches made of cane stalks.

a year-round temperature of 54°F. — also preserved many remains of the Indian culture for present-day archaeologists to find.

Archaeological research conducted deep underground differs in several ways from archaeology done on the earth's surface. The biggest difference is our continual need for artificial light, because the inner recesses of a cave are a realm of perpetual and absolute darkness. The lights must provide dependable illumination lasting from 3 to 15 hours and also must be sturdy and easy to carry. We use battery lamps, gas lanterns, and miners' hardhats with headlamps. Each person also carries a flashlight, candles, and matches.

Another problem is the rugged terrain. Visitors in caverns open to tourists stroll through passages that have been cleared out and paved with smooth walkways. In its natural state, however, a cave is littered with piles of boulders and broken rocks of all sizes. The only way to get past most of these is by climbing over or around them. Also, many sections of caves can be reached only by crawling through small openings or *chimneying* up and down narrow vertical passages — moving slowly by pressing your back against one wall and your feet against the opposite wall.

As you may well imagine, maneuvering through a cave can be dangerous. There are many places where you can fall or get stuck. I once lost my footing on a rock shelf and fell about 10 feet, but fortunately I was not injured. My colleagues and I sometimes marvel at how the ancient cave dwellers were able to get to some of the remote ledges and crawlways where we have found their traces, especially since at least some members of each party had to use one hand to carry a torch. The Indians were terrific cave explorers.

Once we reach the cave area we have chosen to investigate and have set up our lights, we use the same techniques and tools as other archaeologists. We first make a thorough search of the cave floor for prehistoric artifacts and debris. Whatever we find is photographed and identified, and its location is mapped. We then sometimes dig one or more trenches in the sand and clay sediment of the cave floor in search of buried material.

The closer we excavate to the cave entrance, the more debris and artifacts we find, because the Indians lived in the *vestibule* — the entry chamber just inside the mouth of the cavern. But even deep inside the cave, we find considerable evidence of the Indians' presence, especially traces of their mining activities. These findings include remnants of their torches and campfires and the soot smudges those blazes made on walls and ceilings. Occasionally, we come upon artifacts that were discarded or forgotten by the Indians, such as the moccasins they wove from plant fibers. Once, we found a ladder — or more precisely a climbing pole — left in a passage by an ancient miner. The pole is simply the trunk of a small tree with its branches chopped down to stumps to serve as footholds.

Here and there, we find Indians' footprints preserved in the dust or still-soft mud of a passage floor. Nothing makes the cave dwellers seem quite so real to me as seeing the actual impressions of their bare feet. Time seems suspended, and I feel that if I followed the footprints around the next bend in the passage, I would come upon the person who made them.

The cavern vestibules, particularly in Mammoth Cave and Salts Cave, have yielded a great quantity of Indian artifacts. Most of the specimens we find now are fragments; those avid souvenir hunters of years ago removed nearly all of the best-preserved items. (Fortunately, many of those pieces found their way to museums.)

Among the most common artifacts that have been discovered in the vestibule areas are specimens of woven or braided plant fibers. In addition to moccasins, these items include baskets, cloth, bags, and ropes. The Indians fashioned these objects from fibers they obtained from the tough inner bark of several kinds of trees and from the stems and leaves of various plants. On the whole, such articles were probably quite durable, with the possible exception of the moccasins. Most of the moccasins we have found have holes worn in the toes or heels, and they probably had to be repaired or replaced quite often. The preserved footprints reveal that the Indians often went barefoot in the caves, most likely to improve their foothold on sloping surfaces. But some Indians may have been barefoot simply because their moccasins fell apart.

Trenches dug in the cave vestibules have produced spearpoints, various kinds of stone tools, food remnants, and numerous fragments of human and animal bones. We can determine the relative ages of these artifacts by noting the depth at which each is found — an item just a few inches below the surface is usually considerably younger than one that is buried several feet deep. We can also determine the actual ages of many objects fairly accurately by subjecting them to *radiocarbon dating*, a scientific technique that has become indispensable to archaeologists (see HOW ARCHAEOLOGISTS DATE THEIR DISCOVERIES, page 150). All the excavated materials that we have tested with this method have been dated at from 4,000 to 2,000 years old, enabling us to determine the period when prehistoric people began to live in the Mammoth Cave system.

Human bones uncovered in some of our excavations are often broken and burned and are found mixed with animal bones in what are unquestionably ancient garbage heaps. This evidence points to the possibility that the cave dwellers may sometimes have been cannibals. A few archaeologists have suggested that the Indians resorted to cannibalism because they were unable to obtain enough food from hunting and fishing. I think that is rather unlikely, though, because our digs have turned up the bones of many animals — deer, rabbits, turkeys, small rodents, and fish — indicating that wildlife was plentiful in the area.

Another possibility is that the ancient cave dwellers ate human

Everyday Life at a Cave

On a warm day, a group of prehistoric Indians living in a cave
entrance tend to their daily tasks. As a man roasts fresh game
over a fire, his daughter feeds two children. Two women are
weaving plant fibers, the younger one in the foreground mending
moccasins while her mother puts finishing touches on a basket.
Outside the cave, a young boy watches two men barter – a visitor
offers an animal skin in exchange for mineral salts mined from
the cave walls. At the edge of the forest, a woman harvests gourds
and squash from a small garden while her younger sisters
pick wild berries. Beyond them, a young hunter practices throwing
his spear. Such activities were probably typical during the
2,000 years that Indians lived in the Mammoth Cave area.

How Archaeologists Date Their Discoveries

Archaeologists determine the age of debris from ancient societies with a procedure called *radiocarbon dating*, developed in the late 1940's by chemist Willard F. Libby. This technique can be used on any material that once was alive, such as wood, bone, and food remnants.

All living tissues are composed of molecules containing atoms of the element carbon. Plants obtain carbon by absorbing carbon dioxide (CO_2) from the air. Using the energy of sunlight, they break the CO_2 molecules apart and then recombine the carbon atoms into more complex molecules. Animals get carbon by eating plants or other animals that have eaten plants. Therefore, all the carbon in living things was originally derived from CO_2 in the air.

Almost all carbon atoms in the air are in the form of an *isotope* called carbon 12. Isotopes of an element are atoms having the same number of protons but a different number of neutrons. The nucleus of carbon 12 is made up of 6 protons and 6 neutrons. About one out of every trillion carbon atoms is the isotope carbon 14. This isotope is produced when cosmic rays in the form of neutrons strike nitrogen atoms in the atmosphere. Such a collision causes a nitrogen atom, which contains 7 protons and 7 neutrons in its nucleus, to gain an extra neutron and lose a proton — thereby becoming an atom of carbon 14, with a nucleus composed of 6 protons and 8 neutrons. The extra neutrons make the carbon 14 atom unstable and thus radioactive.

Carbon 14 has what scientists call a *half-life* of 5,700 years. This means that in any given number of carbon 14 atoms, half will decay, or break down into nitrogen, about every 5,700 years. Therefore, the bones of an animal that has been dead for 5,700 years would have half as much carbon 14 as the bones of a living animal. Bones that are 11,400 years old would have one-fourth as much carbon 14, and so on.

To find out the age of a specimen, scientists — using special instruments — simply measure its proportion of carbon 12 to carbon 14. Radiocarbon dating is most accurate when a specimen is between 500 and 50,000 years old. In a specimen less than 500 years old, too little carbon 14 has decayed to get an accurate reading. After 50,000 years, not enough carbon 14 remains for a precise measurement.　　[P.J.W.]

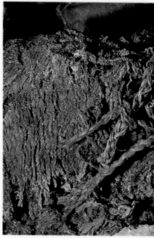

Using radiocarbon techniques, archaeologists have determined that artifacts discovered in the caves are from 2,000 to 4,000 years old. Among the items found are, *left to right,* a basket made of woven strips of cane, a fragment of a moccasin fashioned from twisted plant fibers, and cane stalks cut by the Indians for torches and left in a passage.

flesh as part of a ritual. Even in the mid-1900's, anthropologists found isolated groups of people, such as the Fore tribe of New Guinea, who practiced cannibalism. Some of these people ate the bodies of their dead relatives as a sign of respect. Others ate the hearts and brains of enemy warriors they had slain in battle, hoping to gain strength and wisdom. However, the human remains found at the caves do not seem to fit either practice. For one thing, the careless disposal of the bones indicates a complete lack of reverence for the dead. Moreover, many of the bones are those of children, meaning that if the cave dwellers feasted on their enemies, they did not limit themselves to warriors. My colleagues and I think the evidence suggests that the Indians sometimes raided enemy encampments and killed people of all ages. If so, then they probably ate the bodies of their victims to show their hatred and contempt for them.

Despite many lingering uncertainties about the cave dwellers, there is much that we have learned about them—enough, in fact, for us to reconstruct their appearance and daily life with a fair degree of confidence. From studies of mummies, skeletons, and bones, we know that the Indians were of medium height—an average of about 5 feet 5 inches for men, and just over 5 feet for women. Like all American Indians, they had brown skin and straight black hair, which they probably wore loose or tied in a knot at the back of the head. They no doubt dressed in clothing made of animal skins during the winter, switching in the spring to a wraparound garment of woven fibers that covered just the midsection of the body. Children most likely went naked during warm weather.

The evidence indicates that no more than about 15 people from two or three families that probably were related lived in a cave vestibule at any one time. They probably spent the winter there but left periodically in warm weather to gather food that they could not get near the caves, such as various kinds of nuts and plants, and *mussels* (a type of shellfish) and fish from the Green River.

The cave people also ate whatever animals they could kill in the surrounding forests, and the seeds of various plants they were beginning to cultivate, such as sunflowers and two herbs called sumpweed and goosefoot. In addition, the Indians grew gourds and gourdlike squash, from which they fashioned bowls and bottles. We know this because we have found such containers within the caves, perfectly preserved by the stable cave environment. The gourds and squash were another source of nutritious seeds.

The "farming," as well as the gathering of wild plant foods, was probably the work of the women and girls. Their small garden patches were most likely set among the nearby trees. The cave dwellers probably learned this primitive form of agriculture from Indians living far to the south. The kinds of gourds and squash found in the Kentucky caves were grown in Mexico as long as 10,000 years ago. The knowledge of how to cultivate these plants seems to have spread slowly northward, reaching some parts of North America by at least 7,000 years ago and the Green River area some 2,500 years after that. However, once the North American Indians had learned the basics of agriculture, they were able to use that knowledge to cultivate native plants, such as the sunflowers and other plants grown by the Kentucky cave dwellers.

Hunting was probably the privilege of the men and older boys of the group. Armed with stone-tipped wooden spears and darts and handheld throwing sticks that hooked onto the end of a spear and increased the force with which it was hurled, the hunters would set off into the woods in search of game. Perhaps their wolflike dogs — their only domesticated animals — accompanied them. Some days, no doubt, the hunters returned to the cave empty-handed, or with just a fish speared in the river. Other times, they came back laden with game. After successful hunts, the cave must have been filled with the aroma of meat roasting over a fire.

Sometimes, the cave dwellers ventured deep into the caves, carrying torches of dry twigs or cane stalks cut from a bamboolike plant that grew along the river. We have found that three dried pieces of cane 3 feet long and about as thick as a little finger will burn nicely as a torch for about an hour, its orange flame giving a soft, pleasant light. Other than for sport and curiosity, the Indians explored the caves so thoroughly because they were searching for mineral crystals to mine and also perhaps because they thought the underground world was the home of spirits.

Mining seems to have been the most common reason for going underground. In addition to gypsum, the Indians mined *mirabilite* (sodium sulfate) and *epsomite* (magnesium sulfate). These are better known as Glauber's salt and Epsom salt. All three compounds grow as beautiful crystals on cave walls and ceilings, and gypsum also forms as a thin white crust. These minerals have several uses, which the Indians must have discovered through trial and error. Powdered gypsum can be made into white paint by adding water or grease. Epsom salt and Glauber's salt are laxatives, and the latter, which has a salty taste, can be used as a food seasoning as well.

Because of these properties, the minerals would probably have been a valuable trade item. In the 1930's, archaeologists digging in an area about 50 miles west of Mammoth Cave found copper from what is now Michigan and seashells from the Gulf of Mexico. The Mammoth Cave Indians may have bartered their minerals for these and other articles. The fact that they obtained goods from such far-away places indicates that the Indians of the Green River area were part of an intricate and far-reaching trade network.

Some of the caves occasionally served another purpose — as a place to bury the dead. The Indians' methods for disposing of their dead varied considerably from place to place. Many of the complete skeletons that have been unearthed in various locations in the Mammoth Cave area had obviously been buried with considerable ceremony. Typically, the corpse had been laid on its side with the knees drawn up toward the chin and carefully placed in a hole in the ground. In contrast, in another system of caves, just a short distance from Mammoth Cave, local cave explorers found vertical pits into which bodies had been thrown helter-skelter.

The care a person's body received after death was probably related to how important that person had been in life. The Mammoth Cave dwellers, we believe, had the kind of social system that anthropologists call a *big man society:* Everyone was supposedly equal, but some people were — so to speak — more equal than others. The bodies of those who were less equal may have been thrown into pits. But it is more likely that these were the bodies of enemies.

However, all such interpretations of the evidence are mostly guesswork. Since the Indians painted no pictures on the cave walls, it is difficult for us to reconstruct this part of their lives. We do know, though, that by the time of the Early Woodland Period, about 3,000 years ago, most Indian societies had developed a number of elaborate rituals, including some for the burial of the dead. We have found relatively few graves in the Mammoth Cave area, but that does not necessarily mean that ceremonial burials were rare. Perhaps most bodies were buried outside in places that have not yet been discovered or where they were destroyed by the elements.

For some 2,000 years, the cycle of life and death at the caves continued. Then, at about the time of the birth of Christ, the Indians stopped going into the caves. There are probably several reasons why they did so. They may have exhausted most of the easily mined mineral deposits in the caves, or perhaps the minerals lost their barter value. Then again, trade routes may have changed, leaving the upland Indians "off the beaten track." Any of these things may have occurred, but the most important reason for the Indians' departure, we think, is that they and their culture had changed and living in the uplands did not suit their new way of life. Agriculture was becoming increasingly important throughout the region, with corn being grown in some areas. Many of the upland Indians probably resettled in the river valleys, where the land was level and the soil was rich, becoming part of the society of settled farming tribes that was emerging in Eastern North America.

As the cave dwellers' descendants moved to new areas and intermarried with other groups, the memory of the caves must have faded. And after hundreds of years, when new Southeast Indian tribes had arisen — the Choctaw, the Cherokee, and other peoples encountered by European settlers — only legends remained of an underworld populated by supernatural beings. Unknown to anyone, the debris of 2,000 years of day-to-day living lay scattered in the caves, waiting for present-day archaeologists to interpret its fascinating story.

New methods of taking pictures of the inside of the body have led to dramatic improvements in medical diagnosis.

New Ways to Look Inside the Body

BY HOWARD WOLINSKY

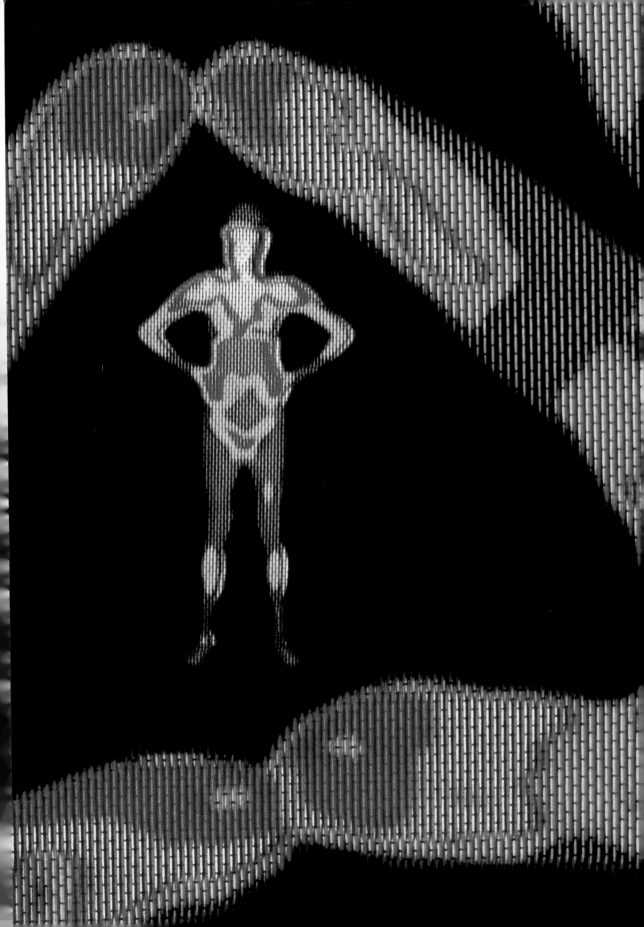

Donald's condition baffled his doctors. His legs were so wobbly that he could hardly stand by himself, and he suffered from severe headaches and a stiff neck.

The doctors suspected that a tumor might be growing near Donald's spine, pressing on nerves that control his legs. So they sent him to Brent M. Greenberg, a radiologist in Highland Park, Ill. Radiologists are physicians who use X-ray machines and other devices to take pictures of the inside of the body to help diagnose diseases.

First, Donald received an *angiogram* — an X-ray examination of blood vessels. A doctor inserted a *catheter*, a thin, flexible tube, into an artery in Donald's groin and carefully pushed it up to the arteries that supply blood to the head and neck. A dye was then injected through the hollow catheter into the artery. The dye made the blood vessels show up clearly in X-ray pictures of Donald's head and neck. Blood vessels that supply healthy tissue look different from vessels leading to tumors, but Donald's pictures appeared normal.

The radiologist then performed a *computerized tomography* (*CT*) *scan* — also called a CAT scan — a computerized X-ray procedure that produces detailed pictures of cross sections of the body. When the CT pictures also failed to show diseased tissue, Greenberg decided to try a *nuclear magnetic resonance* (*NMR*) *scan*, which used magnetism and radio waves to take pictures of the soft tissues in Donald's neck.

NMR, which is more sensitive than CT to disease in soft tissue, produced pictures of what appeared to be a half-inch tumor. When surgeons operated, they found the tumor exactly where the scan indicated it would be.

Donald benefited from a revolution in medical imaging. This revolution includes CT and NMR scanning; *ultrasound scanning*, the use of sound waves to make pictures; and *positron emission tomography* (*PET*), a technique that uses high-energy gamma rays.

The science of medical imaging began in 1895, when German physicist Wilhelm K. Roentgen discovered X rays. The scientist stunned the world with his X-ray "photographs of the invisible."

Word of Roentgen's discovery spread quickly. In 1896, about 50 books and 1,000 scientific papers about X rays appeared. Researchers soon discovered that X rays also have a dangerous side. The first cases of burns from X rays surfaced in 1896. Seven years later, the first skin cancers caused by X rays appeared. Over the years, however, scientists have made X-ray equipment safer. Today, routine X rays such as those taken of the teeth and the chest require only small amounts of X radiation.

X rays pass through or are absorbed by the body to form pictures on film, just as light forms images on film in a camera. Bones absorb a great deal of radiation and so they appear as unexposed or clear areas in the negative X-ray picture. Soft tissue, such as lungs, absorbs fewer rays, and thus looks darker than bone. Air spaces in the body let the most rays through and thus look darkest of all.

The use of X rays radically changed the practice of medicine. For

The author:
Howard Wolinsky is a medical writer for the Chicago *Sun-Times.*

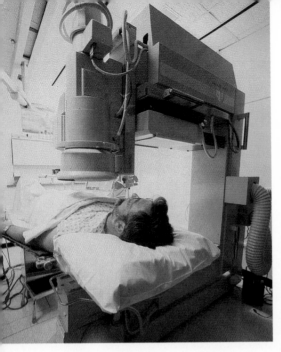

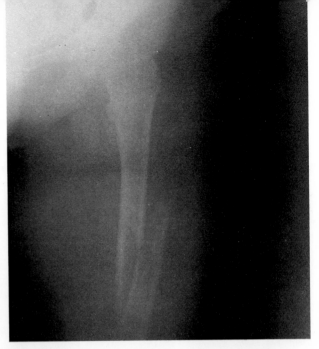

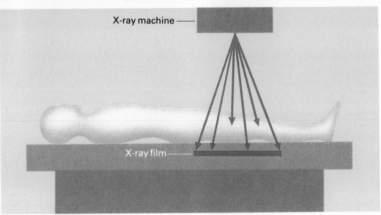

X-ray machine

X-ray film

Photographing with X Rays

An X-ray camera, *left and above left,* takes a picture of the bone in a patient's leg by sending high-energy rays through the patient. Bone absorbs more X rays than does soft tissue. The X rays that pass through the patient's soft tissue create an image on photographic film under the patient. So when the film is developed, *above,* the image of a broken bone appears as a clear area, the soft tissue as dark areas.

the first time, doctors could see the effects of disease and injury inside the body without opening the patient surgically. Within just a few months after Roentgen's discovery, doctors were using X rays to examine broken bones. X rays also came into use in the diagnosis of tuberculosis, lung and stomach tumors, cavities in teeth, and other diseases.

Despite the benefits of X-ray pictures, doctors sought better ways of using X rays. They looked for ways to X-ray parts of the body that are invisible or hard to see in conventional X-ray pictures. Blood vessels, certain tumors, and organs such as the kidneys, liver, and gall bladder absorb the same amount of radiation as surrounding tissue and do not show up in conventional X-ray pictures. In addition, some parts of the body are difficult to see in X-ray pictures because other body parts block them. The ribs, for example, block out parts of the lungs and the heart.

Glossary

Angiography: The examination of blood vessels with X rays after a dye has been injected into the vessels.

Computerized tomography (CT) scanning: A computerized X-ray procedure that produces images of cross sections of the body. Formerly called CAT scanning.

Digital subtraction angiography: A technique in which a computer produces a clear picture of blood vessels. The computer subtracts an X-ray image taken before an injection of dye into the vessels from an X-ray picture taken after the injection.

Electromagnet: A device that becomes a strong magnet when electric current is passed through it.

Electromagnetic radiation: Rays of energy made up of traveling electric and magnetic fields. Radio waves, visible light, X rays, and gamma rays are forms of electromagnetic radiation.

Gamma ray: A form of electromagnetic radiation that has more energy than an X ray.

Magnetic field: The space around a magnet in which the magnet's powers of attraction and repulsion are effective.

Nuclear magnetic resonance (NMR) scanning: The use of magnetic fields and radio waves to produce pictures of the inside of the body.

Positron emission tomography (PET) scanning: The use of gamma rays emitted by radioactive substances injected into the body to produce images of cross sections of the body.

Radioactive: Giving off energy by emitting gamma rays or subatomic particles as atomic nuclei break up.

Ultrasound: Sound that is too high for human beings to hear.

X ray: A form of high-energy electromagnetic radiation used to take pictures of the inside of the body.

Researchers solved the first of these problems in the early 1900's when they learned how to use dyes to darken organs so that the organs show up clearly in X-ray pictures. By the 1930's, researchers developed angiography, the dye technique that was used on Donald. This technique enabled doctors to find heart defects and blockages of the coronary arteries and other major blood vessels.

All these X-ray techniques helped improve diagnosis, but radiology's biggest advance since the discovery of X rays came in the 1970's, when the problem of one body part blocking another was solved by the introduction of the CT scan. CT — computerized tomography — is a marriage of X rays and computers, and it produces cross-sectional images of the body.

When Donald had his CT scan, he lay on a table by a large ring-like machine. When the machine was turned on, the table slid into the ring, which held an X-ray emitter and an X-ray detector. These devices were then switched on, and a small motor began to rotate the ring. As the ring made one complete revolution, the emitter sent X rays through Donald's body from points all around a circle. The detector gathered the X-ray images as the ring revolved and fed the images into a computer, which converted the images into *digits* (numbers) of computer language. The computer then used the digits to produce the cross-sectional images. Each picture from a CT scan shows a "slice" of the body. The pictures are displayed on a TV monitor or on ordinary X-ray film.

Solving the problem of one body part blocking another has made certain diagnoses much easier. For example, if a doctor sees evidence of an apparently enlarged heart on a conventional X-ray picture, a CT scan can reveal whether the heart muscle itself is enlarged or whether there is an overlying tumor. Similarly, CT can show abnormalities in the brain, such as tumors, while regular X rays show only the skull bones.

One drawback to CT scanners is their cost — about $1 million. However, radiologists maintain that CT has often reduced medical costs by eliminating the need for other tests, exploratory surgery, and many hospital stays.

The marriage of X rays and the computer has brought other gains in medical imaging. Today, electronic equipment converts all kinds of X-ray images into digits. Doctors store the digitized pictures on magnetic tape for later viewing on a TV monitor.

Digital imaging is used mainly in *digital subtraction angiography* (*DSA*), a major improvement over conventional angiography. In DSA, a radiologist takes an X-ray picture of blood vessels in the patient's head, neck, heart, lungs, abdomen, arms, or legs. In this picture, tissue and bone near the vessels show up clearly, but the vessels themselves are extremely faint or invisible. A catheter is then inserted into a vein in the patient's arm, and a dye is injected through the catheter. After the dye reaches the blood vessels that

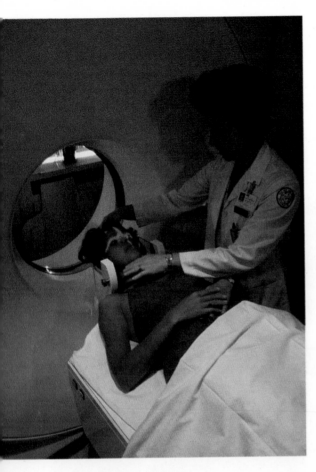

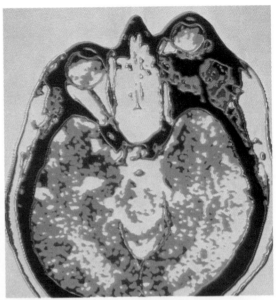

CT Scan: Shoot and Compute

A computerized tomography (CT) scan, *left and below,* shoots X rays from an emitter in a rotating ring into a patient's body. Rays that pass through the patient strike detectors that are also built into the ring. As the ring rotates, the detectors send the X-ray images to a computer, which produces a cross-sectional picture. A CT scan image of a head, *above,* reveals a large tumor behind a patient's right eye.

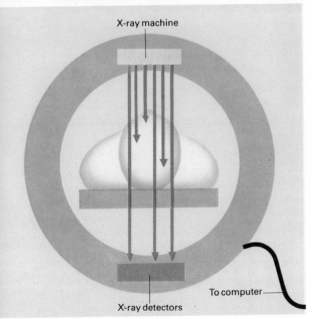

X-ray machine

X-ray detectors

To computer

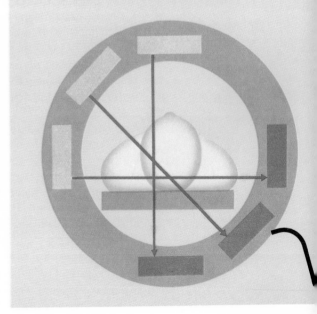

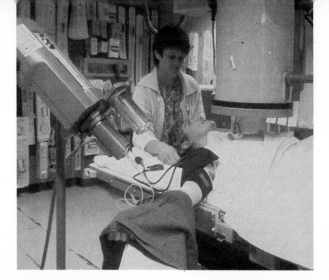

A Picture Minus a Picture

Digital subtraction angiography, a computerized study of blood vessels, begins with an ordinary X-ray picture of the vessels, *below left.* Vessels do not show up well in such pictures, so a technician next injects a dye into the patient's bloodstream, *left,* and takes another picture of exactly the same area, *below center.* Because of the dye, the vessels now photograph well. A computer process then removes from the second picture everything in the first, leaving a computer-enhanced image of the vessels, *below right.*

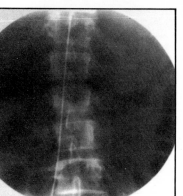

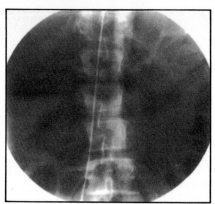

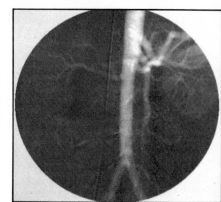

the radiologist wishes to photograph, the radiologist takes another X-ray picture showing exactly the same area as the first picture. The second picture, thanks to the dye, gives a slightly better image of the blood vessels than did the first. Then electronic equipment comes into play, digitizing both images for a computer. The computer removes from the second picture everything that is in the first picture. With the neighboring tissue and bone gone, the vessels show up clearly. DSA is less painful and safer than conventional angiography. It is safer because the digital technique does not require insertion of a catheter into an artery. Inserting a catheter into an artery can cause severe bleeding. The catheter occasionally can trigger a stroke or heart attack by causing an arterial spasm or by breaking loose a waxy deposit of cholesterol from an artery wall, creating a blockage. (Deposits do not build up on the walls of veins.) Furthermore, DSA requires less exposure to radiation. And DSA costs less than conventional angiography. A conventional angiogram costs about $2,000 plus the expense of one or more days in the hospital, compared with about $500 for a digital angiogram, which is usually done without hospitalization.

In recent years, radiologists have developed imaging techniques

How Much
Is Too Much?

Authorities agree that medical testing should be done only if it is likely to benefit the patient. This is especially important in the case of X rays, because X rays damage tissue.

X-ray radiation is a form of *ionizing radiation*. Ionizing rays knock electrons out of their orbits around atoms that make up tissue, converting the atoms into electrically charged particles called *ions*. These ions disrupt the normal chemical processes of living cells, causing the cells to grow abnormally or to die. Because of this, X rays that strike the reproductive system can not only damage the individual but also cause physical or mental defects in his or her future offspring by rearranging genetic material in a sperm or egg cell.

Cells may be able to repair the damage produced by only a few ions. However, they usually do not recover from large amounts of ionizing radiation.

Our bodies are bombarded constantly by small amounts of *background radiation* — ionizing radiation from radioactive minerals in the earth and in cosmic rays. In the United States, the average annual dose of background radiation received by a person is 0.084 rad. A *rad* is a measure of the energy deposited by ionizing radiation as it passes through a substance. A single X ray of the chest deposits 0.1 rad, slightly more than the average annual dose from background radiation. A series of X rays of the skull deposits up to 2 rads, about 24 times the background dose. A typical computerized tomography brain scan of 10 "slices" would deposit from 1 to 10 rads, depending upon the tomography equipment. Conventional X-ray angiography, for picturing blood vessels, leaves 10 rads in the body.

Gamma rays used in positron emission tomography (PET) also ionize atoms in tissue. PET exposes the patient to radiation equal to about 6 rads.

How damaging are such doses of ionizing radiation? Scientists do not yet know.

Researchers have studied the effects of X rays on human tissue, but "most of the data on human effects occur in the high-dose range of 100 rads or more," according to Richard P. Chiacchierini, director of the Statistics Branch, Division of Life Sciences, in the Office of Science and Technology of the Center for Devices and Radiological Health (CDRH) in Rockville, Md. These data came from studies of survivors of the atomic bomb blasts during World War II, patients undergoing radiation therapy, and workers who were exposed for long periods of time to radioactive substances.

To gather data on the effects of low doses, experimenters have irradiated animals and animal and human tissue samples. They have found that increasing the amount of radiation increases the amount of biological damage. However, they disagree on whether biological damage is directly proportional to the amount of radiation. Nevertheless, to be on the safe side, government agencies that are responsible for protecting the public assume that low doses of ionizing radiation have the potential to cause problems. So the United States government has issued a standard requiring that people who work almost daily with X rays — such as radiologists, dentists, and other medical personnel — should receive no more than 5 rads per year on the job.

Ultrasound scans do not produce ionizing radiation. However, ultrasound of long duration and high intensity can damage tissue by such mechanical effects as heating.

At the levels used in medical imaging, ultrasound has no proven damaging side effects. Nevertheless, patients are advised to avoid unnecessary tests, especially for monitoring fetal development. In February 1984, a panel of the National Institutes of Health said that ultrasound should be used for this purpose only when medically justified.

In March 1984, the Food and Drug Administration (FDA) granted two companies permission to sell nuclear magnetic resonance (NMR) scanners. Little is known about the risks of NMR, which uses radio waves and magnetic forces. Health physicist Robert A. Phillips, chief of the Radiologic Devices Branch of the CDRH, says that "research hasn't found anything [unhealthy with NMR] yet, but that doesn't mean it isn't there. We're still studying NMR's effects."

As a precaution, researchers and radiologists in the United States do not perform NMR scans on patients who wear heart pacemakers, because the strong magnetic fields would interfere with the devices; patients with artificial limbs and other body replacements containing metal, because the metal might heat up; and pregnant women, because so little is known about the effects of NMR on fetuses.   [H.W.]

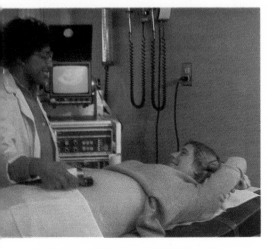

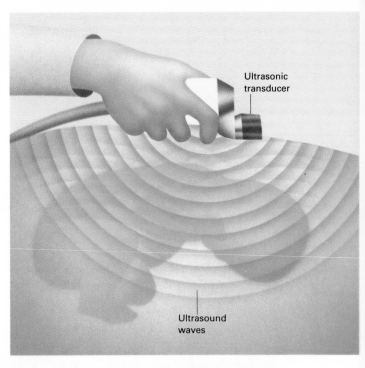

Ultrasonic
transducer

Ultrasound
waves

Taking a Picture with Sound

The handheld transducer of an ultrasound
machine, *above and right,* emits sound
waves that pass through a pregnant
woman's abdomen, bounce off the fetus,
and return to the transducer. A computer
in the machine then converts these echoes
into a picture of the fetus, *below.*

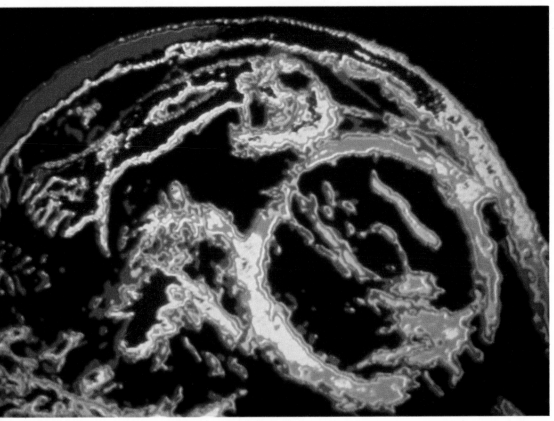

that do not use X rays. These methods—ultrasound scanning, NMR, and PET—not only avoid exposing patients to X rays, but some of them also provide images that X rays cannot supply.

Ultrasound scanning probes the body with sound waves that are too high for us to hear. Medical researchers began to investigate ultrasound after World War II. The United States Navy had found *sonar* (*so*und *na*vigation *a*nd *r*anging) useful for locating enemy submarines. Sonar works by bouncing sound waves off underwater objects. Echo detectors and other devices convert the returning waves to pictures. Researchers found that a similar technique could help doctors detect disease. Since the late 1960's, doctors have used ultrasound to diagnose such abnormalities as cysts and tumors in the liver and other organs. Physicians also use ultrasound to examine the head, the eyes, and even the beating heart.

To create ultrasound medical images, a *transducer*—a device that converts electricity to sound—is placed on the patient's body. As the sound waves pass through the body, some of them encounter the patient's inner organs and bounce back like an echo. A detector picks up the echoes and converts them into images.

Ultrasound provides more detail on the internal structure of organs than does CT scanning. Ultrasound also provides details of blood vessels without the use of dye. Futhermore, ultrasound scanning is much less expensive than CT scanning. A typical ultrasound scan costs $45 or more.

Ultrasound examinations of pregnant women have become more and more common because the technique shows good detail in soft fetal tissue and because it avoids exposing the fetus to X rays. Low-powered ultrasound used for diagnosis has no known harmful side effects. However, the National Institutes of Health (NIH) recommends caution in using ultrasound to examine fetuses. In February 1984, the NIH said that doctors should not use the technique routinely for this purpose but only when there is a medical reason to do so.

One disadvantage of ultrasound is that it cannot penetrate bones such as the skull. However, surgeons at the University of Chicago have developed methods of viewing the brain with ultrasound as their "flashlight" after opening the skull surgically.

The second of the new non-X-ray techniques—nuclear magnetic resonance (NMR) scanning—reveals differences among soft tissues better than do X-ray and ultrasound methods. The differences in anatomy that NMR reveals depend upon molecular differences between healthy tissue and diseased tissue. NMR detects these differences by manipulating the body's most common atom, hydrogen, in the molecules of tissue.

An NMR scanner looks somewhat like a CT scanner. Like a CT patient, an NMR patient lies on a table that slides into a ring. But instead of X-ray equipment, the NMR ring contains a powerful elec-

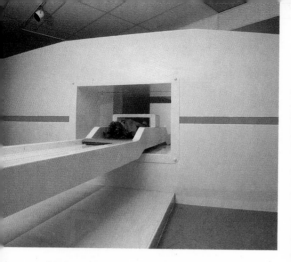

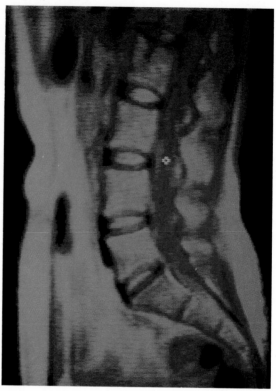

Lining Up for a Picture

A nuclear magnetic resonance (NMR) scanner, *above,* uses magnetic and radio energy to take pictures of the inside of a patient's body, *diagrams below.* Before the scanner magnet is turned on, hydrogen nuclei in the body spin on axes that are not aligned (A). These nuclei are magnetic, so switching on a magnet aligns them (B). A transmitter then emits radio energy, which nuclei absorb (C) and re-emit. A receiver detects re-emitted energy (D) and sends data to a computer, which produces an image of spine curvature, *right.*

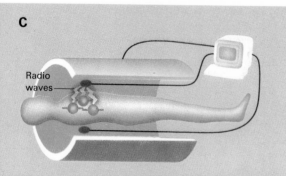

A

Magnet

Computer
and control

Radio
transmitter

Nonaligned
hydrogen nuclei

Radio
receiver

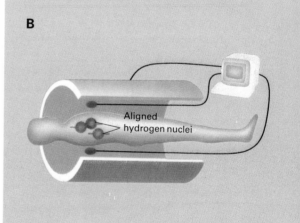

B

Aligned
hydrogen nuclei

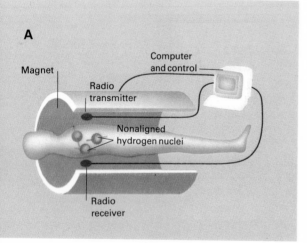

C

Radio
waves

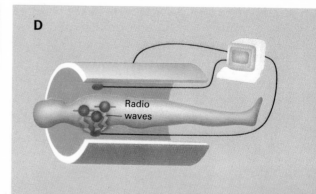

D

Radio
waves

tromagnet, a radio transmitter, and a radio receiver. When the electromagnet is turned on, it produces an intense magnetic field that forces hydrogen nuclei in the patient's body to line up in the same direction. (A hydrogen atom's nucleus spins on its own axis, just as the earth spins. Ordinarily, the axes of a group of neighboring hydrogen nuclei point randomly in many directions.)

Then the radio transmitter is turned on, emitting low-frequency radio waves. The nuclei absorb energy from the waves. And when the transmitter is turned off, the nuclei release the absorbed energy as signals that are picked up by the radio receiver. Hydrogen atoms in healthy tissue emit the radio signals at different rates and intensities than do hydrogen atoms in diseased tissue. A computer then converts the signals from the nuclei into images. NMR is more sensitive than CT to abnormal soft tissue, even though NMR pictures are not as sharp as CT images. In addition, NMR slices can be taken at any angle to the length of the body, while CT scans can produce only certain cross sections. On the other hand, NMR is not sensitive to bone, but CT is, so CT is better than NMR at detecting tumors that affect bone.

Scientists have used NMR devices to analyze chemicals for the past 30 years, but the first NMR image of a living person was produced only in 1977. While NMR is still considered experimental for medical imaging, physicians generally consider it safe for use on patients. The technique is being used, for example, to detect brain tumors and multiple sclerosis plaques—areas of hardened tissue that interfere with nerve function. Physicians are evaluating NMR as a method of detecting disease in the breasts, heart, liver, and pancreas, and as a technique for measuring blood flow. However, there are some restrictions on its use. For example, uncertainty about damage from the powerful magnets prevents doctors from using NMR on people who wear heart pacemakers.

NMR has an added drawback in its cost. A complete NMR machine costs about $3 million, compared with $1 million for a CT machine and $15,000 to $100,000 for an ultrasound machine.

The third new method of imaging, positron emission tomography (PET), is devoted solely to revealing chemical activity in tissue. Abnormal chemical activity may indicate disease. For example, patients with a mental illness called schizophrenia have regions in their brains that absorb glucose—a form of sugar—more slowly than normal.

A PET scanner has the familiar table-and-ring design. Like the rings in CT and NMR machines, the PET scanner's ring contains radiation detectors. The detectors in the PET scanner respond to gamma rays, which are like X rays but have more energy.

Unlike CT and NMR scanners, however, the PET machine does not originate the radiation that strikes the detectors. Instead, the radiation originates inside the patient.

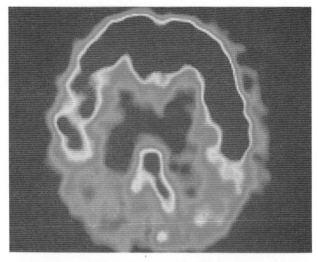

Scanning with PET

A patient receives a positron emission tomography (PET) scan of the brain, *above,* inside a ring of gamma-ray detectors. Radioactive glucose injected into the bloodstream goes to the brain, where, *below, left to right,* a radioactive atom emits a particle called a positron; this particle meets an electron; and the two particles destroy each other, emitting gamma rays that strike detectors. A computer combines data from all the detectors to produce a picture.

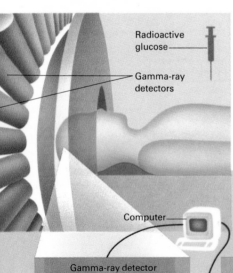

Radioactive glucose

Gamma-ray detectors

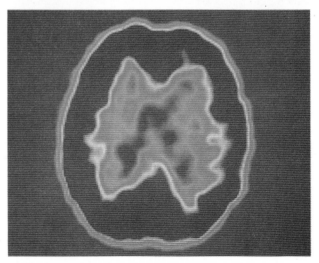

A PET scan reveals that the brain of a patient with Alzheimer's disease, *top,* takes up glucose (in red) slower than does a normal brain, *above.*

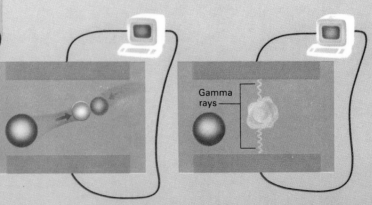

Computer

Gamma-ray detector

Positron

Electron

Radioactive atom in glucose

Gamma-ray detector

Gamma rays

The patient inhales or is injected with radioactive forms of substances that the body normally uses. For a PET scan showing the brain's absorption of glucose, for example, the patient receives radioactive glucose mixed with ordinary glucose. The brain uses glucose as its major source of energy and so, when glucose passes into the blood vessels of the brain, the sugar is absorbed rapidly.

Meanwhile, the radioactive glucose emits particles called positrons. When a positron meets an electron, the two particles destroy each other, giving off gamma rays.

Detectors in the PET ring measure these gamma rays from many angles, then relay the measurements to a computer, which produces cross-sectional pictures. These images show the rate at which various parts of the brain are using the glucose. The PET images of the brain resemble those produced by CT and NMR scanners in that all three show the overall structure of a "slice" of the brain. However, only PET enables doctors to see ongoing metabolism — the process by which food such as sugar is broken down into energy and living tissue.

The brain has been the focus of most PET research, but experimenters also have used PET to study the use of chemicals by the heart muscle and to determine how rapidly the blood delivers chemicals to certain parts of the body. PET is considered safe because the radioactive chemicals leave the body quickly.

PET scanning is extremely expensive. Setting up a PET facility costs as much as $5 million. Furthermore, few hospitals own or have access to particle accelerators, machines necessary to prepare the radioactive chemicals needed for PET scanning. The accelerators must be at or near the hospital because some chemicals used in PET lose their radioactivity within a few minutes. So, for the next few years at least, PET probably will continue to be used mainly for research into the chemistry of disease.

Patients will continue to benefit from the new information PET provides. Doctors will combine this information with data gathered from the other existing imaging techniques — and perhaps new techniques to come. No single imaging technique can presently provide all the answers that doctors are looking for. Rather, it is the combined use of all these techniques by informed scientists and doctors that will be most effective in diagnosing and helping the Donalds of the future.

For further reading:

Arehart-Treichel, Joan. "Fetal Ultrasound: How Safe?" *Science News*, June 12, 1982.
Dagani, Ron. "Positron Tomography," *Chemical & Engineering News*, Nov. 9, 1981.
Pykett, Ian. "NMR Imaging in Medicine," *Scientific American*, May 1982.
Thomsen, Dietrick E. "X-Rays and the Number Crunchers," *Science News*, June 12, 1982.

Zoologists and other scientists have launched programs to save endangered wild animals by breeding them in zoos.

How Science Is Saving Wild Animals

BY EUGENE J. WALTER, JR.

In July 1981, officials at the Bronx Zoo in New York City waited nervously for Flossie, a Holstein cow, to give birth. For months they had waited and watched while Flossie carried her unborn calf, and by July, their tension had grown as her delivery date drew near.

It might seem odd that so much attention was paid to an ordinary dairy cow at a place like the Bronx Zoo. But when Flossie gave birth on Aug. 11, 1981, she delivered not a Holstein calf but a robust 73-pound gaur, a wild ox of southern Asia. For the first time ever, a procedure called *embryo transfer* — placing a fertilized egg from one female into the womb of another female — was successfully used in the reproduction of a wild mammal. With proper maternal instinct, Flossie immediately began to lick the newborn calf, who was named Manhar — a word in the Hindi language meaning "one who wins everyone's heart."

Manhar has since outgrown his substitute mother, but his revolutionary birth serves as one sign of how far zoo officials have progressed in their mission to breed some endangered species and thus help save them from extinction. Zoo officials throughout the world today play a vital role in protecting endangered species — animals whose numbers are so small that they may die out. Some endangered species now exist only in zoos. And with their varied collections of wildlife and their staffs of biologists and animal managers, zoos are also uniquely suited to breed endangered animals.

Scientists estimate that thousands of species of all kinds — including insects, reptiles, and fishes — are threatened worldwide. Deciding which endangered species to save is a very difficult task. Zoos, with their limited space and financial resources, can play a role in helping to save only a small percentage of all the endangered species. Most of the rescue efforts are centered on mammals and birds — such as gaurs, pandas, white rhinos, and condors.

Wild animal populations are vanishing for a variety of reasons — including the natural dying out of species — but the major reason is human population growth. Animal habitats disappear as more and more people build bigger settlements, both in industrialized and in developing nations. They clear land for farming, cut down forests, dam rivers, and drain marshes.

For example, once the gaur, the largest of the world's wild cattle, was plentiful, but today its population in such places as southern India, Nepal, Burma, Thailand, Laos, Cambodia, and Vietnam has dwindled. Cutting down timber for farming and other land development destroyed much of its natural habitat. Pursued by hunters and exposed to the diseases of domestic cows, the gaur's only chance of survival in the foreseeable future is in preserves specially set aside for it and other wild animals.

Early conservation efforts

The first efforts on the part of zoos to save endangered wildlife began in the late 1800's. A few far-sighted conservationists, including some European and United States zoo officials, recognized that the Père David's deer, the European bison, the Mongolian wild horse, the mountain zebra, and the American bison, or buffalo, faced extinction. They gathered as many representatives of these species as they could find, brought them into captivity, and created breeding programs that saved them. But these pioneering efforts were the exception.

Public awareness of the plight of vanishing animals spread slowly, even among zoo officials. For most of their history, zoos were designed as places to exhibit wild animals simply to show the public what these creatures looked like. Few of these institutions actively engaged in captive breeding. When births did occur, they were regarded mainly as pleasant attractions to draw more visitors.

That attitude began to change in the 1960's. Zoo officials realized it was becoming more difficult to find wild animals for their collections. Experts who lived close to wild animals, such as biologists studying animal behavior, pointed out that the natural habitats of wild animals were vanishing. Zoo officials realized they had not only a problem but also a major responsibility on their hands. They began revising their management methods extensively.

Before the 1960's, animal collections at zoos were like stamp collections. Large zoos kept one or two animals from a wide variety of species. Often they did not have male and female pairs. Beginning

The author:
Eugene J. Walter, Jr., is editor in chief of *Animal Kingdom* magazine and curator of publications for the New York Zoological Society in New York City.

in the mid-1960's, however, zoo officials began to scale down collections. When they had only one animal of a particular species, they sent it to a zoo that had members of the opposite sex. For example, the Bronx Zoo in 1968 kept some 2,600 animals of 1,100 different species. By 1983, the zoo exhibited about 3,300 animals representing only 642 species.

In the early 1970's, the informal trading that was typical of the 1960's developed into formalized breeding loans. To avoid mating closely related animals — a potentially dangerous phenomenon known as *inbreeding* — zoologists (biologists who specialize in studying animals) adopted the practice of keeping records documenting the parents of each animal. Inbreeding can cause many problems including a condition known as *infertility*, which means the animal cannot reproduce. Record-keeping was expanded and simplified in 1974 when the Animal Association of Zoological Parks and Aquariums, based in Wheeling, W. Va., created the International Species Inventory System (ISIS). Located at the Minnesota Zoo outside Minneapolis-St. Paul, ISIS keeps track of most of the animals in 186 zoos around the world. ISIS consolidates such vital statistics as how many animals are kept at what location, their ages, sex, parents, number of births and deaths, and any transfers from one zoo to another. ISIS has made matchmaking considerably easier, replacing uncontrolled, random breeding with long-range, planned breeding.

Breeding and behavior studies

Attempts to breed the giant panda in captivity have attracted a great deal of attention. The first captive birth of a giant panda outside China did not occur until August 1980, when a cub was born at Chapultepec Zoo in Mexico City. But the cub was accidentally smothered by his mother, Ying-Ying. On July 21, 1981, Ying-Ying gave birth again, and this time the cub, a male, survived. In September 1982, a female panda at a zoo in Madrid, Spain, gave birth to twins, but one died. In the United States, Ling-Ling, a giant panda at the National Zoological Park in Washington, D.C., gave birth in July 1983, but the tiny male cub died the same day of pneumonia. By May 1984, Ling-Ling had apparently become pregnant again.

Experience with the giant panda and other animals demonstrated that breeding captive animals involves far more than arranging for a male and female to meet. Zoo officials have learned that successful breeding involves understanding the animal's natural behavior, helping along natural biological processes in some cases, and creating the proper environment. They have also experimented with techniques used successfully in domestic-animal breeding, such as artificial insemination and embryo transfer.

Zoologists have learned to pay particular attention to an animal's natural behavior. For example, the cheetah's reproductive rate in captivity improved once scientists better understood how this wild cat behaves in its natural home in eastern and southern Africa.

The Mongolian wild horse, *right,* and the Père David's deer, *below,* are alive today thanks to timely action on the part of European zoos and a few private individuals. In the early 1900's, the last remaining animals of these species were placed in protected preserves where they flourished. But none of these animals are found today in the wild.

In 1979, zoologists classified the cheetah as *vulnerable*, meaning it would become an endangered species if its numbers continued to decline. The cheetah is the fastest mammal in the world, capable of speeds of 45 to 50 miles per hour. Some observers believe they can attain speeds of up to 70 miles per hour. In 1983, they numbered fewer than 25,000 in all of Africa.

In zoos, cheetahs were usually kept in male-female pairs. Cheetahs first reproduced in a zoo in 1956, but after that there were few births, and even then, the newborn cubs often died. Zoologists observing the natural behavior of wild cheetahs found that females are solitary animals and almost always hunt alone. Taking note of this solitary behavior, officials at Whipsnade Park, the Zoological Society of London's 765-acre country zoo about 40 miles northwest of London, abandoned the practice of keeping cheetahs in pairs. Instead, they put the females in areas by themselves, except during the mating season. The number of births rose significantly. Between 1962 and 1981, 73 cheetah cubs were born at Whipsnade Park.

Other zoos failed to match Whipsnade's achievement, however. So again, biologists observing cheetahs in the wild provided more clues to improve captive breeding. They noted that in the wild, young male cheetahs often hunted in groups of two to seven. When a pack encountered a female during the breeding season, they pursued her, often fighting for her favors until she permitted one to mate with her. Zoologists theorized that zoos might improve their cheetah birth rate if they gave the female a choice of two or more competing suitors.

Success with cheetahs and rhinos

Several zoos adopted the idea, but the National Zoological Gardens of South Africa in Pretoria carried the natural-breeding concept one step further. Zoologist D. Jack Brand, the zoo's director, established a cheetah breeding and research center at DeWildt, outside Pretoria.

At DeWildt, females live alone in pens of more than 1 acre each, giving them plenty of space. Cheetahs may become jittery if they feel hemmed in. Males live in another area, out of sight and sound of the females. From time to time, the zoo staff releases six to eight males into a long strip of land next to the area where females live. When the males pick up the scent of a female ready to breed and the female responds, the zoo staff takes over. They select the male they think is best for breeding and release him into the female's enclosure, leaving the pair together for two or three days. Since the late 1970's, an average of about 20 cubs has been born and raised to maturity every year at DeWildt.

Understanding natural behavior also played a crucial role in helping to reverse the near extinction of the southern white rhinoceros. The white rhino is the third largest of the world's land mammals, after the African and Asian elephants. Adults weigh in at 3 to 4 tons

A cheetah surveys its territory at the New York
Zoological Society, *above*. Cheetahs rarely reproduced
in captivity until zoologists discovered that female
cheetahs need to be alone and choose their mates.
The evidence of a successful breeding program, a
cheetah cub, *below,* weighs in at the Phoenix Zoo.

A keeper at the San Diego Zoo, *left,* examines a southern white rhino calf born at the zoo. The zoo began breeding southern white rhinos in the early 1970's after the rhinos were allowed to live in a herd. Group living appears to stimulate mating. Part of the herd, *below,* grazes in a section of the 94-acre rhino exhibit area.

and stand more than 6 feet high at the shoulder. Despite its huge size, the white rhino is usually relatively easy to approach and kill. Hunting rhinos with guns began in the late 1800's. By the 1960's, the southern white rhinos had been reduced to a small population, living in isolated areas of southern Africa.

In contrast to the solitary nature of the female cheetah, the southern white rhino is a fairly social animal that usually lives in herds. "A male white rhinoceros will mate only if he is the dominant male in a large territory with several females and a few male rivals to make a contest out of it," according to Kurt Benirschke, who directs reproductive research at the Zoological Society of San Diego.

White rhinos had never mated in captivity until zoo officials in Pretoria, South Africa, in the mid-1960's provided a large exhibit area for a group of white rhinos, rather than the standard enclosure for a pair. The animals quickly responded to this new situation, and the first captive white rhino baby was born in 1967; more births followed in subsequent years.

Similarly, in 1971, San Diego zoo officials imported a herd of 20 white rhinos from South Africa and installed them in a 94-acre exhibit at the society's San Diego Wild Animal Park in nearby San Pasqual, Calif. Zoo officials sent Mandala, a male white rhino who had ignored his female companion in the San Diego Zoo for nine years, to join the herd at San Pasqual. Once in the herd, Mandala courted most of the females. The first calf was born on Oct. 11, 1972, and, by the end of 1983, Mandala's offspring totaled 53.

Although a few of the zoos that have kept white rhinos in pairs have recorded births, those zoos that have kept them in herds have had more success. Aside from San Diego and Pretoria, Whipsnade Park in England maintains white rhinos in a herd that has reproduced consistently. Group living may not be the sole stimulus, but evidence suggests that it helps.

Helping nature along

Understanding an animal's natural breeding behavior may not be enough, however. When a species' population has been reduced to a perilously low level, zoo officials sometimes are able to help along natural biological processes to increase the reproduction rates.

A technique called *double-clutching* has become standard procedure to boost the reproduction of birds at faster-than-normal rates. This technique has been applied to a large variety of bird species. After a female bird lays a *clutch* — or nest of eggs — and begins incubating them, she will not lay eggs again until the next mating season. The time it takes for this reproductive shut-down to begin varies by species, anywhere from 1 day for quail to 42 days for condors. If the eggs are broken or if a predator takes them before the shut-down begins, the pair will mate again, and the female will lay a second clutch. Zoologists found that by removing eggs from a nest before the shut-down began, they could trigger a second clutch.

When an animal mother rejects her baby, zoo officials must step in and raise it themselves. At the San Diego Zoo, a staff member feeds a baby gorilla from a bottle, *left,* while a hand puppet resembling a condor's head is used to feed a California condor chick, *below.* Use of the puppet keeps human contact with the chick to a minimum and lessens the chances of imprinting, in which the animal thinks that humans are its parents.

Meanwhile, they could hatch the first clutch artificially in an incubator, thereby doubling the number of birds born.

Double-clutching paid off when the Bronx Zoo started a breeding project for Andean condors early in the 1970's in cooperation with other zoos. Condors are very particular about their mates, and during the early stages of the project, the female selected as best potential breeder, Miss McNasty, failed to get along with any of the prospective partners supplied by other zoos. Finally, after two years of unsuccessful matchmaking by zoo officials, a young male condor from the Los Angeles Zoo caught Miss McNasty's fancy. In 1976, the couple produced a chick, but they were not interested in being parents. They ignored the chick and refused to feed it, and the chick died. In 1977, the couple produced another chick, but they fought over rights to care for it. This time, zoo officials hand-reared the chick. In 1978, each time Miss McNasty laid an egg, zookeepers removed it for hatching in an incubator, causing the couple to mate again. Eventually, three healthy chicks were hatched. Normally, condors lay only one egg every other year. Young condors need two years to develop and become independent, and they begin breeding only after they are 7 or 8 years old. Consequently, the zoo's double-

Penguins roam a subfreezing world built for them at Sea World in San Diego. Sea World officials set out to copy the penguins' native habitat in Antarctica. They even keep the lights on 24 hours a day during the months corresponding to the Antarctic summer, when the sun shines all day. This reproduction of its natural habitat helps the penguin to breed in captivity.

and triple-clutching techniques created a modest population boom for a bird with such a slow natural rate of reproduction.

However, if humans raise newborn animals, as happened with the condor chicks, there is the danger that a newborn will regard people — rather than members of its own species — as its parents. This process, known as *imprinting*, means that if humans do the feeding, the young animal will be unable to recognize or mate with its own species once it is grown. To avoid this danger, the Bronx zoologists devised hand puppets to look like adult condors and used them to feed the little condors, minimizing human contact. The device worked. In 1980, the Bronx Zoo, working with the U.S. Fish and Wildlife Service (FWS), released four puppet-reared condors in Peru. They continue to thrive just as if they had been hatched and reared in the wild by natural parents.

Imitating life in the wild

Another successful bird-breeding program involved the extremely rare California condor. In 1978, only about 20 California condors survived in the wild, chiefly in southern California. Their numbers had been depleted by hunting, the loss of natural habitat, and poisoning from pesticides. Zoologists feared that the California condor faced extinction by the end of the 1980's.

Only one California condor lived in captivity in the early 1980's, so the National Audubon Society and the FWS devised a breeding plan to collect eggs from nests in the wild and hatch them in captivity. On Feb. 23, 1983, FWS biologists removed eggs from condor nests found in the wild north of San Diego and took them by helicopter to the San Diego Zoo. Keepers placed the precious cargo in an incubator and began a 24-hour watch, monitoring temperature and humidity and turning the eggs at regular intervals just as a condor parent would.

On March 27, one chick began trying to break through its shell. The keepers played tapes of condor sounds and tapped on the shell periodically, as a parent condor would. After three days, the chick still had not broken through. The little bird needed help, so keepers chipped the shell and peeled it away with surgical tools. They timed it just right. On March 30, a healthy chick emerged. Five days later, keepers helped a second chick from its shell. Ultimately, four bald, fluffy little condors — one male and three females — hatched. Two hatched that year in the wild, and the total of six was three times the usual reproduction rate for the wild condor population alone.

Zoos have developed other ways to help animals breed in captivity. One of the most important of these is creating an artificial environment for the animal that resembles its natural habitat. This may involve something as subtle as lighting. For example, many bird species receive their cues to breed from the length of the day, rather than from other seasonal changes such as temperature, rainfall, or the color of leaves. *Photoperiod* — the amount of time an animal is

Keepers at the Phoenix Zoo capture an Arabian oryx for shipment to Jordan. The ultimate goal of zoo breeding programs is to return animals to the wild when their numbers are restored and they are no longer in danger of extinction.

exposed to daylight — was a factor that scientists took into account when they began a breeding program for Adélie penguins of Antarctica. Although the Adélie is not classified as endangered, the National Science Foundation began a breeding program at Sea World in San Diego in the late 1960's as part of a study of Antarctic birds.

Teams of Sea World scientists spent several summers studying penguins in Antarctica, where the seasons occur in reverse order of those in the Northern Hemisphere. The scientists collected 86 pairs of Adélie adults and shipped the entire group to California in refrigerated aircraft. The Sea World staff copied all the comforts of the natural penguin habitat. They set up a 4,000-square-foot building, equipped it with two saltwater pools, and kept it at constant subfreezing temperatures. Each day they added 12,000 pounds of crushed ice to the floor. To keep human contact to a minimum, remote-control television cameras monitored the penguins 24 hours a day.

Adélie penguins construct nests of stones that prevent eggs from rolling away and keep them dry should a thaw occur. Every October, which is springtime in Antarctica, the Sea World staff spreads 10,000 pounds of rock over a third of the exhibit area, creating a *rookery* or breeding place. The Adélies move in promptly. Pairs stake out territories, mate, and lay eggs. At the same time, the staff lengthens the time the lights remain on. By mid-December, hatching time, the lights at Sea World provide 24 hours of daylight just as the sun would in Antarctica. Since 1976, several hundred Adélies have been hatched and raised.

Returning the oryx to the desert

The ultimate goal of nearly all zoo breeding programs is to one day return a species, its population on the upswing, to the wild. One endangered species reached the ultimate goal within a relatively short span of time. The Arabian oryx, a whitish antelope with long spearlike horns, once lived in large numbers throughout the Arabian Peninsula. The oryx was prized as a symbol — killing one was regarded as a manly deed because the oryx was wary, fleet-footed, and often escaped hunters on foot or on camelback. But in the 1950's, as oil exploration brought new wealth to the region, a new kind of hunter pursued the oryx across the desert in four-wheel-drive vehicles and gunned it down with automatic weapons.

A census late in the 1950's estimated the Arabian oryx population at only 100 to 200 animals in what was then Aden (now called Yemen [Aden]). Early in 1961, a hunting party slaughtered at least 28 of the only known herd, then returned and killed another 48.

Zoologists are reluctant to remove the last representatives of an endangered species from its native habitat unless the species is in extreme danger. And time was running out for the Arabian oryx. Even in zoos, only a few existed. A British conservation organization, the Fauna Preservation Society (FPS), mounted an expedition to capture some oryxes for breeding. The expedition searched 8,000 square miles of Arabian desert and, in May 1963, captured three. Meanwhile, the London Zoo donated a female, and the rulers of Kuwait and Saudi Arabia sent oryxes from their private herds.

To offer the antelopes the best conditions, FPS transported nine animals to the Phoenix Zoo in Arizona, where the environment is similar to their native habitat. Unmolested, the oryxes multiplied and herds were created at other zoos. Late in the 1970's, U.S. zoos shipped a small herd to Oman, where the sultan established a preserve. On Jan. 31, 1982, zoo officials realized their ultimate goal — 10 white oryxes were released back into the desert wilds.

Advanced breeding techniques

What does the future hold for endangered species? Reproductive biologists and zoo veterinarians are actively engaged in research that may help certain species overcome serious problems in breeding. For example, they have borrowed techniques used with domestic animals, such as *artificial insemination*. This involves fertilizing a female's eggs with previously collected sperm.

Artificial insemination has been used successfully with such mammals as the giant panda, a small antelope called Speke's gazelle, and cougars, but not on a regular basis. In general, the procedure has yielded better results with birds, notably cranes and pheasants. Crane mating is a highly ritualized affair. Prior to mating, the birds perform a vigorous dance with much flapping and leaping, accompanied by loud almost-constant nasal-sounding calls. The activity prepares the male to release sperm at the same time the female is ready to release her eggs.

However, when a female crane has imprinted on humans that raised her from the time she emerged from an egg, she is unable to respond to the dance of other cranes. Her instinct to perform the ritual is unchanged, but she will cooperate only with a human dance partner. So ornithologist George Archibald, director of the International Crane Foundation in Baraboo, Wis., learned to imitate as closely as possible the crane's intricate mating dance. His best-known courtship was with Tex, a female whooping crane who had been imprinted on people when young and wanted nothing to do with male whoopers. Beginning in 1976, Archibald spent countless hours dancing with Tex, establishing their unorthodox relationship. After each dance, Tex was artificially inseminated, but each season she laid eggs that were infertile or easily broken. Finally, on May 3, 1983, Tex produced an egg that hatched on May 31. The result was a downy youngster named Gee-Whiz.

Another technique adopted from domestic breeders that holds

A researcher at the New York Zoological Society, *below,* puts into an incubator a batch of unfertilized eggs taken from a dead zoo animal. Later, when the eggs mature, a dye test, *below right,* determines which eggs can be artificially fertilized. The usable eggs will be frozen for future use.

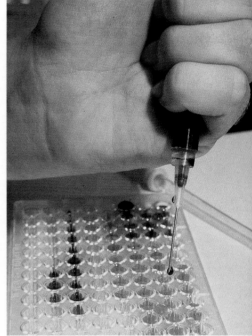

Veterinarians and staff members of the New York Zoological Society perform an embryo transfer operation on a female gaur, a wild ox from southern Asia, *left.* The zoo team took an embryo from the gaur and put it in the womb of Flossie, a Holstein cow. The revolutionary breeding technique proved successful when Flossie gave birth to Manhar, a male gaur. Flossie then nursed Manhar, *below,* just as a natural mother would.

promise for wild animals is the embryo transfer, the process that allowed Flossie, a Holstein cow, to give birth to Manhar, the wild gaur at the Bronx Zoo. Embryo transfer permits a single female to produce many offspring in the same time she would normally produce one because the female's fertilized eggs are transferred to several substitute mothers. This procedure is useful when the species is endangered and requires a faster rate of reproduction to restore its numbers. Cincinnati Zoo veterinarians have performed successful embryo transfers with African elands, the largest of the world's antelopes, as well as with gaurs. And at the Louisville (Ky.) Zoo, an embryo transfer experiment used a horse as a substitute mother to produce a Grant's zebra calf in May 1984. This zebra species is not endangered, but zoo officials hope eventually to apply the technique to the Grévy's and mountain zebras, which are endangered.

Researchers in the Bronx, Cincinnati, and San Diego zoos also are freezing fertilized embryos of various species in order to implant them in substitute mothers at later dates. Although success has been limited so far, scientists have high hopes for the technique. If the wild population of a particular species drops to an alarmingly low level in the future or even becomes extinct, a supply of these microscopic packages of frozen cells could literally resurrect the species.

Opposite page:
The setting sun silhouettes George Archibald, director of the International Crane Foundation in Baraboo, Wis., as he spreads his arms in imitation of the mating dance of the whooping crane. His dance partner, a female whooper, responds to the courting gestures that are crucial preparation for breeding by artificial insemination. Thanks to efforts like these, the sun may never set on the whooping crane.

Cautious hope for the future

However, Janet Stover, veterinarian in charge of reproductive research at the Bronx Zoo, cautions that these new techniques are still in the experimental stage for wild animals. "With domestic cattle, breeders experimented with thousands [of animals] before they got the technique down to a science," she says. "Zoos don't have thousands [of animals] available, and our animals are not research animals. It takes many tries to perfect things like artificial insemination and embryo transfer."

Even without these exotic experimental techniques, however, zoos have had enormous success. Today, they are producers of wildlife where only a few decades ago they were consumers, obtaining most of their animals from the wild.

Zoo scientists and officials hope that, managed properly, some of the animals they save may be returned to the wild. And of these, some may one day provide food for undeveloped nations; or they may supply the research key that solves a medical problem. But most of these are distant hopes and not the primary motivation for the men and women involved in trying to preserve endangered species. Perhaps their vision is best expressed by naturalist Charles William Beebe, the first curator of birds at the Bronx Zoo, who said, "The beauty and genius of a work of art may be reconceived, though its first material expression be destroyed; a vanished harmony may yet again inspire the composer; but when the last individual of a race of living beings breathes no more, another heaven and another earth must pass before such a one can be again."

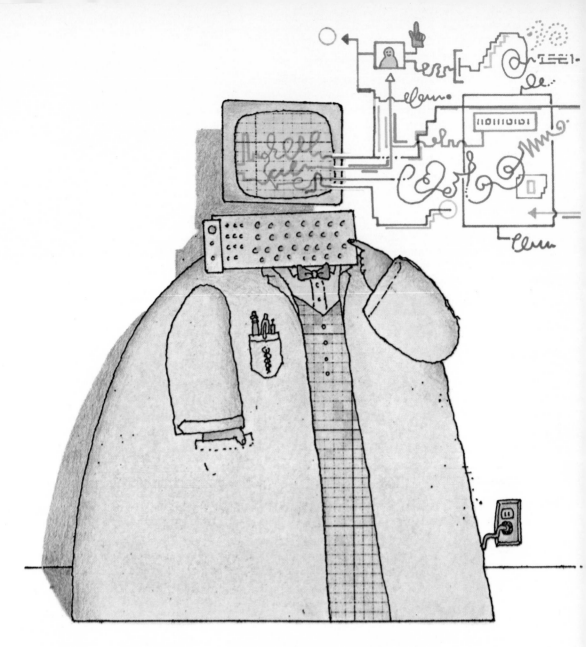

Sophisticated computer programs called expert systems
can rival the experience and reasoning of human experts.

Computers That
Give Advice

BY WILLIAM J. CROMIE

The physician was not sure how to treat the cancer patient she would be seeing in less than 30 minutes. The patient had been receiving drugs and radiation therapy for cancer spreading through her *lymph system* — the network of vessels that carry fluids from body tissues to the bloodstream. Armed with recent test results and the patient's medical records, the doctor decided to seek the help of an expert.

The expert, at Stanford University Medical Center in Palo Alto, Calif., asked questions about the patient's medical history, the drug and radiation treatments, and recent test results. The physician, tired and rushed, gave a wrong answer to a question about the patient's blood. The expert challenged the answer, and the doctor corrected her mistake. At the end of a five-minute interview, the expert recommended precise doses of four drugs and several tests to be done.

The expert was not a doctor specializing in cancer treatment. He, or rather "it," was not a doctor at all but an *expert system,* a computer programmed with knowledge about a subject and with rules for using that knowledge. This system is known as ONCOCIN, from the Greek word *onkos,* meaning *tumor.* It is one of a new breed of advisers being used in medicine, chemistry, geology, computer design, and a growing number of other fields. ONCOCIN's machine "colleagues" include PUFF, which diagnoses lung problems; R1, which designs minicomputers; and PROSPECTOR, which helps geologists find mineral deposits. Other systems play chess, help lawyers make decisions, fill out income tax forms, and solve problems for oil-well drillers.

Trying to mimic intelligence

Expert systems are the offspring of a science called artificial intelligence (AI), which originated in the mid-1950's. After developing computers that could calculate much more rapidly than people, engineers realized that computers can also handle symbols other than numbers. These symbols could represent facts and objects that could be combined and manipulated in ways that imitate human thought. Some of the engineers envisioned silicon chips crowded with transistors that would be the equivalent of brain cells connected in ways that would equal, or improve upon, human intelligence.

The researchers, however, found that they could not mimic human intelligence because they could not program the quality of *generality* into a computer. An intelligent person learns something in one area and applies it to problems in other areas. No one has been able to build a machine that does this as generally or as broadly as a person. But expert systems do perform as well as or better than human beings in specific areas.

By 1983, 56 expert systems were in various stages of development, according to Edward A. Feigenbaum, a computer scientist at Stanford University. All are — or will be — limited to specific applications, ranging from designing gene-splicing experiments to solving water-resource problems and managing nuclear reactors. In mid-1984, fewer than a dozen of them were in commercial use.

The author:
William J. Cromie is executive director of the Council for the Advancement of Science Writing.

Both calculating and expert programs convert information into series of digits — 0's and 1's. In calculating systems, the digits represent numbers that are stored and later retrieved to create, for example, a monthly billing or a prediction of how much money a company will earn in a year. In expert systems, the digits represent objects, facts, and ideas and ways of using them that imitate human reasoning.

Instructions in an expert system often take the form of *if-then* rules. The *ifs* are sets of facts that, when true, lead to a *then* — an action or conclusion. For example, PUFF, the expert system for lung diagnosis, "reasons" that *if* a patient has trouble getting air into his lungs and *if* his ability to get oxygen into his blood is below a certain level, yet *if* his lungs can hold a larger than normal amount of air, *then* he probably has emphysema.

To develop an expert system, a human expert works with a *knowledge engineer*, a programmer who translates the expert's "thinking out loud" into instructions for the computer. This work is difficult because human experts cannot always describe precisely how they use information to make a decision or solve a problem. Consequently, the first, second, or even third version of an expert system often does not work as planned. Correcting or "debugging" a system may take years.

Jack D. Myers, a specialist in internal medicine at the University of Pittsburgh School of Medicine, with the aid of computer scientist Harry E. Pople, Jr., has put his expertise and that of other physicians into an expert system called INTERNIST. This system contains information on more than 550 diseases and disorders that account for about 75 per cent of the major medical problems that afflict human beings.

To test how well INTERNIST works, its developers matched it against two panels of physicians — specialists and nonspecialists — in the diagnoses of 43 tricky cases. The patients already had been diagnosed correctly and were responding to treatment, but none of the doctors in the test knew the diagnoses. INTERNIST provided 28 correct answers, the nonspecialist physicians got 25 right answers, and the specialists were accurate 35 times. The test showed that expert systems can perform as well as most human beings in a specific area.

More and better expert systems

Researchers at Carnegie-Mellon University in Pittsburgh, Pa., developed R1, an expert system that custom-designs minicomputers made by Digital Equipment Corporation (DEC) of Hudson, Mass. A customer tells a DEC designer what he or she wants the computer to do. After the designer feeds this information into R1, the expert system lays out the computer components and connections in a way that will meet the customer's requirements. In one three-month period during which R1 worked on 3,000 orders, more than 85 per cent of its designs were flawless, and most of the remainder needed only minor corrections.

Another expert system, called PROSPECTOR, aids geologists in their search for valuable minerals. PROSPECTOR uses information from maps, reports, and the answers to questions it asks geologists. It compares this information with data on existing ore deposits, then it draws conclusions about where minerals can be found.

PROSPECTOR, developed at SRI International in Menlo Park, Calif., successfully predicted the location of a copper ore deposit on

Dialogue with an Expert

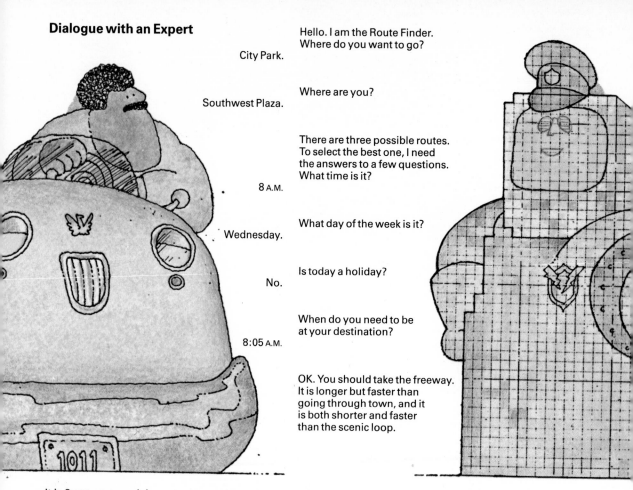

Hello. I am the Route Finder. Where do you want to go?

City Park.

Where are you?

Southwest Plaza.

There are three possible routes. To select the best one, I need the answers to a few questions. What time is it?

8 A.M.

What day of the week is it?

Wednesday.

Is today a holiday?

No.

When do you need to be at your destination?

8:05 A.M.

OK. You should take the freeway. It is longer but faster than going through town, and it is both shorter and faster than the scenic loop.

It is 8 A.M. on a weekday morning and a driver who is running late for an appointment on the other side of town seeks the aid of an expert computer system in determining the best route to take. The expert asks some questions and uses its internal system of *if-then* rules to determine the best route.

Vancouver Island in Canada. It also located a deposit of molybdenum that geologists had missed near Mount Tolman in eastern Washington state.

As good as these expert systems are, researchers want to develop better ones that handle more general and complex tasks. They want medical systems, for example, that can spot trends in diseases, explain the reasons for recommending a certain treatment, find gaps and errors in the information fed into them, separate facts from assumptions, and determine the goals and experience of the people using the systems.

To carry out such activities, expert systems must:
- acquire larger amounts of knowledge more quickly;
- organize the knowledge in new ways;
- process the knowledge more rapidly;
- communicate with users in natural languages, rather than computer codes;
- hear, speak, and see.

Researchers at the University of Illinois in Urbana-Champaign believe that they can get an expert system to acquire knowledge more quickly by building a dictionary into it. "We want to translate

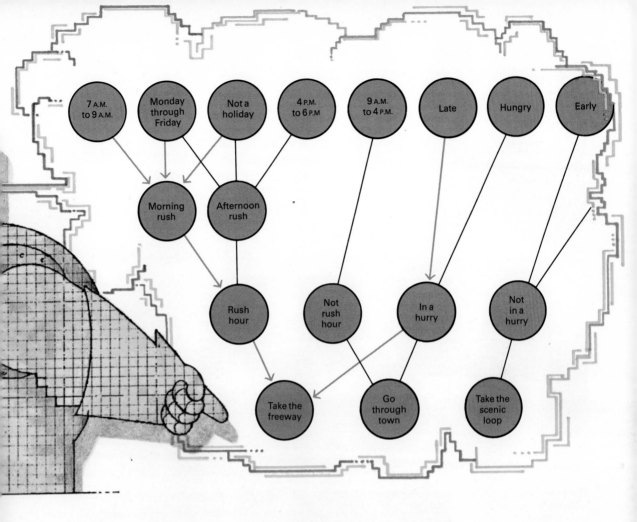

a minimum of 5,000 words into machine-readable form," explains computer scientist David L. Waltz. The system designer would feed each word, its definition, and rules for using it into the system. These words and rules then would be used to define all other words to be used by the system. Rules that apply to the words of the definition would also apply to the new word. As a result, the expert system could "learn" new words rapidly.

Other researchers work on systems that organize or reorganize information fed into them to create new concepts. One such system, developed by computer scientist Douglas B. Lenat of Stanford, "discovered" laws of mathematics. Lenat fed the computer a set of mathematical concepts and if-then rules. The rules combined the concepts in various ways and then evaluated the results. Most combinations were nonsense, but a few of them turned out to be extremely interesting. For example, when Lenat combined 100 mathematical concepts with 250 rules in a program called AM (*Automatic Mathematician*), the expert system discovered how to perform addition, subtraction, multiplication, and division.

If-then rules themselves are concepts, so they can be combined to produce new rules of reason or judgment. A Lenat-designed system

Computers programmed
with expert human
knowledge and with
rules for using that
knowledge challenge
human skills in such
activities as chess,
above, and can help
technicians perform
complex tasks, such
as repairing a
locomotive, *right.*

called EURISKO processed concepts so well that the rules it produced led to a new design for a high-speed electronic switch. Also, EURISKO discovered strategies of ship design that were superior to those of human engineers. In 1981 and 1982, a hypothetical fleet of warships designed by EURISKO defeated fleets designed by human beings in war games conducted by the United States Navy.

Teaching the machines new tricks

Feigenbaum and another Stanford computer scientist, Bruce G. Buchanan, developed a system that learns directly from scientific experiments instead of from experts. It starts with another computer program that identifies unknown molecules by the way they break up in a *mass spectrometer*, a device that separates fragments by mass and electric charge. Combining many examples of how the mass spectrometer fragments molecules with if-then rules, the expert system produced a set of general rules to describe which chemical bonds break in certain molecules and to identify the fragments that result. Buchanan claims that the computer-generated rules are as good as those generated by human experts. "This is the first case in history," says Buchanan, "of a theory successfully generated by a machine."

Getting large amounts of knowledge into a computer rapidly does not solve any practical problems unless a person has quick access to the precise information that is needed for a task. Today, all com-

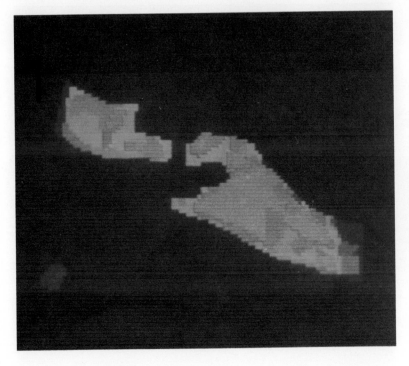

After a computer was programmed with geological information about known ore deposits, it produced a map that correctly identified other likely locations of deposits of the metal molybdenum. Exploration verified the locations, shown on the map in pink, in the area around Mount Tolman in Washington.

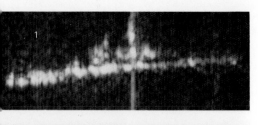

Gun

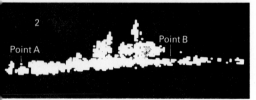

Weapons launcher

1

2

Point A   Point B

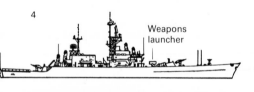

5

Top to bottom: An expert system is asked to identify a warship from its radar image (1). The system translates the image into a pattern of squares (2) and looks for identifying points. A *Belknap*-class cruiser (3), for example, would have a gun at Point A, while a *Bainbridge*-class cruiser (4) would have a weapons launcher at Point B. Because the radar picture indicates something at Point A but not at B, the system concludes that the unknown warship is a *Belknap*-class cruiser (5).

puters perform one operation at a time. For example, an expert system with thousands of if-then rules checks one "if" at a time to determine whether the "if" applies to a given problem. This method of operation, called *serial operation*, is like going through a dictionary one word at a time, starting with *aardvark*, when you want to know what *zymurgy* means.

To process information faster, researchers are building experimental computers that perform many operations simultaneously, or *in parallel*. These machines contain a number of microprocessors, each of which works on a different part of a problem at the same time.

Researchers at New York University in New York City have designed a system with more than 4,000 parallel microcomputers. Getting such a system to work, however, is difficult. Like people, microcomputers working together need to coordinate their efforts so that two of them are not doing the same task. To date, no one has built a system that coordinates the operation of dozens, let alone thousands, of microcomputers.

Friendly machines

Designers of advanced hardware and programs also want their machines to be "friendly," a computerese term that means "easy to use." They want people to be able to communicate with computers in *natural language* — plain English or some other language — instead of the complex computer languages or codes used today. Jaime G. Carbonell, a computer scientist at Carnegie-Mellon, envisions a system that would combine natural-language ability and rules of speech analysis to adjust its response to the knowledge and experience of a user. For example, it would give different answers to the same question depending on whether it was asked by a high school student or an expert in the field.

At present, all "conversations" with expert systems take place in computer codes because many words and phrases in natural language have more than one meaning and are difficult to define in terms of 0's and 1's. Japanese and American scientists already are working on computers that will correspond in natural language.

Progress, so far, is confined to systems that can

deal only with narrow subject areas. A Carnegie-Mellon program called XCALIBUR, for example, allows keyboard communication in plain English with R1 and another expert system used by DEC salespeople to write orders that are filled by R1.

Several other systems allow limited conversations in plain English. These systems store information in computer code, but electronic translators enable the machines to respond in English to such questions as, "How many salespeople in our Chicago branch sold more than $100,000 worth of widgits in 1983?"

Other systems in the development stage understand spoken as well as typed English and can "speak" with users. However, their vocabularies are severely limited, and most recognize only isolated words, not continuous speech. They also must be "trained" to understand each speaker who uses the system. The training involves typing and then saying each word. One of the earliest successful natural-language systems, developed at Carnegie-Mellon and called HARPY, recognized 1,000 words of continuous speech. However, only certain words could follow other words, speech was limited to a specific subject, the system had to be trained, and the program required a large, expensive computer.

Systems that will speak, hear, and see

Ronald Cole, a psychologist-turned-computer-scientist at Carnegie-Mellon, invented a system that does not have to be trained by each speaker, but it cannot understand continuous speech. Computer engineer Harvey F. Silverman of Brown University in Providence, R.I., is developing a similar system that recognizes statements such as, "The computer is not working." Silverman claims that the problem of constructing a system that understands continuous speech is not insurmountable. "In a few years," he says, "we expect to develop one that will have a vocabulary of 5,000 words and will understand most conversations in plain English." Ordinary speech combines thousands of words in millions of ways, so an expert system with a 5,000-word vocabulary must store a tremendous amount of rules and definitions, and it would require parallel processing to quickly check all the possible combinations of words.

Friendly computers of the future will be able to see as well as hear and speak. Such systems could respond to drawings, photographs, and live action. The machine would view this material by means of a television camera or other light-sensitive device, compare the picture with information stored in its memory, and respond to the comparison according to a computer program. Manufacturers could use such capability, for example, to control a robot that assembles automobiles or other products.

Robots now in use view objects as silhouettes. These systems identify only objects that match silhouettes stored in their memories. Several companies have developed devices that recognize various shades of gray, but these have not yet been put to commercial use.

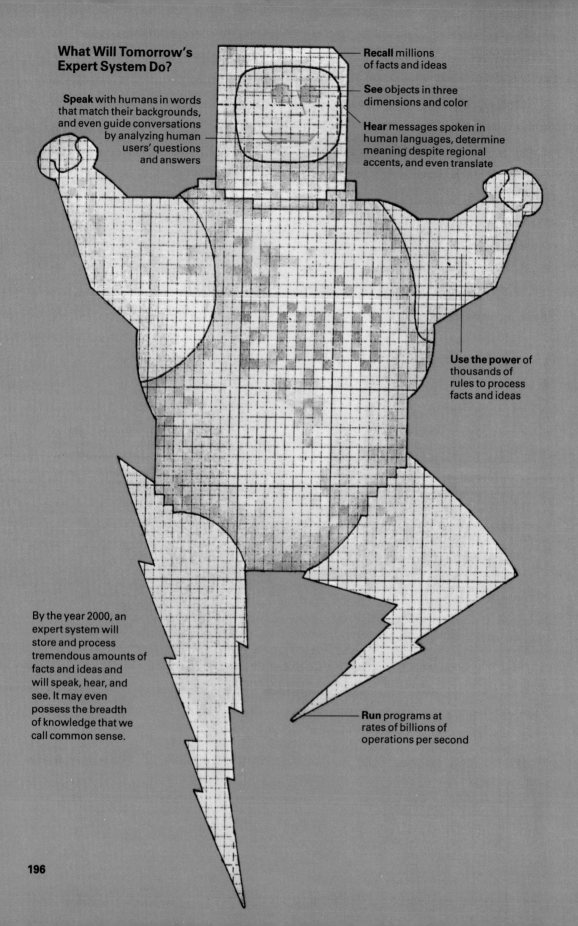

What Will Tomorrow's Expert System Do?

Speak with humans in words that match their backgrounds, and even guide conversations by analyzing human users' questions and answers

Recall millions of facts and ideas

See objects in three dimensions and color

Hear messages spoken in human languages, determine meaning despite regional accents, and even translate

Use the power of thousands of rules to process facts and ideas

By the year 2000, an expert system will store and process tremendous amounts of facts and ideas and will speak, hear, and see. It may even possess the breadth of knowledge that we call common sense.

Run programs at rates of billions of operations per second

Systems with stereo vision, which would enable robots to see in three dimensions, also remain in the experimental stage. Most of them combine images from two cameras in much the same way that the brain combines pictures from the left and right eyes. These systems are much slower than human beings, however. For example, a vision system developed at the Massachusetts Institute of Technology in Cambridge takes 15 seconds to produce a three-dimensional image that the computer can recognize. This compares with about one ten-thousandth of a second for a human brain.

Machine vision is so slow because each scene must be divided into thousands of parts, each of which is processed in series. Someday, banks of microprocessors working in parallel may process three-dimensional images as quickly as do people. The Japanese government plans to develop a computer that will store 100,000 charts, drawings, X rays, and photographs, and will retrieve any of them in one-tenth of a second for comparison with what the cameras view.

The fifth generation and beyond

Progress in solving problems such as human-language understanding and machine vision certainly will lead to expert systems that operate near or beyond the levels of human beings in specialized areas. But how far will artificial intelligence go? Japan expects to produce so-called *fifth generation computer systems* by 1995 that will converse in natural language (Japanese or English), see, hear, learn without human aid, and even possess the breadth of knowledge that we call common sense. Even if the Japanese experts succeed, however, most scientists believe that computer systems will never have the broad range of intelligence, motivation, skills, and creativity possessed by human beings.

Meanwhile, the pursuit of artificial intelligence is providing us with a valuable by-product: knowledge about knowledge. To make an intelligent machine, you have to know about how human beings acquire knowledge, how they organize it in their minds, and how they use it to solve problems and create new ideas. The more we learn about these basic processes, the better we should be able to solve many complex problems of individuals and society, and to improve human capabilities.

For further reading:

Boden, Margaret. *Artificial Intelligence and Natural Man.* Basic Books, 1977.
Feigenbaum, Edward A., and McCorduck, Pamela. *The Fifth Generation.* Addison-Wesley Publishing Co., 1983.
McCorduck, Pamela. *Machines Who Think.* W. H. Freeman Co., 1979.

Better math and science education is critical
to both career scientists and other citizens.

Closing In on the Math and Science Gap

BY FRANK PRESS

Education has been a matter of public concern in the United
States for many years, but it has recently engaged the national interest to a surprising degree. We can hardly read a newspaper or
watch the television news without learning about another new study
critical of the American educational system. As a result, the public
perceives that the system is in a state of deterioration, that students
study less and learn less of the basic subjects, that teachers are less
effective than they used to be, and that unemployment due to a lack
of working skills will pose a serious problem in the years ahead.

Such concerns are not new. In 1957, the launch of the *Sputnik 1*
space satellite by the Soviet Union triggered a national concern for

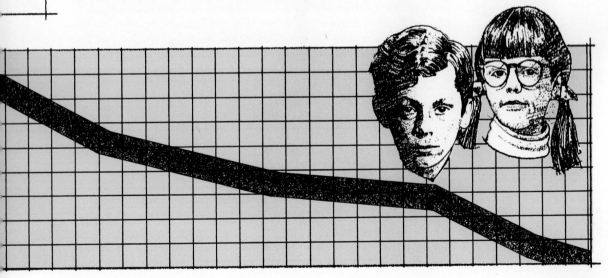

education on national security grounds — based on the fear that Soviet leadership in space and technology would lead to world dominance. Today, the fear of economic domination by Japan and the large industrial democracies in Western Europe has heightened U.S. concern for education on national *economic* security grounds.

This new fear has given rise to a particular national concern about how well American students are being schooled in science and mathematics. Most Americans know about the new, rapidly growing industries spawned by science and technology. The public is aware of the astonishing developments in electronics and computers, new materials, and the automation of manufacturing. People speak of the remarkable advances in applying technology to biological science — and the potential this has for transforming agriculture and food production, controlling disease, finding new sources of energy, and developing new industrial processes.

Can the United States do well in this time of rapid growth of new scientific and technological knowledge? Not if its young people are ill served by their schools. Not if they graduate, as they do, with such a poor understanding of science and mathematics that they consistently score lower on international achievement tests than students in other leading industrialized nations.

It is not surprising that the American public is worried and confused. It is not surprising that a flood of studies and reports critical of the state of American education has saturated the news media and that many states and communities have begun to introduce major changes in their educational programs.

Most of the reports deal with the general problems of education in the United States, such as financial support — and the roles of the federal, state, and local governments; teachers — their training, classroom effectiveness, performance evaluation, and salary structure; the curriculum — what it is and what it should be; and the role of parents and business in improving the schools. Studies by the National Academy of Sciences (NAS), the National Academy of Engineering (NAE), the National Science Board (NSB), and various other professional societies single out the special problems of mathematics, science, and technology education.

In an important sense, however, it is impossible to separate out mathematics, science, and technology education as an issue distinct from the general problems of American schools. One can hardly teach science — or any other subject — to students who have difficulty writing, reading, and reasoning, and whose curiosity and interest in learning have been stifled by their preschool and school environments. Nevertheless, the special problems of teaching mathematics, science, and technology justify special attention to education in these fields.

The seriousness of these problems was highlighted at an important meeting in Washington, D.C., in May 1982. The NAS and the

The author:
Frank Press is president
of the National
Academy of Sciences.

". . . as one speaker put it, 'We are raising a new generation of Americans that is scientifically and technologically illiterate.' "

NAE cosponsored a convocation attended by some 600 leaders of education, science, engineering, business, and government. At that meeting, federal Cabinet officers, business executives, educators, and scientists listed national goals that could not be achieved because, as one speaker put it, "we are raising a new generation of Americans that is scientifically and technologically illiterate." Perhaps the most chilling facts discussed at the convocation were these:
■ The average science and mathematics scores in standardized college entrance tests have been dropping steadily for 20 years.
■ Children in elementary schools average only 1½ hours of science and 3¾ hours of arithmetic per week.
■ Only one-third of the United States school districts require more than one year of mathematics and one year of science for graduation from high school.
■ Enrollments in high school science courses dropped from 60 per cent of all students in 1960 to 48 per cent in 1977.
■ In two-year community colleges, 42 per cent of the mathematics courses are remedial.
■ Students do not particularly like science as it is now taught. According to national studies, by the end of the third grade, only slightly more than half of all students feel they would like to take more science. By the eighth grade, only one-fifth have a positive attitude toward science.

Equally disturbing is the 1983 report *Educating Americans for the 21st Century* issued by the NSB's Commission on Precollege Education in Mathematics, Science and Technology. The NSB warns, "We must not provide our children a 1960's education for a twenty-first-century world." This warning carries special weight because the NSB is the governing body of the National Science Foundation — the chief government agency for the support of American science and science education. The NSB report points out that all upper-secondary students in Japan, West Germany, and the Soviet Union take at least one course of mathematics and one of science each year. The NSB contrasts this with data indicating that 84 per cent of American students do not take physics, 65 per cent do not take chemistry, 62 per cent do not take calculus, 48 per cent do not take geometry, and 23 per cent do not take biology. A stunning comparison is the fact that the *average* Japanese secondary school student spends three times more hours in science classrooms than do U.S. high school students who intend to *major* in science.

Like the NSB report, most of the other studies express serious

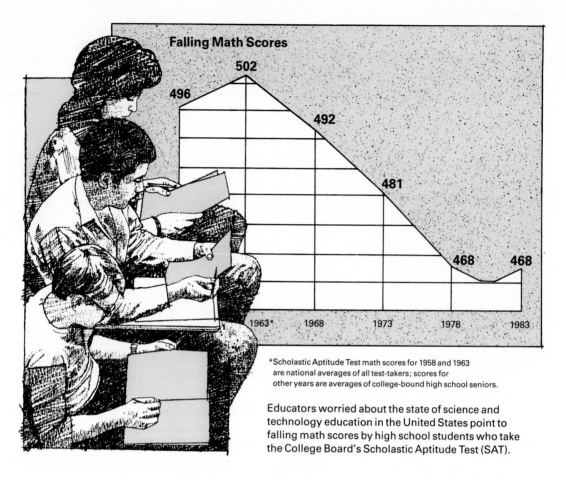

Falling Math Scores

496
502
492
481
468   468

1963*   1968   1973   1978   1983

*Scholastic Aptitude Test math scores for 1958 and 1963
are national averages of all test-takers; scores for
other years are averages of college-bound high school seniors.

Educators worried about the state of science and
technology education in the United States point to
falling math scores by high school students who take
the College Board's Scholastic Aptitude Test (SAT).

concern not only about the amount but also about the quality and
style of teaching mathematics and science in the United States. Although parents, after-school programs, museums, newspapers, television, magazines and books, and the business sector all have much
to contribute to education, the teacher is the most important element. A teacher can motivate students and instill in them a lifelong
interest in learning — or do the opposite. And, of course, the
teacher must impart the latest knowledge and teach with the confidence and up-to-date methods that characterize a professional.

Considering the critical role that teachers play, it is tragic that a
substantial number of America's elementary-school teachers are deficient in mathematics and science and lack the ability and interest
to teach these subjects effectively and imaginatively. It is astonishing
that 51 per cent of elementary-school teachers say their college undergraduate training did not prepare them to teach the science they
are required to teach and that 71 per cent have never had in-service
training in science. The problem is compounded when poorly prepared elementary school graduates arrive at secondary schools and
all too often find more unqualified or underqualified mathematics,
science, and technology teachers. Studies by the National Science

"The reports have succeeded in sounding the alarm but have left [us uncertain] about what to do . . . and how to pay for it."

Teachers Association, for example, show that half of the new teachers hired in 1981 to teach high school mathematics and science were unqualified. So few college students with qualifications in mathematics and science have been entering the teaching profession that school systems have had to fill the vacancies with unqualified instructors licensed on an emergency basis.

The reports speculate on the reasons for the decline in both the number and the quality of mathematics and science teachers. They speak of deteriorating classroom conditions, with inadequate equipment and facilities and problems of student discipline. They also point to the low public esteem in which teachers are often held, the low pay, the cumbersome teacher-certification process that does not necessarily provide any assurance of quality, the lack of financial rewards for superior teaching, and the lack of incentives and opportunities for teachers to upgrade their skills and knowledge. It is no wonder that fewer and fewer superior college students are entering the teaching profession and that many qualified teachers of mathematics and science are seeking new and more attractive careers in business.

Almost all of the reports characterize the situation in math and science as one of crisis, and there are some notable similarities in their diagnoses of the problems and their recommendations. Unfortunately, very few of them spell out the specific, detailed steps needed to solve the problems they describe so well. The reports have succeeded in sounding the alarm but have left the 16,300 school districts and the millions of parents and students in a state of uncertainty about what to do, how to do it, and how to pay for it.

There are some exceptions, notably the report of the NSB commission and the studies — and actions — of some professional organizations. The NSB commission, for example, not only calls for "sweeping and dramatic changes" but also puts a price tag on the federal government's share of the total cost — $1.51 billion. The largest portion of the federal funds would pay for a network of *exemplary* schools or programs in mathematics, science, and technology that would serve as examples for upgrading all schools. The NSB recommends that at least 1,000 such schools be established at the elementary level and 1,000 at the secondary level throughout the United States at a cost of $829 million. Another NSB recommendation, requiring $349 million, calls for the federal government to organize programs to upgrade teacher skills in mathematics, science, and technology.

"[We need] . . . a new approach . . . one that puts more emphasis on using math to solve real-world practical problems."

Among the professional organizations already taking action is the American Association for the Advancement of Science, which — with support from private industry — is establishing a program to involve scientists and engineers in volunteer work in schools. Five other professional groups — the American Chemical Society, the American Geological Institute, the American Physical Society, the Mathematical Association of America, and the Institute of Electrical and Electronics Engineers — are undertaking programs to provide schools with career-information materials, guidelines for teacher training and continuing education, and detailed descriptions of the subject matter that courses should contain. The National Science Teachers Association is studying outstanding science programs in elementary and secondary schools throughout the United States to determine what has made these programs work successfully. The dissemination of this kind of program information enables school districts to use what works rather than repeat costly mistakes. The National Council of Teachers of Mathematics is recommending a new approach to math education — one that puts more emphasis on using math to solve real-world practical problems instead of focusing on computational skills that have little to do with everyday life.

Professional groups are not alone in taking action to improve education. Many states have begun to implement some of the recommendations that appear in the reports and surveys. In some cases, of course, states took action even before the reports appeared. A number of the states were driven by their interest in attracting new industries, especially those in the high-technology sector. These states view the availability of a skilled and technologically literate work force and a pool of well-trained scientists and engineers as inducements for industry to locate within their boundaries.

Programs that are being recommended or placed in operation by states include scholarships and forgivable loans to future mathematics and science teachers, and new certification requirements that call for math and science teachers to take more courses in the subjects they plan to teach and fewer courses in *how* to teach. Other programs involve summer institutes for teacher retraining, arranging summer employment for teachers with local advanced-technology firms, knowledge of computers as a new requirement for teacher certification, competency testing for teachers, and higher pay scales for mathematics and science teachers. Some states are restructuring the curriculum for kindergarten through grade 12 to increase the number of mathematics and science courses.

Also on the state level, a number of universities are raising requirements for undergraduate admission in an effort to pressure high schools into upgrading their educational programs. Some universities are going so far as to require of all incoming students four years of high school English with an emphasis on composition, three years of mathematics, three years of natural sciences including one year of laboratory work, two years of social sciences, and two years of a foreign language.

The growing interest of business and industry, too, in the quality of the nation's elementary and secondary schools is a recent and welcome trend, since most new employees entering the work force are not college graduates. Industry's primary concern is that these new employees have the attributes leading to success on the job — learning skills, problem-solving abilities, and a good attitude toward work. But those industrial sectors that employ scientists and engineers are particularly interested in science and mathematics education, of course, both the precollege instruction and the university programs for educating professionals. Many companies, therefore, are providing schools with computers and scientific equipment, giving grants to young faculty members, offering summer jobs for students, and making available other resources.

What do the trends in science and technology mean to the career prospects of young people seeking jobs after high school gradua-

A sharp decline in the number of science and math teachers produced by U.S. colleges means that some school systems have had to fill vacancies with unqualified instructors.

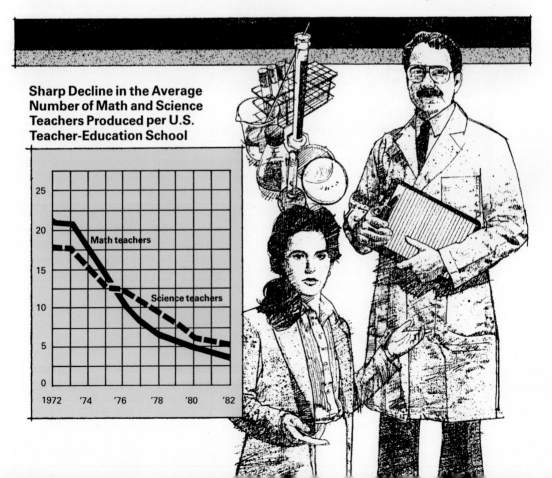

Sharp Decline in the Average Number of Math and Science Teachers Produced per U.S. Teacher-Education School

Math teachers

Science teachers

25

20

15

10

5

0

1972   '74   '76   '78   '80   '82

"Workers will be able to retain their jobs only if they have the ability to acquire the new or different skills required."

tion? The NAS and the NAE address this issue in a report titled *High Schools and the Changing Workplace: The Employers' View.* The report points out that technological change will spread through the workplace of the future, as it has in the workplace of the past. Several general developments are certain to happen. Wider use of computers and automation will increase the worker's productivity and the quality of the product. The nature of many jobs will change as a result of the technological innovations that will be introduced in the workplace, and the job skills required will be different than in the past — though they will not necessarily always be higher skills. Workers will be able to retain their jobs only if they have the ability to acquire the new or different skills required. People in declining industries or occupations may find themselves looking for new jobs, possibly in new industries or modernized old ones.

Perhaps the most important statement in *High Schools and the Changing Workplace* is that "the successful high school graduate will be the one with a firm grounding in the fundamentals of knowledge, with mastery of the basic skills that create an intellectual foundation to which new knowledge may be added." Unfortunately, it is precisely those basic intellectual skills in which many graduates of American schools are deficient. These skills include the ability to draw proper inferences from information; the ability to understand oral or written instructions; the ability to express ideas coherently and effectively; the ability to analyze a situation and develop alternatives and draw conclusions; and the ability to apply such basic skills to the problems found in the workplace. "The need for adaptability and lifelong learning dictate a core of fundamental competencies critical to the career success of high school graduates," the report says. "These include the ability to read, write, reason and compute; an understanding of American social and economic life; knowledge of the basic findings and techniques of physical and biological science; experience with cooperation and conflict resolution in groups; and attitudes and personal habits that make for a dependable, responsible, adaptable, and informed worker and citizen."

In trying to understand the problems of education in the United States, we should distinguish between the needs of those students who will become professionals in the use of mathematics, science, and technology and those nonspecialists who will enter the work force in other fields after leaving high school or college. Something like 200,000 professionals in science and technology leave our colleges and graduate schools each year to work as scientists or engi-

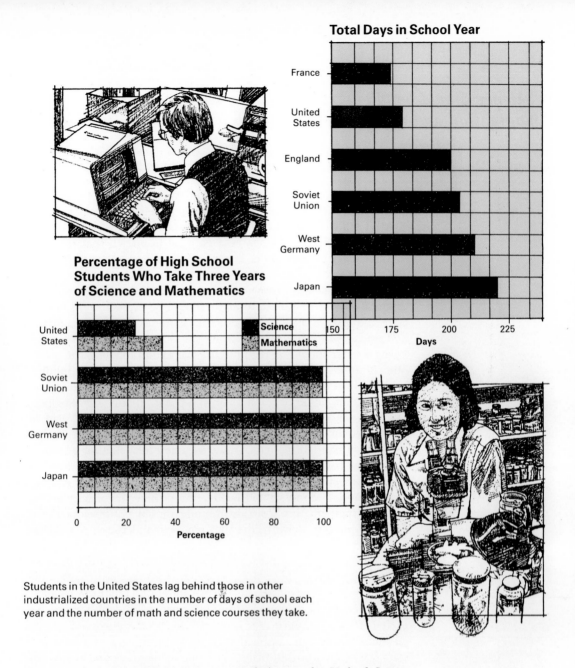

Total Days in School Year

Graph showing total days in school year:
- France
- United States
- England
- Soviet Union
- West Germany
- Japan

Days: 150, 175, 200, 225

Percentage of High School Students Who Take Three Years of Science and Mathematics

Legend: Science, Mathematics

- United States
- Soviet Union
- West Germany
- Japan

Percentage: 0, 20, 40, 60, 80, 100

Students in the United States lag behind those in other industrialized countries in the number of days of school each year and the number of math and science courses they take.

neers. In a nation with as large a population as the United States has, it will always be possible to find enough adequately prepared students to meet the nation's needs. The nonspecialists are another matter. Another NAS and NAE report, *Science for Non-Specialists: The College Years,* criticizes the state of undergraduate science education for those students who will become, for example, journalists, lawyers, managers, legislators, theologians, or teachers. The math and science needs of these individuals so important to American life are largely left unfulfilled, due to inadequate teaching and narrowly defined courses of study. The report recommends raising the mathematics and science requirements for college graduation to two one-year courses, including laboratory exercises and demonstrations relevant to the needs and experiences of nonscience majors.

After studying all of the reports, recommendations, and actions, one can see the beginnings of a national approach that could be effective over the next 10 or 20 years. It would consist of the following elements:

■ **The improvement of teaching as a profession.** The qualifications of teaching should be raised, teachers should be evaluated for knowledge and effectiveness, teachers' salaries should increase in general, and teachers with higher proficiency should receive higher rewards. Every teacher should be required to have a substantial college major other than education, with science and math requirements fulfilled in the college's science and math departments, and with education courses taken either as a minor or in a postgraduate year. Prospective high-school teachers should major in the subject they plan to teach and should be encouraged to take a master's degree in that subject, with added monetary rewards suited to such a high level of professional attainment.

■ **Improvements in high schools.** The science requirement for graduation from high school should include three full years of science and three of mathematics. Courses of study should be developed that generate interest, are effective and modern, and reflect the excitement and utility of mathematics and science in terms of everyday life. In-service training for teachers should be a key feature of these new curriculums.

■ **Changes in elementary schools.** Science should be taught to elementary students with imagination and effectiveness and with a sense of excitement. To achieve this, a teacher must take good college science courses and be supplemented by a visiting master science resource teacher who can bring enrichment materials and new techniques to the classroom. I believe it is possible to devote an hour a day each to mathematics and science in the elementary schools.

The question of how to pay the bill to reform America's schools will have to be confronted. The total amount now spent annually on public elementary and secondary education is about $115 billion, with 10 per cent provided by the federal government and 90 per cent by state and local governments and other sources. Spending on national defense in 1984 totaled about $237 billion. The social security and health care expenditures by the federal government amounted to some $271 billion, and there are many other categories of government expenditures. These allocations of tax funds are decided as part of the political process. If the United States wants to spend more on education by transferring money from other activities or by raising taxes, it can do so.

The reports and studies of the past few years have made a strong case for new investments in education. To implement the kinds of programs they suggest would require additional funds for education in the amount of a few tens of billions of dollars. Not all of this need be new money, however. For example, some organizational changes can be made in America's education system to reduce costs in certain categories and free sizable funds for upgrading teachers' salaries. Only 41 per cent of all public school expenditures now go to pay teachers. And, of course, it doesn't cost anything for students to work harder.

There is some reason for optimism about increased spending for education. One indication already is apparent: Only 47 per cent of new school-bond issues were approved by voters in 1972, but the approval rate had increased to 73 per cent in 1982. The expected economic growth for the remainder of the 1980's will lead to increased state revenues and, therefore, to possible increased state commitments to education. The new phenomenon of a broad coalition of politicians, business leaders, and parents working in support of education can lead to pressures for reform. And with reform will come a greater national commitment to the schools and a citizenry that is better educated and better able to participate in the new industrial revolution that lies ahead.

For further reading:

An Agenda for Action: Recommendations for School Mathematics of the 1980s. National Council of Teachers of Mathematics, 1980.

America's Competitive Challenge: The Need for a National Response. Business-Higher Education Forum, 1983.

Education in the Sciences: A Developing Crisis. American Association for the Advancement of Science, 1982.

High Schools and the Changing Workplace: The Employers' View. National Academy Press, 1984.

National Commission on Excellence in Education. *A Nation at Risk: The Imperative for Educational Reform.* The Commission, 1983.

National Research Council. Committee on the Federal Role in College Science Education of Non-Specialists. *Science for Non-Specialists: The College Years.* National Academy Press, 1982.

National Science Board. Commission on Precollege Education in Mathematics, Science, and Technology. *Educating Americans for the 21st Century.* The Commission, 1983.

Raizen, Senta A. *Science and Mathematics in the Schools: Report of a Convocation.* National Academy Press, 1982.

Science File

Science Year contributors report on the year's major developments in their respective fields. The articles in this section are arranged alphabetically by subject matter.

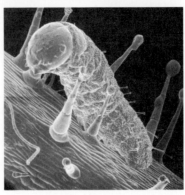

Agriculture

In February 1984, the United States Environmental Protection Agency (EPA) banned the use of the pesticide ethylene dibromide (EDB) after traces of the chemical were found in ground water, grain, and fruits. EDB, which has been used by U.S. farmers since 1948, has been found to cause cancer in laboratory animals.

Scientists and public health officials do not yet know whether low levels of EDB pose a threat to human health. Many such experts thought that people had become unduly alarmed about the pesticide. Most environmentalists, on the other hand, said the EPA should have acted in the mid-1970's, when the possible cancer risk first became known. See ENVIRONMENT (Close-Up).

Frost-free bacteria. Agricultural scientists were stopped by a federal court in 1983 and 1984 from testing bacteria genetically engineered to prevent frost damage to crops. The court held up the tests until it could be determined whether the bacteria pose any threat to the environment.

The bacterium is a strain of *Pseudomonas syringae*, which creates frost in plants by acting as a "seed" around which ice crystals form. Scientists do not know which part of the bacterium serves as the ice seed, but they learned that several genes are responsible for giving the bacterium this property.

Researchers at Advanced Genetic Sciences in Greenwich, Conn., working with plant scientist Steven F. Lindow of the University of California in Berkeley, created a strain of *P. syringae* with the ice-forming genes removed. The scientists wanted to test the genetically engineered bacteria by spraying them on crops early in the growing season. They hoped the new bacteria would become the established strain and squeeze out the ice-forming strain. Without the ice-forming bacteria, plants can stand temperatures as low as −5°C (23°F.) without freezing.

In the summer of 1983, the National Institutes of Health (NIH) in Bethesda, Md., authorized tests of the bacteria in a remote part of northern California. However, several citizens'

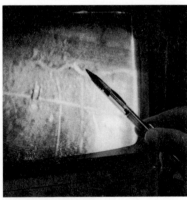

Investigators at the Southern Plains Cotton Research Laboratory in Lubbock, Tex., use an underground viewer to record video images of the roots of wild Mexican cotton plants, *left*. The images are later studied on a monitor, *above*, to learn how the plants resist drought – a trait the researchers hope to breed into commercial cotton plants.

A Trichogramma wasp, *left,* prepares to lay eggs on and thus destroy the egg of a cotton bollworm, a pest that feeds on cotton bolls, *below.* In a new pest control program, the wasps will be used to control the bollworm and its cousin, the tobacco budworm, which together cause about $1 billion in crop damage each year.

Agriculture

Continued

groups brought suit against the NIH in federal court, and the spraying was delayed. Scientists hoped to convince the court that the bacteria are not dangerous so testing could proceed late in 1984. See MOLECULAR BIOLOGY.

Drumsticks and pork chops. People in the United States are eating more turkey and pork than ever before. Americans consumed a record 5 kilograms (11 pounds) of turkey per person in 1983, a quantity far exceeding that of any other nation. Once considered a holiday dish, turkey is rapidly becoming a year-round food item.

Pork producers are following the lead of poultry producers by moving toward the complete industrialization of their industry. Most hogs are now kept indoors from birth until they are sent to market, their feeding computer-programmed and automated. One result of these controls is that pork is now leaner than it used to be, which might account for pork's increased popularity.

Animal scientists at the University of Illinois in Urbana-Champaign re-

ported in March 1984 that when hogs are allowed to play, they are less aggressive and grow more quickly than hogs not given the opportunity to play. Hogs seem to especially enjoy playing with red bowling balls. Some pork producers are now providing bowling balls for their hogs.

Scientists and pork producers long recognized the advantages of *boars* (normal male hogs) over *barrows* (castrated male hogs) for commercial pork production. Boars gain weight faster, grow larger, and have leaner meat than barrows. Their main drawback is "boar odor," an undesirable smell that boar meat gives off when heated.

Animal and food scientists at Michigan State University in East Lansing showed in November 1983 that the odor is caused by chemicals that function as *pheromones* (sex attractants to female hogs). The scientists are searching for a way to block the formation of the boar pheromones and still maintain the growth rate of the animals.

Farm mechanization. Fruit and vegetable farmers in the United States hire

Engineers at the University of Western Australia in Nedlands clip the wool from a sheep with an experimental robot shearing machine. The machine shears about 70 per cent of a sheep's wool, but a new model under development will remove up to 95 per cent at a cost below that of hand shearing.

Agriculture

Continued

many illegal immigrants to harvest their crops. The availability of unskilled alien workers has caused many farmers to postpone buying modern harvesting equipment.

In October 1983, agricultural economist Philip L. Martin of the University of California at Davis warned that the reluctance of farmers to mechanize is making the $18-billion U.S. fruit- and vegetable-growing industry increasingly vulnerable to foreign competition. He said the survival of this industry will depend upon machines taking the place of alien farmworkers.

Maximum yields. Agricultural scientists are learning how to "fine-tune" the cultivation of crops — to make all the growing conditions as ideal as possible — and are producing ever larger harvests. Using these experimental farming techniques, Ray C. Flannery, a researcher at the New Jersey Agricultural Station in New Brunswick, produced a record yield of 292.6 bushels per hectare (118.4 bushels per acre) for irrigated soybeans in the fall of 1983. Milo B. Tesar of the Michigan

Agricultural Experiment Station in East Lansing recorded a two-year average yield of 22.4 metric tons per hectare (10 tons per acre) for alfalfa. Tesar's harvests were the highest documented experimental yields for non-irrigated alfalfa in the United States.

Kill weeds, not crops. Scientists at the University of Guelph in Ontario, Canada, reported in January 1984 that they had bred strains of rape plant resistant to the chemical atrazine, the most widely used weedkiller in North America. Rape is a plant in the mustard family grown as a pasture crop for livestock.

The Canadian researchers, under the direction of molecular biologists William Beversdorf and Vince Souza-Machado, crossed rape plants with a closely related atrazine-resistant weed, the wild turnip. Canadian farmers are expected to grow 405,000 hectares (1 million acres) of the new variety of rape in 1985.

Plant scientists at Michigan State University in East Lansing said, also in January, that there are many other kinds of atrazine-resistant weeds that could be crossed with related crop plants to create crops able to withstand the weedkiller.

Natural weed control. The *residues* — the dead stems and leaves — of many plants contain natural weedkilling chemicals, plant scientist Alan R. Putnam of Michigan State University reported in August 1983. Putnam and his colleagues found that the residues of rye, barley, wheat, and sorghum plants can be used to control weeds in fields of tomatoes, lettuce, beans, and most large-seeded vegetables.

Rebecca B. Wolf, a plant physiologist at the Northern Regional Research Center in Peoria, Ill., announced in July 1983 that she had found a compound in the seeds of papaya, a tropical fruit, that stops the growth of velvetleaf, a weed that grows in corn and soybean fields. Wolf said the substance does not hurt the crop plants.

Supertrees. Canadian researchers at several institutions and agencies reported in December 1983 on how to get thousands of offspring from a single "supertree." A supertree is a tree with superior genetic characteristics — it is stronger and grows faster.

The scientists said spring buds from such trees can be grown in laboratory culture and continually subdivided. In this way, each bud will produce as many as 1,000 "daughter" plants, or explants. The explants are then grown in greenhouses until they are big enough to be planted. Using this technique, tree farmers could grow large stands of supertrees, including fruit trees.

Several new crop plants were introduced in 1983 and 1984. A "sweet sandwich onion," developed by plant breeder Clinton E. Peterson of the University of Wisconsin in Madison, was widely acclaimed for its superior taste. Reliance, a red seedless grape, was announced by researchers at the Arkansas Agricultural Experiment Station in Fayetteville. And scientists at Louisiana State University in Baton Rouge developed a strain of soybean resistant to tiny worms that infest plant roots. [Sylvan H. Wittwer]

Anthropology

A jaw fragment found in February 1983 in Kenya is believed to be the oldest fossil from a *hominid* (human ancestor) discovered so far. An expedition led by paleoanthropologist Andrew P. Hill of Harvard University's Peabody Museum of Archaeology and Ethology in Cambridge, Mass., found the specimen at Tabarin, near Lake Baringo, about 320 kilometers (200 miles) northwest of Nairobi.

According to anthropologists David R. Pilbeam of Harvard and Richard E. Leakey of the National Museums of Kenya, codirectors of the research project, the lower jaw fragment, which contains two molar teeth, is similar to fossils found in Ethiopia. These fossils, which have been classified as *Australopithecus afarensis*, include "Lucy," the 3-million-year-old hominid skeleton found in 1974.

The jaw fragment is estimated to be about 5 million years old. This date is based on the similarity of volcanic rocks from Tabarin to other rocks found in the same region that have been firmly dated at nearly 5 million years old. Other fossil animal remains found with the jaw fragment were dated at more than 4½ million years old. If the age of the jaw fragment is confirmed, the fossil would be more than 1 million years older than similar fossils found elsewhere.

The missing link? Fossils discovered in Kenya and estimated to be more than 17 million years old may represent the common ancestor of humans and apes. If so, the earliest ancestors of humans and apes may have resembled orangutans, rather than chimpanzees, as scientists have believed.

The new fossils were discovered in August and September 1983 at Buluk, a desolate region in northern Kenya, by a group of anthropologists led by Leakey and paleontologist Alan C. Walker of Johns Hopkins University in Baltimore. The Buluk fossils, representing nine individuals, appear to be identical to fossils found earlier in Pakistan. Those were classified as *Sivapithecus. Sivapithecus'* close resemblance to modern orangutans led many anthropologists to conclude it was an an-

Anthropology

Continued

cient orang ancestor. Until the discovery of the Buluk fossils in Africa, anthropologists believed that *Sivapithecus* lived only in Asia.

The Buluk fossils are several million years older than the Pakistani fossils. Some anthropologists believe this suggests that the Buluk specimens represent a very ancient African ancestor of the orangutan, which later spread to Asia.

Walker suggests the Buluk fossils may represent a common ancestor of all apes and humans. According to this theory, *Sivapithecus* arose in Africa and spread to Asia. The Asian branch changed little and survives now as the orangutan. The African branch, however, split into three groups that eventually gave rise to human beings, gorillas, and chimpanzees. Walker suggests modern orangutans are therefore an excellent model for understanding the common ancestor of apes and human beings.

Ramapithecus from China. In an analysis of ancient primate teeth, published in November 1983, two anthro-

pologists concluded that an earlier theory that *Sivapithecus* and *Ramapithecus* are two separate groups is correct. The two extinct species of primate closely resemble each other. Until recently, most anthropologists believed that the two species were separate, with *Sivapithecus* representing an apelike creature and the smaller *Ramapithecus* being a possible human ancestor.

However, new finds of *Sivapithecus* fossils in the late 1970's and early 1980's caused some scientists to change their mind. They contended that the fossils belonged to just one group — *Sivapithecus* — with the larger fossils representing males and the smaller fossils representing females. In addition, they argued that *Sivapithecus* was more closely related to apes, particularly orangutans, than to humans.

Anthropologists Wu Rukang of the Institute of Vertebrate Paleontology at Academia Sinica in China and Charles E. Oxnard of the University of Southern California in Los Angeles analyzed the measurements of more than 1,000 teeth from *Sivapithecus* and *Ramapithe-*

The discovery in Egypt of four more skulls of *Aegyptopithecus zeuxis,* a tree-dwelling primate that lived about 32 million years ago, has strengthened arguments that the cat-sized creature represents the earliest known ancestor of all modern primates, including monkeys, apes, and human beings.

Anthropology

Continued

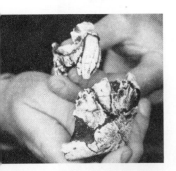

Fossil jaws and teeth of a 17-million-year-old primate found in Kenya may represent the common ancestor of apes and human beings, indicating that the ancestor of apes and humans split from monkeys earlier than was previously thought.

cus fossils found in Yunnan Province in China. They concluded that the differences between the teeth are sufficient to support the claim that the two groups are separate, even when size differences between males and females are taken into consideration. Although the two scientists agree that *Ramapithecus* is the more humanlike of the two forms, they believe that there is not enough clear evidence to establish a direct ancestral relationship between *Ramapithecus* and human beings.

Hominid from Nepal. A team of scientists led by geologists Jens Munthe of Mobil Oil Corporation's Exploration and Producing Division in Denver and Bishnu Dongol of Tribhuwan University in Kathmandu, Nepal, reported in May 1983 on the discovery of the first hominid fossil found in Nepal, a kingdom in south-central Asia. The fossil, an upper molar, was found at Tinau Khola in southwestern Nepal. Estimated to be 9 million to 9½ million years old, the tooth has been classified as belonging to either *Ramapithecus* or *Sivapithecus*.

Dating Yuha man. Research published in October 1983 indicates that "Yuha man"—a skeleton found in the Yuha Desert of California in 1971—is much younger than was previously thought. Yuha man was originally estimated to be from 21,500 to 23,600 years old. At that age, Yuha man would have been the oldest skeleton found in North America.

In 1980, the skeleton was stolen from the California laboratory where it was being studied. However, samples of bone had already been removed from the skeleton. Thomas Stafford, a graduate student in geochemistry at the University of Arizona in Tucson, ran bone samples and samples of calcium carbonate from the soil in which the skeleton was found through the university's particle accelerator. This device enables scientists to determine the age of materials containing carbon by *radiocarbon dating*—measuring the rate at which carbon 14 has decayed to carbon 12. Stafford found that the Yuha skeleton was only 2,000 to 4,000 years old.   [Charles F. Merbs]

Archaeology

Old World. An analysis, published in September 1983, of ancient pieces of copper found in Yugoslavia has confirmed that metalworking skills arose independently in Europe. Until the 1970's, most archaeologists believed that metalworking and the development of more complex metalworking skills, such as smelting and *alloying* (mixing two or more metals), arose first in the Near East, particularly in Mesopotamia, then spread to the rest of the Old World.

Archaeologist Petar Glumac of the University of California at Berkeley analyzed 300 copper fragments found by other scientists in 1978 at Selevac, a late *Neolithic* (New Stone Age) site. The fragments consisted mainly of pieces of malachite ore, one of the chief ores from which copper is obtained. Among the fragments, however, were three copper beads and a piece of *slag*—waste given off during the smelting of the malachite into copper. The slag provided the main evidence that the ore was smelted into workable copper at Selevac.

The fragments were excavated from the debris of burned and collapsed houses, which have been radiocarbon dated to 4600 to 4000 B.C. The oldest evidence of working with copper ores in the Near East dates from about the same time.

The Selevac fragments provide some of the earliest evidence of copper production in a European village. Most early copper fragments found in Europe have been discovered in graves or hoards buried for future use. Archaeologists were uncertain whether the people of that area manufactured the copper used in the artifacts or obtained the metal elsewhere.

No Asian connection. Research reported in August 1983 by archaeologists Charles Higham of Otago University in New Zealand and Amphan Kijngam of the Northeast Thailand Archaeological Program cast serious doubt on the theory that Southeast Asia was the source of tin used in Mesopotamia beginning in the 2000's B.C. to manufacture bronze. Bronze is an alloy commonly made of copper and

Plaster statues of human beings found in Jordan may have been used in ancestor worship or a death cult. The statues, 90 centimeters (3 feet) tall, date from more than 8,000 years ago.

Archaeology

Continued

tin, though it is sometimes made of copper and zinc. Tin is not found in Mesopotamia, so the bronze workers there must have imported it.

Some archaeologists theorized that the tin used in Mesopotamia came from Southeast Asia. Their theory was based on a discovery in the early 1970's of bronze-metalworking technology and nearby deposits of tin at Ban Chiang, an ancient settlement in northeast Thailand. Archaeologists estimated that the settlement dated from the 2500's B.C.

To establish a more precise date for Ban Chiang, Higham and Kijngam dated layers of sediment at Ban Nadi, a nearby settlement that existed about the same time. The scientists chose to study the layers of sediment at Ban Nadi because, unlike those at Ban Chiang, the Ban Nadi layers are clearly defined.

At the lowest level of the excavations at Ban Nadi, the scientists found evidence of a bronze-casting kiln and workshop along with artifacts of the same type as those found at Ban Chiang. Using carbon-14 dating methods, Higham and Kijngam calculated that the lowest level of sediment at Ban Nadi dated from about 1500 B.C., not 2500 B.C. Therefore, their discovery provides evidence that Ban Chiang was settled too late to have been the source of tin used by earlier Mesopotamian bronze workers.

Chinese chariots. In April 1984, Chinese scientists reported on their analysis of two bronze chariots unearthed in 1981 at the tomb of Qin Shi Huang (Chin Shih Huang) near Xian (Sian), China. Qin, the first emperor of China, unified the country in 221 B.C. The two bronze chariots, which had collapsed into many pieces, are among the finest examples of the skill of ancient Chinese metalsmiths.

The scientists found that one of the chariots consisted of 3,462 separate parts of cast silver, bronze, and gold, alloyed in various ways according to the required strength and appearance. The metal was finished by engraving, polishing, and painting to produce a lifelike effect.   [Ruth Tringham]

Archaeology

Continued

New World. In May 1984, an expedition led by anthropologist Richard E. W. Adams of the University of Texas at San Antonio announced the discovery of a 1,500-year-old Maya tomb at Río Azul in the jungles of northern Guatemala. Because the tomb was undamaged by looters and in nearly perfect condition, scientists consider it a major find.

In the tomb, the scientists found the skeleton of a man they believe may have been the blood relative of a Maya ruler buried in a large pyramid nearby. Covering the walls of the tomb are brilliant red *hieroglyphs* — pictures representing words or sounds — that the scientists hope will provide clues about the occupant's identity. Also found in the tomb were 15 undamaged pieces of pottery, including cylindrical jars with tripod legs and a remarkable blue-green pot with a twist-top lid.

Prehistoric rock art. In January 1984, archaeologist Donald E. Weaver, Jr., of the Museum of Northern Arizona near Flagstaff reported on the re-

sults of extensive research on the prehistoric rock art of the Colorado Plateau. This region, covering parts of Arizona, New Mexico, Utah, and Colorado, has a rich record of ancient rock paintings and carvings, many of which are thousands of years old.

Weaver believes that the rock art is neither a primitive form of writing nor just idle scribbling. Instead, he suggests that the paintings represent attempts by ancient native Americans to influence their environment through magic. For example, Weaver theorizes that the Indians may have painted certain symbols or scenes to try to ensure good hunting or plentiful rain for their crops. Many scenes of deer, buffalo, and bighorn sheep lend support to this hypothesis. Weaver also suggests that human figures depicted in the rock paintings wearing masks and ceremonial dress may be *shamans* (medicine men) or religious leaders.

A major problem facing rock art scholars in the Colorado Plateau and elsewhere in North America is the increased destruction of these sites.

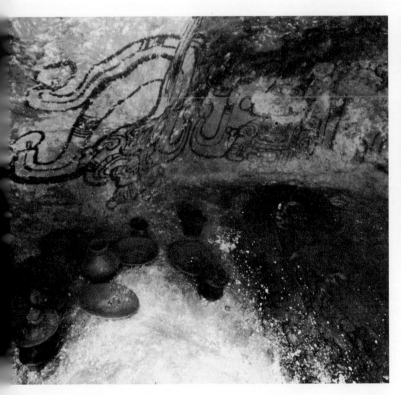

Untouched for 1,500 years, a Maya tomb containing the skeleton of a man was found in northern Guatemala in May 1984, *left*. Its treasures included brilliant wall paintings, pieces of pottery, and a jar with a twist-top lid, *above*.

Cataloging America's Attic

Counting national
treasures

As of June 1983, the Smithsonian Institution in Washington, D.C., was at last able to answer a question asked by thousands of tourists each year: Exactly how many objects do the institution's nine largest museums have in their possession? The answer — 100 million, give or take a few million —was determined by an $8-million, five-year inventory of the Smithsonian possessions.

Seven million beetles, 8,000 turtles, 4,500 meteorites, 3,238 sea slugs, 3,618 leeches, 114,429 bird eggs, 110,664 rocks, 50,000 flies, and 35,594 skeletons are among the items tallied by the staff of the National Museum of Natural History alone. The tally sheets also showed that the National Museum of American History has 872,780 costumes and the National Air and Space Museum has 283 airplanes, 125 missiles, and 63 satellites.

The final statistics from the inventory provide dramatic proof of the wide range of objects in what has been called "the nation's attic." One Smithsonian branch in New York City, the Cooper-Hewitt Museum of Design and Decorative Arts, has 110,000 prints and drawings, as well as 21,050 textiles and 7,000 samples of wallpaper. In Washington, D.C., the National Museum of American History has nearly 13 million stamps, 2,000 pieces of lace, and 8,500 pill bottles and apothecary jars. The Freer Gallery of Art, Hirshhorn Museum and Sculpture Garden, National Museum of American Art, and Museum of African Art, along with the National Portrait Gallery, share more than 82,000 works of art. Other national treasures that are listed in the inventory are an acorn from a tree planted at Mount Vernon by George Washington, Theodore Roosevelt's teddy bear, and Dwight D. Eisenhower's red pajamas with five stars on the shoulders — indicating his rank of five-star general.

Few sensational discoveries turned up as employees wandered the halls with checklists, poking into corners and cabinets. But the auditors had several unexpected encounters. Eight whale skeletons and a stuffed buffalo were found in a hidden room above the enormous dome in the museum's grand entrance. The auditors also discovered 75 reindeer skulls, complete with antlers, tucked above some public display cases.

The survey had several important goals beyond the satisfaction of tourists' curiosity. One was simply a "housekeeping" goal. The Smithsonian, which acquires roughly 1 million objects every year, had never taken a thorough inventory of the items in its possession. Lacking such an inventory, museum and government officials long feared that priceless artifacts could be lost or stolen without anyone's knowledge.

These concerns were intensified in the late 1970's by plans to ship many of the Smithsonian's holdings — some of which were in serious danger of damage from bugs, heat, and humidity — from its museums in downtown Washington to a new storage and conservation building in Suitland, Md. The inventory, which included minerals, gems, fossils, and marine animals, helped ensure that nothing got waylaid in transit.

Another goal of the inventory was to assist scientific researchers, who occasionally had to interview several curators to locate important specimens. With the help of experts such as paleontologist Gary Gautier, who directs the data-processing department at the Museum of Natural History, the auditors transferred the records of Smithsonian possessions from ledgers to indexed and cross-referenced computer files. Once the move to the new warehouse is complete, researchers should be able to find the items they need in just an hour.

Despite the impressive catalog of Smithsonian treasures, Gautier admits that there may be less in the count than meets the eye. In some instances, the number of individual museum specimens was merely estimated, because an exact count would have taken decades. "Knowing that you have 1.2 million specimens is not that meaningful if you are discussing, say, worms," he says. "It's a bit like counting the blades of grass in your lawn."

No one could say exactly how many blades of grass the Smithsonian has, but one official noted that its holdings do include several million specimens of soil.   [R. Jeffrey Smith]

Archaeology

Continued

A diver hoses down the coral-encrusted anchor of the Union ironclad *Monitor,* recovered in August 1983 off the coast of North Carolina, where it sank in 1862.

Many of the canyon walls and shallow caves where the paintings are found have fallen victim to excavations for towns, mines, roads, and dams. Especially appalling is the destruction caused by vandals, who have spray-painted some sites and scrawled their names across the prehistoric symbols. Weaver notes that rock art sites on public and federal property are protected by laws that call for stiff fines and jail terms for vandals.

Underwater city. In January 1984, anthropologist Don L. Hamilton and nautical archaeologist Robyn P. Woodward of Texas A&M University in College Station reported discoveries at Port Royal, Jamaica, a submerged 17th-century city. Hit by an earthquake and tidal wave on June 7, 1692, the city literally sank into Kingston Harbor. More than 4,000 people died.

Founded in the 1660's as a haven for privateers, Port Royal was a bustling place, and reputedly the "wickedest city on earth." By the late 1600's, Port Royal was the mercantile center of the Caribbean and covered more than 20 hectares (50 acres), with 2,000 buildings and 6,500 inhabitants.

Working with the Jamaican government, the Texas scientists began their research in 1981. The remains of the submerged city, covered by 90 centimeters (36 inches) of silt and coral, were cleared away in 1981 with a special water vacuum.

In 1982, the scientists, working underwater, excavated a multiroom building, which they believe was once part of the Port Royal fish and meat market. One room contained bones of butchered animals, meat hooks, and tools. The presence of many liquor bottles in another room led the scientists to conclude that that room was probably a warehouse associated with the market.

Because the destruction of the city occurred quickly, many everyday objects were left behind or dropped as the inhabitants fled. As a result, the scientists believe the underwater site offers a remarkable opportunity for studying the daily life of this Caribbean city.   [Thomas R. Hester]

Astronomy

Solar System Astronomy. In February 1984, two astronomers reported their findings on the makeup of Pluto's atmosphere. S. A. Stern of the Laboratory of Atmospheric and Space Physics in Boulder, Colo., and Laurence Trafton of the University of Texas in Austin showed how atmosphere is related to the planet's complex and harsh climate.

Of the nine known planets, Pluto is farthest from the sun. In May 1984, Pluto was 4.3 billion kilometers (2.7 billion miles) from the sun, about as close as it gets, and its surface temperature was $-140°C$ ($-284°F$.). When Pluto is at its farthest point from the sun, some 130 years from now, the planet's temperature will drop to $-191.6°C$ ($-377°F$.).

Pluto's *polar axis* (an imaginary line between the two poles) is tilted 118 degrees. (By comparison, Earth's polar axis is tilted 23 degrees.) Because of the angle of its polar tilt, when one pole points closest to the sun, the hemisphere of the other pole gets no sunlight and is completely dark.

The two worst times of the year on Pluto—where one year equals roughly 248 Earth-years—are midsummer and midwinter, those points in the planet's orbit when either the north pole or the south pole points closest to the sun. So the most extreme weather is not necessarily dependent on when the planet is farthest from the sun. Under these conditions, the two astronomers calculated that all of the gases in Pluto's atmosphere on the night, or dark, side could "collapse"—freeze solid and fall onto the planet's surface—unless enough heat energy is released by the melting and freezing of nitrogen ice on the surface.

Stern and Trafton also reported that methane gas, which was detected earlier on the planet, is probably only a minor gas in Pluto's atmosphere. They concluded that the most abundant gas is nitrogen.

In addition, the two researchers studied Pluto's wind patterns. They believe that the same type of violent windstorms or cyclones that occur on Earth also occur on Pluto. In the Spe-

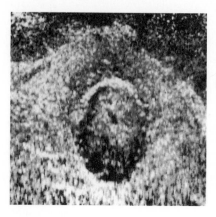

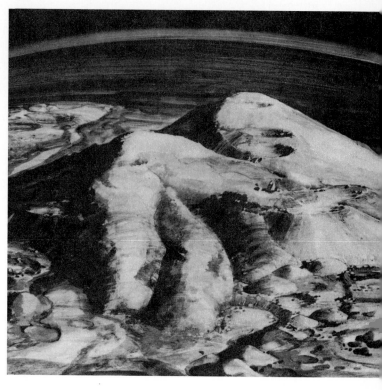

A radar image of the surface of Venus, *above,* taken by Soviet spacecraft in October 1983, reveals what many scientists believe is a volcanic crater. Based on mounting evidence of volcanoes on Venus, an artist's conception of one volcanic region, *right,* might be correct.

Astronomy

Continued

cial Reports section, see PROBING THE SECRETS OF ATMOSPHERES.

Visit to a comet. In December 1983, the *International Sun Earth Explorer* satellite got a new name and a new course. Renamed the *International Cometary Explorer (ICE),* the National Aeronautics and Space Administration (NASA) satellite was redirected on December 22 to pass within 120 kilometers (75 miles) of the moon. The moon's gravity then hurled *ICE* onto a new course that will take it to a meeting with Comet Giacobini-Zinner in September 1985, six months before the first of several European, Japanese, and Soviet spacecraft reach the more spectacular Halley's Comet.

ICE mission engineers were uncertain about the precise position of Comet Giacobini-Zinner in space, because it was last seen in 1979 and is known to undergo unpredictable orbital changes.

In April 1984, however, a team of scientists working at Kitt Peak National Observatory in Tucson, Ariz., found the comet was only 9,700 kilometers (6,000 miles) away from the position that NASA had targeted. As a result, *ICE* will require only a minor change in course.

Halley's Comet. In mid-1984, Halley's Comet continued to move closer to the sun and was already well within the orbit of Saturn. Observations with telescopes in Hawaii, Arizona, and Chile indicated that the brightness of the comet varies strongly, probably due to the rotation of its nucleus, or central core. A team of French scientists at the Mauna Kea Observatory on Hawaii estimated that the nucleus of the comet makes a complete revolution every 8 hours and 10 minutes, much faster than was previously thought.

In April 1984, scientists at Kitt Peak National Observatory for the first time obtained data about the comet's *spectrum* (the colors of its light) and determined that the surface of the nucleus is bright red. The red color was not a complete surprise. Other icy bodies in the outer solar system, such as the Trojan asteroids, are also known to be red. In the case of the Trojan asteroids, scientists believe the red color is caused by kerogen, a little-understood mix of complex *organic* (carbon-bearing) molecules. Kerogen is also found in certain types of meteorites and was probably present when the solar system formed. On Earth, it is found in *oil shale* (a fine-grained rock) and in coal tar. Now scientists think kerogen may also exist on Halley's Comet.

Deadly comet showers. In 1983 and 1984, a number of astronomers joined the ongoing and highly speculative discussion on what causes periodic mass extinctions on Earth, including the disappearance of the dinosaur some 65 million years ago (see EARTH SCIENCES [Paleontology]). Studies done in 1982 by paleontologists David M. Raup and J. John Sepkoski, Jr., of the University of Chicago and in 1977 by geologists Alfred G. Fischer of Princeton University in Princeton, N.J., and Michael A. Arthur of the University of Rhode Island in Kingston indicated that mass extinctions occur every 26 million years. In 1979, a group of scientists at the University of California and at

Lawrence Berkeley Laboratory, both in Berkeley, Calif., linked the mass extinction that occurred 65 million years ago with the impact of a large asteroid or comet striking Earth.

Finally, geologist Walter S. Alvarez and astronomer Richard A. Muller, both of the University of California, Berkeley, examined the ages of the few impact craters found on Earth. They concluded that the various craters were caused by meteorites that struck at different times—about 28 million years or so apart. The dates of the craters and of the periodic mass extinctions are remarkably close.

In February 1984, several groups of astronomers came up with a startling explanation for this. They proposed that the vast cloud of some 100 billion comets that is part of the outer solar system is somehow disturbed every 26 million years. As a result, a billion comets rain down on the inner solar system for a million years. Such a comet shower would lead to many comet impacts on Earth. In the early 1980's, physicists at the California In-

Drawing by Chas. Addams; © 1983
The New Yorker Magazine, Inc.

"Maynard, I do think that just this once
you should come out and see the moon!"

Astronomy

Continued

stitute of Technology in Pasadena estimated that the impact of a comet 10 kilometers (6.2 miles) in diameter on the surface of Earth would be like exploding more than 100 million 1-megaton atomic bombs.

The groups of scientists offered various explanations for what could cause this type of comet shower. In April 1984, planetary geologists Michael R. Rampino and Richard B. Stothers of NASA's Goddard Institute for Space Studies in New York City and astronomer Richard D. Schwartz and physicist Philip R. James of the University of Missouri in St. Louis theorized that such showers are a result of the sun's motion in the Milky Way galaxy. As the sun moves in its orbit around the center of the Galaxy, it passes above and below the *plane of the Galaxy* (an imaginary two-dimensional layer that divides the Galaxy horizontally). The plane of the Galaxy contains dense clouds of dust and gas, and the sun passes through this dense material every 33 million years. Rampino and his colleagues proposed that during this passage, the sun will collide with a massive interstellar cloud of gas and dust, triggering a comet shower.

Another tantalizing suggestion, also introduced in April, came independently from two research teams. One team included astronomers Daniel P. Whitmire of the University of Southwestern Louisiana in Lafayette, and Albert A. Jackson of Computer Sciences Corporation in Houston. The other included astronomers Marc Davis and Richard A. Muller of the University of California in Berkeley, and Piet Hut of the Institute for Advanced Study in Princeton, N.J. These researchers believe that the sun may have a faint companion star, which one group named Nemesis. Nemesis is in a distant orbit and passes closest to the sun every 26 million years, they theorized. Such a companion could exist and yet remain undetected because of its extreme faintness. According to this theory, the star would pass through the outer solar system's comet cloud once every orbit, causing a massive comet shower to be unleashed toward Earth. They predict the next such comet shower will occur in 15 million years.   [Michael J. S. Belton]

Galactic Astronomy. One of the most significant developments of the year was the successful mission of the *Infrared Astronomical Satellite* (*IRAS*), which ended on Nov. 22, 1983. Observations from *IRAS* will provide important data about the hidden regions where new stars form, the envelopes of dust around stars, and the coldest forms of interstellar matter. The *IRAS* results will take years to analyze completely. In the Special Reports section, see A New View of the Universe.

Most powerful star. In May 1983, astrophysicists at the University of Kiel in West Germany reported that they had detected extremely high-energy gamma rays from Cygnus X-3, the third X-ray star to be found in the constellation Cygnus. Their findings were verified in October 1983 by astrophysicists at the University of Leeds in England.

Since the early 1970's, astronomers have known that Cygnus X-3 is a remarkable, variable X-ray star. (An X-ray star gives off most of its energy in the form of high-energy X rays. A variable star is one that varies in brightness.) With the detection of gamma rays, Cygnus X-3 has set the record for the most energetic radiation ever detected from a star.

Gamma rays, X rays, visible light, and radio waves are all forms of electromagnetic radiation that differ only in the amount of energy that each wave packet of radiation contains. X rays, for example, carry up to a thousand times more energy than does visible light. The gamma rays from Cygnus X-3 observed by the West German and English scientists carry up to 1 thousand trillion times as much energy as visible light.

The West German scientists used Earth's atmosphere as a kind of telescope for making their measurements. Gamma rays produce an extremely faint glow of visible light over large areas when they enter our atmosphere. Using sensitive light detectors on the ground, the astrophysicists measured the glow in the upper atmosphere to determine the energy level of the gamma rays and to find their approximate source. Each gamma ray is extremely powerful, but there are very few of them. As a result,

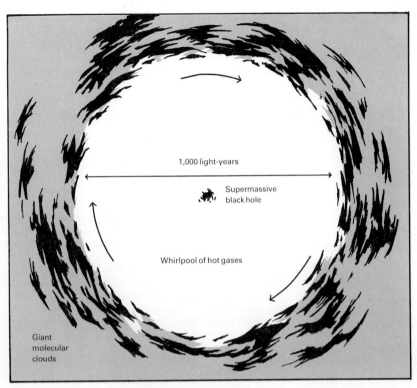

1,000 light-years

Supermassive
black hole

Whirlpool of hot gases

Giant
molecular
clouds

Streams of hot gas
spiraling toward the
center of our Galaxy
are revealed in a radio
image, *above,* taken with
the Very Large Array
Telescope near Socorro,
N. Mex. The gases may
be falling into a black hole
so dense not even light can
escape, *right.*

Astronomy

Continued

the study took 3,838 hours of observing time over a four-year period. Their findings indicate that Cygnus X-3 produces more than 1,000 times the total power of our sun just in the form of the highest-energy gamma rays.

In November 1983, astrophysicist Robert J. Gould of the University of California, San Diego, said that the West German scientists might have underestimated the gamma ray production by Cygnus X-3. Some of the gamma rays coming from the star will be absorbed before they reach Earth as they pass through the low-energy radiation that fills space. By allowing for this absorption, Gould estimates the power of Cygnus X-3 must be at least three times greater than the West German observations indicated.

Cygnus X-3 also occasionally produces an enormous burst of radio waves. In October 1983, a group of radio astronomers led by Barry J. Geldzahler of the Naval Research Laboratory in Washington, D.C., reported on their observations of a recent burst of radio waves. The astronomers used a

nationwide network of telescopes, including the National Radio Astronomy Observatory's Very Large Array near Socorro, N. Mex., and a smaller array at Green Bank, W. Va. The most startling result was a direct measurement of a burst of radio waves over a two-month period. Astrophysicist John M. Dickey of the University of Minnesota in Minneapolis suggested in a recent study that Cygnus X-3 is at least 35,000 *light-years* away. (A light-year is the distance light travels in one year at a speed of 186,282 miles per second.) If this is the case, then material blown off in the burst of radio waves is expanding at greater than one-third the speed of light, according to Geldzahler. A significant amount of material moving at this speed is one more indication of the enormous energy being given off by Cygnus X-3. Nothing like this has ever been seen before, and consequently, astronomers are perplexed as to exactly what powers Cygnus X-3.

Protoplanet or protostar? The star T Tauri in the constellation Taurus is a

Astronomy

well-known example of a young, recently formed star. It is still embedded within interstellar matter left over from the cloud of dust and gas that evidently condensed to form it. In the last few years, observations of infrared and radio radiation revealed that T Tauri has an invisible companion — an object too faint or too deeply buried in dust and gas to be seen in visible light. When looking at this region, astronomers have detected two objects that emit infrared and radio waves. One is a weak source; the other, a strong one. However, researchers were unable to determine which of the radio and infrared sources — the weak one or the strong one — corresponds to the visible star known as T Tauri.

In July 1983, astronomer Robert B. Hanson and his colleagues at the University of California's Lick Observatory on Mount Hamilton published some interesting suggestions about T Tauri's invisible companion. They made a careful reexamination of the exact position of T Tauri and concluded that it corresponds with the position of the weaker source. The scientists found that T Tauri lies slightly north of its invisible companion.

Hanson and his team proposed that the invisible, strong infrared companion might be a *protoplanet* (a planet in the process of forming). The mysterious object has a temperature of only about 500°C (932°F.), but it has an infrared power output 1½ times the total power output of our sun. The California astronomers suggest that this is just what would be expected from an orbiting protoplanet that is growing larger as more and more material falls onto it. The material could be supplied by a thin doughnut-shaped cloud of gas and dust around T Tauri. This interpretation fits in well with some theories that describe the formation of our own sun and solar system. It also makes T Tauri a good subject for the study of how planets form. In the Special Reports section, see PROBING THE SECRETS OF ATMOSPHERES.

However, in October 1983, astronomer Claude Bertout of the Institute of Astrophysics in Paris proposed an al-

Technicians in England grind the giant 4.2-meter (165-inch) primary mirror of the William Herschel Telescope to be located at a new international observatory on La Palma in the Canary Islands. When completed in 1986, the British optical telescope will be the world's third largest.

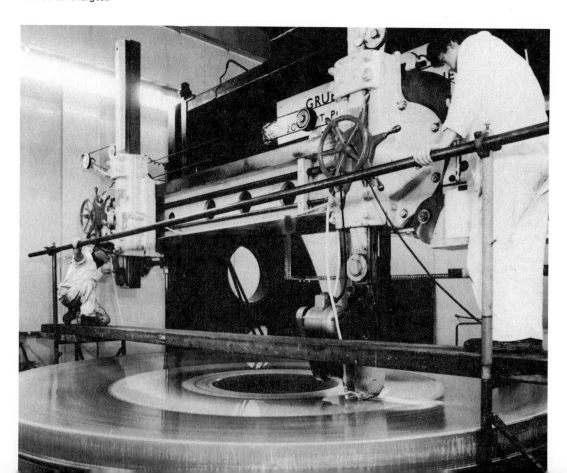

Astronomy

Continued

ternative explanation. He theorized that the invisible infrared companion is a much larger object—a *protostar* (a star in the process of forming). The essential difference between the two proposals is that a protostar would be much more massive than a protoplanet. Further research will be required to establish which of the two theories for T Tauri's companion is correct, or whether an entirely different idea will be needed.

X rays from a dark cloud. Astrophysicists at the Center for Nuclear Studies in Gif-sur-Yvette, France; the Observatory of Meudon, France; and the Harvard-Smithsonian Center for Astrophysics in Cambridge, Mass., reported in June 1983 that a dark cloud near the star Rho Ophiuchi contains a large number of X-ray sources. Between 1978 and 1981, when the X-ray telescope in orbit aboard the *Einstein* observatory spacecraft was in use, this team of scientists detected approximately 50 weak sources of X rays near the central region of this dark cloud. After analyzing the data gathered by the spacecraft, they concluded that the X rays probably arise in young stars that have formed inside the cloud within the last 100,000 years.

Young stars tend to vary rapidly in their X-ray brightness, probably as a result of occasional flares that last a few hours. The X rays coming from each star are only a small fraction of the power that it radiates in the form of visible and infrared light. However, the combined X-ray emission from all these stars may have important effects on the temperature of the cloud. The dark clouds of interstellar gas and dust where new stars form are usually considered extremely cold, calm places. However, when stars begin to form, they can heat up such clouds. X rays may also speed up the cloud's collapse, alter the chemistry of its gases, and affect its ability to form more stars. One important conclusion of this work is that variable X-ray emission is probably a common occurrence in recently formed stars and not a rare event. Therefore, future studies of star formation must take X rays into account. In the past, the usefulness of X-ray astronomy to the study of star formation was ignored. [John H. Black]

Extragalactic Astronomy. The search for *gravitational lenses* continued in 1983 and 1984. A gravitational lens is formed by the gravitational field of a massive object, such as a galaxy, when it deflects light coming from a more distant object. The light bends around the edges of a galaxy, for example, in two or more places. This causes an observer on Earth to see more than one image of the distant object. Usually, the more distant object is a quasar, an object that gives off large amounts of radiated energy. Astronomers can detect the lens effect when they find two or more quasar images that are very close together and have identical *spectra*, or bands of distinguishing characteristics in the colors of their light.

The discovery of two gravitational lenses was announced during a January 1984 meeting of the American Astronomical Society (AAS). One of these new lenses was discovered by astronomer C. R. Lawrence of the Massachusetts Institute of Technology in Cambridge and colleagues from several other institutions, including the California Institute of Technology in Pasadena and Princeton University in Princeton, N.J. This was the first gravitational lens to be detected by a radio telescope, the Very Large Array near Socorro, N. Mex. The finding was later confirmed by observations with an optical telescope at the Lick Observatory at Mount Hamilton, California.

The astronomers knew that the gravitational lens effect was at work in this case because the two quasar images had nearly identical optical spectra, and their *red shifts* indicated that their light had taken the same amount of time—at least 10 billion years—to reach us. (Red shift means that when an object is moving away from Earth, the light coming from the object will be shifted toward the red, or longer, wavelength end of the electromagnetic spectrum. The faster the object is moving away from Earth, the more its light is red-shifted.) The third object in the gravitational lens system is a galaxy that is believed to be the brightest member of a cluster of galaxies. This cluster is the massive object whose gravitational field is producing the images of two quasars. The cluster lies

227

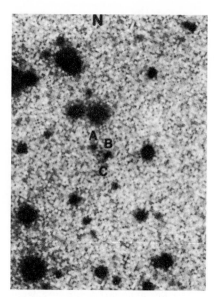

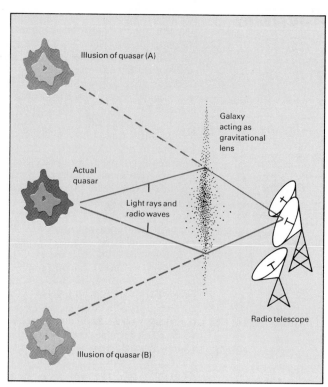

Images A and B, *above,* are optical illusions created when a galaxy or a cluster of galaxies, C, acts as a gravitational lens by bending the light of a single quasar, *right,* so that two images appear to an observer on Earth.

Astronomy

Continued

between what is actually a single, very distant quasar and Earth.

At the same AAS meeting, astronomers Stanislav Djorgovski and Hyron Spinrad of the University of California, Berkeley, reported their discovery of a second gravitational lens system. These discoveries bring to four the total number of gravitational lenses found since the first was discovered in 1979. Scientists are excited about these discoveries because gravitational lenses enable them to make calculations about the scale of distances in the universe. If enough gravitational lens systems are detected, their calculations will provide a more detailed map of the universe. Then, it will be possible to estimate the distribution of matter in the very distant universe, to measure the rate at which the universe is expanding, and even to measure the rate at which the expansion may be slowing down (in the Special Reports section, see THE FIRST SECOND).

Quasars near or far? Gravitational lenses also add fuel to arguments over whether quasar red shifts actually in-

dicate distance. Most astronomers believe that quasars are the most distant objects in the universe based on observations that their light is highly red-shifted. However, some researchers believe they have found evidence indicating that some quasars are associated with nearby galaxies, even though the light from the quasar is highly red-shifted and the light from the nearby galaxy is only slightly red-shifted. These astronomers question whether red shifts do, in fact, indicate an object's speed and, therefore, its distance from Earth. The red shifts may be caused by something near the quasar, they argue, perhaps by a gravitational field or by some phenomenon not yet understood.

One astronomer in particular, Halton C. Arp of Mount Wilson Observatory near Pasadena, Calif., has argued that not all quasar red shifts need to be related to the distance the light has traveled. This ongoing controversy was the subject of several new studies in 1983 and 1984.

In August 1983, astronomers E. J.

Astronomy

Continued

Zuiderwijk of the Royal Greenwich Observatory in England and H. R. deRuiter of the Institute of Radio Astronomy in Bologna, Italy, analyzed a number of galaxies that seem to have a nearby quasar, according to photographs made with optical telescopes. The astronomers wanted to see if these objects are physically associated — that is, actually close together in space. Simply because two objects appear near each other on a photograph produced by an optical telescope does not mean they are physically close, since the photographs are two-dimensional. Actually, the two objects may be separated by immense distances because one is much farther out in space. The scientists in England and Italy used a list of galaxy-quasar combinations generated by Arp and applied careful statistical tests to see whether these associations happen by chance. They found that there was about a 1 per cent chance that the observations could be due to accidental associations of images of galaxies with images of quasars. These findings would tend to support Arp's view that quasars are associated with nearby galaxies. However, the two astronomers in England and Italy presented a number of other explanations that do not require the quasars to be physically close to the galaxies. Most important among these is the possibility that current statistics regarding the number of quasars and their positions in the sky are inaccurate because of the multiple images that gravitational lenses produce from a single object.

New perspectives. In June 1983, astronomers Howard B. French of the University of Oklahoma in Norman and James E. Gunn of Princeton University Observatory investigated the quasar-galaxy association from another perspective. They searched for faint galaxies in the vicinity of quasars that are relatively near Earth, the opposite of the approach taken by Arp, who searched for quasars near galaxies. French and Gunn found that images of faint galaxies tend to cluster around quasars. In this case, both objects had similar red shifts. This finding suggests a physical closeness between these nearby galaxies and quasars, as Arp maintains, but at the

same time, it does not require a new understanding of red shifts — that is, red shift can still be understood as a measure of distance.

In October 1983, a group of astronomers, including Arp, presented new evidence that red shifts are not always indicators of distance. They discovered six quasar images near galaxy NGC 1097. Finding images of so many quasars around a galaxy is unlikely unless quasars are associated with the galaxy. In addition, the red shifts of the six quasars are all different, indicating that their red shifts may not be caused by the speed at which they are traveling away from Earth. However, the possibility that gravitational lenses may be causing multiple quasar images to appear near this galaxy was not ruled out.

One possible conclusion from all these observations is that there may be two types of red shifts. One type indicates an object's distance. The second type has nothing to do with speed or distance, but is caused by some unknown factor in the object's environment. Such an explanation has been suggested before, but it cannot be proven or disproven without a method of telling the difference between these two possible types of red shifts. As a result, the controversy is likely to continue.

Pancakes in the sky. The large-scale structure of the universe is an area of increasing interest to astronomers who have detected superclusters of galaxies on scales of hundreds of millions of *light-years*. (A light-year is the distance light travels in one year, about 9.6 trillion kilometers or 6 trillion miles.) Astronomers have also found giant voids in the universe that are practically empty of galaxies.

In November 1983, astronomer Stanislav Djorgovski analyzed the orientation of galaxies in the Coma Cluster, a collection of thousands of galaxies bound together by gravity. Galaxies in the Coma Cluster tend to be elliptical, or oval shaped. The Coma Cluster is itself elliptical in shape. To determine how the galaxies are arranged in relation to each other, Djorgovski drew an axis, or imaginary line, between the longest points of their ellipses. He did this to determine how

Analysis of new satellite data suggests that the bright center of Seyfert galaxy NGC4151 may contain a black hole, in this case a dense object with 100 million times the mass of our sun. Since Seyfert galaxies are similar to quasars, the finding indicates that both classes of objects are powered by stars and gases falling into a central black hole.

Astronomy

Continued

the galaxies were aligned — that is, in what direction the axis was pointing. Djorgovski was able to study the alignment of 4,000 galaxies and found that the galaxies tended to be aligned in the same direction as the cluster — in an east-west direction in the sky. These observations lend support to the so-called *pancake theory* for the formations of galaxies and clusters of galaxies that was originally proposed in 1970 by Soviet astrophysicists Yakov B. Zel'dovich and Rashid Sunyaev of the Institute of Applied Mathematics in Moscow. This theory states that large collections of matter in the early universe collapsed into flattened shapes — pancakes — and that later galaxies formed from the material in these pancakes. These galaxies copy the properties of the pancake from which they formed —for example, the direction of their axes and their shapes.

An opposing theory by astrophysicist P. James E. Peebles of Princeton University holds that galaxies formed first in the universe and later collected into clusters. However, Djorgovski's observations cast doubt on this theory, because there would not have been enough time since the birth of the universe for the galaxies to become aligned.

In February 1984, astronomers Neta A. Bahcall of Princeton University and Raymond M. Soneira of the Institute for Advanced Study, both in Princeton, N.J., also reported findings consistent with the Zel'dovich pancake model. Their catalog of superclusters indicated that a large fraction of all clusters belong to superclusters. These superclusters are several hundred million light-years across and form the largest structures yet observed in the universe. These superclusters also form the boundaries of the large voids in space where very few galaxies have been detected. The pancake theory predicts this large-scale distribution of galaxies. However, Peebles' competing theory can also be made to fit these observations, and other data favor the galaxies forming first. The controversy over these competing theories is likely to continue.   [Stephen S. Murray]

Books of Science

Here are 25 outstanding new science books suitable for the general reader. They have been selected from books published in 1983 and 1984.

Archaeology and Anthropology. *In Pursuit of the Past: Decoding the Archaeological Record* by Lewis R. Binford shows how archaeological evidence is used to explore the past. (Thames & Hudson, 1983. 256 pp. illus. $18.50)

Margaret Mead and Samoa: The Making and Unmaking of an Anthropological Myth by Derek Freeman looks carefully at American anthropologist Margaret Mead's famous 1928 study of Samoan society and offers alternative conclusions. Freeman draws on his own experiences in Samoa for evidence. (Harvard Univ. Press, 1983. 379 pp. illus. $20)

Astronomy. *The Moment of Creation: Big Bang Physics from Before the First Millisecond to the Present Universe* by James S. Trefil explains new theories that describe the earliest moments of the universe. Trefil concludes with a discussion of the moment of creation and the need to create a new definition of time. (Scribner, 1983. 234 pp. illus. $15.95)

100 Billion Suns: The Birth, Life, and Death of the Stars by Rudolf Kippenhahn, translated from the German by Jean Steinberg, tells the story of the stars in our Galaxy, including white dwarfs, X-ray stars, pulsars, binary stars, and our own sun. Kippenhahn describes how stars get their energy, how they are born, and how they die. (Basic Bks., 1983. 264 pp. illus. $25)

The Ultimate Fate of the Universe by Jamal N. Islam speculates about what will eventually happen to the universe, noting that it may go on expanding forever or may collapse upon itself. (Cambridge Univ. Press, 1983. 155 pp. illus. $13.95)

Biology. *Aristotle to Zoos: A Philosophical Dictionary of Biology* by P. B. Medawar and J. S. Medawar is patterned after the *Philosophical Dictionary* by Voltaire, a French philosopher of the 1700's. The Medawars present 200 short, reflective articles on a wide range of topics related to biology. (Harvard Univ. Press, 1983. 305 pp. $18.50)

A Slot Machine, A Broken Test Tube: An Autobiography by Salvador E. Luria tells of the professional, artistic, emotional, and political events in the life of this Italian-born American scientist, who won the Nobel Prize for physiology or medicine in 1969 for his pioneering work in molecular biology. (Harper & Row, 1984. 229 pp. $17.95)

Earth Sciences. *The Search for Our Beginning: An Enquiry, Based on Meteorite Research, into the Origin of Our Planet and of Life* by Robert Hutchison explains how the study of meteorites yields knowledge of Earth's early history and of the solar system. (Oxford Univ. Press, 1983. 164 pp. illus. $16.95)

Sunsets, Twilights, and Evening Skies by Aden Meinel and Marjorie Meinel describes numerous atmospheric phenomena, including the *green flash*, a flash of vivid green light seen when the sun is just below the horizon; and *zodiacal light*, a faint glow that appears in the sky soon after twilight or just before dawn. The book also explains how volcanic activity and other Earth-bound events affect such atmospheric displays. (Cambridge Univ. Press, 1983. 163 pp. illus. $29.95)

Mathematics. *The Visual Display of Quantitative Information* by Edward R. Tufte illustrates the many useful, artistic, and informative ways in which graphs display numbers. The book also includes the history of graphs and the theory that underlies graphic illustration. (Graphics Press, 1983. 197 pp. illus. $34)

Wheels, Life and Other Mathematical Amusements by Martin Gardner is his 10th collection of games, riddles, amusements, and diversions. The author, who originally wrote these articles for his "Mathematical Games" column in *Scientific American*, has supplemented each article with the solutions, comments, and accidental discoveries sent in by readers. (W. H. Freeman, 1983. 216 pp. illus. $15.95)

Medicine. *The Black Death: Natural and Human Disaster in Medieval Europe* by Robert S. Gottfried traces the history of the outbreak of bubonic plague in Europe during the 1300's, its impact on European society, and its effect on the development of modern medicine. (Free Press, 1983. 203 pp. $16.95)

Princes and Peasants: Smallpox in History by Donald R. Hopkins is a history

Books of Science

Continued

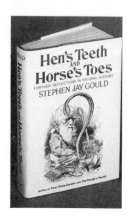

of the disease from prehistoric times to its elimination in 1980. Hopkins tells how smallpox killed many prominent persons and thus influenced the course of history. (University of Chicago Press, 1983. 380 pp. illus. $25)

Natural History. *Australia: A Natural History* by Howard Ensign Evans and Mary Alice Evans surveys the characteristics of the Australian continent, including its climate, geography, and plant and animal life. The book also describes the relationship of the Australian Aborigines to their land. (Smithsonian Institution Press, 1983. 208 pp. illus. $39.95)

A Desert Country near the Sea: A Natural History of the Cape Region of Baja California by Ann H. Zwinger provides a comprehensive view of the wildlife, vegetation, and settlements of the southern tip of Lower California, or the Baja peninsula. (Harper & Row, 1983. 399 pp. illus. $24.95)

Philosophy of Science. *Evolution from Molecules to Men*, edited by D. S. Bendall on behalf of Darwin College, Cambridge, England, consists of 28 papers written for a 1982 conference observing the 100th anniversary of the death of British naturalist Charles R. Darwin. The essays represent the range of implications that Darwin's theory of evolution has for biology, sociology, and philosophy. (Cambridge Univ. Press, 1983. 594 pp. illus. $29.95)

Hen's Teeth and Horse's Toes by Stephen Jay Gould is the third collection of essays on Darwin and evolutionary theory drawn from Gould's column in *Natural History* magazine. The author seeks to show how evolutionary theory can be used to explain a wide range of natural phenomena. (Norton, 1983. 413 pp. $15.50)

Scientists Confront Creationism, edited by Laurie R. Godfrey, consists of 15 essays written by scientists responding to creationist arguments on such topics as the age of Earth, gaps in the fossil record, and the Biblical story of the great flood. (Norton, 1983. 324 pp. $19.50)

The Secular Ark: Studies in the History of Biogeography by Janet Browne shows how early investigations into the distribution of plants and animals throughout the world influenced Darwin's

thinking. (Yale Univ. Press, 1983. 274 pp. illus. $27.50)

Technology. *Revolution in Time: Clocks and the Making of the Modern World* by David S. Landes explains why the development of timekeeping remained a European monopoly for 500 years. Landes describes the improvements made in timekeeping devices over the centuries and identifies the people who made them. (Harvard Univ. Press, 1983. 482 pp. illus. $20)

Taming the Tiger: The Struggle to Control Technology by Witold Rybczynski looks at the ways in which new technologies have been received, and often opposed, by the societies in which they have been introduced. Part of this reaction has been a struggle to control machines, rather than be controlled by them. The author argues for a new perspective acknowledging that human beings are an intimate part of the environment of technology. (Viking, 1983. 247 pp. $15.95)

The Tower and the Bridge: The New Art of Structural Engineering by David P. Billington identifies the best works of structural engineering of the past 200 years. Billington argues that these works constitute a new art form and names the Eiffel Tower and the Brooklyn Bridge as among the masterpieces. (Basic Bks., 1983. 306 pp. illus. $24.95)

Zoology. *Animal Thought* by Stephen Walker argues that the possibility of organized thought in animals other than human beings must be considered. (Routledge & Kegan Paul, 1983. 437 pp. $35)

Animals as Navigators by E. W. Anderson describes how the navigational skills of animals can be related to their need to find their way, to hunt for food, and to avoid predators. (Van Nostrand Reinhold, 1983. 207 pp. illus. $19.50)

A Beast the Color of Winter: The Mountain Goat Observed by Douglas H. Chadwick describes the mountain goat, one of the least studied big-game animals in North America, from its birth to adulthood, including its social behavior and feeding patterns. Chadwick observed these animals, often under hardship conditions, for seven years. (Sierra Club Bks., 1983. 208 pp. illus. $15.95)   [William G. Jones]

Botany

In November 1983, a botanist at the University of Wisconsin in Madison published a new theory of the origin of corn, a question that plant scientists have debated and puzzled over since the early 1930's. Corn — or maize, as it is often called — is a domesticated crop, a plant that depends on human cultivation for its continued existence. The seeds of corn — the kernels on the corncob — are not released to the soil when they mature but instead remain inside the *husks* (leaves). Thus, corn plants cannot reproduce easily by themselves. Furthermore, there are no wild plants that produce an *ear* (a corncob covered with rows of kernels) like that of corn. So how did corn first come into being?

Botanists have suggested several theories to account for the origin of corn. Most botanists agree that modern corn developed from a closely related plant called teosinte that grows wild in Mexico and Central America.

According to one theory, farmers living in the Tehuacan Valley of south-central Mexico about 7,500 years ago began to crossbreed different strains of teosinte, eventually producing a plant similar to modern corn. But many researchers point out that the hard kernels of the teosinte would probably not have interested ancient farmers in the first place. A plant resembling modern corn must have been in existence for farmers to begin domesticating it. Now, botanist Hugh H. Iltis of the University of Wisconsin has proposed a new theory — catastrophic sexual transmutation — as an explanation for the origin of corn.

On corn plants, male flowers form a tassel at the tip of a single stem. The female flowers, which develop into the ears, are located on short branches. On the teosinte plant, male flowers form tassels at the tip of each branch as well as on the main stem. Female teosinte flowers, which develop into very simple ears with only two rows of kernels, are situated on the same branches as the male flowers but closer to the main stem.

Iltis theorized that, in response to some sort of environmental stress

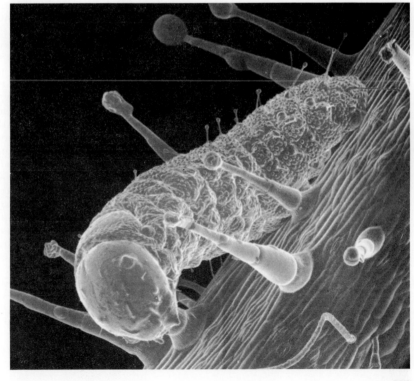

A newly hatched alfalfa weevil larva is trapped in the sticky hairs of a new type of alfalfa, produced by crossing several alfalfa species. The hybrid alfalfa may enable farmers to control the weevil without using insecticides.

Botany

Continued

thousands of years ago, the male tassels of a teosinte plant developed much closer to the main stem than usual and in so doing became female flowers. These sexually changed flowers then developed into a new and larger ear — the first corn.

According to Iltis' theory, this transformation happened within a short period of time, so the change was *catastrophic*. Since the change was from male to female, it was a *sexual transmutation*. Genes that made the change possible had to be present in the teosinte plants so the characteristics could be passed on to future generations of plants. Iltis suggests that ancient Mexican farmers selected the new form of teosinte for cultivation because its tightly clustered kernels made it much more edible. And thus corn became an established crop.

Ancient magnolias. For more than 200 years, botanists have tried to answer a basic question about the origin of plants: Which modern group of plants most resembles the first ancestor of the flowering plants? Some botanists think that plants such as willows or cattails are most similar to the primitive plants. Others believe that the earliest flowers were more like buttercups and magnolias. The fossil record is not much help because the most ancient plant fossils are of leaves or stems and are often impossible to identify.

In June 1983, botanists James W. Walker and Audrey G. Walker of the University of Massachusetts in Amherst and geologist Gilbert J. Brenner of the State University of New York at New Paltz reported that they had found extremely old pollen grains in rocks taken from Israel's Negev Desert. The rocks were from about the middle Cretaceous Period, some 105 to 110 million years ago — about the time that flowering plants first begin to appear in the fossil record.

The researchers identified the grains as members of the Winteraceae family, which is closely related to magnolias and buttercups. Pollen grains in this family are highly distinctive, so the researchers feel certain that they have properly classified the grains. Thus, magnolias and buttercups — or plants very much like them — may have been Earth's first flowers.

Plant growth. Much of the research in botany today is on plant growth processes. In 1983 and 1984, botanists tested two long-held, but unproved, theories of how *auxin*, a substance important to plant growth, moves within plant tissues.

In the 1920's, soon after auxin was discovered, botanists learned that the substance travels from the tip of a plant stem to its base but not in the opposite direction. They suggested, therefore, that plant cells contain a special protein in the membrane on the bottom of the cell that carries auxin through the membrane. The auxin then enters the next cell on its own power, to be once again carried through the bottom of that cell by the auxin-transporting protein.

In June 1983, plant scientists Mark Jacobs and Scott F. Gilbert of Swarthmore College in Pennsylvania announced that they had discovered just such a protein. Using biochemical "tags" that enabled them to track molecules through plants, the researchers found that the protein occurs only in the membrane at the bottom of the cell, just as they had suspected.

Botanists Rüdiger Mertens and Elmer W. Weiler of Ruhr University in West Germany reported on another important question in plant development: why horizontal plant stems bend upward when they grow. Researchers in the 1920's theorized that plant tissues, responding in some way to Earth's gravity, move auxin to the bottom side of a horizontal stem, stimulating cell growth on that side of the stem. The increased growth causes the stem to bend upward.

Mertens and Weiler measured the concentration of auxin and other plant growth substances in the stems, roots, and *coleoptiles* (the first leaf of young grass plants) of several plants. The researchers found more auxin on the bottoms of horizontal coleoptiles in oat plants, but they could find no significant differences in auxin levels between the tops and bottoms of any other plant tissues.

This finding argues strongly against the theory that auxin is responsible for plant bending. Botanists must now create a new theory to account for that phenomenon.   [Frank B. Salisbury]

Chemistry

It now seems more likely that we will find life elsewhere in the universe, according to an August 1983 announcement by chemist Cyril Ponnamperuma, director of the University of Maryland's Laboratory of Chemical Evolution in College Park. He announced that a meteorite discovered in Australia in 1969 contains all four of the substances called bases found in *deoxyribonucleic acid (DNA)* — the material of which genes are made. Genes contain the code that tells cells how to function, and they also transmit hereditary traits. DNA bases had been detected in other meteorites, but this is the first time all four have been found in one meteorite.

The presence of all four bases in a single meteorite indicates that the chemical setting essential for life to develop from nonlife exists in outer space. It also helps confirm the theory of chemical evolution of life on Earth by demonstrating that the bases can form before there is life. To confirm this further, Ponnamperuma created a laboratory environment that was similar to Earth's environment more than 3 billion years ago, when life probably began. This environment included a mix of simple chemicals that are known to have been on Earth at that time. Ponnamperuma found that the four bases formed from this mix.

A ribonucleic acid (RNA) base, uracil, was also found in the meteorite and in the laboratory mixture. RNA helps DNA produce proteins.

The Maryland chemist hopes to find an area on Earth where prelife chemistry exists today and where bases and other important biological chemicals are being formed. One possibility is the hydrothermal vents, or openings, in the ocean floor. Water heated under the floor escapes through these vents, along with gases containing chemicals needed to form bases.

Cyanide before protein. In April 1984, chemists Clifford Matthews and Robert Ludicky of the University of Illinois in Chicago reported evidence for a new theory on how proteins first formed. The traditional theory proposes that amino acids developed from

" . . . That's 'H' as in hexadecyltrimethylammonium . . . "

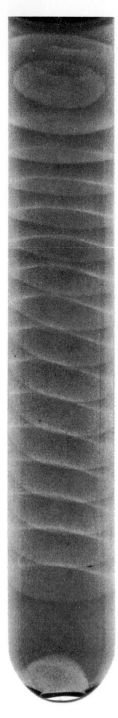

Chemical waves created by certain unstable reactions were photographed for the first time in 1983 by Scottish researchers.

simpler chemicals and that these acids, in turn, assembled themselves into proteins.

However, this course of events is very unlikely from a chemical standpoint. The amino acids form readily enough, but it requires too much energy for them to join together spontaneously to form protein.

The Illinois scientists proposed that amino acids were not the first links in the primitive protein chain. Instead, cyanide molecules, which were very common on the primitive Earth, began the processes by linking themselves together in chains. These chains then reacted chemically with water, transforming their links into chemicals that resembled amino acids and turning the chain into a primitive protein. The natural formation of these chains is very likely chemically, and the Illinois chemists found them in laboratory mixtures that duplicated those in the early environment of Earth.

The analysis of such chains within a mixture has become possible only recently, with advances in a technique called *nuclear magnetic resonance*. This method uses radio waves and powerful magnetic fields to determine the chemical makeup of molecules without removing the molecules from their surroundings. Other techniques that the chemists might have used would have required them to remove the chains from the mixture. But this could change the chains chemically, interfering with the experiment's results.

The chemists suggested that the cyanide process is so likely that the early Earth may have been "knee-deep" in primitive proteins, making the beginning of life almost inevitable on our water-rich world. Furthermore, the scientists claimed that their analysis of the mixture strongly supports the idea that living matter has evolved elsewhere in the universe. Cyanide has been found not only on Earth but also in the atmospheres of Jupiter, Saturn, and Saturn's largest satellite, Titan. If there are other planetary systems in the universe that resemble our solar system chemically, then their planets and satellites probably had large amounts of both cyanide and water in their early environments. Perhaps life developed and then died out on some

of them. In the Special Reports section, see PROBING THE SECRETS OF ATMOSPHERES.

Chemistry by ultrasound. In September 1983, chemist Phillip Boudjouk of North Dakota State University in Fargo announced that certain chemical reactions require less energy than normal when they occur in the presence of ultrasound. Ultrasound is sound that is too high for human beings to hear (in the World Book Supplement section, see ULTRASOUND). Ultrasound waves passing through a liquid create tiny bubbles, many of which collapse and form highly energetic shock waves that break molecules apart.

In the simplest experiments, Boudjouk placed a 100-milliliter (3.38-fluidounce) vessel containing liquid forms of the chemicals to be reacted in a special ultrasound container filled with distilled water. Ultrasound heats liquids rapidly, so — to prevent the chemicals from becoming too hot — Boudjouk added ice to the water for most reactions. Then he turned on a device called a *transducer* that is mounted on the container. The transducer sent ultrasound waves through the water and into the vessel, where they created bubbles in the liquid chemicals. The collapsing bubbles stimulated the reaction by providing the needed energy to the molecules.

In other experiments, Boudjouk also put filings of the metal palladium into the vessel to serve as a *catalyst*, a substance that regulates the rate of a chemical reaction while itself remaining almost unchanged. If the reaction had taken place without ultrasound, unwanted chemicals would have built up on the filings, destroying their effectiveness. But the ultrasound waves vibrated the filings constantly, preventing excessive buildup.

Boudjouk said that ultrasound chemistry eliminates the need for high pressures and temperatures, while providing more energy-efficient reactions and increased yields because fewer undesirable by-products are formed. Many reactions that Boudjouk aided by ultrasound are important in the production of drugs, petrochemicals, dyes, and molecules that could become useful as insulation or replacements for parts of the human body.

 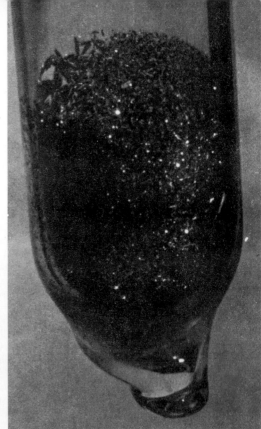

Chemistry

Continued

Germanium selenide gas in a space shuttle experiment cooled to form crystals, *above left,* that are up to 100 times as large as crystals grown on Earth, *above right.* The chemist who designed the experiment, Heribert Wiedemeier of Rensselaer Polytechnic Institute, suspects that the space crystals are bigger because the lack of gravity enabled them to grow as they floated in the test tube.

New shark repellent. Chemists at the University of Miami in Florida have discovered that sharks hate sodium dodecyl sulfate (SDS), a common ingredient of shampoos and dishwashing liquids. Samuel Gruber and Eliahu Zlotkin reported in September 1983 that lemon sharks, a species known to attack people, rejected food treated with the detergent. In another test, very small amounts of SDS distressed the sharks so much that they leaped out of the water.

The chemists had analyzed a natural shark repellent produced by the Red Sea flatfish and found that the substance had detergentlike properties. This discovery led them to test 15 other detergentlike compounds as shark repellents. SDS performed better in tests than Shark Chaser — the repellent used by the United States Navy.

SDS is inexpensive, highly stable, and easy to work with chemically. SDS alone cannot make swimming in shark-infested waters safe, but it provides a good starting point for developing shark repellents that will be safe for human beings and effective against several species of sharks. The scientists believe a product could be on the market within three years.

Method for purer drugs. Chemists at Purdue University in West Lafayette, Ind., announced a major breakthrough in synthetic chemistry in March 1984. Herbert C. Brown, co-winner of the 1979 Nobel Prize for chemistry, and Bakthan Singaram developed a way to *synthesize*, or manufacture, chemicals that are almost 100 per cent *optically pure*. This kind of purity had previously been almost impossible to obtain.

An optically pure chemical is made up of molecules that have one of two "mirror-image" forms. These forms differ from each other as your right hand differs from your left.

Many biologically active chemicals, including 12 of the 20 most prescribed drugs, can exist in both forms. It is especially desirable to get only one form of the mirror-image molecules in a drug, because the other form may be

Chemistry

Continued

less effective and may even cause undesirable side effects.

A good example is propranolol, a drug that is commonly prescribed for high blood pressure and *angina* (chest pain). Propranolol is sold as a mixture of its two optical forms, but the right-handed form is 100 times as potent as the left-handed form.

Brown and Singaram's method could allow commercial manufacture of optically pure propranolol and other drugs for the first time, making them safer and less expensive. The new method is convenient, and an important ingredient, (alpha)-pinene, is already made commercially. The method might also be used to make agricultural chemicals, industrial chemicals, and food additives.

Pickled violins. In April 1984, biochemist Joseph Nagyvary of Texas A&M University in College Station presented the results of 20 years of research into the methods of master violin makers of the Renaissance, a period of history that began about A.D. 1300 and lasted about 300 years. As part of Nagyvary's presentation, two violins, a viola, and a cello made according to what he had learned of the old methods competed against concert-quality instruments and were given high praise by a panel of experts. The instruments were played by the Landolfi String Quartet in St. Louis, Mo., at the 187th national meeting of the American Chemical Society.

Using a variety of techniques, including examination of wood with an electron microscope, Nagyvary has spent years trying to solve the mystery of how such masters as Italian violin maker Antonio Stradivari produced stringed instruments of such stunning quality that some sell today for as much as $1 million. One of Nagyvary's discoveries was that the wood used to make the instruments had been *pickled*, or soaked in mineral solutions. Also, the varnish was made with chitin, the hard outer covering of beetles, crickets, and other creatures, creating a much stiffer material than today's ordinary varnishes.

Breakthrough for polymers. Chemists at E. I. du Pont de Nemours & Company in Wilmington, Del., announced in August 1983 what may be the biggest advance in polymer science in 30 years. Polymers are long chains of small molecules called *monomers*. The familiar plastic polyethylene is a polymer made up of thousands of ethylene molecules linked together. Biological molecules such as proteins, DNA, and RNA are also polymers.

The Du Pont chemists—Owen Webster, Walter R. Hertler, Dotsevi Y. Sogah, William B. Farnham, and T. V. RajanBabu—developed a method that provides outstanding control of polymer formation. The method, called *group transfer polymerization* (GTP), enables chemists to control precisely the size and structure of polymers. GTP also enables them to change the type of monomer being linked to the end of the chain during the process of polymer formation. This kind of switch is not possible with previous methods of polymerization, except under conditions of extreme cold.

In the new process, a chemical called the *initiator* is always placed at the growing end of the chain. The initiator keeps the chain primed for new additions only at this end.

If the initiator were not there, many monomers would join links in the middle or at the wrong end of the chain; and some chains would bend back on themselves, with one end sticking to a middle link. The result would be polymers of irregular shapes and sizes. Furthermore, when a chemist changed monomers, the new monomer would not necessarily link up at the proper end of the chain.

A key to keeping the initiator at the end of the chain is a catalyst, a charged molecule called bifluoride ion, which was discovered by accident. When the chemists were testing catalysts, they accidentally exposed one of them, fluoride ion, to humid air, resulting in the formation of the bifluoride ions.

The chemists tested it and, to their surprise, it performed beautifully. GTP will be used in the manufacture of acrylic paints, particularly those used on automobiles. Acrylic paints made by GTP require less heat to harden, and need less solvent, which is composed of organic chemicals that can evaporate and pollute the air. So the new paints are better for the environment.   [Peter J. Andrews]

Notches in a human hair were etched by pulses of ultraviolet light from a finely tuned laser. The light broke chemical bonds that held molecules in the hair together.

Deaths of Scientists

Notable scientists and engineers who died between June 1, 1983, and June 1, 1984, are listed below. An asterisk (*) indicates that a biography appears in THE WORLD BOOK ENCYCLOPEDIA.

Abell, George (1927-Oct. 7, 1983), astronomer whose many discoveries included the Abell galaxy. His books include the *Abell Catalogue of Clusters*.

Adams, Sir John Bertram (1920-March 3, 1984), British particle physicist who headed the European Organization for Nuclear Research (CERN) in Geneva, Switzerland, from 1976 to 1981. He was the architect of CERN's giant atom smasher.

Antonov, Oleg K. (1906-April 4, 1984), Russian aircraft designer whose work included the An-72, a military transport plane, and the An-2, a light biplane used for agricultural spraying and also for high-altitude weather research.

Astin, Allen V. (1904-Feb. 4, 1984), physicist who directed the National Bureau of Standards from 1952 to 1969. During World War II, he helped develop the proximity fuse, which used radar to detonate shells in midair, thus showering entrenched troops with shrapnel.

Barghoorn, Elso S. (1915-Jan. 28, 1984), geologist whose research on fossils pushed back estimates of the origin of life on Earth to more than 3.4 million years ago.

Bloch, Felix (1905-Sept. 10, 1983), Swiss-born physicist, co-winner of the 1952 Nobel Prize for physics for his work on nuclear magnetic resonance (NMR), a technique for analyzing chemicals and for making images of the human body that uses strong magnetic fields combined with radio waves. NMR has recently become a powerful diagnostic tool in medicine. Bloch taught at Stanford University in California from 1934 to 1971.

Bok, Bart J. (1906-Aug. 5, 1983), Dutch-born astronomer who was considered a leading authority on our galaxy, the Milky Way.

Cole, Kenneth S. (1900-April 18, 1984), physiologist and biophysicist noted for his research on the measurement of the action potential of the nerve impulse. He was one of the first scientists to apply the concepts of physics to the study of living cells.

Crohn, Burrill B. (1884-July 29, 1983), gastroenterologist noted for his pioneering work in diagnosing and treating *ileitis* — the intestinal inflammation that is also known as Crohn's disease.

Debus, Kurt H. (1908-Oct. 10, 1983), German-born electrical engineer who helped develop the V-2 rocket used against Great Britain during World War II. He served as director of the United States National Aeronautics and Space Administration's John F. Kennedy Space Center from 1963 to 1974, and during that time he supervised the launch of the first U.S. Earth-orbiting satellite and the first U.S. moon landing.

Dorf, Erling (1905-April 16, 1984), geologist, known for his research on primitive plants in Wyoming, Maine, and Newfoundland, Canada, and for his work on the petrified forests of the Yellowstone Park region. He taught at Princeton University in Princeton, N.J., from 1926 to 1974.

Dunham, Theodore, Jr. (1897-April 9, 1984), astronomer who discovered in 1932 that the atmosphere of Venus contains a large portion of carbon dioxide. He developed ways of using invisible light to study the chemical makeup of cells and was also noted for his research on interstellar cosmic rays and for his work on the development of better telescopes.

Forbush, Scott E. (1904-April 4, 1984), geophysicist who discovered the *Forbush effect* — a decrease in cosmic rays bombarding Earth. This was attributed to magnetic fields within clouds of gas ejected by the solar flare.

*Fuller, R. Buckminster (1895-July 1, 1983), engineer and designer whose work included such innovative structures as the lightweight, prefabricated geodesic dome.

Green, John (1905-March 27, 1984), Canadian aeronautical engineer, head of the Canadian Aeronautics and Space Institute from 1972 to 1978.

Harish-Chandra (1923?-Oct. 16, 1983), Indian-born physicist and mathematician who proposed a theory used in quantum mechanics that is important in studying the motions of particles and waves.

Kahn, Herman (1922-July 7, 1983), physicist and mathematician who in

Sir John Bertram Adams

Felix Bloch

Bart J. Bok

Deaths of Scientists

Continued

R. Buckminster Fuller

Pyotr Kapitsa

Alfred Kastler

1961 founded the Hudson Institute, a center for research and national security. His books include *On Thermonuclear War*, in which he took the controversial position that nuclear war can be limited.

*Kapitsa, Pyotr (1894-April 8, 1984), Russian physicist, co-winner of the 1978 Nobel Prize for physics for his work in the transformation of gases, such as oxygen and helium, into extremely low-temperature liquids. He headed the Soviet *Sputnik* space satellite program in the 1950's and was also considered one of the world's experts in the fields of magnetism, microwaves, and electronics.

Kaplan, Henry S. (1918-Feb. 4, 1984), radiologist whose research led to the successful treatment of Hodgkin's disease, a previously incurable form of cancer. He was co-inventor of the first medical linear accelerator in the United States.

Kastler, Alfred (1902-Jan. 7, 1984), French physicist who won the 1966 Nobel Prize for physics for his work on optical resonance techniques, which led to the development of the laser.

Kunkel, Henry G. (1916-Dec. 4, 1983), physician, renowned for his work in the study of diseases linked to defects in the immune system.

Little, Elbert P. (1912-July 19, 1984), physicist and teacher who helped devise a program to modernize the teaching of physics in secondary schools.

Merrill, John P. (1917-April 4, 1984), physician who led the medical team that performed the first kidney transplant in 1954. He also helped develop the artificial kidney.

Monroe, Marion (1898-June 25, 1983), psychologist who coauthored the Dick and Jane schoolbooks that instructed millions of Americans to "see Spot run."

Nachmansohn, David (1899-Nov. 2, 1983), Russian-born biochemist who identified and analyzed the chemicals involved in the complex process by which nerve impulses are generated along nerve and muscle fibers. His studies added greatly to knowledge of the human nervous system, particularly in relation to Parkinson's disease.

Odishaw, Hugh (1916-March 4, 1984), executive director of the U.S.

National Committee for the International Geophysical Year from 1953 to 1963.

Philips, Frederick S. (1916-March 24, 1984), biologist, one of the first research scientists to study the effects of poisonous gases in the treatment of malignant tumors and other cancers.

Roos, Sven E. (1908-May 15, 1984), Swedish-born oceanographer who conducted tests of the floor of the Pacific Ocean on Admiral Richard E. Byrd's expedition to Antarctica in 1933.

Rowe, Wallace P. (1926-July 4, 1983), physician and virologist whose research provided insights into how retroviruses use the cells they infect to grow and reproduce and how such viruses could produce cancer.

Sachar, Edward J. (1933-March 25, 1984), psychiatrist, an authority on the roles of brain chemicals in mental illness. He was noted for his research on the relationship between psychological processes and hormones.

Simons, Joseph H. (1897-Dec. 30, 1983), chemist who discovered one of the first practical ways to synthesize fluorocarbons.

Tietze, Christopher (1908-April 4, 1984), Austrian-born physician and demographer, an authority on the hazards of contraceptives and pregnancy. He was a critic of attempts to limit access to abortion.

Ulam, Stanislaw M. (1909-May 13, 1984), Polish-born mathematician who developed a method using computer-generated random numbers to predict the probable outcome of atomic chain reactions. His work was crucial in the development of the hydrogen bomb.

Upton, John (1899-Sept. 16, 1983), gynecologist who designed the portable blood transfusion unit used in World War II to treat thousands of Allied wounded.

Verbit, Lawrence P. (1935-Dec. 31, 1983), professor of chemistry at the State University of New York at Binghamton and a contributor to THE WORLD BOOK ENCYCLOPEDIA, THE WORLD BOOK YEAR BOOK, and SCIENCE YEAR.

Whitehead, Elizabeth A. (1928-Aug. 3, 1983), archaeologist who was considered a leading authority on classical, North American, and Chinese archaeology. [Irene B. Keller]

Drugs

Advances in the pharmaceutical, or drug, industry during 1983 and 1984 promised to change the meaning of the phrase *taking your medicine* — long associated with something necessary but unpleasant. The traditional bad-tasting pills and liquids or painful shots not only produce discomfort but also cause other and perhaps more important problems. Pills, liquids, or shots at first introduce a high level of medication into the body, followed by a steady decline until the next dose. Sudden high doses of drugs tend to produce side effects, which can be dangerous or unpleasant; and at low levels, a drug may not be effective.

These problems have led to attempts to develop new drug-delivery systems — ways that allow patients to take their medicine less frequently, and yet get steadier doses of the drug.

Rx: through the skin. One of the new drug-delivery systems is the *transdermal technique*. In this method, an adhesive patch worn on the body delivers small, steady doses of a drug through the skin. In January 1984, physician Mi-

chael A. Weber and co-workers at the University of California at Irvine reported success in treating *hypertension* (high blood pressure) with the drug *clonidine* administered through an adhesive patch applied to the skin. Ordinarily, the patient would have to take clonidine pills two or three times a day. Many patients taking these pills complain of side effects, including drowsiness, fatigue, a dry mouth, and dizziness. In addition, if a patient stops taking the clonidine pills or forgets several doses, the person's blood pressure will rise rapidly, often to levels higher than before treatment. Although this rise, called *rebound hypertension*, is temporary, it can be dangerous for the patient.

Weber and his colleagues treated 20 patients with a patch system that slowly released clonidine into the body through the skin. The researchers found that a single patch would give good control of blood pressure for seven days. They also noted that fewer patients complained of side effects, and none chose to stop the treatment.

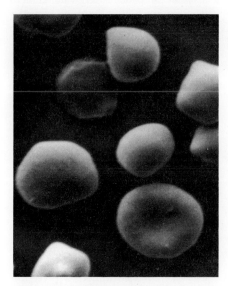

Drug-Carrying Red Cells
Red blood cells, *above,* may be used as time-release capsules. The cells are made to swell, *right,* so drugs can enter through pores in the cell wall. When the drug-loaded cells return to normal size, they are injected into the bloodstream.

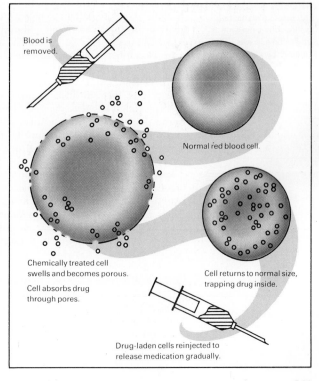

Blood is removed.

Normal red blood cell.

Chemically treated cell swells and becomes porous.

Cell absorbs drug through pores.

Cell returns to normal size, trapping drug inside.

Drug-laden cells reinjected to release medication gradually.

Drugs

Continued

An electronic device in the cap of a medicine bottle shows the time when the cap was last removed and replaced. This tells patients when they last took the drug.

Transdermal systems on the market in 1984 included those for the drugs *scopolamine* — for motion sickness — and *nitroglycerine* — for *angina pectoris*, a pain caused by the heart muscle receiving too little blood. Future transdermal systems may include birth control pills and anticancer drugs.

Time-release capsules. Another approach to drug delivery has been the development of pills or tablets that do not release all the medication they hold at once, but instead release it over a period of up to 24 hours. This has long been a popular technique for cold-symptom medications.

Pharmaceutical companies have developed a number of variations on the time-release technique. In April 1983, *propranolol* — a drug used for the treatment of hypertension, angina pectoris, migraine headaches, and irregular heartbeat — became available in a slow-release capsule. The new propranolol capsule allows one pill a day to replace the usual regimen of two to four pills daily.

In February 1984, the United States Food and Drug Administration (FDA) approved two new preparations of *theophylline* — a drug for the treatment of asthma — for marketing. Both preparations allow the patient to take a single daily dose instead of one pill every 8 to 12 hours.

In December 1983, researchers at Georgetown University Medical Center in Washington, D.C., reported on a slow-release form of an angina pectoris drug called *isosorbide dinitrate*. They found that the time-release form benefited patients for eight hours. Ordinarily, isosorbide dinitrate is effective for four to six hours.

New ulcer drug. In addition to finding new ways to give old drugs, researchers found some important new drugs during 1983 and 1984. *Ranitidine*, which became available in July 1983, is the second drug in a group called *histamine-2 receptor blockers*. These drugs inhibit the secretion of stomach acid. As a result, they have been used for the treatment of both duodenal ulcers, which develop in the upper small intestine, and gastric ulcers, which form in the stomach.

The first drug in this group, *cimetidine*, was marketed in 1977 under the trade name Tagamet and has become the largest-selling prescription drug in the United States. Cimetidine can cause side effects, however. These include confusion, particularly in older patients, and in male patients increased breast size and a drop in sperm count. Ranitidine, which is sold under the trade name Zantac, appears to have fewer side effects than cimetidine. In addition, some patients whose acid secretion does not respond to cimetidine get results with ranitidine.

Transplant wonder drug. At the First International Congress on Cyclosporine held in Houston in May 1983, researchers reported encouraging results with this drug, which suppresses the part of the immune system that normally attacks foreign tissue and causes rejection of a transplanted organ. Unlike other immunosuppressive drugs, cyclosporine does not shut down parts of the immune system that enable the body to resist infection.

In October 1983, *The New England Journal of Medicine* reported the results of a five-year Canadian study that compared cyclosporine to a standard immunosuppressive drug called *azathioprine* in patients receiving kidney transplants. Both groups of patients also received *prednisone*, one of a group of drugs called *steroids* used to reduce inflammation and suppress immunity. The Canadian researchers reported a one-year transplant success rate of 80.4 per cent in patients receiving cyclosporine, compared with only 64 per cent in patients who received azathioprine. Patient survival at one year was also better in the cyclosporine group — 96.6 per cent versus 86.4 per cent.

In November 1983, the FDA approved cyclosporine for human use. However, certain problems with the drug remain, including a tendency for it to cause kidney damage. See also INTERNAL MEDICINE.

New painkiller. In May 1984, the FDA approved a pain reliever called *ibuprofen* for sale without a prescription. Until then, the only nonprescription painkillers sold in the United States were aspirin and *acetaminophen,* marketed under such names as Tylenol and Datril. The new drug was to be sold under the brand names Advil and Nuprin.   [B. Robert Meyer]

Earth Sciences

Geology. The discovery of the oldest known grains of rock formed on Earth, reported in May 1983, has helped earth scientists fill in some gaps in the early history of Earth. The grains, which are from 4.1 billion to 4.2 billion years old, seem to indicate that Earth's continental crust began to form much earlier than scientists had thought.

Although earth scientists agree that Earth formed 4.6 billion years ago, the previous oldest-known rocks, found in Greenland, appeared to be only 3.8 billion years old. Scientists believed that all earlier rocks had been destroyed by erosion and by large meteorites that bombarded Earth until about 3.9 billion years ago. The oldest grains are bits of zircon. They were discovered in sandstones from Mount Narryer in Western Australia by geochemist William Compston and co-workers at the Australian National University in Canberra. The zircons may have survived because they are highly resistant to erosion.

The Australian scientists dated the zircon grains using *ion probe microanalysis* — a new technique that can determine the composition of a single grain of a mineral. The scientists determined the amounts of two isotopes, or forms, of uranium and two isotopes of lead in the grains. The uranium isotopes decay to lead at a slow but steady rate over time. Therefore, by measuring the relative amounts of the isotopes, the scientists determined the age of the zircon. The great age of the grains seems to indicate that by about 4.2 billion years ago, when Earth was only 400 million years old, it had cooled enough to form rocks.

Mantle and crust. Scientists seeking to understand the separation of Earth into the crust and the mantle should use the moon as a model, according to a report published in June 1983 by petrologist Ann Hofmeister of the California Institute of Technology (Caltech) in Pasadena. The crust, Earth's outer layer of solid rock, sits atop the mantle, a region of hot, semi-molten rock.

Scientists have long believed that

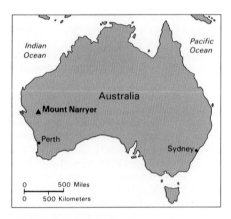

Tiny grains of zircon found at Mount Narryer in Western Australia and dated to about 4.2 billion years old are the oldest rocks ever found.

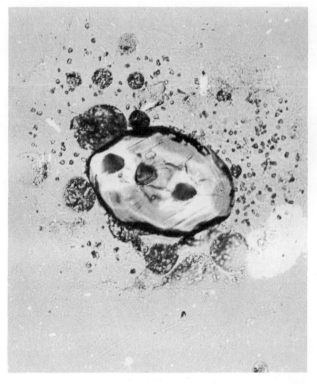

Earth Sciences

Continued

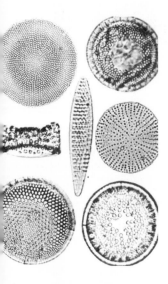

Tiny marine fossils, 3 million years old, were found high in the Transantarctic Mountains of Antarctica. They indicate that, contrary to traditional belief, the Antarctic icecap has not remained stable since it first formed but has advanced and retreated several times.

shortly after Earth formed about 4.6 billion years ago, it was covered by a fiery ocean of *magma* (molten rock). However, they have no direct evidence that such an ocean existed because no rocks from that early period survive. However, rocks of that age have been found on the highlands of the moon. These rocks consist chiefly of plagioclase, a light rock also plentiful in Earth's crust. The plagioclase crystals formed from magma as the moon began to cool. Because the plagioclase crystals were lighter than the magma, they floated on the surface of the early moon's magma ocean and eventually formed a crust.

Hofmeister theorizes that the same thing happened on Earth. She suggests that two types of crystals formed from Earth's magma — plagioclase and olivine, which is a denser rock. Earth's mantle consists chiefly of olivine. Hofmeister believes that the plagioclase crystals formed an early crust, while the denser olivine crystals sank and accumulated at the bottom of the magma ocean, forming the bulk of Earth's mantle.

Ancient mantle. In July 1983, French scientists reported evidence supporting the theory that Earth's mantle consists of two separate layers of hot rock that do not generally mix. Claude J. Allègre and co-workers from the Institute de Globe of the University of Paris based their report on an analysis of isotopes of helium and xenon in basalts from Hawaii and several other volcanic islands. Basalt, the most common type of volcanic rock, results from melting of Earth's mantle.

The French scientists discovered that the island basalts contained unusually large amounts of helium 3, a very light gas present when Earth began to form. No helium 3 has formed on Earth since then. Basalts normally contain only a small proportion of helium 3 because most of the gas has escaped into the atmosphere.

Allègre theorized that the helium 3 was trapped within Earth when it formed from a cloud of dust and gas about 4.6 billion years ago. He argued that the presence of large proportions of the gas in the island basalts indicates that the helium 3 remained trapped in a separate deeper layer of the mantle.

Otherwise, it would have escaped into the atmosphere along with most of the helium 3 in the upper mantle. Allègre believed the island basalts formed when rock containing helium 3 in the deep mantle layer rose into the upper mantle layer and melted.

The French scientists also reported that the high proportion of another isotope, xenon 129, in the island basalts provides evidence of when the two mantle layers separated. Basalts normally contain only a small proportion of xenon 129. Some xenon 129 was trapped within Earth when it formed. Some, however, resulted from the decay of iodine 129, an isotope that — like helium 3 — was present when Earth formed but which has not formed since then. Allègre argued that because iodine 129 decays rapidly, all the xenon 129 in the island basalts must have formed within the first 100 million years of Earth's history. Therefore, he concluded, the mantle must have separated into two layers during that period.

More extinction evidence. Research reported in 1983 and 1984 provided additional support for the theory that the iridium and other heavy metals present in 65-million-year-old rocks came from a meteorite. These metals are rare on Earth but plentiful in extraterrestrial objects. Some scientists have theorized that the bombardment of Earth by comets or asteroids 65 million years ago, at the end of the Cretaceous Period and the beginning of the Tertiary Period, caused the extinction of many plant and animal species, including dinosaurs.

In November 1983, geochemist Karl K. Turekian and geologist Jean-Marc Luck of Yale University in New Haven, Conn., reported on their analysis of rock samples from the Cretaceous-Tertiary boundary taken from sites in Denmark and Colorado. They found that the ratio of different isotopes of the heavy metal osmium in the samples did not match the ratios of osmium isotopes in most rocks found on Earth. However, the ratio is the same as that found in meteorites, particularly iron meteorites. Although dust from some volcanic eruptions contains high levels of osmium, Turekian and Luck argued that a volcanic eruption is

A geologist watches in March 1984 as Mauna Loa, the world's largest active volcano, on the island of Hawaii, erupts for the first time since 1975.

Earth Sciences

Continued

an unlikely source for the metal. They contended that the amount of material spewed from a volcano would have to be impossibly large for so much osmium to accumulate in such a short time.

In March 1984, geologist Walter S. Alvarez of the University of California, Berkeley, and five co-workers reported on their detailed examination of the fossil record of mass extinctions at the end of the Cretaceous Period. The scientists found that beginning about 10 million years before the end of the Cretaceous Period, the total number of plant and animal species began to decline. However, the decline occurred gradually. The scientists contended that these extinctions could not have been caused by the impact of an extraterrestrial body because they were not abrupt and occurred before the layer of iridium was laid down, according to the record in the rock.

However, the fossil record of many other species ends abruptly at the Cretaceous-Tertiary boundary, where the corresponding rock layer contains

high levels of iridium. Alvarez concluded that this evidence supports the theory that the extinctions were caused by a meteorite impact.

Seismic gaps. In October 1983, geophysicists Allan Lindh and William Ellsworth from the U.S. Geological Survey in Menlo Park, Calif., predicted that there is a 75 per cent chance for a moderately severe earthquake in the Los Angeles area in the next 20 years. The researchers based their conclusion on an analysis of sediments from an area near Los Angeles by seismologist Kerry E. Sieh of Caltech.

Seismologists operate on the premise that large earthquakes occur periodically along 160-kilometer (100-mile) lengths of seismically active *faults* — cracks in Earth where blocks of the crust are moving past one another. The earthquake releases stress that has developed along the fault since the previous severe earthquake. Typically, such earthquakes occur about every 100 years. Thus, sections of an active fault that have not slipped for a long time, called *seismic gaps*, are likely locations for future severe earthquakes.

Sieh examined 1,500-year-old sediments from a seismic gap near Los Angeles. He found 10 *offsets* — shifts in the sediment indicating that an earthquake with a magnitude of 8 or above on the Richter scale had taken place. The earthquakes had occurred about every 150 years. Thus, Lindh and Ellsworth contend that the next major earthquake should occur by 2007, since the last earthquake of that magnitude occurred there in 1857.

Antarctic icecap. An analysis of *forminifera fossils* — fossils of tiny, shelled marine organisms — from ancient sediments on the ocean floor has challenged the belief that the Antarctic icecap formed only 15 million years ago. Kenneth Miller and Richard Fairbanks of Columbia University's Lamont-Doherty Geological Observatory in Palisades, N.Y., in February 1984, and other researchers working independently, have concluded that an icecap had formed by 30 million years ago.

Fossils of forminifera and other marine organisms reflect changes in the chemical composition of the ocean. For that reason, scientists study these fossils for clues about ancient ocean environments.

For example, scientists studying forminifera have noted that there were periodic shifts in the ratio of the isotope oxygen 18 to the isotope oxygen 16 in ancient seawater. The amount of oxygen 18 in seawater increases when ice forms or when water temperatures drop. However, most scientists believed that any oxygen 18 increases before 15 million years ago resulted solely from drops in ocean water temperatures.

Miller and Fairbanks analyzed forminifera fossils from 30-million-year-old ocean sediments. The two scientists contend that colder water temperatures cannot completely account for the increase in oxygen 18 levels. They argue that such increases could not have occurred unless water temperatures had dropped to an impossibly low $-2°C$ (28°F.). Instead, the researchers suggest that the Antarctic icecap had begun to form 30 million years ago. They believe it was then one-third to one-half the size of the present icecap. [Robert W. Kay]

Paleontology. Theories about large-scale extinctions — times in Earth's history when many species of plants and animals suddenly died out — continued to dominate paleontology during 1983 and 1984. Perhaps the most exciting new theory about mass extinctions was reported in August 1983 by J. John Sepkoski, Jr., and David M. Raup of the University of Chicago. The two paleontologists discovered an apparent pattern of mass extinctions occurring about every 26 million years during the past 245 million years. Their analysis of the fossil record of marine animals revealed that during that time there were five major and five minor periods of extinction. The major periods occurred at about 245 million, 218 million, 65 million, 40 million, and 14 million years ago.

A number of theories were proposed to explain this 26-million-year cycle. One hypothesis, proposed in March 1984 by astronomer Richard A. Muller of the Lawrence Berkeley Laboratory in California, suggests that the sun has an as-yet-undiscovered companion star, whose elongated orbit brings it close to the solar system about every 26 million years. During its closest approach, the star disturbs the cloud of comets surrounding the solar system, causing a shower of comets to hurtle toward Earth. However, many scientists doubt this explanation because they believe a star with an orbit so highly elongated that it has not been seen from Earth would soon be pulled off course by other stars and away from the sun.

Another hypothesis links the extinctions to the up-and-down movement of the solar system as it orbits the center of the Milky Way Galaxy. About every 33 million years, the solar system passes through the central plane of our disk-shaped Galaxy. Astronomers Michael R. Rampino and Richard B. Stothers of the Goddard Institute for Space Studies in New York City suggest that when the solar system passes through the plane of the Galaxy, it encounters clouds of cosmic dust. The gravitational pull of the clouds disrupts the orbits of comets, triggering comet or asteroid showers on Earth.

Mammoth ending. One extinction that was almost certainly not related to

Earth Sciences

Continued

A previously unknown, 200-million-year-old reptile called *Postosuchus*, whose fossil bones were found in November 1983 in Texas, may have been the ancestor of *Tyrannosaurus rex*. The discovery of adult and juvenile fossils together has led scientists to conclude that the ferocious reptile, which measured 4 meters (13 feet) from head to tail and weighed 270 kilograms (600 pounds), hunted in packs and cared for its young.

extraterrestrial events was the disappearance of many species of large mammals, such as mammoths, mastodons, and woolly rhinos, about 10,000 years ago, at the end of the last ice age.

In August 1983, Russell B. Graham of the Illinois State Museum in Springfield suggested that the extinctions were related to the appearance of a warmer climate and the changes this caused in the growth patterns of vegetation. Some plant species died out in certain areas, and there was a general shift from forest vegetation adapted to a cold climate to grassland vegetation typical of milder climates. Thus, the extinction of the large mammals may have occurred because they lost their traditional food sources.

Other researchers believe that hunting by human beings led to the demise of these big animals. Evidence for this theory — cuts and scrapes made by tools on the fossil bones of mastodons — was presented in March 1984 by paleontologist Daniel C. Fisher of the University of Michigan in Ann Arbor. Fisher theorized that prehistoric

people butchered mammoths and mastodons.

But did human beings kill these animals or simply butcher animals that were already dead? Fisher compared mastodon bones without butcher marks with the bones of butchered animals. By counting growth rings in the tusks — similar to the growth rings in trees — he established that most of the mastodons whose bones did not have butcher marks had died in late winter or early spring. In contrast, all the animals whose bones had butcher marks had died in the early autumn. Fisher suggests that sick animals are more likely to die in the late winter or early spring, after the long period of cold. However, animals are less likely to die of natural causes in early fall when food is plentiful. Therefore, Fisher concluded that the butchered animals were killed by ancient hunters and that the hunting took place in the fall of the year as they gathered food for the winter.

A surprising nursery. In December 1983, a team of scientists headed by

Sepkoski and paleontologist Peter Sheehan of the Milwaukee Public Museum challenged traditional thinking on the evolution of new marine species. Because offshore areas have many diverse animal species and nearshore areas have few species, scientists believed that new species were more likely to arise in offshore environments. However, the new research seems to indicate that three large groups of marine organisms appeared in shallow-water areas first.

The first group, which appeared about 560 million years ago, was dominated by *trilobites* — extinct, segmented marine animals distantly related to horseshoe crabs. The second group was characterized by such animals as *brachiopods* (lamp shells), *bryozoans* (sea moss animals), and *crinoids* (sea lilies). The third and most recently evolved group was dominated by *mollusks* and *crustaceans* (forms of shellfish). Each of these animal groups apparently arose in shallow nearshore areas, were eventually displaced by the next group, and then migrated farther out to sea. This pattern of evolving nearshore then migrating to offshore areas flies in the face of traditional evolutionary theory, which holds that evolution is likely to occur in offshore environments.

More Ediacarians. The discovery in northwestern Canada of fossils representing some of the earliest known animals was reported in July 1983 by geologists H. J. Hofmann of the University of Montreal and Guy M. Narbonne of Queens University in Kingston and W. H. Fritz of the Geological Survey of Canada in Ottawa, both in Ontario. The fossils, which were found in rocks more than 570 million years old, are very similar to the fossils of animals with soft bodies first found in the Ediacara Hills of Australia in 1947. The Ediacarian animals, which first appeared about 670 million years ago, are the oldest known multicelled organisms.

The discovery of similar fossils in Canada supports an idea put forth in 1982 by geologist Preston Cloud, Jr., of the University of California at Santa Barbara and Martin F. Glaessner of the University of Adelaide in Australia. Cloud and Glaessner suggested that such fossils represent a unique, worldwide group of animals and so the period during which they existed — from about 670 million until about 560 million years ago — should be classified as a new geological period.

Far from being the ancestors of modern forms of life, the Ediacarian animals may represent an evolutionary experiment that failed, according to paleontologist Adolf Seilacher of the University of Tübingen in West Germany. In the past, paleontologists classified the Ediacarian animals as members of one of a number of groups of modern organisms including jellyfish, soft corals, and worms. Seilacher, however, has reinterpreted the Ediacarian fossils as the remains of a group of flattened, soft-bodied organisms quite different from later life forms. He asserts that unlike modern organisms, which have a small external body surface relative to their total body volume, the Ediacarian animals had a large external surface area relative to low body volume.

If Seilacher is correct, the Ediacarian animals were not the ancestors of later organisms but an early "experiment" in life forms that failed, and their disappearance may represent the first mass extinction. The Ediacarian forms were replaced about 560 million years ago by the Cambrian animals, including trilobites and a wide variety of other marine *invertebrates* (animals without backbones).

Alien land. Trilobite fossils have provided critical evidence that eastern portions of North and South Carolina are parts of an ancient continent that collided with North America about 250 million years ago. In August 1983, geologists at the University of South Carolina in Columbia and the Geological Society of America in Boulder, Colo., reported the discovery of many trilobites in 540-million-year-old slate in South Carolina. These trilobites belong to groups that have not been found anywhere else in North America except eastern Massachusetts and eastern Newfoundland. They have also been found in southern Great Britain. The scientists theorized that these areas and the eastern Carolinas may have been parts of two microcontinents known as the Avalon and Carolinas terranes. [Carlton E. Brett]

The aurora borealis, or Northern Lights, sweeps across the sky in a broad band in this composite picture of North America taken by satellite. Coastal regions of the United States are also apparent.

Earth Sciences

Continued

Meteorology. In 1983 and 1984, scientists continued to learn about large-scale atmospheric patterns that affect the weather worldwide. A warm ocean current called El Niño was the focus of much research. Ordinarily, El Niño appears off the Peruvian coast around Christmas. However, in 1982, El Niño originated in the Pacific Ocean in May, causing severe weather disturbances in 1982 and 1983 around the world.

Studies of the El Niño phenomenon helped confirm the theory that a close relationship exists between weather events in the tropics and events in those parts of the world north and south of the equator known as the midlatitudes.

In December 1983, meteorologists Eugene M. Rasmusson of the National Weather Service in Washington, D.C., and John M. Wallace of the University of Washington in Seattle confirmed that El Niño is closely related to a phenomenon known as the *Southern Oscillation*. This is a major seesawlike shift of air pressure between Indonesia and the eastern South Pacific Ocean. It is

the only major change in the atmosphere that occurs consistently, except for the seasons themselves. The seesaw shift means that when there is relatively high pressure over Indonesia, for example, there tends to be relatively low pressure in the South Pacific. This makes the easterly trade winds in the tropics weaker than normal. Without the winds pushing, there is less movement of warm surface waters. As a result, cold water does not rise to the surface as it normally would near the equator, and unusually warm water develops. Once formed, these warm water currents have a long lifetime. The warmer water may move either eastward or westward depending on complex conditions in the ocean and the atmosphere.

Long-range effects. When the sea-surface temperature pattern shifts, as it did in 1982 and 1983, it alters the large-scale airflow pattern over Europe and North America. A report in July 1983 by atmospheric scientist Jagadish Shukla, then with the National Aeronautics and Space Administration's

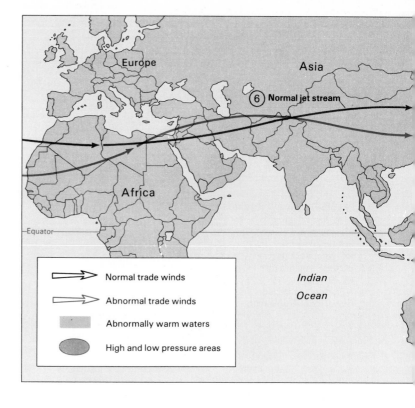

Scientists studying the 1982 El Niño, an unusually warm ocean current, are learning how conditions in the Pacific influence weather around the world. During El Niño, low pressure air over Indonesia shifted eastward (1), allowing high pressure air to move into Australia (2) and causing normal easterly trade winds (3) to fade. Westerly trade winds (4) sped the flow of the Equatorial Counter Current (5), causing El Niño's warm waters, which heated the air and changed the direction of the jet stream (6 and 7) and, with it, the world's weather.

Earth Sciences

Continued

(NASA) Goddard Space Flight Center in Greenbelt, Md., revealed that the warm water in the tropics sets up a series of long waves in the atmosphere that travel slowly northward. Normally, in the upper and middle latitudes, atmospheric circulation — and thus storms — moves from west to east. But these slow-moving waves create long-lasting weather patterns and tend to guide storms along paths they would not otherwise take. Meteorologists have created new computer models to study the long-range weather effects of such ocean temperature and atmospheric waves.

Ozone layer. In March 1984, a panel of the National Academy of Sciences (NAS) presented new estimates of the effects of *chlorofluorocarbons* (CFC's) on climate, and on atmospheric ozone (O_3) in particular. CFC's, also commonly known as Freons, are widely used as cooling agents in air conditioners and refrigerators and in the manufacture of insulating material. Their use in aerosol sprays was banned in the United States in 1978. CFC's do

not combine with other gases or chemicals, so once they are released into the atmosphere, they eventually find their way into the stratosphere, the upper region of the atmosphere about 16 to 48 kilometers (10 to 30 miles) above Earth's surface. The sun's radiation then causes them to decompose, releasing chlorine, which destroys the stratospheric ozone that serves to shield living things on Earth from harmful solar rays. Without this protective ozone layer, plant and animal life probably could not exist.

The NAS report indicated that CFC's are not as great a threat to the ozone layer as was previously feared. In 1979, the NAS had estimated that continued release of CFC's, based on the rate of their release in 1977, would result in an 18 per cent ozone reduction by the end of 1979. In 1982, the NAS lowered this estimate of the yearly ozone depletion rate to 5 to 9 per cent. The 1984 report estimated the projected yearly ozone destruction at an even lower 2 to 4 per cent. The NAS scientists arrived at the lower es-

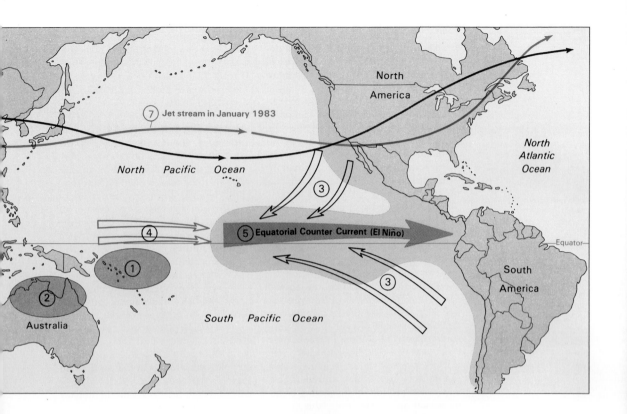

North
America

(7) Jet stream in January 1983

North
Atlantic
Ocean

North   Pacific   Ocean

(3)

Equatorial Counter Current (El Niño)

(4)

(5)

Equator

(1)

South
America

(2)

(3)

Australia

South   Pacific   Ocean

Earth Sciences

Continued

timates by taking into account the effects of other atmospheric gases that may offset the depletion of ozone caused by CFC's. For example, the increased release of oxides of nitrogen by jet aircraft and the increasing atmospheric concentration of both methane and carbon dioxide would tend to raise ozone concentrations by several percentage points. When the chemistry of all of these atmospheric gases is considered together, the scientists concluded, the total concentration of atmospheric ozone is not expected to change very much despite the release of CFC's.

The most dramatic finding in the March 1984 report, however, was the way ozone is distributed at different heights above Earth's surface. Atmospheric scientist Donald J. Wuebbles of Lawrence Livermore National Laboratory in California predicted that due to the release of CFC's and other gases, the peak ozone concentration in the stratosphere at a height of about 40 kilometers (25 miles) would decrease by about 10 per cent. Meanwhile, how-

ever, the maximum ozone concentration in the troposphere — the region of the atmosphere closest to Earth's surface — at a height of about 10 kilometers (6 miles) would increase by about 20 per cent. This vertical redistribution of atmospheric ozone poses serious new questions. Scientists now believe that they may have to make further revisions in their estimates of the long-term effects of CFC's and other gases on Earth's climate.

Nuclear winter. In December 1983, a team of atmospheric scientists released a study predicting that a large-scale nuclear war would have a catastrophic effect on climate, ushering in a *nuclear winter*. According to their findings, a thick cloud of smoke would blanket large portions of Earth, blocking out sunlight and plunging temperatures far below freezing. The team of atmospheric scientists included Robert P. Turco of R and D Associates in Los Angeles and Owen B. Toon, Thomas P. Ackerman, and James B. Pollack of NASA's Ames Research Center at Moffett Field, California.

Earth Sciences

Continued

The study indicated that clouds of smoke and dust from nuclear explosions and resulting fires would spread over the entire Northern Hemisphere in a matter of weeks, assuming that the nuclear war was fought in the Northern Hemisphere. The sun's radiation would be largely absorbed by the smoke in the troposphere. This, along with the continued loss of heat from Earth's surface by infrared radiation, would cause air to become warmer at higher elevations rather than cooler. This large-scale disruption of the normal structure of the atmosphere would drastically alter wind systems and storm paths in both low and high latitudes. Depending upon how long the nuclear winter lasted, there could be widespread loss of plant and animal life. Plant *photosynthesis*, the process whereby plants use sunlight to convert carbon dioxide in the air into oxygen, could cease. The soil might freeze over much of the middle latitudes. The world's oceans would remain warm due to the water's ability to retain heat and would moderate the cooling of air in coastal areas. However, this would set up monsoonlike winds from the continental interiors that would move outward toward the coasts. The scientists' scenario about nuclear winter was based on computer projections, and their conclusions were challenged by other scientists.

Lightning detection. In September 1983, atmospheric scientists Richard E. Orville, Ronald W. Henderson, and Lance F. Bosart of the State University of New York in Albany described the findings they obtained from a lightning-detection network installed in the early 1980's over the Northeastern United States. A system of 10 magnetic direction-finding antennas recorded virtually all of the cloud-to-ground lightning strikes that occurred from Maine to North Carolina and as far west as Ohio. When lightning was detected, its location, time, and strength were automatically recorded.

When used in conjunction with other weather observations, this kind of data will provide new information on the intensity of thunderstorm activity and should aid in the short-term prediction of severe local thunderstorms.   [W. Lawrence Gates]

Oceanography. The drill ship *Glomar Challenger* ended its 15-year mission to probe the sea floor in November 1983. During that time, the ship made 96 voyages and explored more than 600 sites in all of the world's oceans. Scientists believe that findings from those voyages added more to the body of knowledge about the geology of the ocean floor than any other expedition.

For example, while drilling on the floor of the Tasman Sea off New Zealand, the drill ship recovered layers of ash that documented three periods of intensive volcanic activity during the last 18 million years. The islands of New Zealand formed as a result of this volcanic activity.

Drilling in the mid-Atlantic, *Glomar Challenger* uncovered new evidence to help scientists determine a timetable for when the ice ages occurred.

The *Glomar Challenger* also uncovered new sources of oil and gas deposits in the ocean floor. Previously, rich oil fields were found in the continental shelves, the area where land that is part of a continent is submerged below the water. The drill ship, however, revealed that oil and gas deposits in the oceans are not limited to the areas of the continental shelves but can be found in midocean regions.

On its final voyage, scientists unraveled the forces that shape the huge Mississippi fan in the Gulf of Mexico. The fan is a pile of *sediments* (debris from river runoff) 4 kilometers (2½ miles) thick. It stretches seaward off the Mississippi River delta to ocean depths greater than 3,000 meters (10,000 feet). From September to November 1983, scientists recovered cores of sediments from more than 360 meters (1,200 feet) below the seabed. Researchers will use these cores to construct a three-dimensional view of the fan that will help them understand its geological history.

Sea floor storms. In March 1984, oceanographers Charles D. Hollister and Arthur M. Nowell of Woods Hole Oceanographic Institution in Woods Hole, Mass., and Peter A. Jumas of the University of Washington in Seattle reported that powerful underwater storms scrape the sea floor in some areas and dump huge loads of silt and clay in others. They found that bottom

Two U.S. Navy divers equipped with apparatus enabling them to breathe and rebreathe pure oxygen swim in a shallow circular test tank at the State University of New York at Buffalo. Technicians monitor equipment that records the divers' body temperature and oxygen consumption. Use of pure oxygen lets the divers swim longer in shallow water than do other gases, and the rebreathing apparatus eliminates telltale bubbles.

currents can speed up from $\frac{1}{10}$ of a knot to 1 knot or more. At the same time, the amount of sediment in the water increases 10 to 100 times. Such storms are unpredictable, show no strong seasonal pattern, and may last from several days to two weeks.

This finding means geologists must revise their ideas about where to search for underwater oil and gas. Also, because these storms are noisy, naval strategists will have to consider the implications for antisubmarine warfare, which depends heavily on sound detection. In addition, engineers will have to develop new ways to ensure the stability and security of structures and cables placed on the sea floor, which could be dislodged by surging sediments.

Manganese nodules. In February 1984, scientists working in the Manganese Nodule Program (MANOP), set up by the National Science Foundation, summarized the results of their research, which was begun in the 1970's, into how manganese nodules form and grow.

Somewhat like potatoes in shape and size, manganese nodules are mineral formations found on the ocean floor. Many nodules are rich in such minerals as copper, nickel, and cobalt in addition to manganese, and they may one day be mined for their commercial value. Knowing how the nodules form will help scientists predict where they can be found on the ocean floor and what areas of the ocean will have nodules that contain minerals with the greatest commercial value, such as copper and cobalt.

The scientists learned that nodules are found mainly at depths of thousands of meters on the deep ocean floor. They are concentrated in areas where plants and animals grow in the surface waters above. The bodies of these marine organisms contain small amounts of manganese, copper, and other minerals. When these organisms die and decompose, the minerals dissolve in the water and fall to the ocean floor.

A nodule usually forms around the tooth of a shark, which provides a surface on which the dissolved minerals begin to deposit. Layer after layer of the mineral compounds are added around the tooth over long periods of time through a complex chemical process. In some areas of the ocean, it takes 50 million years to produce a nodule 8 centimeters (3 inches) in diameter. In other areas where there is more marine life, decaying organisms provide a faster rate of growth, and the same size nodule could grow in 1 million years.

A major question the researchers tried to answer was why the nodules are on the surface of the sea floor rather than below the surface. The sediments created by decaying marine life pile up on the sea floor at rates a thousand times faster than the nodules grow. Thus, it would seem that the nodules should be buried by the sediments. The only reasonable explanation is that the nodules are kept above the sediments by the actions of bottom-dwelling animals as they burrow in the sediments looking for food and shelter. Over millions of years, their activities may move sediments underneath the nodules and lift the nodules to the surface. MANOP photographs of animal activity on the sea floor, such as tracks and burrows, provided evidence to support this idea.

The MANOP scientists theorize that several chemical and biological processes are involved in the formation of nodules. Those processes are controlled by environmental conditions. The extent to which one process or another is more prevalent will determine the mineral content of the nodules. Altogether, the team found concentrations of 14 elements — including aluminum, barium, cobalt, copper, iron, nickel, and titanium — in nodules from different geographic locations in the Pacific Ocean.

Saving the sea turtles. Nearly the entire species of the Gulf ridley sea turtle nest on a short stretch of beach north of Tampico, Mexico. The sea turtles instinctively return to this beach, their birthplace, when they are ready to mate and make nests. Although they may migrate as far as 3,200 kilometers (2,000 miles), they still manage to find their way back. There, they are exposed to so much illegal hunting that they are in danger of extinction. To reverse this trend, researchers David W. Owens and Mark A. Grassman of Texas A&M University in College Station; James P. McVey of National Marine Fisheries Service in Galveston, Tex.; and Mexican marine biologist Rene Marquez reported in February 1984 on laboratory experiments they conducted to determine whether young turtles can be conditioned to nest on a safer beach on the Padre Island National Seashore in Texas. Their studies centered around a technique called *imprinting*, which is used to condition the senses of young animals to a particular environment. In this case, the researchers wanted to imprint the turtles to the local environment of Padre Island so they would return there to nest when they reached sexual maturity.

In their experiment, the scientists took sea turtle eggs from the Mexican beach and hatched them in the sand at Padre Island. They let the newborn turtles swim in the surf before placing them in laboratory tanks. At 4 months old, the turtles were put in a tank where they could choose among four compartments. These compartments contained seawater and sand solutions from either Padre Island or Galveston Island or two mixes of unfamiliar water. The young turtles moved to the compartment containing the Padre Island solutions much more frequently than to the other compartments. This suggested that they could detect differences in seawater and that this ability might influence their choice of a nesting beach. If so, the turtle can be imprinted or conditioned to nest on a beach other than the one where its ancestors nested. Therefore, captive rearing, combined with imprinting, may be important tools for saving the sea turtle and other endangered marine animals. The best evidence for the success of imprinting would be a mature group of the imprinted sea turtles returning to Padre Island to nest after being released into the ocean. One of the problems, however, is that many sea turtles take well over 15 years to reach sexual maturity. Keeping track of an experimental group of sea turtles over such a long period would be extremely difficult. Consequently, experiments to test this approach must continue in the laboratory. [Feenan D. Jennings and Lauriston R. King]

Ecology

Ecologists Michael H. Madany and Neil E. West of Utah State University in Logan reported in August 1983 on why rangelands in the Western United States, which in the early 1800's were covered with vast expanses of tall grass, by 1900 were covered mainly by shrubs and trees.

Ecologists had earlier proposed two main explanations for that change. Some thought it started when settlers began putting out prairie fires, usually started by lightning. The fires destroyed shrubs and trees but did not damage the roots of the grass. The roots, fertilized by the ashes of the burned vegetation, would then produce a lush new growth of grass. Other ecologists theorized that the decline of grass was caused by livestock, whose grazing reduced the sod layer.

Madany and West studied rangelands in Utah's Zion National Park. They compared the ecology of two sections of the park: Horse Pasture Plateau, which is part of a large forest and grassland area; and Church and Greateast mesas — flat, elevated areas bounded by steep cliffs and rocks. They found that most of the ground on the mesas is covered with grass, whereas the plateau has many trees and a great deal of underbrush.

Because the tops of the mesas are hard to reach, they were never used for grazing. The plateau, on the other hand, was intensively grazed in the late 1800's and early 1900's and has been swept by fire periodically.

But fires that burned the rangeland below the mesas did not spread onto the mesas themselves. So the ecologists concluded that grazing — and not a lack of fire — was the major reason for the decline of grass on the rangelands. They theorized that livestock pulled up sod with their teeth and damaged it with their hoofs. With less competition from grass for soil moisture and nutrients, trees and shrubs gained an ecological foothold and thrived.

Rhesus monkeys in India are dying off due to modern development programs, according to a study reported in June 1983 by ecologists John R. Oppenheimer of the City University of New York's College of Staten Island, M. Farooq Siddiqi of Aligark Muslim University in India, and Charles A.

Southwick of the University of Colorado in Boulder. The researchers found that the number of rhesus monkeys in the Ganges River Basin of northern India — an area studied by Southwick in 1959 and 1960 — decreased greatly from 1960 to 1980. The basin is a region of explosive population growth, industrialization, and urban and agricultural development.

In his earlier study, Southwick found that most groups of rhesus monkeys live near villages and along roadsides and canals. So the researchers concentrated on these areas.

Their findings were grim. Wherever they checked, the populations of the monkeys had been drastically reduced. Along roadways, the number of groups of monkeys had declined by about 77 per cent, and in some such areas there were almost none left.

The investigators thought the monkeys might still be plentiful along the banks of canals, which are an ideal home for the animals. Canals are frequently bordered by trees and agricultural fields. Moreover, there are few people and no motorized vehicles. Even so, monkey groups had declined in those areas, too, by about 75 per cent. The greatest reduction in monkey groups — about 87 per cent — occurred in the vicinity of villages.

The ecologists said one reason for the disappearance of the monkeys is that Indians, who once had been fond of the animals, now consider them a nuisance and often kill them. Another reason is that forests are being cut down to make way for agriculture, industry, and human habitation. The decline of rhesus monkeys, the scientists said, is an almost inevitable consequence of the modernization of India.

Tree communication. When attacked by leaf-chewing insects, trees apparently emit chemicals to warn other trees, according to a June 1983 report by botanists at the University of Washington in Seattle and Dartmouth College in Hanover, N.H. The scientists noted that nearby trees that receive such a warning seem to respond by changing the chemical makeup of their leaves to make them less attractive to the insects.

The researchers came to this conclusion after studying several kinds of

A plant scientist at the Fort Keogh Livestock and Range Research Laboratory in Miles City, Mont., burns a test plot of rangeland, *top,* to determine the effect of fire on vegetation growth. Fall burning decreased the growth of silver sagebrush, *above,* a shrub that hinders cattle from grazing and competes with grasses for water. Spring burning stimulated the growth of the sagebrush.

trees that were infested with caterpillars. They found that the leaves underwent a chemical change and that the leaves of nearby trees — though free of caterpillars — changed in a similar manner. This finding indicated that the neighboring trees were receiving an airborne warning signal from the caterpillar-infested trees.

If the scientists are correct, their discovery could have important applications in pest control. The warning chemical could be sprayed on trees that are threatened by insects. The trees would then change their leaf chemistry to repel the bugs.

The Dartmouth scientists learned that the same chemicals are given off by leaves that are damaged by tearing or cutting. They are now trying to isolate the warning chemical. The University of Washington scientists are conducting similar studies.

Metal in the rings. Trace amounts of metals in the growth rings of a tree provide information about air quality during the tree's lifetime, according to a report made by ecologists at Oak Ridge National Laboratory in Oak Ridge, Tenn., in May 1984.

The scientists, Charles F. Baes III and Samuel B. McLaughlin, measured the metal content of more than a dozen kinds of hardwood and evergreen trees in eastern Tennessee. They found that tree rings formed between 1863 and 1912 were narrower than normal — indicating stunted growth — and contained higher levels of several metals, including iron and titanium. During those years, a copper-smelting plant 55 miles (88 kilometers) upwind from the trees released vast amounts of pollution into the air.

Baes and McLaughlin also examined tree rings formed between the mid-1950's and 1983, the period during which acid rain became a problem in much of the United States and Canada. They discovered that the metal content of the wood increased steadily from the 1950's to the early 1970's and rose at an even higher rate from the 1970's to 1983. The metals, the scientists concluded, originated in fossil fuels burned by electrical generating plants — one suspected cause of acid rain. [Stanley I. Auerbach]

Electronics

Advances in electronics made possible a wide range of consumer products introduced in 1983 and 1984. They included a new video system, more personal computers, and electronics for the car.

New home video. Eastman Kodak Company of Rochester, N.Y., in January 1984 introduced Kodavision 2000, a lightweight videotape system. The system includes a 2.4-kilogram (5.3-pound) color camera-recorder (camcorder) and a device called a cradle into which the camcorder is placed to play tapes on a TV set. The cradle also has electric circuits for recharging two 60-minute batteries for the camcorder.

The recording cassette for the Kodak system is slightly larger than a standard audio cassette. Kodavision tape is 8 millimeters (0.3 inch) wide, compared with the 13-millimeter (½-inch) width of VHS and Beta videotapes. However, its advantages are somewhat offset by its shorter maximum recording time—only 90 minutes, compared with 8 hours on a VHS tape. The 8-millimeter video movies can be copied onto VHS or Beta tapes by plugging the cradle into a video cassette recorder (VCR).

The camcorder has an electronic viewfinder and a power zoom lens. Other features include fast forward and reverse, speeded-up visual search, and high-fidelity sound. A deluxe model focuses automatically, displays still frames, fades frames in and out, and even enables the viewer to write information on the tape electronically. An optional TV tuner and timer is available to tape TV programs. Other firms introducing 8-millimeter recorders in 1984 included General Electric Company of Schenectady, N.Y.; Sanyo Business Systems Corporation of Moonachie, N.J.; Fisher Corporation of Los Angeles; and Toshiba America Consumer Division of Wayne, N.Y.

In late 1983, Konica of Japan introduced a 0.7-kilogram (26-ounce) video camera that uses VHS, Beta, or 8-millimeter tape. In January 1984, RCA Corporation of New York City demonstrated a 1-kilogram (35-ounce), palm-sized, color-video camera that

A digital disk system for autos, developed by Mitsubishi Corporation, fits neatly underneath the car's dashboard, plays high-fidelity sound through four speakers, and will sell for about $800.

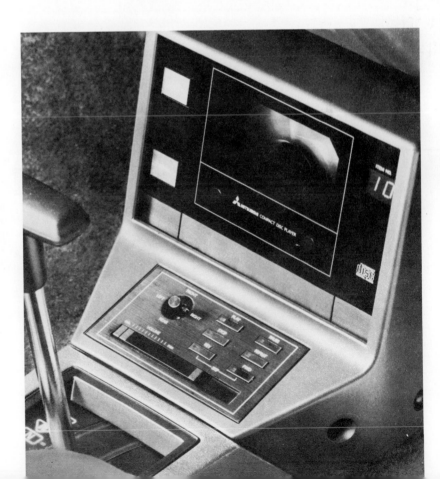

Electronics

Continued

records with an electronic chip instead of a conventional camera tube.

Peanuts and apples. A personal computer made by International Business Machines Corporation (IBM) of Boca Raton, Fla., called "Peanut" during its development, broke out of its shell and came on the market in late 1983, christened PCjr. The price for a basic PCjr system was $700. The PCjr has a 0.7-kilogram keyboard that operates the central processing unit (CPU) at distances up to 7.6 meters (25 feet) without a connecting cable. The CPU can store 65,536 *bytes* (64K), or characters, of information in its *random-access*, or temporary, memory (RAM). The CPU also accommodates an optional 32K *read-only*, or permanent, memory (ROM) cartridge and an optional disk drive. For an additional $600, a buyer also receives a built-in double-sided disk drive with 128K RAM. An optional device called an RF modulator enables the PCjr to display pictures on any color or black-and-white TV set.

A major advantage of the PCjr is that it can run programs designed for the IBM PC, a more expensive computer introduced in 1982, primarily for business use. These include thousands of programs for word processing, business accounting, and financial planning.

Two drawbacks to the PCjr are its keyboard with small keys spaced far from one another and the lack of a provision for a second disk drive. Several firms introduced improved keyboards to ease word processing with the PCjr.

In January 1984, Apple Computer, Incorporated, of Cupertino, Calif., unveiled the Macintosh computer, priced at $2,500. The Macintosh has borrowed a movable control called a *mouse* from Apple's Lisa, a professional-level computer introduced in January 1983. The mouse is a plastic box about the size and shape of a bar of soap with a button on its top. It is connected by a slim cable to the computer.

When the user inserts a program disk into the computer and turns the computer on, a picture of a desk appears on the computer's display screen

Drawing by Stevenson; ©1983 The New Yorker Magazine, Inc.

"Here's the story, gentlemen. Sometime last night, an eleven-year-old kid in Akron, Ohio, got into our computer and transferred all our assets to a bank in Zurich."

Call from Your Car

A phone on wheels

The dream of having a phone in the family car came closer to reality in late 1983, as a new type of mobile phone service went into operation in Chicago in October and in the Washington-Baltimore region in December. The service became available in Los Angeles in May 1984 and in New York City and Philadelphia in June. It was expected to be in operation in about 30 cities in the United States by the end of 1984.

The Federal Communications Commission (FCC) set the stage for this development in 1982 by authorizing a new kind of communications network, a cellular telephone system. A conventional mobile phone service can accommodate only a few thousand subscribers in each city, but a cellular system can handle millions of subscribers.

A conventional system uses a single, high-powered radio transmitter that operates on a limited number of channels — only 12 in some major cities. A telephone call on one of these channels is broadcast throughout the city, so no other subscriber can use the channel until the callers hang up. Furthermore, signals miles from the transmitter are weak. And interference from hills and buildings can create background noise or disrupt calls.

By contrast, a cellular system is divided into a honeycomb of geographic regions called *cells*. At the center of each cell is a radio receiver and a low-powered, computer-controlled radio transmitter that broadcasts strong signals throughout the cell. Each cell can serve at least 48 channels. Each cell's computer is wired into a central computer, which, in turn, is connected to the local telephone network. When you dial a number from a telephone mounted in a car or truck, or from a portable phone, a tiny microcomputer in the phone communicates by radio with computers in your cell and nearby cells. The cell computers evaluate the strength of the radio signals from your microcomputer and select the best cell for the call — usually the cell you are in. When the party you have dialed answers the phone, the central computer assigns a two-way channel to the call so that you and the other party can talk at the same time, as you would in a normal telephone conversation.

If you drive from one cell toward another, the cell computers detect this movement as a change in the strength of the signals reaching their receivers. Instantly, they switch the call to the cell you are approaching and assign it another two-way channel. The channel you had been using is available immediately to other callers in the first cell. This constant switching and reuse of channels makes it possible for cellular services in many urban areas to handle hundreds of thousands of new subscribers.

The American Telephone and Telegraph Company (AT&T) tried to establish cellular systems throughout the Bell System in the early 1970's. However, AT&T ran into strong opposition from radio common carriers — firms that compete with local telephone companies for mobile service. After a decade of court battles, the FCC settled the conflict by setting aside a new band of 666 channels for cellular systems in each city. The channels were equally divided — 333 for a common carrier and 333 for the local phone company. No single cell in a common carrier's or a phone company's system uses all 333 channels because there must be at least a one-channel separation between calls in adjacent cells to avoid radio interference. At sites served by two firms, 100 clear channels may be available at any time, enough for 100 simultaneous conversations.

Even though mobile phone service has greatly expanded, the cost keeps it out of reach for most people. In Chicago, for example, a mobile radio phone costs $2,000 to $3,000. There is a $100 to $200 installation charge and a monthly service charge of $150 to $300.

The cost is expected to limit the number of initial subscribers to about 1.5 million nationwide, mostly business and professional people. But as mobile and portable phone prices fall during the next few years, the demand is expected to soar. The number of subscribers will grow to 30 million or more by the late 1990's, according to some estimates. So one day, the mobile car telephone may be as common as any stationary telephone extension in the home. [John Free]

Electronics

Continued

Two experimental electronic devices developed in 1983 and 1984 help handicapped people use words. A specially wired glove, *above,* translates the sign language of the deaf into printed English for people who do not understand sign language. The Tactile Image Generator, *above right,* scans printed words and converts them into raised images that a blind person can read by feel.

along with an *icon,* or sketch, of each program on the disk. A user wanting to work on a mailing list, for example, would roll the mouse along the desktop and watch as the pointer on the computer's display screen moved to the icon representing the list. The user would then press the button to feed the list program into the computer's memory. The mouse thus enables the user to by-pass the keyboard for routine operations. The Macintosh has 64K of RAM and an 8.9-centimeter (3½-inch) disk drive for storing an additional 400K of RAM.

Many consumers find the Macintosh attractive. However, the PCjr's appeal has prompted most suppliers of programs and *peripheral equipment* such as printers and *modems* — instruments that interconnect computers via telephone lines — to concentrate their attention on PCjr. And, unfortunately for Macintosh owners, programs and peripheral equipment built for one of the two machines will not work on the other.

Custom computers. Also in January 1984, Commodore Business Machines,

Incorporated, of West Chester, Pa., introduced Model 264 productivity tools, a line of special-purpose computers. Each computer has a built-in *productivity package* — a ROM unit that contains one program. A writer who wants a word processor, for example, rather than a general-purpose computer, would buy a Model 264 with a built-in word-processing program. On the other hand, a business executive probably would be more interested in a machine with a spreadsheet program, which calculates and displays rows and columns of financial data.

Portable computers have evolved from too small to too big to just right. Handheld, or pocket, computers introduced in 1981 were limited by memory size, had tiny keyboards, and displayed only one line of data. Such computers are still practical for engineers, scientists, and students. However, they cannot handle word processing or business spreadsheets, two major areas of computer use.

In 1982, Osborne Computer Corporation of Hayward, Calif., unveiled a

Electronics

machine at the other extreme — a sewing-machine-sized computer with 64K RAM, two disk drives and a 14-centimeter (5½-inch) video monitor that displayed 24 lines of 80 characters each. This machine handled word processing and spreadsheets, and it was portable. However, it weighed 13 kilograms (28 pounds), and it did not run on batteries.

In 1983 and 1984, several companies introduced lightweight, notebook-sized computers that can run on batteries and can handle word processing and spreadsheets. These machines do not display data on video monitors. Instead, they use *liquid crystal displays* (*LCD*'s), devices that form numbers and letters when electric current is passed through them. Prices range from under $800 to over $8,000.

The TRS-80 model 100, introduced by Tandy Radio Shack of Fort Worth, Tex., for $800 early in 1984, measures 20 by 30 by 5 centimeters (8 by 12 by 2 inches). It weighs less than 2 kilograms (4 pounds) and has a typewriter-style keyboard.

In May 1984, Hewlett-Packard Company of Palo Alto, Calif., announced the Portable, a $3,000 computer that weighs 4 kilograms (9 pounds), measures 25 by 33 by 8 centimeters (10 by 13 by 3 inches), and can run on battery power for 16 hours without a recharge. The Portable has 272K of RAM and 384K of ROM, a full-sized keyboard, and a pop-up LCD display with 16 lines of 80 characters each.

In the $4,000 range is the Gavilan Mobile Computer, introduced in late 1983 by Gavilan Computer Corporation of Campbell, Calif. This machine is small enough to slip into a briefcase. A pop-up LCD screen provides an 8-line, 66-character display. A cordless touch panel between the keyboard and the screen can be used to control a pointer on the screen. The user simply moves a fingertip along the panel surface, and the pointer follows the finger motion. The $8,150 Grid Compass, made by Grid Systems Corporation of Mountain View, Calif., weighs 4 kilograms (9 pounds). It has 256K of ordinary RAM, which loses its stored in-

The Aerobics Joystick controller made by Suncom, Incorporated, of Wheeling, Ill., links an exercise bicycle to a computer game that creates the illusion on a TV screen of pedaling down a country road.

Electronics

Continued

formation when the power to the computer is turned off, and 384K of nonvolatile RAM, which retains data even when the power is switched off. The Compass has a built-in modem.

In the car. Electronic circuits have helped the United States automobile industry meet strict state and federal exhaust-emission standards. For example, diesel engines have been cleaned up by a control module supplied by TRW Incorporated of Cleveland for 1984 Oldsmobiles sold in California. The module controls the recirculation of exhaust gas.

In early 1984, the Chrysler Corporation announced a prototype electronic control for automatic transmissions. A small computer within the control compares the speed of the transmission's turbine with that of the vehicle. If the transmission needs to shift from one speed range to another, the control sends an electric signal to electromechanical devices that open or close the channels through which the transmission fluid flows, shifting the range.

Chrysler 1984 models also have an electronic fuel-injection system. Electronic sensors monitor manifold pressure, engine temperature, throttle position, and the oxygen content of the exhaust, and send information to computer circuits that determine the exact amount of fuel needed and the timing of spark-plug firing. The sensors also monitor engine malfunctions. Technicians can use data stored in the computer to diagnose engine problems.

To help motorists on long trips, Volkswagenwerk A.G. of West Germany began testing its Autoscout, a dashboard-mounted automatic navigation system designed by Siemens Company of West Germany. The driver feeds map coordinates of his or her location and destination into the Autoscout, while a magnetic device supplies data on the car's exact direction. The Autoscout's computer uses the two sets of data to determine the proper direction for the car and the distance to the destination, and then shows the results on a compasslike LCD on the dashboard.   [Howard Bierman]

Energy

During the summer of 1984, the United States Department of Energy (DOE) began to dismantle the historic nuclear power plant at Shippingport, Pa., the first large nuclear power station built in the United States. It operated from 1957 until 1982. The Shippingport plant is the first major nuclear facility ever to be dismantled, and the process is expected to take four years. The reactor vessel, which weighs 700 metric tons (770 short tons), will be loaded onto a barge on the adjacent Ohio River and transported down the Ohio and Mississippi rivers, through the Panama Canal, and up the Pacific coast to Washington's Columbia River. The vessel will be buried 9 meters (30 feet) underground at the DOE's Hanford nuclear storage facility near Richland, Wash. The piping, valves, and other components will be shipped to this site by truck.

The DOE estimated that 20 commercial nuclear power plants will be *decommissioned*, or taken out of service, by the year 2000. However, instead of being dismantled, a decommissioned plant could be *moth-balled*, or stored, by removing the nuclear fuel from the plant and installing instruments to monitor the plant's radiation level. People would be kept away from a moth-balled plant for 30 years. During this time, components in the plant would lose a great deal of their radioactivity, simplifying the eventual dismantling.

Melt tester. The world's largest facility for testing the interaction of molten fuel with reactor core structures began operations at Sandia Laboratories in Albuquerque, N. Mex., in the spring of 1983. The facility can imitate how reactor fuels would melt in a major accident. The Large-Scale Melt Facility (LMF) can melt 500 kilograms (1,100 pounds) of uranium oxide and then heat it to temperatures above 2800°C (5072°F.), which is much higher than the melting point of steel. Such molten material then drains rapidly into a chamber containing concrete, steel, liquids, gases, or other materials that molten reactor fuel might encounter during a major accident.

Energy

Continued

An unusual "windmill" in Spain consists of a 200-meter (650-foot) tower that juts up through a 4.7-hectare (11½-acre) greenhouse, *above*. Sunlight creates temperatures in the greenhouse that are hotter than those at the top of the tower. As a result, the heated air rushes up the tower to turn a propeller, *above right*, that drives a generator, producing up to 70 kilowatts of electric power.

The first experiments investigated what might happen if molten reactor fuel escaped from a reactor vessel and fell onto the floor of the containment building, which houses the reactor. Most containment building floors are made of concrete. The molten fuel would cause the concrete to decompose chemically, producing extremely hot carbon dioxide gas and steam. These hot gases, in turn, might react chemically with the molten fuel to form equally hot hydrogen and carbon monoxide gases. In a major accident, all four gases would transfer heat from the molten fuel to the surrounding structures. Scientists have been trying to develop flooring materials that would be less likely to react this way.

To test one such material, LMF scientists heated 230 kilograms (500 pounds) of a mixture of uranium dioxide and zirconia to a temperature of 2600°C (4710°F.) and then dumped it onto bricks made of magnesia, a material being considered for reactor flooring. The experiment produced no detectable hydrogen. The heat made

hairline cracks in the bricks, but the molten materials did not flow deeply into the cracks.

Last of the breeder. The controversial Clinch River Breeder Reactor project came to an end in October 1983 when the United States Senate turned down a budget request for its continuation. A breeder reactor is a nuclear power plant that *breeds*, or produces more nuclear fuel than it uses.

In 1972, the U.S. Congress had authorized the construction and operation of a breeder reactor to determine how economical it would be for electric companies to use such reactors as energy sources and how the reactors might affect the environment. The original cost estimate of the reactor, which was to be built on the Clinch River in Tennessee, was $400 million.

Although France, Great Britain, and the Soviet Union are already operating breeder reactors, the Clinch River project in the United States has been extremely controversial. Opponents were concerned about the possibility that the plutonium fuel produced by the reactor would be used to make nuclear weapons.

In 1977, President Jimmy Carter vetoed the bill to fund the reactor. However, President Ronald Reagan reactivated the project in 1981.

By 1983, the U.S. government had spent $1.7 billion for design, engineering, excavation, and construction of major components. About $2.5 billion was needed to complete the project. The Reagan Administration asked the electric utilities to contribute $1 billion, and put the remaining $1.5 billion into its budget request. On Oct. 26, 1983, the Senate voted 56 to 40 to delete the $1.5 billion from the budget.

Fusion breakthrough. A major event in fusion power research occurred on Nov. 3, 1983, at the Massachusetts Institute of Technology (MIT) in Cambridge, when the Alcator C Tokamak fusion reactor exceeded the *Lawson Product*, a mathematical calculation based on a certain combination of fuel concentration and fuel confinement time. A fusion-power reactor must exceed the Lawson Product in order to produce more energy than it consumes. Nuclear power plants in operation today produce energy by *fission*, the splitting of a heavy atomic nucleus into two nuclei. Researchers are trying to develop a commercial reactor that produces energy by the opposite process, *fusion*.

In a fusion reaction, the nuclei of two atoms are fused together. The reaction produces one nucleus that has less mass than the two original nuclei, and converts the remaining mass into energy. The first fusion reactors probably will obtain energy from the fusion of deuterium and tritium, two *isotopes*, or forms, of hydrogen.

Because all nuclei are positively charged, and like charges repel one another, nuclei must travel at very high speeds to overcome their mutual repulsion so that they can collide and fuse. Heating the nuclei makes them travel faster. To fuse deuterium and tritium nuclei, the temperature must be about 200 million°C (360 million°F.).

A tremendous amount of energy is

Technicians inspect the reactor chamber in the world's first pebble-bed nuclear reactor, scheduled to begin operating near Dortmund, West Germany, in 1985. The nuclear fuel is embedded in graphite-coated spheres rather than conventional rods, making nuclear accidents less likely.

Energy

Continued

Panels of silicon cells convert sunlight directly into electricity at a solar-energy plant near San Luis Obispo, Calif. The plant began operating in November 1983 and was expected to provide 6.5 megawatts of electric power when completed in 1984.

required to reach such a temperature. Furthermore, nuclei that travel rapidly enough to combine are very hard to contain. The only thing that will hold them is a *magnetic bottle*, a container made up of powerful fields of magnetic energy. Magnetic bottles that are sufficiently leak-proof for reactor nuclei are extremely difficult to generate and maintain.

Because of these problems, researchers have not yet produced a controlled fusion reaction that has reached the *break-even point* by producing more energy than required to start and maintain the reaction. To achieve break-even with deuterium and tritium, the temperature must be 200 million°C (360 million°F.), and the Lawson Product, the mathematical product of the number of nuclei per cubic centimeter and the number of seconds during which the fuel is confined in the magnetic bottle, must exceed 60 trillion. The Lawson Product is named after British physicist John D. Lawson, who calculated it in 1955.

In the MIT experiment, conducted with deuterium nuclei only, the Lawson Product was 60 trillion to 80 trillion. However, the temperature was only 17 million°C (31 million°F.).

Superconducting generator. In early 1983, a team of scientists headed by research engineer Trifon E. Laskaris of the General Electric Research and Development Center in Schenectady, N.Y., successfully tested an electric generator that uses a superconducting electromagnet. Superconducting magnets are made of material that conducts electricity almost without resistance at temperatures near absolute zero (−273.15°C or −459.67°F.).

In an electric generator, an electromagnet built into the rotor—the major rotating part—produces a rotating magnetic field that causes electric current to flow in wire windings mounted on the inside of a stationary frame surrounding the rotor. Superconducting magnets can produce a much stronger magnetic field than can conventional magnets, so a superconducting generator can be smaller than a conventional generator with the same electric power output. Another advantage of a superconducting generator is that the flow of electricity in the rotating electromagnet does not cause a loss of energy as it does in a conventional generator because of electrical resistance. In a superconducting commercial generator, operating costs would be reduced by millions of dollars.

The rotating magnet of a conventional generator has wire windings made of a copper-silver alloy. In the General Electric design, the windings are made of a new niobium-titanium alloy. Liquid helium cooled to a temperature of $-269°C$ ($-452°F.$) constantly bathes the windings of the rotor, which is 4 meters (13 feet) long. The windings in the stationary frame are made of copper and are water-cooled, as are similar windings in conventional large generators.

The superconducting generator has been tested over a wide range of operating conditions. At full capacity, the experimental generator produced 20.6 kilowatts of electricity — enough for a community of 20,000 people and about twice as much electricity as can be produced by a conventional generator of about the same size.

Wind power. The Hawaiian Electric Company during the year prepared to install the world's largest wind turbine, the MOD-5A, in late 1984 on the hills above Kahuku on the north shore of Oahu. The turbine is rated at 7.3 *megawatts* (million watts) and was manufactured by the General Electric Company. The MOD-5A is expected to generate 30 million kilowatt-hours of electricity annually, enough for 3,500 homes.

The MOD-5A is the third generation of large wind-powered turbines designed and tested by engineers at the Lewis Research Center of the National Aeronautics and Space Administration in Cleveland and paid for by the DOE. The MOD-5A has two gigantic blades with a distance between blade tips of 122 meters (400 feet). The blades are mounted on a cylindrical tower that is 73 meters (240 feet) high. Made of laminated wood and epoxy, the blades are lighter and cheaper than earlier hollow steel blades. The outer 17 meters (56 feet) of the blades can swivel to control

speed and turning force exerted on the blades by the wind.

The turbine begins to generate electricity at wind speeds greater than 22 kilometers per hour (kph), or 14 miles per hour (mph), and produces 7.3 megawatts of power in 51-kph (32-mph) winds. At wind velocities between 51 and 97 kph (32 and 60 mph), output remains constant at 7.3 megawatts. At 97 kph, the wind pressure becomes so high that it might damage the turbine, and so the blades are *feathered* — that is, swiveled so that their broad surfaces no longer face the wind. When the blades are feathered, the turbine's power output falls to zero.

Farming the wind. Windmills now play an important role in the generation of electricity in California. By the end of 1983, about 3,600 small wind turbines, averaging a 75-kilowatt output each, were generating electricity for utilities in California. Many of these were on "wind farms," sites where more than one wind turbine is located.

California is an excellent place for wind turbines. During the spring, summer, and early fall, the valleys heat up and, as the hot air rises, it meets cooler, heavier air from the Pacific Ocean moving through the mountain passes, creating strong wind currents. In Altamont Pass and Tehachapi Pass, for example, the annual wind velocity averages about 27 kph (17 mph).

In addition, federal and state tax laws favor individuals who invest in California wind farms that supply electricity to utilities. Independent energy producers get a federal tax credit of 15 per cent for renewable energy projects plus a California tax credit of 25 per cent. Federal law requires public utilities to purchase all the electricity generated by small power producers at the price the power would have cost if it had been produced by the utility. Pacific Gas and Electric Company (PG&E) in northern California paid an average price of 7 cents per kilowatt-hour for electricity purchased in 1983.

California utilities in 1983 bought more than 50 million kilowatt-hours of electricity from wind farms. The capacity of U.S. wind farms was 230 megawatts. [Marian Visich, Jr.]

Environment

The spread of airborne pollutants to areas far from their sources became a major environmental concern in the United States during 1983 and 1984. Cities that had reduced pollution output from factories and motor vehicles found that many pollutants still blew in from areas upwind. Similarly, many rural areas in the United States began to experience significant air pollution that originated 1,000 to 10,000 kilometers (600 to 6,000 miles) away.

Tracing a pollutant to its source is difficult because an air mass picks up pollutants from many sources as it moves across the countryside. However, in January 1984, atmospheric chemists Kenneth A. Rahn and Douglas H. Lowenthal of the University of Rhode Island in Narragansett reported significant progress in determining the sources of pollutants.

The two scientists collected and analyzed about 100 air samples from each of six locations around the world. They measured the amounts of more than 40 different polluting elements in each sample. Rahn and Lowenthal found that six of these elements — antimony, arsenic, indium, manganese, vanadium, and zinc — varied considerably among the 100 samples. By using these six elements as tracers and measuring their levels in each sample in comparison to selenium, which is present in similar quantities in all air, the scientists could identify where the sample was collected.

Using their system, Rahn and Lowenthal made some interesting discoveries about the sources of air pollution. They found, for example, that the pollutants in the air over Barrow, Alaska, come largely from Europe and Asia rather than North America.

Saving the Chesapeake. An important example of comprehensive efforts to reduce pollution was the plan, launched in 1983, to clean up Chesapeake Bay. Chesapeake Bay is an arm of the Atlantic Ocean that divides Maryland into two parts. It is a major source of fish and shellfish, supports a variety of wildlife, and is a major commercial fishing and recreational area. But water pollution has greatly re-

Instruments on a tower measure amounts of dry sulfur and nitrogen compounds deposited – a dry form of acid rain. When these compounds mix with moisture in the air, they form acids. But scientists believe the dry deposits may do as much damage as acid rainfall.

duced the bay's fish supply and its recreational value.

In September 1983, the United States Environmental Protection Agency (EPA), the chief federal agency working to control pollution, issued an action plan for cleaning up the bay. The EPA identified the bay's two most significant problems as increased rates of nutrient enrichment and contamination by toxic substances.

Nutrient enrichment, also called *eutrophication*, occurs when large amounts of nutrients, such as nitrogen and phosphorus, pour into a body of water from treated sewage or from fertilizers washing off farmland. The excess nutrients stimulate the growth of algae, producing far more than fish and other aquatic creatures can eat.

This so-called *algal bloom* sets off a complex ecological chain reaction that removes huge quantities of oxygen from the water. By late summer, the amount of dissolved oxygen in some nutrient-enriched bodies of water may be so low that fish and shellfish suffocate and die. In Chesapeake Bay, the problem has become so severe that the deeper waters of the bay have no oxygen from May to September.

In January 1984, a group of scientists led by marine geologist Charles B. Officer of Dartmouth College in Hanover, N.H., reported findings that explained why Chesapeake Bay's oxygen loss begins so early in the year, long before the season's algae have grown to their peak. The scientists found that huge numbers of dead algae and other organisms, which grow in Chesapeake Bay's nutrient-enriched waters during the summer, settle to the bottom of the bay each fall. There they remain intact over most of the winter. As the waters warm in early spring, bottom-dwelling organisms — mostly bacteria, fungi, and *invertebrates* (animals without backbones), such as worms and snails — consume the dead organisms and begin to use up oxygen in the deep waters by their own respiration.

Adding to the problem, rivers carry fresh water from melted snow into Chesapeake Bay as early as February and March. When this fresh water meets the heavier salt water of the bay, it floats on top, cutting off the deeper waters from the surface. As a result, the deeper waters cannot take in new oxygen by mixing with the oxygen-rich surface waters. The mixing of deeper waters and surface waters does not occur until autumn, when colder air temperatures cause the surface waters to cool and become denser. But, at the same time, the summer's growth of algae begins to settle on the bottom of the bay, where its decay in spring will again remove oxygen from the deep waters. Each year, as the cycle repeats itself, the oxygen shortage caused by nutrient enrichment grows worse.

Chesapeake Bay's other category of pollutants, toxic substances, include pesticides, herbicides, oil, and polychlorinated biphenyls (PCB's) — a type of industrial waste. Together with excess nutrients, these contaminants have caused marked declines in the number of such important commercial marine animals as the blue crab and the striped bass. In his State of the Union message in January 1984, U.S. President Ronald Reagan announced that he would propose funding for a major cleanup in Chesapeake Bay.

The greenhouse effect. Another continuing concern during 1983 and 1984 was the expected warming of global temperatures caused by a build-up of carbon dioxide in the atmosphere — a process called the greenhouse effect. Carbon dioxide is a gas that occurs naturally in the atmosphere. It is also produced by burning fossil fuels — coal, oil, natural gas, and gasoline.

Carbon dioxide traps heat within Earth's lower atmosphere because of how it absorbs and reflects different forms of radiant energy from the sun. Both light and heat are forms of radiant energy and move through space in patterns called *waves*. Carbon dioxide allows most of the light waves from the sun to reach Earth's surface. Earth absorbs some of this energy and radiates some of it back as light and some of it back as heat. But carbon dioxide in Earth's atmosphere, like the glass on a greenhouse, reflects the heat waves back to Earth's surface rather than allowing them to escape into space. The more the carbon dioxide levels in the atmosphere rise, the more heat is trapped.

Analyses of the carbon dioxide dissolved in the ancient ice of Green-

EDB: Old Pesticide, New Worry

EDB-tainted cabbage

No other environmental problem in the United States in 1984 captured the public's attention as much as the discovery of widespread contamination by *ethylene dibromide* (*EDB*), an extensively used pesticide. By the end of January, EDB had been found in ground water, citrus fruit, and flour and other grain products manufactured under nationally known brand names.

Americans' concern about EDB intensified when public health officials raised the possibility that a significant portion of the U.S. grain supply was tainted. In February, the U.S. Environmental Protection Agency (EPA) banned further use of EDB on grain and set maximum levels for food supplies. The EPA allowed a maximum concentration of 30 parts per billion (ppb) in ready-to-eat foods.

Despite these federal limits, some states imposed even more stringent standards and pulled many packaged foods off grocery shelves. New York state, for example, imposed a 10-ppb standard for ready-to-eat foods. New York public health officials contended that, based on animal studies, EDB concentrations allowed by the federal government could lead to possible birth defects as well as to a higher risk of cancer. Other states that imposed tougher standards were Massachusetts, Maine, Ohio, California, and Florida. These actions created a great deal of confusion among consumers about the potential health risks from small amounts of EDB.

EDB is an effective and versatile pesticide. For the past 40 years, farmers have used EDB to protect stored grain from insect infestation. More recently, farmers in the Southeast and Southwest have injected EDB into the soil to kill *nematodes* (tiny worms) before planting crops, and citrus growers in California, Florida, and Texas have fumigated oranges and grapefruit with EDB to kill fruit flies.

Government authorities now realize that the extensive use of EDB has led to a widespread problem. For decades, scientists believed that EDB evaporates completely after being applied and therefore would not leave residues in water or food. But in the mid-1970's, they discovered that EDB does leave residues, and in the early 1980's, they learned that EDB injected into the soil contaminates ground water.

The danger to human beings from low-level, long-term exposure to EDB is not yet clear because there is no way of knowing whether any human cancers, birth defects, or other problems have been caused by the chemical. However, animal experiments have shown that EDB causes cancer and genetic changes in rats and mice. Because of these findings, the EPA moved in 1977 to regulate EDB. EPA officials said that if EDB were a new chemical, its use would never be approved now. But because EDB was already in widespread use, the agency moved slowly and took seven more years—until 1984—before it actually banned the chemical for most agricultural applications.

The EPA predicted that its new regulations will eliminate EDB from all stored grain within three to five years. The agency determined that only about 2 per cent of the total U.S. grain supply was actually contaminated. Citrus fruits contaminated with EDB were sold only in California, Florida, and Texas.

To some extent, therefore, the public may have become unduly alarmed about EDB. Bruce N. Ames, a biochemist at the University of California in Berkeley, said there is little danger of developing cancer from low-level EDB exposure. But many people were not convinced, and officials looked for alternatives to EDB.

The EPA suggested that food could be bombarded with radiation to kill insects. But this process—even though no radiation remains in the food—is unlikely to gain wide public acceptance in the near future. Scientists, too, are uncertain whether it is a good idea, because it is not known what changes radiation causes in food molecules.

For now, other chemicals are being used as substitutes for EDB—aluminum phosphide to fumigate stored grain and methyl bromide to kill fruit flies in citrus fruit. However, these chemicals are also being studied for their long-term health risks, and many experts fear that the problems with EDB are only the tip of the iceberg as pesticide use continues. [Marjorie Sun]

269

An underground vault near Richland, Wash., *left,* provides an area for testing how nuclear waste can be stored in rock deposits. Technicians check instruments in the vault wall, *above,* for measuring how heat and radiation from the waste affect the rock.

Environment

Continued

land's glaciers indicate that concentrations of the gas have risen since the last ice age, which ended about 10,000 years ago. Then, carbon dioxide was at a concentration of about 190 parts for every 1 million parts of other gases — or 190 ppm. By the mid-1980's, it had risen to 340 ppm. The build-up of carbon dioxide has been more rapid since about 1900, in part because people have burned more fuel in their homes and factories.

Both the EPA and the National Research Council, an arm of the National Academy of Sciences, issued reports during 1983 concerning the greenhouse effect. By the year 2050, mean global temperatures are expected to rise 2 to 4 degrees Celsius (3.5 to 7 degrees Fahrenheit). The warming will have the greatest effect on polar regions. Within 100 years, polar ice could melt enough to raise the sea level by 5 meters (16 feet), flooding parts of such coastal cities as New York City and Los Angeles. Climatic zones would shift, affecting agriculture. For example, the wheat- and corn-growing belt now in Iowa and Indiana would shift north into Saskatchewan, Canada. The natural vegetation would change over vast areas, severely disrupting wildlife.

According to a December 1983 report by a group of ecologists from Ecosystems Center in Woods Hole, Mass., and the University of New Hampshire in Durham, fossil fuels are not the only important source of excess carbon dioxide. The ecologists reported that the cutting of trees to clear land for farming, mainly in the tropics, accounted for most of the carbon dioxide released to the atmosphere between 1860 and 1960. Since then, tree cutting may have accounted for 22 to 43 per cent of the total. Just as fossil fuels produce carbon dioxide when they burn, living plants release the gas when they are cut and burned or allowed to decay. In addition, trees and other living plants remove carbon dioxide from the air. These findings indicate that forest conservation and replanting would reduce the greenhouse effect.   [Walter E. Westman]

Genetics

Researchers at medical centers in the United States and Venezuela announced jointly in November 1983 that they had found a way to identify persons who carry the gene that causes Huntington's disease, an inherited disorder that destroys brain cells. Their discovery is expected to lead to a procedure for diagnosing the disease.

Huntington's disease is one of the most serious genetic diseases. Its symptoms — mental disturbances and the loss of muscle control — usually begin after age 30, and the victim dies within 10 to 20 years. There is no known cure. Each child of a person with Huntington's disease has a 50 per cent chance of developing the disease. However, until now, there has been no way of knowing which children carry the Huntington's disease gene before the symptoms appear. By that time, they may have children of their own who have inherited the disease.

The research group, headed by molecular biologist James F. Gusella of Massachusetts General Hospital and Harvard University Medical School in Boston, found a *genetic marker* that makes it possible to identify persons who carry the Huntington's disease gene. A genetic marker is a variation of some kind in deoxyribonucleic acid (DNA) associated with a certain gene. DNA, the chemical that genes are made of, carries the "blueprint" for life. It is contained in chromosomes, of which there are 23 pairs in the nucleus of a human cell.

Human DNA contains billions of smaller units called *nucleotides*, which are connected end to end to form a long strand. There are many different sequences or arrangements of these nucleotides among individuals that determine inherited characteristics, such as eye color and facial appearance. However, there are a few differences in nucleotide sequences that have harmful effects, such as the one that causes Huntington's disease.

In developing genetic engineering techniques, scientists learned that DNA contains many short sequences that are "targets" for *restriction enzymes,* chemical "scissors" that cut the DNA molecule at those sites. The location of the sites targeted by a particular enzyme may be at different places in different people's DNA. If that is true of the target sites in the neighborhood of the Huntington's disease gene, the scientists reasoned, then the difference would provide a genetic marker. The DNA sequence containing the Huntington's disease gene would, when cut at the target sites by a restriction enzyme, be longer or shorter than the same sequence from normal individuals. The length of the DNA would be the genetic marker for Huntington's disease.

To find a target site that would indicate the Huntington's disease gene, the researchers used *DNA probes* — pieces of human DNA that the scientists "tagged" with a radioactive substance. A probe, when added to a solution of DNA, will stick to any piece of DNA that has the same, or nearly the same, sequence of nucleotides. The combined molecule can then be detected on X-ray film by its radioactive "glow."

The length of the piece of DNA that a probe sticks to is determined by the distance between the DNA's target sites, where the molecule can be cut by the enzyme. If the target sites are close, the DNA piece — or sequence of nucleotides — will be short. If the sites are far apart, the DNA will be long.

In other experiments of this type, scientists use probes containing known genes. But Gusella's team did not know which chromosome contained the Huntington's disease gene. They therefore had to use several hundred probes — of unidentified DNA sequences — from different chromosomes in the hope that one of the probes was from a location close to the Huntington's disease gene. They were looking for a probe that would stick to a DNA piece of one length when added to the DNA of Huntington's disease victims, and to a DNA piece of a different length — but in roughly the same location — when added to the DNA of normal individuals.

Although the researchers' strategy was sound, they nonetheless were searching for a needle (the right probe) in a haystack (the huge amount of DNA unrelated to the Huntington's disease gene). But they found it — a probe that evidently lies very close to the fatal gene.

The geep, a cross between a goat and a sheep, was created by scientists at the Animal Research Station in Cambridge, England, who joined the embryo of a goat with the embryo of a sheep. The animal, a male, has only sheep sex cells, so its offspring should all be normal lambs.

Genetics

Continued

To confirm this finding, the scientists needed to test whether the probe worked consistently in the DNA of a large number of people with the Huntington's disease gene. The best group for such a study, they knew, would be a large family in which some members have the Huntington's disease gene and others do not. They found such a family in Venezuela. After much testing, the researchers found that the probe always links differently with the DNA of family members who have Huntington's disease and the DNA of normal family members (persons over age 60 with no symptoms). Gusella and his colleagues had definitely found the marker they had been looking for.

Because the probe was from chromosome 4, Gusella and his colleagues concluded that the Huntington's disease gene must be located on the same chromosome. The next step will be to isolate the gene and learn what it normally codes for. Once the working of the gene is understood, scientists may be able to develop a cure for Huntington's disease.

ID sequences. Researchers at Scripps Clinic in La Jolla, Calif., reported in March 1984 that they had discovered an important clue to solving one of the greatest mysteries in genetics — how each cell in the body can "turn on" only the genes it needs.

The human body contains about 200 different types of cells. Every kind of cell contains the same genes, but most of the genes in a cell are turned off. Because each type of cell has its own active group of genes, geneticists realized that genes must be "labeled" in a way that allows a cell to recognize the genes it needs.

The researchers discovered how genes that are turned on in brain cells are labeled. They found that each active brain cell gene contains an identical sequence of 82 nucleotides. This sequence, called an identifier (ID) sequence, is not found in genes that are inactive in brain cells or in genes that are active in other kinds of cells. Geneticists must now determine how cells recognize ID sequences and turn on genes. [Daniel L. Hartl]

Immunology

Researchers at the National Cancer Institute (NCI) in Bethesda, Md., announced in April 1984 that they had identified a virus that may cause acquired immune deficiency syndrome (AIDS), a disease that severely weakens the body's immune system. Virologist Robert C. Gallo, director of the NCI research team, said the virus is called HTLV-3. It is similar to the human T-cell leukemia virus, HTLV-1, which causes a type of blood cancer.

AIDS, which first appeared in 1979, makes its victims susceptible to a rare skin cancer called Kaposi's sarcoma and to a variety of infections that would be no threat to a person with normal immunity. The disease affects mainly homosexual and bisexual men, intravenous drug addicts, Haitian immigrants, and *hemophiliacs*, people whose blood does not clot properly. By May 1984, more than 4,000 Americans had developed the disease and nearly 1,800 had died. No AIDS victims had been cured.

Shortly before the NCI announcement, scientists at the Pasteur Institute

in Paris reported that a virus they called LAV was the probable cause of AIDS. Both LAV and HTLV-3 are *retroviruses* (a type of virus that reproduces by inserting its genes into the genetic material of a cell). Because LAV and HTLV-3 are similar, many immunologists think that they are the same virus. Studies are in progress to confirm this.

Most immunologists had suspected that a virus is responsible for AIDS. A retrovirus was an especially likely candidate because such viruses are not transmitted as easily as other viruses, such as flu viruses. And AIDS does not seem to be transmitted easily but only through intimate contact. Furthermore, these viruses can infect and destroy a certain type of white blood cell that is deficient in AIDS victims.

Scientists believe homosexuals contract the disease through sexual contact. Drug addicts probably get the virus by sharing needles with infected addicts, while hemophiliacs apparently are infected when they receive blood-clotting factor that has been extracted

David, the boy who lived for 12 years in a sterile plastic "bubble" at Texas Children's Hospital in Houston because he was born without normal immunity, is prepared for a bone-marrow transplant in October 1983. The operation failed to correct the boy's condition, and he died of severe complications in February 1984.

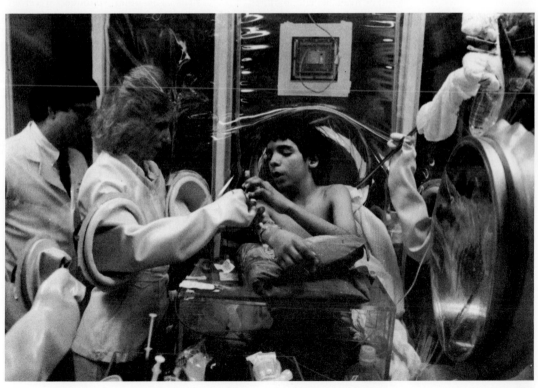

from AIDS-contaminated blood. By May 1984, 83 Americans had contracted AIDS from virus-infected blood transfusions or blood-clotting factor. Scientists are not certain how AIDS spreads among Haitian immigrants. But they suspect that AIDS first came to the United States from Haiti. Immunologists note that HTLV-1 — from which HTLV-3 evolved — has been found with increasing frequency in residents of Caribbean islands.

Gallo's research team found HTLV-3, or *antibodies* to HTLV-3, in the blood of more than 80 per cent of the AIDS victims tested. (Antibodies are molecules created by the immune system to combat foreign substances, such as viruses and bacteria.) To prove that HTLV-3 causes AIDS, immunologists plan to infect animals — probably apes — with the virus and see if they develop AIDS. If HTLV-3 is definitely found to cause AIDS, work can begin on a vaccine against the virus.

Meanwhile, Gallo's research may soon block one avenue of AIDS transmission — contaminated blood. It was hoped that a simple test to detect the presence of HTLV-3 in donated blood would be available late in 1984.

The new findings have had little effect on the treatment of AIDS victims, however. Physicians have been treating AIDS patients with drugs that strengthen the immune system. These substances, usually the natural infection-fighters interferon and interleukin-2, are produced by white blood cells in response to viruses and tumors. AIDS victims are deficient in interferon and interleukin-2, so doctors hope that giving these substances to AIDS patients will bolster their immune response. As yet, however, there is no evidence that AIDS victims have been significantly helped in this way.

New vaccines against flu and chicken pox were tested by researchers in 1984.

The first test of a new influenza vaccine was announced in March by the National Institute of Allergy and Infectious Diseases in Bethesda. Officials reported that the experimental vaccine, which is given in nose drops rather than by injection, was highly effective in protecting volunteers against influenza.

The vaccine was made from a virus created by scientists at the University of Michigan in Ann Arbor. To make the virus, the Michigan researchers used two strains of influenza A, the most common type of flu virus. One strain was a natural, flu-causing variety of the virus. The other strain, created in the laboratory, did not cause flu because it thrived at lower temperatures than are found in human cells.

The new virus has six genes from the harmless virus and two genes from the flu-causing virus. The two genes from the flu-causing virus direct the production of proteins that form part of the virus's outer surface. These proteins are detected by the immune system and cause the body to mount an attack on the virus. Thus, the new virus, with the two proteins on its "overcoat," stimulates an immune response but cannot cause flu.

The nose-drop vaccine was tested on 81 student volunteers at the University of Maryland in Baltimore and the University of Rochester in Rochester, N.Y. Sixteen of the volunteers were given a full dose of the vaccine and later exposed to the flu-causing strain of the virus. The other volunteers received no vaccine, a smaller dose of the vaccine, or a conventional flu shot. Then they were also exposed to the virus.

The researchers found that all of the volunteers who received a full dose of the nose-drop vaccine were completely protected against the flu. Many other volunteers developed flu symptoms.

The vaccine must now undergo more extensive testing. The researchers reported that the vaccine should be ready for commercial production within five years and that other viruses could be created to combat different strains of influenza A.

In May, medical scientists at the University of Pennsylvania in Philadelphia announced that a vaccine against chicken pox was highly effective in protecting children in a test group against that disease. The vaccine — developed by Merck, Sharp, & Dohme, a West Point, Pa., pharmaceutical company — was made from a virus isolated in the 1970's by Japanese researchers. The company said it hoped to have the vaccine on the market by the end of 1985.   [Paul Katz]

Medicine

Dentistry. Tooth decay could be significantly reduced if more dentists coated children's back teeth with sealants, an advisory panel to the National Institutes of Health in Bethesda, Md., concluded in December 1983. Sealants are plastic materials applied to teeth to prevent food and bacteria from lodging in the pits and *fissures* (grooves) of molars and premolars, the most common areas of decay in children. Although sealants are safe and painless to apply and have been available since the early 1970's, few dentists use them. According to the panel, sealants, which remain in place for at least five years, are more effective than fluoride in reducing pit and fissure cavities.

Antibiotic surprise. In September 1983, a team of researchers at the State University of New York in Stony Brook reported that antibiotics may provide an effective treatment for some forms of gum disease, but not for the reason they expected. Diabetics are particularly susceptible to an advanced form of gum disease in which *collagen* — the main protein in the fibers of connective tissue — in the gums breaks down. This breakdown results from high levels in the gum tissue of *collagenase*, an enzyme normally present in body tissue that breaks down collagen. The researchers theorized that the bacteria that cause the gum disease give off harmful chemicals that stimulate the production of high levels of the enzyme.

To test their hypothesis, the researchers gave antibiotics to two groups of diabetic laboratory rats. One group had gum disease. The other was germ-free and so their gums were free of the bacteria. The researchers found that the levels of collagenase in the gums of the diseased rats fell. But they were surprised to find that enzyme levels in the gums of the germ-free rats also dropped. The researchers concluded that the antibiotics may block the production of collagenase and so may provide an effective way to treat and, perhaps, prevent gum disease resulting from the destruction of collagen in nondiabetics as well as in diabetics.

[Paul Goldhaber]

Plastic sealants prevent food and bacteria from lodging in the pits and grooves of teeth. Sealant is applied to teeth, *below,* then hardened with intense light beams, *below right.*

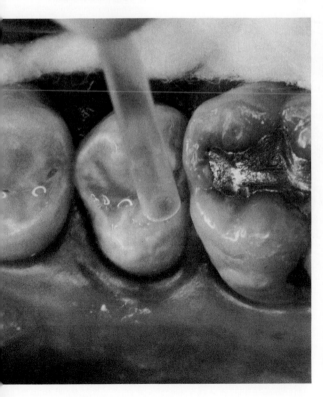

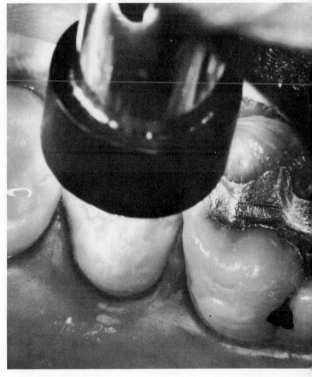

Internal Medicine. Evidence confirming a connection between heredity and malignant melanoma, a particularly deadly form of skin cancer, was reported in October 1983 by a team of scientists led by epidemiologist Mark H. Green of the National Cancer Institute, part of the National Institutes of Health (NIH) in Bethesda, Md. The researchers based their conclusion on data from a registry at the NIH that records information about cancer victims and their families.

Twenty-five of the 1,000 families listed in the registry when the study began had at least 2 members with malignant melanoma. Malignant melanoma originates in moles and often spreads quickly throughout the body. Of the 401 family members studied by the researchers, 69 had developed at least one cancerous mole and 74 had at least one mole of the type likely to become cancerous.

The researchers were unable to account for the cases of malignant melanoma that develop in people with no family history of the disease. However, they suspect that environmental factors, such as overexposure to the sun, may influence the development of the disease. In the Special Reports section, see THE SKIN WE LIVE IN.

New stroke treatment. In January 1984, researchers at the University of Pennsylvania's Children's Hospital of Philadelphia and the Cerebrovascular Research Center in Philadelphia reported a new approach in the treatment and prevention of stroke in patients with sickle cell disease. Sickle cell disease is an inherited disease, found chiefly among blacks, in which red blood cells become deformed and stick in the blood vessels, blocking the flow of blood. Victims of the most severe form of the disease suffer from a variety of serious problems, including strokes.

Researchers examining arteries in the heads of young sickle cell victims who had suffered a stroke discovered that deformed blood cells had caused serious damage to the walls of the arteries. Pediatric oncologist Marie Oliver Russell and her associates theo-

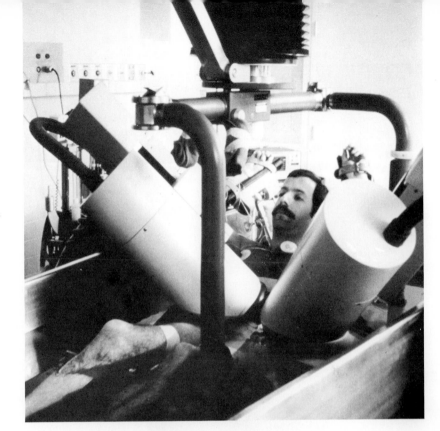

A shock-wave bathtub is a new way to destroy kidney stones. Large tubes containing electrodes are aimed toward the kidneys of an anesthetized patient in a special tub. Sparks from the electrodes vaporize surrounding water, setting up shock waves that shatter the patient's kidney stone without damaging the tissue of his kidneys.

Medicine

Continued

rized that rapid transfusions of whole blood would "wash out" deformed cells sticking to the artery walls and thus permit the blood vessels to heal. They hoped that this healing would increase the rate of recovery from stroke and help prevent it from recurring.

To test their idea, the investigators divided 23 young black sickle cell victims who had suffered a stroke into two groups. All 23 children had at least two damaged arteries. Seventeen of the children were given transfusions of whole blood every three to four weeks for at least one year, and the remaining 6 children were given no transfusions.

The researchers reported that 22 per cent of the group that did not receive transfusions died and of the survivors in that group, 67 per cent had at least one more stroke. In contrast, none of the patients who received transfusions died, and only 10 per cent suffered another stroke.

Further research on this treatment must be done to predict which sickle cell stroke patients would benefit, how

long treatment should be administered, and what hazards, if any, might be involved.

New blood pressure guidelines. A panel of experts convened by the National Heart, Lung, and Blood Institute recommended in April 1984 that physicians should place greater emphasis on nondrug treatments for the mildest cases of high blood pressure, or hypertension. Hypertension, which affects an estimated 35 million Americans, increases the risk of heart disease, stroke, and kidney disease. The panel recommended that people with mild hypertension lose weight and cut back on the amount of sodium they consume daily. The panel also recommended drinking fewer alcoholic beverages, establishing a regular exercise program, and using relaxation techniques, such as meditation.

The panel suggested that physicians prescribe drugs to lower blood pressure in mildly hypertensive patients only after determining that nondrug treatments are ineffective. The experts also recommended that nondrug treat-

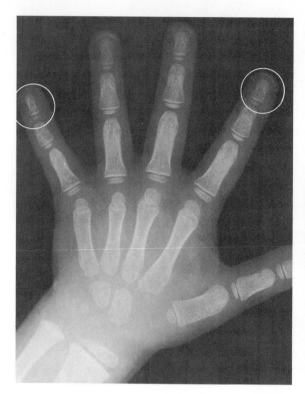 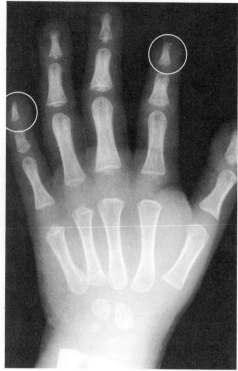

Medicine

Continued

X rays of children's hands may enable physicians to detect fetal alcohol syndrome (FAS), a pattern of birth defects caused by drinking during pregnancy. The fingertip bones of children with FAS, *above right*, especially in the index and little fingers, are narrower and shorter than those of normal children, *above left*.

ments be used in combination with drugs for more severe hypertension.

The new guidelines were issued as a response to increasing concerns about the harmful side effects of drugs used to lower blood pressure. The experts stressed that nondrug treatments alone would probably be successful only for people with the mildest form of high blood pressure.

Cutting amputations. A program consisting of careful and conscientious examination of the feet and vigorous early treatment of foot ulcers in diabetics has sharply reduced the number of amputations at the largest diabetic clinic in the United States. The program was developed by orthopedic surgeon Paul W. Brand of the National Hansen's Disease Center in Carville, La. It has been used for 13 years at the diabetes clinic at Emory University's Grady Memorial Hospital in Atlanta, Ga. In January 1984, John K. Davidson, director of the clinic, reported that the annual rate of amputations fell by 50 per cent between 1971 and 1983.

Diabetics with a severe form of the disease may suffer nerve damage that leads to a loss of sensation in their feet. As a result, they may neglect or even fail to notice minor problems, such as blisters and calluses. The problem is complicated by the deteriorating eyesight that often accompanies diabetes. If unattended, these minor problems may develop into serious infections and ulcers. Ulcers of the feet are particularly difficult to heal, and gangrene often sets in. At that point, the foot or the ulcerated part of it must be amputated.

To solve this problem, Brand developed a program involving prevention, early detection, and treatment. Each diabetic patient's feet are regularly examined by clinic personnel for potential sources of trouble. In addition, an impression is made of the feet to reveal pressure points where circulation is poor and ulcers may develop. Patients may then be fitted with special insoles or "rocker" shoes that distribute the weight on the foot evenly and relieve stress on pressure points. Patients are also taught proper foot care.

Brand developed a "total contact" foot cast for patients whose foot ulcers have been surgically removed. The cast improves circulation in the foot, allowing the wound to heal. Physicians at the Duke University Medical Center in Durham, N.C., where the cast has been extensively used, report a 73 per cent cure rate for deep ulcers involving damage to the tendons and bones and a 97 per cent cure rate for less serious ulcers.

Ultrasound limits. Physicians should stop ordering ultrasound examinations for pregnant women unless there is a specific medical reason for believing that the procedure would help in the care of the mother or unborn child, according to a panel of experts convened by the NIH. In an ultrasound examination, high frequency sound waves are beamed into the mother's womb. The reflections of the fetus are then converted into a picture, which can be used to determine the fetus' age and sex, measure its head and bones, and check for certain birth defects.

Surveys have indicated that from 15 to 40 per cent of pregnant women in the United States have at least one ultrasound examination.

The panel said that there was no evidence that ultrasound examinations had harmed human mothers or fetuses. However, they also said that neither the benefits nor the safety of the procedure had yet been proven. Some studies with laboratory animals have indicated that ultrasound may slow prenatal growth or cause deformities.

A trigger for heart spasms. A chemical produced in the body and often associated with hay fever may be an important cause of spasm—a sudden contraction—of the coronary arteries that may lead to a heart attack. The chemical, histamine, is one of several chemicals that cause the sniffling and watery eyes that may occur during allergic reactions. It also causes smooth muscles, such as those in blood vessels, to contract.

In March 1984, pharmacologists Stanley Kalsner and Robert Richards of the University of Ottawa in Canada

---

The Verdict on Cholesterol

Checking blood cholesterol

After years of uncertainty about the role of cholesterol in heart disease, the verdict is finally in: Reducing blood cholesterol levels can help to prevent a heart attack.

A heart attack is the final result of a process called *atherosclerosis*—the gradual clogging of the small coronary arteries by fatty deposits called *plaques*. One of the substances contained in plaques is cholesterol—a waxy substance found in many foods and also produced by the liver.

Scientists have known for some time that such risk factors as cigarette smoking, high blood pressure, and high levels of cholesterol in the blood are associated with atherosclerosis. Patients who stopped smoking and reduced their blood pressure lowered their heart attack risk, but doctors were unable to prove that the same was true of lowering cholesterol.

In 1974, the National Heart, Lung, and Blood Institute in Bethesda, Md.,

began a major study to determine the benefits of lowering blood cholesterol. Researchers studied more than 3,800 middle-aged men with cholesterol levels greater than 265 milligrams per 100 milliliters of blood. Normal is about 210 milligrams.

The men were divided into two groups. Both groups were placed on a low-cholesterol diet, and one group also received cholestyramine, a cholesterol-lowering drug. After 10 years, both groups had a lower death rate from heart disease than would be expected, statistically. The diet-and-drug group had the best results—19 per cent fewer heart attacks and 24 per cent fewer deaths.

However, the research did not completely settle the cholesterol issue because all the men studied had high levels of cholesterol. Whether people in the normal range should also strive to lower their cholesterol is still open to debate.   [Michael H. Alderman]

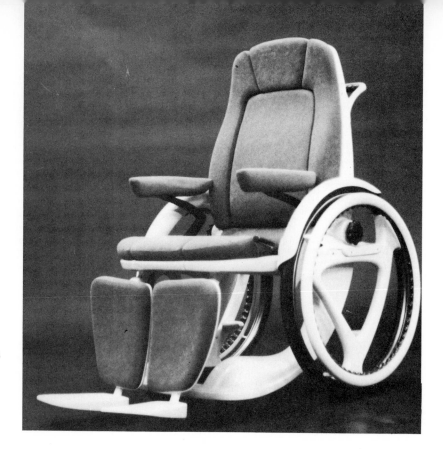

A futuristic design in wheelchairs features spokeless wheels for better handgrip, armrests that retract to allow the user to get up on either side, and removable cushions so the chair can be wheeled into a shower.

Medicine

Continued

reported on their study comparing the coronary arteries of people who died of heart attack with the arteries of a control group of people of similar age who died suddenly of other causes. The researchers found that the arteries of the heart attack victims contained much higher levels of histamine than did the arteries of people in the control group. In addition, the arteries of the cardiac patients contracted much more strongly when injected with histamine than did the arteries from the control group. When a coronary artery contracts, less blood can flow to the wall of the heart. A heart attack may occur when the coronary arteries become so narrow that the heart muscle receives an insufficient supply of blood.

Most heart specialists had long believed that heart attacks were always caused by a blockage — a blood clot or a build-up of *plaque* (a fatty substance) — in one or more coronary blood vessels. However, in the 1970's, researchers began finding that in many heart attack victims, no blockage

existed. They theorized that a spasm could also cause a heart attack.

This idea has puzzled researchers because they believed that if a spasm occurred, it would occur within the narrow part of the artery, which is embedded in the wall of the heart muscle. However, in that case, the damaged cells in the heart wall would give off waste products that would immediately cause the closed artery to open. Kalsner and Richards suggest, however, that if the spasm occurs in the part of the coronary artery that rests on the surface of the heart, the waste products would not reach the artery and the spasm could continue, possibly causing a heart attack.

The new findings suggest that high levels of histamine in the coronary arteries of people with heart disease may increase the risk of heart attack. The researchers suggested that a variety of allergic reactions, ranging from hay fever to reactions to food, which raise histamine levels in the body, may trigger a spasm that might produce a heart attack. [Michael H. Alderman]

Medicine

Continued

Surgery. An experimental surgical procedure using a laser to remove an obstruction in a coronary artery may eventually replace coronary by-pass surgery, according to some experts. Internist Daniel S. J. Choy of St. Luke's-Roosevelt Medical Center in New York City conducted the first tests of the technique, called *laser coronary angioplasty*, on heart patients at the University of Toulouse Medical Center in France in September 1983. The United States Food and Drug Administration has not yet approved the procedure for use in America.

After testing the procedure on animals and human cadavers, Choy performed the laser surgery on four French patients undergoing coronary by-pass surgery. In by-pass surgery, a vein is grafted onto the coronary arteries to by-pass a blockage in the arteries caused by fatty deposits.

Choy hopes someday to perform the laser surgery without opening the patient's chest. But because it is still experimental, Choy and his team of French surgeons performed the laser surgery with the patient's heart and coronary arteries exposed.

After the heart was exposed and the coronary artery opened in preparation for the by-pass graft, Choy inserted a *catheter* (a slender tube) into the blocked artery. He then fired an argon laser connected to the catheter. The intense beam of light from the laser traveled through the catheter and vaporized the fatty deposit in the artery.

After the laser treatment, the French surgeons completed the usual by-pass surgery. This was done so that if the artery became blocked again, the patient would not be harmed.

In the second stage of his research, Choy plans to use the laser treatment alone — without the by-pass — but the patient's chest will be open so that Choy can monitor the laser effect. In the final stage of the experiments, Choy will use the laser procedure without opening the chest and exposing the heart. The catheter will be inserted into an artery in the groin, then guided to the blocked coronary artery. However, further research is needed

Tiny metal beads, *right*, cover a metal stem implanted into a thighbone to anchor an artificial hip joint. Bone grows into the implant, *far right*, eliminating the need for cement, which often weakens over time, causing pain and a loss of mobility.

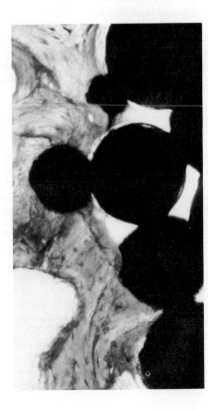

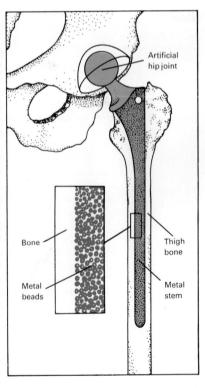

to ensure that the artery would not be injured by the laser beam.

Removing fat. A new plastic surgery technique developed in Europe literally sucks out *subcutaneous fat* — the fat found below the skin. Although it was developed for cosmetic purposes, it may have other uses, according to a report issued in October 1983 by a panel of experts from the American Society of Plastic and Reconstructive Surgeons, who observed the technique, called *suction lipectomy*, in France.

In suction lipectomy, a metal tube 1.9 centimeters (0.75 inch) or less in diameter is inserted into the subcutaneous fat and moved back and forth. This movement breaks up the fat, which is then sucked out through the tube. Because the incision the surgeon makes to insert the tube is small, suction lipectomy causes much less scarring than the incisions of traditional plastic surgery. In addition, the procedure is less expensive and the patient does not lose as much blood.

The procedure requires a great deal of skill. If the metal tube pierces the layer of muscle underlying the fat, this may cause severe bleeding. If the tube gets too close to the skin layer, it may cause damage that blocks the flow of blood to the skin tissue, possibly causing gangrene.

So far, suction lipectomy has been used chiefly on young patients to remove fat deposits from the abdomen, buttocks, and thighs. These patients were not necessarily obese but had fat deposits that were considered a cosmetic problem. The technique is most effective with young patients because their skin is still elastic enough to shrink after the fat is removed. Because the amount of fat removed during the procedure is very small, the patient does not lose much weight.

In November 1983, plastic surgeon Stephen H. Miller of Oregon Health Sciences University in Portland reported using suction lipectomy to remove a *benign* (noncancerous) tumor from the cheek of an 8-year-old girl. Because the tumor covered almost the entire cheek, conventional surgery would have left her with a huge scar. Miller was able to remove the tumor with an incision only 1.5 centimeters (0.6 inch) long. Also in November,

plastic surgeon Eugene H. Courtiss of Newton-Wellesley Hospital in Newton, Mass., reported using suction lipectomy on a young woman to remove about 40 benign tumors.

Some surgeons also have begun using suction lipectomy to shape the skin after surgery. The removal of tissue during some types of surgery, such as the removal of a tumor from the neck, leaves a depression in the skin. The surgeon fills the depression with a "flap" of tissue taken from another area of the patient's body. The flap consists of skin, subcutaneous fat, and muscle.

However, because the flap is usually bigger than the depression, additional surgery is needed to remove excess tissue. Several surgeons have reported using suction lipectomy to remove excess fat from flaps. They report that the new procedure enables the surgeon to shape the tissue more precisely.

Killing cancer with heat. In May 1983, neurosurgeon Robert Rand of the University of California, Los Angeles, reported on trials of an experimental surgical technique in which iron particles are used to speed the destruction of cancer cells by heat. Since the late 1960's, surgeons have used heat, either by itself or with radiation, to destroy cancerous tumors. However, the procedure has had limited use because raising the body's temperature more than a few degrees — to 45° or 46°C (113° or 114°F.) — can cause death. Unfortunately, such temperatures are usually too low to completely destroy cancer cells.

Rand's procedure is designed to raise the temperature of tumors without increasing overall body temperature. To accomplish this, Rand either injected iron particles into the tumor or set the particles close to the tumor during surgery. He then placed the patient in a magnetic field. The attraction between the iron and the magnetic field heated the iron particles. By using the particles, Rand was able to raise the temperature of the tumor to 55° to 65°C (131° to 149°F.), well above temperatures that can be used when heating the entire body. Rand reported that patients treated with this new technique suffered no side effects.

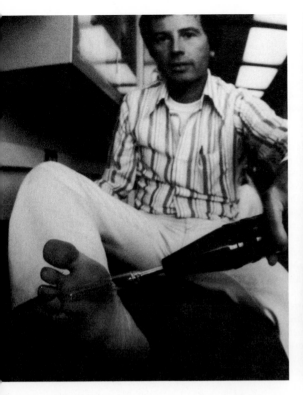

Medicine

Continued

A spark of electricity from a glass electrode, *above,* held close to a wart, *above right,* seems to kill the viruses that cause warts, thus eliminating the growth.

New spinal surgery. In 1983 and 1984, surgeons at a number of medical centers in the United States reported success using a new surgical technique to repair protruding — or slipped — disks in the lower back, the most common cause of severe back problems. Spinal disks are pads consisting of tough gristlelike tissue surrounding a soft core. They separate and cushion the spinal vertebrae. When a disk ruptures, the soft core protrudes through the gristlelike tissue into the spinal cord, putting pressure on the spinal nerve and causing pain.

In the past, the surgical removal of slipped disks involved cutting away the muscle and part of the bone surrounding the spinal cord. In 1958 in Canada and 1983 in the United States, surgeons began injecting slipped disks with chymopapain, an enzyme commonly used in meat tenderizers. The enzyme breaks down the *collagen* — the main protein in the fibers of connective tissue — in the disks, causing them to soften and shrink. However, patients treated with chymopapain injec-

tions suffer a great deal of pain afterward. In addition, injections frequently must be repeated.

The new technique allows surgeons to remove the protruding disk while leaving the muscles and bone around the spinal cord intact. The spine is first examined with a computerized tomography (CT) scanner, an X-ray device that provides cross-sectional images of the inside of the body (in the Special Reports section, see NEW WAYS TO LOOK INSIDE THE BODY).

The CT scan allows the surgeon to pinpoint the location of the ruptured disk. The surgeon then makes a small incision near the disk and, while viewing the area through a special operating microscope, inserts microsurgical instruments into the opening. These instruments, which are designed for operating in tiny areas, allow the surgeon to reach around the muscles and bones to remove the disk. Surgeons believe the new technique is safer than conventional disk surgery and reduces the time needed for the patient to recover.   [Frank E. Gump]

Molecular Biology

Scientists reported in January 1984 that ribonucleic acid (RNA) can act as an *enzyme*, a substance that speeds up biochemical reactions. Previously, all known enzymes had been proteins. The discovery was made by researchers at Yale University in New Haven, Conn., and the University of Colorado Medical Center in Denver, led by molecular biologist Sidney Altman.

RNA is a complex molecule that "reads" the genetic code from deoxyribonucleic acid (DNA), the master molecule of heredity, and directs the production of *proteins*, long chainlike molecules. Enzymes are one type of protein, but there are many other kinds, such as hormones and the proteins that make up skin and muscles.

Enzymes are of great importance in biology. Without enzymes, almost none of the biochemical reactions that make life possible would occur fast enough to enable cells to function properly. And because all the reactions occurring within cells are dependent on enzymes, cells can control the precise rates of those reactions — and even their locations — by controlling the release of enzymes.

Molecular biologists have long tried to understand how enzymes are controlled by a cell's genes, how they are distributed to the correct places within cells, and how they accomplish their highly specific tasks. After studying thousands of enzymes, molecular biologists had become convinced that enzymes were always proteins, folded into a vast number of different shapes. How enzymes function depends upon the particular shapes into which they are folded. Now it will be necessary to enlarge the concept of an enzyme to include RNA molecules, which apparently can also fold themselves in such a way that they can act as enzymes.

The work that led to this finding began in 1977, when Altman discovered that ribonuclease P, an enzyme found in bacteria, contains both a protein chain and an RNA molecule. At first, many molecular biologists suspected that the enzyme had somehow become "contaminated" with RNA.

However, Altman and his colleagues

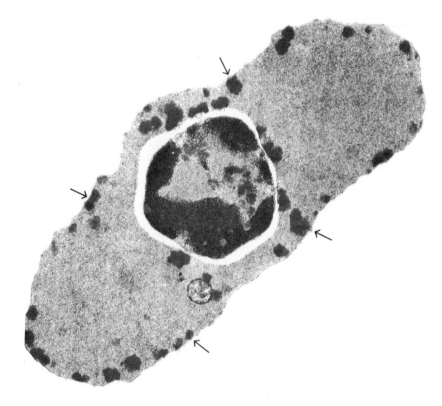

Dense, grainy masses called Heinz bodies (arrows) in the red blood cell of a herring gull (26,800 times actual size) provide evidence of how birds are poisoned by eating crude oil. Heinz bodies are a common feature of a type of anemia caused by toxic chemicals, such as oil spilled into the ocean by supertanker accidents.

"Forget enlightenment. I want you to concentrate
on the structure of the protein molecule."

Molecular Biology

Continued

were eventually able to prove that the enzyme would work only when RNA was present. Most molecular biologists concluded that the RNA must somehow help the protein to stay in the right shape to carry out the ribonuclease P enzyme activities. Altman was as surprised as anyone else when his research team found that it is actually the RNA portion of the molecule that carries out the enzyme function of ribonuclease P and that the protein plays a relatively minor role. In fact, the scientists learned that under certain conditions, ribonuclease P can function as an enzyme even when only the RNA portion is present.

Cells contain many RNA molecules whose functions are not completely understood. For example, a large part of a *ribosome* — the complex particle on which proteins are assembled — is made up of RNA. Although molecular biologists previously thought that this RNA was only the scaffolding on which various proteins carry out their functions, it now seems likely that some RNA's in ribosomes — and per-

haps other RNA's of unknown function — also act as enzymes.

Cancer genes. Scientists have made tremendous progress in the early 1980's in understanding changes in cells that lead to the development of cancer. One of the most important advances has been the discovery that animals and human beings possess *oncogenes*, or cancer genes, that can cause cells to become malignant. In August 1983, researchers at the Massachusetts Institute of Technology (MIT) reported that at least two cancer genes must act together to cause cancer.

In making this discovery, the MIT research team — headed by molecular biologists Hartmut Land, Luis F. Parada, and Robert A. Weinberg — helped to clarify a crucial question: why cancer genes cause malignant changes more easily in some cells than in others. The question centered around how to interpret one of the most important experiments used to study cancer genes. This experiment involves purifying the DNA from cancer cells and adding it to laboratory cul-

285

Molecular Biology

Continued

An ice crystal, *below,* forms around *Pseudomonas syringae* bacteria (arrow). Ice damage to crops, such as oranges, *below right,* is often caused when such bacteria act as "seeds" for ice formation. Scientists have produced a strain of this bacteria that does not cause ice to form, and they hope that when sprayed on crops it will force out the ice-forming variety.

tures of noncancerous cells. If the cells become cancerous, the DNA presumably contains a cancer gene.

The biggest controversy with this type of experiment involved the nature of the cultured cells, which are usually mouse cells that have been maintained in the laboratory through many cell divisions. The best results have been obtained with a particular mouse cell line known as NIH3T3 cells and named for the National Institutes of Health in Bethesda, Md., where they were first cultured. Scientists have been able to create cancerous changes in NIH3T3 cells by adding DNA from a wide variety of mouse and human cancer cells.

However, when the same DNA is added to normal mouse cells that have not been previously grown in culture, no cancerous changes occur. Many biologists therefore speculated that some critical early steps in cancer formation have already occurred in NIH3T3 cells and that the cancer gene or genes in the DNA may be just tipping the balance. If so, this type of experiment

would be of little help in understanding the steps that change a normal cell into a cancer cell.

As molecular biologists debated the meaning of these experiments with NIH3T3 cells, the MIT group found that it is possible to take normal cells from rat embryos and convert them to cancerous cells simply by adding DNA containing known cancer genes. But the MIT group added two specific cancer genes at the same time—the *myc* and the *ras* cancer genes. They found that both these genes had to be present to produce cancer.

The names *myc* and *ras* are derived from the names of the animal cancer viruses in which these cancer genes were discovered. The *myc* gene was found in a virus that infects birds; the *ras* gene, in a rat virus.

Scientists believe that cancer genes originated in the DNA of animals and were copied by the viruses in the distant evolutionary past. These genes are now present in the DNA of all mammals, including human beings. Cancer genes seem to have a normal

Molecular Biology

Continued

function in many cells. They become capable of causing cancer only when their structure is altered or when they somehow function abnormally.

Apparently, NIH3T3 cells are so easily changed into cancer cells because they already contain an improperly functioning *myc* gene. Only a *ras* gene must be added to complete the transformation of NIH3T3 cells into cancerous cells. This finding fits well with growing scientific evidence indicating that the change of a normal cell into a cancer cell is a complex process with many steps. Also, the fact that cancer becomes much more common as people grow older suggests that it usually takes a long time for all the required genetic changes to accumulate in a given cell.

Researchers have a great deal of work ahead of them. They must identify and analyze all the steps leading to cancer. They must also determine which changes in a cell actually cause the cell to become cancerous and which changes are simply a result of the cancer process. However, the MIT discovery is a tremendous advance toward the understanding of cancer.

Artificial chromosomes. One of the most extraordinary processes in biology is the reproduction of *chromosomes* — the structures within the cell nucleus that carry genes. Every time a cell divides, in a process called *mitosis*, it has to reproduce its entire set of chromosomes. The new chromosomes must then split into two groups so that each new "daughter" cell receives a complete set of chromosomes — 23 pairs of chromosomes in the case of human cells. Even more complex is the process known as *meiosis*, in which the reproductive cells — sperm in males and egg cells in females — are formed. The chromosomes must be distributed in such a way that each reproductive cell obtains only one of each pair.

Until recently, little was known about the structures in chromosomes that regulate their reproduction and distribution during mitosis and meiosis. However, research at Harvard University Medical School in Boston has begun to clear up this mystery. Harvard scientists reported in September 1983 that they had created an artificial yeast chromosome that behaved almost like a natural chromosome. By observing this chromosome, the researchers learned much about how all chromosomes operate.

Biologists had long known that one particular part of a chromosome was likely to be of special importance. This area is called the *centromere*. Tiny fibers within the cell attach to the centromere during mitosis and meiosis. These fibers pull the duplicate chromosomes apart and toward opposite sides of the cell before it divides.

In addition to centromeres, the scientists investigated regulatory roles of two other types of chromosome structures, *replication origins* and *telomeres*. A replication origin is a point on the DNA molecule where the reproduction of the DNA begins. Telomeres are special DNA sequences on the ends of chromosomes. Their function is to ensure that even the very last unit of DNA is duplicated correctly. (DNA is made of hundreds of millions of small units called *base pairs*.)

In the early 1980's, a number of other researchers, working with yeast cells, found that all three structures — centromeres, replication origins, and telomeres — are located at specific sites on the yeast DNA molecule. They also showed that these structures cause a complete chromosome to form spontaneously around the DNA if the DNA is placed in a yeast cell.

The Harvard scientists, headed by molecular biologists Andrew W. Murray and Jack W. Szostak, followed up on that finding. Using pieces of natural yeast DNA, they assembled an artificial yeast chromosome containing about 50,000 base pairs. The artificial chromosome was only about one-fifth as big as the smallest natural yeast chromosome, but it contained a centromere, a replication origin, and telomeres. When placed in yeast cells, the artificial chromosome divided just like natural chromosomes.

Careful measurements, however, showed that the artificial chromosome was slightly defective when compared with normal chromosomes. For example, although the artificial chromosome reproduced and divided correctly more than 99 per cent of the time during mitosis, it made errors about 100 times more frequently than

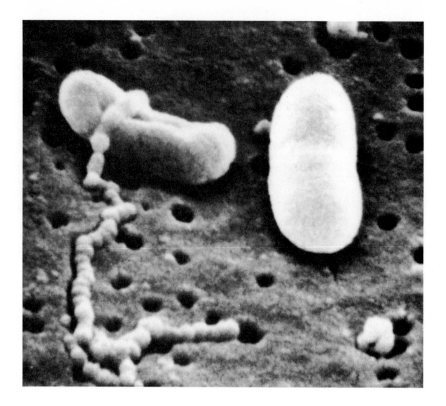

Industrial uses may soon be found for bacteria such as *Alcaligenes eutrophus,* which secretes a resin that could replace petroleum as the basic ingredient in some types of plastic.

Molecular Biology

Continued

natural chromosomes do. Presumably, natural chromosomes have acquired very precise behavior patterns as the result of billions of years of evolutionary fine-tuning. Nonetheless, the success of this experiment suggests that just three kinds of structures are required for chromosome function, and that the assembly of chromosomes within cells is triggered simply by the presence of these components at specific sites on the DNA molecule.

Clotting factor. In April 1984, California scientists announced that they had produced a substance vital to the clotting of blood, a protein called factor VIII. Factor VIII is lacking in many *hemophiliacs,* persons whose blood does not clot easily. Factor VIII is the largest and most complicated molecule so far created with genetic engineering techniques.

The protein was made by researchers at Genentech Incorporated in South San Francisco, Calif. They isolated the human gene that directs the production of factor VIII and inserted it into the genetic material of animal

cells in laboratory cultures. The cells then manufactured factor VIII. In laboratory experiments, the protein enabled blood taken from hemophiliacs to clot properly.

Genentech officials said clinical trials of the artificially produced factor VIII may begin in late 1985 or early 1986. But before testing can start, the scientists must develop methods for producing large quantities of the protein and for purifying it.

The artificial clotting factor will be of great benefit to hemophiliacs, who now must inject themselves with factor VIII extracted from the blood of thousands of donors. This procedure not only is very expensive — $5,000 to $10,000 for the 30 to 50 injections a year needed by many hemophiliacs — but it also carries a health risk. Factor VIII obtained from blood donors may carry hepatitis B virus or the virus that causes acquired immune deficiency syndrome (AIDS), which destroys the immune system. Artificially produced factor VIII will be free from such dangers. [Maynard V. Olson]

Neuroscientists at the National Institute of Mental Health (NIMH) in Bethesda, Md., reported in November 1983 that they had produced Parkinson's disease symptoms in laboratory monkeys. Parkinson's disease destroys brain cells and causes rigid muscles, trembling, and mental disturbances. The cause is unknown, but a drug called L-dopa helps relieve the symptoms by increasing the brain's supply of dopamine, a chemical produced by the adrenal glands. Parkinson's disease destroys the cells that produce dopamine.

Scientists have been hampered in developing improved medicines for Parkinson's disease because drug-testing has been limited to what can be safely done on humans. Until recently, scientists had not been able to cause the disease in laboratory animals.

The breakthrough made by the NIMH researchers — Richard S. Burns, Chang C. Chiueh, Irwin J. Kopin, and their colleagues — resulted from a tragic error made by some drug addicts who had been trying to manufacture a heroinlike drug. Instead, they produced a toxic chemical, called NMPTP, that when injected caused severe brain damage, similar to Parkinson's disease. The NIMH scientists discovered that monkeys injected with NMPTP developed the same symptoms and brain damage suffered by the addicts. The researchers concluded that the drug-produced disease is a form of Parkinson's disease because L-dopa relieved the monkeys' symptoms.

Now that researchers have learned how to cause Parkinson's disease in monkeys, they will be able to investigate the disease more thoroughly and develop better methods to treat it. They also hope to discover what causes the disease and how to prevent it.

Huntington's disease. The discovery of a specific genetic variation that will make it possible to diagnose Huntington's disease was announced in November 1983 by molecular biologist James Gusella and his associates at the Massachusetts General Hospital and Harvard University Medical School in Boston. Huntington's disease is a hereditary brain disorder that causes mental disturbances and involuntary muscle movements. Symptoms of this fatal disease generally do not appear until after the age of 30, so the children of Huntington's disease victims grow up without knowing whether they have inherited the disorder.

The Boston researchers discovered a unique sequence of deoxyribonucleic acid (DNA) — the master molecule of heredity — located close to the gene that, when defective, causes Huntington's disease. This DNA sequence is different from the DNA sequence that lies close to the normal version of the gene in persons who run no risk of getting the disease. The unique segment of DNA is a sort of genetic signpost that indicates the Huntington's disease gene is present. See GENETICS.

Brain tissue transplants. Brain cells, once damaged or destroyed, do not grow back as do cells in most other parts of the body. In the past few years, however, researchers have experimentally transplanted brain tissue from one animal to another to learn whether brain injuries may be treated by replacing lost cells.

In July 1983, neuroscientists Donald G. Stein, Randy Labbe, and Arthur Firl of Clark University in Worcester, Mass., and Elliott Mufson of Harvard University Medical School reported the results of their studies on rat brains. The researchers transplanted brain tissue from the frontal *cortex* (outermost layer of brain cells) of unborn rats into the brains of adult rats whose frontal cortex had been surgically removed.

The brain cells in the implants made connections with the cells in the adult rats' brains. As a result, the implants improved the learning ability of the brain-injured rats. Rats receiving these brain tissue implants learned much more quickly how to find their way through a maze than rats that had received no implants or implants from the back part of the brain.

Brain tissue transplants offer hope for the treatment of brain injuries. Neurosurgeons may someday use this technique to restore normal functioning in brain-damaged patients.

Smoking and the brain. Research reported in January 1984 by scientists at Johns Hopkins University in Baltimore showed that pregnant rats exposed to low levels of carbon monoxide (CO) — one of the gases in cigarette smoke — give birth to offspring with inferior memory and learning ability. The research indicates that pregnant women who smoke may also be harming their unborn babies.

The investigators, headed by neuroscientists Laurence D. Fechter and Charles F. Mactutus, performed the experiment on 32 pregnant rats. The rats had identical living conditions except that half breathed clean air while the others were exposed to CO.

Large amounts of CO can be fatal. However, the amount of CO in the experiment was just enough to cause about 15 per cent of the rats' *hemoglobin* — the part of the blood that carries oxygen — to combine chemically with the toxic gas. (From 5 to 16 per cent of the hemoglobin of heavy smokers is chemically combined with CO.)

At birth, the litters of both groups of rats appeared normal except for a slightly lower average birth weight among the pups of the mothers exposed to CO. The scientists trained both groups of pups at different stages of development to avoid an electric shock. They later retested the young rats to measure how well the animals remembered to avoid the shock. At every age, the rats whose mothers had been exposed to CO were less successful in the tests than the rats whose mothers had breathed clean air.

Scientists cannot make a direct comparison between rats and human beings. But this experiment shows that smoking may have a damaging effect on unborn human offspring.

Inadequate nutrition, as well as smoking, may impair brain development early in life, Tennessee researchers reported in April 1984. Scientists at St. Jude Children's Hospital in Memphis said their studies with rats showed that a lack of proper nutrition hinders the formation of *myelin*, the fatty covering that surrounds and insulates nerve fibers. The researchers said a "myelin deficit" early in life might lead to an irreversible damaging of brain function, a possibility they are now investigating.   [George Adelman]

Nutrition

Zinc, an essential nutrient, may prove to be an effective and safe treatment for the common cold. In January 1984, nutritionists at the University of Texas at Austin reported on the first clinical trial using zinc to reduce the duration of colds. Zinc inhibits the reproduction of several viruses.

The investigators conducted a study of 146 people who had a common cold to determine the effect of zinc tablets compared with *placebos* (tablets with no active ingredient). Each volunteer took either a placebo or a tablet containing 23 milligrams of zinc every two waking hours. After seven days, cold symptoms had disappeared in 86 per cent of the 37 volunteers who received zinc. Only 46 per cent of the volunteers who received the placebo were free of symptoms. Overall, the zinc shortened the duration of a common cold by seven days.

About one-half of the volunteers who received zinc reported unpleasant side effects, including altered food tastes, mouth irritation, and nausea. Other forms of zinc than that used in the clinical trial need to be explored to find some less unpleasant to take.

Because this study involved people who already had colds, it did not show whether zinc would prevent the common cold. The investigators warned against long-term use of zinc supplements, which may be hazardous.

Diet and heart disease. In January 1984, United States government researchers reported the first conclusive evidence of something scientists had long suspected: Lowering cholesterol levels through diet and drugs dramatically reduces the risk of heart disease. Cholesterol is a fatty substance manufactured by the human body and also obtained from such foods as eggs, butter, and meat. The body needs some cholesterol, but the government study proved that an excess of the substance increases the risk of heart attacks. See MEDICINE (Internal Medicine [Close-Up]).

It also seemed that not only adults suffered from high cholesterol levels. In March 1984, a group of 37 heart specialists warned that cholesterol lev-

A food scientist at the University of Georgia in Athens collects human milk for a milk bank that will serve babies who are allergic to formula but whose mothers cannot breast-feed them.

Nutrition

Continued

els in American children were too high and should be lowered through changes in the children's diets. The ideal average level of cholesterol in children's blood, the experts said, should be about 100 milligrams per 100 milliliters of blood. However, the group reported that the average level in the blood of American children is about 160 milligrams. Because cholesterol levels tend to rise with age, this could put many children at high risk of a heart attack later in life.

The heart experts recommended that poultry and fish be substituted for red meat as much as possible in children's diets. They also urged that youngsters drink low-fat or skim milk instead of whole milk.

Vitamin poisoning. In August 1983, a group of physicians reported that high doses of vitamin B_6, also called *pyridoxine*, may cause toxic effects. Pyridoxine is a *water-soluble vitamin* — one that dissolves in water. It is generally regarded as safe and had never before been associated with poisoning. The vitamin, sold at health-food stores, is used by many body builders, and by women who believe it will reduce premenstrual swelling.

The physicians, led by neurologist Herbert H. Schaumburg of Albert Einstein College of Medicine in New York City, reported loss of muscle coordination and numbness or loss of sensation in seven adults between the ages of 20 and 43. These patients had consumed 2 to 6 grams of pyridoxine daily — about 1,000 times the minimum daily requirement — over a 2- to 40-month period. They developed serious symptoms, including difficulty in walking; tingling in the legs and soles of the feet; difficulty in handling small objects; and lessening of several senses, including those of touch and temperature. Studies of their sensory nerves, which carry information from the sense organs to the brain, showed that the functioning of such nerves was significantly diminished.

After approximately seven months of withdrawal from pyridoxine, all seven patients improved greatly, though some nerve damage remained.

Cancer and Cuisine

Researchers have uncovered some bad news and some good news about diet and cancer: Some foods may increase your chances of developing cancer, but others may provide you with one of the most effective means of preventing the disease. In February 1984, the American Cancer Society (ACS) issued dietary guidelines designed to lower the risk of developing cancer. These guidelines are almost identical to recommendations made in 1982 by the National Research Council (NRC), an agency of the National Academy of Sciences. According to the ACS, diet may be related to 35 per cent of cancer cases reported annually. Cancer is the second leading cause of death, after heart disease, in the United States.

The ACS guidelines advised people to keep their weight down to normal and to eat less fat and more high-fiber foods, such as vegetables, fruits, and whole-grain cereals. The ACS particularly recommended *cruciferous* vegetables (plants of the mustard family), such as broccoli, Brussels sprouts, and cauliflower, because these vegetables seem to block the action of some *carcinogens* (cancer-causing chemicals). The guidelines also recommended a decreased consumption of alcohol — no more than two drinks daily — and less smoked, salt-cured, and nitrite-treated foods, such as bacon and ham.

The link between cancer and diet has been hotly debated for decades. Although the connection is still not ironclad, research has turned up increasingly convincing evidence. Among the most persuasive studies are those of the differences in cancer rates among different ethnic groups. For example, women in Japan have a low rate of breast cancer. However, the breast-cancer rate among Japanese women who have migrated to the United States nearly equals that among American-born women.

The ACS reported that certain eating habits may increase the risk of developing the disease. For example, the link between cancer and fats seems to be the strongest. People who eat a diet rich in fatty foods develop more colon and breast cancer.

Obesity is another factor. An ACS study of 750,000 people between 1960 and 1972 revealed that cancer rates were 55 per cent higher among obese women and 33 per cent higher among obese men than among people of normal weight. Heavy alcohol consumption, especially when combined with smoking, greatly increases the risk of cancer of the mouth, throat, esophagus, and liver.

In addition, certain foods contain substances that may be altered during digestion to produce carcinogens. For example, nitrites in bacon, ham, and beer may be converted in the body into cancer-causing nitrosamines.

The ACS guidelines make no recommendations about browning foods. However, the NRC and many researchers believe that browning foods by broiling or even toasting may cause the formation of *mutagens* (substances that cause changes in genes).

Foods containing substances that may protect against cancer include those rich in vitamin A. Vitamin A foods — such as milk, liver, eggs, and green and yellow vegetables — seem to lessen the risk of developing cancer of the lungs, cervix, bladder, and colon. Some studies indicate that beta-carotene, a substance the body converts to vitamin A, may be the chief protective substance.

Foods rich in vitamin C — citrus fruits, tomatoes, and leafy vegetables, for example — seem to provide protection against cancer of the stomach and esophagus. Selenium, a mineral found in whole-grain cereals, egg yolks, and milk, may lessen the risk of developing cancer of the digestive tract.

However, because large amounts of vitamin A and selenium are toxic, health experts warn against overdosing on vitamin and mineral supplements. In addition, there is no evidence that vitamins and minerals taken as supplements would provide the same protection as vitamins consumed in food.

Someday, scientists may be able to determine which people are susceptible to certain types of cancer and design a diet to minimize the risk. Until then, experts recommend that people eat moderately and follow the new guidelines. At the very least, the guidelines offer sound nutritional advice and may also lessen the risk of heart disease.   [Eleanor A. Young]

Cancer-fighting vegetables

Examination of the patients showed that pyridoxine was the sole cause of their illness.

The reporting physicians stressed that high doses of pyridoxine are dangerous. They suggested that limits should be placed on the use of pyridoxine and that researchers should perform further studies to establish safe levels of the vitamin. Their findings underscore the importance of medical supervision whenever large doses of presumably "safe" nutrients are taken.

Undernutrition in adolescents. A study reported in September 1983 in *The New England Journal of Medicine* said that the negative attitude toward obesity in modern American society can have harmful effects on the eating practices of children. Researchers headed by pediatrician Michael T. Pugliese of North Shore University Hospital in Manhasset, N.Y., reported on a study of 201 children who were short for their age or late in entering *puberty*, or both. (Puberty is a period of rapid growth that marks the end of childhood and the start of physical and sexual maturity.)

Fourteen of the children — nine boys and five girls, aged 9 to 17 years — showed no organic causes for their failure to grow. Extensive testing revealed that the major cause of delayed growth in these children was self-imposed malnutrition due to a fear of obesity. The children had reduced their food intake by skipping meals and eating mainly low-calorie foods. On the average, they consumed only about half the ideal calories for their age. All 14 children were underweight, short in stature, and retarded in sexual development.

With appropriate counseling and dietary therapy, all the patients gained weight. After one to three months of weight gain, all but one of the children began to grow rapidly in height. One female patient did not get taller because her bone ends, where growth occurs, had already fused. Her growth was permanently stunted at a height of about 140 centimeters (4 feet 7 inches). [Eleanor A. Young]

Physics

Atoms and Nuclei. In 1983 and 1984, physicists made important breakthroughs in laser spectroscopy. Since the late 1800's, the prime tool of atomic research has been *spectroscopy*, the study of how atoms emit and absorb light and other forms of electromagnetic radiation. These processes cause electrons orbiting the atomic nucleus to change their energy levels and patterns of motion. The wavelength of the radiation emitted indicates the amount of energy increase or decrease; other features give clues to the electrons' motion.

In the past, spectroscopy was restricted to visible light, with wavelengths between about 400 and 700 nanometers (nm). (One nanometer equals one-billionth of a meter.) Today, spectroscopy uses radiation ranging from centimeter-length radio waves to X rays a fraction of a nanometer long. This progress has stemmed mainly from the development of new sources of radiation.

One such source is the laser, which emits radiation of only one wavelength, rather than a mixture of wavelengths, as is the case with ordinary light. Laser light makes it possible to study changes in an atom, one at a time, and to measure how rapidly they occur. But until 1983, no one had developed lasers that emit light in the extreme ultraviolet range, shorter than 104 nm. Air blocks out ultraviolet light below 200 nm, so a scientist who wishes to employ a beam whose wavelength is less than this value must project the beam into a vacuum. This would seem easy to do. The scientist would merely install a vacuum pipe between the laser and the target that the laser beam was supposed to hit. The laser light would be generated in a gas that emits extreme ultraviolet light. The gas would be sealed inside the laser, and the beam would come out through a window in the laser.

However, light below 104 nm in wavelength will not pass through any solid substance, so there is no material that can serve as a window.

In 1983, however, physicists at the University of Illinois in Chicago; Bell

Laboratories in Murray Hill, N.J.; Stanford University in Palo Alto, Calif.; and the University of California, Berkeley, worked their way around the 104-nm barrier. The scientists built lasers in which the beam comes out through a small uncovered hole. Gas that leaks through the hole is pumped out rapidly from the vacuum pipe. The Bell laser set a world record for the shortest wavelength—35.5 nm.

Mutual interest. It became apparent in 1983 that nuclear physicists now need high-energy accelerators as much as particle physicists do. Scientists who study atomic nuclei parted company with scientists studying the particles nuclei are made of in the 1950's, when the first multibillion-volt particle accelerators went into service. At these energies, physicists learned that the protons and neutrons in nuclei are merely the most stable members of a vast family of subatomic particles. Producing and studying the other, relatively unstable particles became the focus of research with high-energy accelerators, while lower-energy accelerators were used to determine how neutrons and protons are arranged in nuclei, how they move, and how they absorb and emit energy.

Progress in both fields has now brought the two groups of scientists closer together. The structure of ordinary nuclei is well understood, and nuclear particles are known to be made of smaller objects called *quarks* held together by *gluons*. All the particles in the subatomic family to which protons and neutrons belong are merely different arrangements of quarks, locked in a tight embrace that has so far proved unbreakable. No one has yet liberated an individual quark.

There are still unanswered questions, however. A question that interests experts in both areas is: What happens when nuclei are compressed so that protons and neutrons overlap? This can happen when heavy nuclei collide at very high speeds. Particle theory predicts that such a collision will lead to *quark matter*—a new state of matter in which quarks are temporar-

Quark Matter
Physicists have proposed a theory to explain how matter can become very densely packed as it is in black holes and dying stars. Heavy nuclei such as iron (A) might collide at energies high enough to make the nuclei combine (B). This would cause the boundaries between neutrons and protons to break down, and the quarks of which they are made would form a new state of matter (C) called *quark matter*.

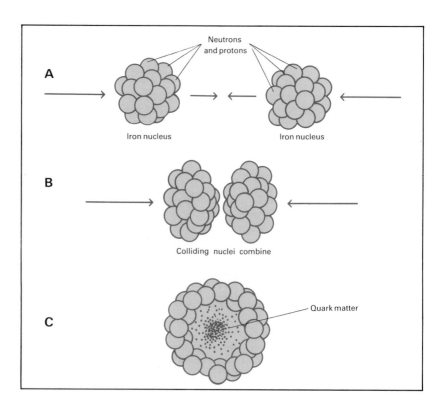

At an Alaska airport, a U.S. Air Force technician installs an atom-powered landing light containing tritium, a form of hydrogen. The runway light needs no maintenance and can operate for up to 10 years at temperatures from $-62°$ to $54°C$ ($-80°$ to $130°F$.). Its radioactive glow can be seen for distances of up to 11 kilometers (7 miles).

Physics

Continued

ily released from their bondage in protons and neutrons to wander freely.

It takes a great deal of energy to make heavy nuclei collide at very high speeds. Most particle accelerators that have been designed for heavy nuclei give the nuclei just enough energy to overcome their mutual electrical repulsion, in hopes that they will stick together long enough for physicists to study the giant nucleus that results.

An advisory panel to the United States Department of Energy in July 1983 gave top priority to producing a high-energy heavy-nucleus accelerator. And in September 1983, a conference at Brookhaven National Laboratory on Long Island, N.Y., brought together particle and nuclear physicists interested in producing quark matter.

Quark matter is also of interest to astrophysicists—scientists who study the physics of stars—because it duplicates conditions in the very early universe when all the matter was densely packed together.

Bare nuclei. Designers of heavy-nucleus accelerators face the major technical problem of how to strip away all the orbiting electrons in order to produce a bare nucleus. Electrons that remain in orbit around nuclei in a beam partially shield the nuclei from the magnets that steer the beam. Therefore, to keep these heavy nuclei under control without investing in more powerful magnets, their speed must be kept relatively low. But bare nuclei are easy to control at high speeds.

In August 1983, physicists at Lawrence Berkeley Laboratory in Berkeley, Calif., produced the first bare nuclei of uranium, the heaviest element naturally present on Earth. Previously, they had been able to strip only 68 of the 92 electrons that orbit the uranium nucleus.

The electrons whose orbits are closest to the nucleus are very hard to remove, because the negatively charged electrons are strongly attracted by the large positive charge of the many protons in a heavy nucleus. The physicists succeeded in removing the last 24 electrons by passing the nuclei through a thin metal foil.   [Robert H. March]

Physics

Continued

Particles and Forces. Throughout 1983 and 1984, particle physicists studied and reviewed the results of experiments in the Super Proton Synchrotron (SPS) accelerator at the laboratory of the multinational European Organization for Nuclear Research (CERN) near Geneva, Switzerland. In May 1983, researchers using this remarkable device announced that they had discovered the long-sought Z particle. In 1982, the SPS had produced a similar particle, the W particle. These particles carry the so-called weak nuclear force, which is responsible for certain kinds of radioactivity. The existence of the W and Z particles had been predicted by a theory that treats the weak force as a form of the electromagnetic force. The scientists who created this theory — Sheldon L. Glashow of Harvard University in Cambridge, Mass.; Abdus Salam of Imperial College in London; and Steven Weinberg, then of Harvard and now of the University of Texas in Austin — were awarded the 1979 Nobel Prize in physics for their work.

The SPS continued to produce data on these particles until July 1983, when it was shut down for improvements. The machine was scheduled to resume operation in October 1984.

The SPS accelerates a beam of protons and a beam of antiprotons in opposite directions around a ring that is 2 kilometers (1.2 miles) in diameter. The beams reach a combined energy level of 640 billion electron volts (GeV), then meet head-on in a collision that converts all their energy into particles, sometimes including a W or a Z. (One electron-volt [eV] is the amount of energy that an electron gains when it moves across an electric field of one volt.) In the Special Reports section, see THE NEW ATOM SMASHERS.

Until the W and Z particles were observed directly, there remained some room for doubt of their existence. But by March 1984, 99 examples of the W and 13 of the Z had been found in data produced by the SPS collisions. Their masses are 87 and 100 *atomic mass units*, close to the theory's predic-

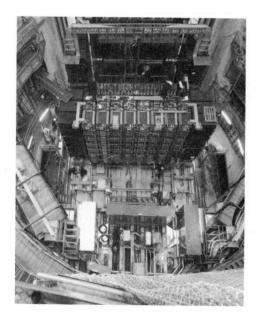

In May 1983, a previously undiscovered particle, the Z, formed when a proton beam collided with an antiproton beam, *right,* inside a huge detector in the CERN collider in Switzerland, *above.* The Z then decayed into a positron and an electron.

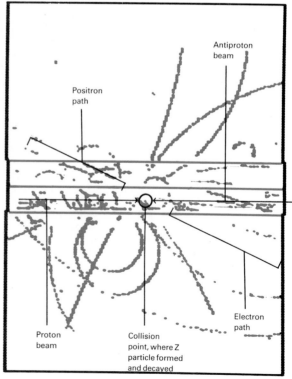

Antiproton beam

Positron path

Proton beam

Collision point, where Z particle formed and decayed

Electron path

tions of 89 and 101. (One atomic mass unit is approximately the mass of a neutron or a proton.)

Breaking up is easy. Particles this heavy are extremely unstable, breaking up in about 10^{-25} second. In most cases, W's and Z's break up into combinations of many lighter particles. However, occasionally they form only two particles that have more energy than any other particle created by the collision and that fly away from each other in opposite directions. It is this distinctive pattern that helps scientists sort out these rare events from data on billions of colliding particles. In fact, the only way experimenters have so far been able to identify W's and Z's is by discovering such two-particle combinations.

Although experimental results are turning out pretty much as the theory predicted, there have been some surprises. For example, three abnormal Z collisions have been discovered in which the two particles are accompanied by a very energetic gamma ray. It is too early to say what physical process could produce these gamma rays.

Detecting the particles. The SPS experiments use two huge electronic particle detectors known as UA-1 and UA-2. More such detectors were being built during the year for three new colliders that are expected to begin service in 1987 or 1988. One of these is the Tevatron at Fermi National Accelerator Laboratory (Fermilab) near Batavia, Ill. The Tevatron, a proton-antiproton machine, will be three times as powerful as CERN's. Another is LEP, a CERN machine that will collide electron and positron beams; and the third is the SLC, an electron-positron device at Stanford Linear Accelerator Center in Palo Alto, Calif.

When particles meet head-on, the debris that emerges can fly in all directions. So the collision point must be surrounded by a detector consisting of many layers of electronic devices. The innermost devices of UA-1, UA-2, and the similar detectors being built track the paths of particles. Other devices identify the particles and measure their energies. All the devices are linked to computers, which sort, relay, and store the data for later analysis on giant computers.

The Chicago Egg, the largest cosmic ray detector ever built for space flight, was scheduled to be launched aboard a space shuttle in the spring of 1985. University of Chicago scientists built the device to measure very-high-energy cosmic rays – atomic nuclei and subatomic particles that speed through our Galaxy.

Search for proton decay. Most particle physicists try to prove or disprove theories by running experiments on huge accelerators. However, some scientists attempt to test theories of physics by searching for rare natural events. One such effort is the ongoing search for evidence of proton *decay*, or breakup.

Some physicists theorize that all matter is very slightly unstable and that, out of many tons of any material, a few protons will decay each year. The energy released in this process would be more than 100 times as great as ordinary radioactivity, and would thus trigger a strong signal in a crude particle detector. However, the perpetual hail of cosmic rays, consisting of protons and other particles from outer space would create so many signals in any such detector on Earth's surface that a proton decay signal would be lost. So these experiments must be conducted in deep mines or highway tunnels, protected from the effects of cosmic rays.

As of mid-1984, there were eight detectors in use, monitoring from several hundred to many thousands of tons of material. Some had logged more than a year of operating time. Although all the detectors had found some unexplained signals, there were as yet no convincing cases of proton decay. As a result, it is possible to rule out the simpler theories, which predict one easily recognized decay per year for every 20 metric tons (22 short tons) of material.

Bigger accelerator projects. Accelerator designers were working during 1983 and 1984 on grandiose plans for more powerful accelerators. Studies for a 20-trillion-electron-volt (TeV) collider were in full swing in the United States. The project, which would require a ring of magnets and vacuum pipes more than 100 kilometers (62 miles) in circumference, would cost more than $1 billion.

Despite this high price, the 20-TeV collider has strong backing from federal science policymakers, who hope to see the United States regain leadership in particle research, which passed to Europe in the late 1970's. However, it will take several years just to decide whether the project is feasible, and to set a budget.   [Robert H. March]

Condensed Matter Physics. Scientists who studied solids, liquids, and gases in 1983 and 1984 discovered an important magnetic phenomenon, learned more about how one surface wets another, and may have solved a major magnetic riddle.

Magnetic whirlpools. Finnish and Soviet researchers led by physicist Marti Krusius of Helsinki University of Technology in Finland announced in October 1983 that a rare form of liquid helium becomes magnetic in an unusual way when chilled to an extremely low temperature and rotated. Liquid helium remains a liquid at temperatures down to absolute zero, $-273.15°C$ ($-459.67°F$.). At temperatures just above absolute zero, it becomes a *superfluid*, flowing without resistance. Various *isotopes*, or forms, of helium become superfluids at different temperatures. The most plentiful isotope, He-4, becomes a superfluid at temperatures colder than $-271.0°C$ ($-455.8°F$.), while the rare isotope He-3 flows without resistance at temperatures within $0.001°C$ ($0.002°F$.) of absolute zero.

When either liquid He-4 or He-3 is rotated, *vortexes* (whirlpools) appear as they do in normal rotating fluids. (The most common example of a vortex is a swirling mass of water going down a drain.)

The Finnish and Soviet scientists found that He-3 vortexes behave like weak magnets. The magnetism of He-3 vortexes is unusual because it is generated in the He-3 atomic nucleus. In most common magnetic materials, such as iron, the magnetic field is generated by electrons, particles that orbit the nucleus.

An He-3 nucleus contains two protons and one neutron. All three particles spin, generating magnetic fields. The protons spin in opposite directions, so their magnetic fields cancel one another. However, there is nothing to cancel the field of the single neutron. So the He-3 nucleus is magnetic.

Whether or not a substance is magnetic also depends on the alignment of its atomic magnets — that is, the direction in which the magnets point. The alignment of He-3 atomic magnets occurs in pairs of atoms that revolve

A More Accurate Meter

On Oct. 20, 1983, delegates at the international General Conference on Weights and Measures in Paris redefined the meter, making it 10 times as precise as it had been. The meter is now defined to a precision of about 0.00000001 per cent.

We do not need a measurement standard anywhere near this precise in our everyday lives. But imagine trying to use radio signals to maneuver a satellite orbiting 2,000 kilometers (1,200 miles) per hour above Earth. You would need a very good clock and a very good standard for distance measurements to be certain that your signals arrived at exactly the right time and place.

The new distance standard is based on the standard for time adopted in 1967. The time standard, for one second, is based on the behavior of an isotope, or form, of a chemical element called cesium-133.

Think of a cesium atom as a tiny spinning ball. If the atom is placed in a magnetic field of a certain strength, its *axis of rotation* — the imaginary line about which it spins — will move around in a circle, much as a child's top moves. The atom's *precession*, as this motion is called, can be detected by a radio signal. If the signal vibrations are set just right, they will energize the atom, pushing its precession in much the same way as correctly timed pushes on a playground swing will get the swing going into a wide arc. The rate of vibration of a radio signal that does this is 9,192,631,770 vibrations per second. So scientists have defined the second as the time it takes the radio waves that make up this signal to vibrate 9,192,631,770 times. Using a sophisticated formula for time and distance, they have now defined the meter as the distance traveled by light in a vacuum in a tiny fraction of a second — $\frac{1}{299792458}$ second, to be precise.

[James Trefil]

Physics

Continued

around one another. The two atomic magnets line up in one of three ways: with both magnets pointing in one direction, called the *up* direction; with both magnets pointing in the *down* direction; or with one magnet pointing up and the other magnet pointing down. The magnetic fields of an up-down pair cancel each other. However, the fields reinforce each other in the up-up pairs and the down-down pairs, so these pairs are magnetic.

When liquid He-3 is chilled to an extremely low temperature but not rotated, the number of up-up pairs is about the same as the number of down-down pairs. As a result, the pairs' fields cancel one another out and the He-3 is not magnetic. However, rotating the He-3 disturbs the orientation of the atomic magnets so that the up-up pairs no longer balance the down-down pairs, and the liquid becomes magnetic.

Wetting: a delicate balance. In 1983 and 1984, scientists from France, Great Britain, and the United States announced unexpected results of experiments on the wetting of surfaces. Anyone who has washed dishes is familiar with the fact that water forms little drops, or beads, on glass. Ordinary water does not *wet* the entire surface of the glass. However, a soap powder will cause the droplets to flatten out and wet the entire surface.

Whether a given *adsorbate* (wetting agent), such as water, will wet a given *substrate* (surface to be wetted), such as glass, depends on the strength of the attraction that the adsorbate molecules have for one another, compared with their attraction to substrate molecules. In the case of water on glass, the water forms droplets if the water molecules are strongly attracted to one another. On the other hand, if the water is strongly attracted to glass, it will spread out on the surface of the glass so that there are as many contacts as possible between water molecules and glass molecules.

Wetting — in the sense that an adsorbate covers a substrate with a thick layer — also occurs when the adsorbate is a solid rather than a liquid. In July

1983, French, British, and United States researchers at the Faculty of Sciences of Luminy in Marseilles, France, reported on experiments conducted to determine how molecular attraction affects the "wetting" of solids by solids. The physicists expected the relationship between attraction and wetting to be the same as it is for the wetting of glass by water—the stronger the attraction between substrate and adsorbate, the greater the wetting.

The scientists experimented with solid graphite substrates and adsorbates of xenon, argon, and neon gases. They chilled the graphite to temperatures of $-263°$ to $-213°C$ ($-441°$ to $-351°F$.). Then they directed streams of each gas against the cold substrates. When the gases touched the graphite, they solidified into films. To determine how well the films wet the graphite, the researchers bounced a beam of electrons off each film and recorded how the films influenced the electron paths. A rough film of crystallites—like beads of water on a dish—produces paths very different from those pro-duced by the thick, smooth film of an adsorbate that thoroughly wets a substrate.

The physicists found that only xenon and argon wet the graphite. Neon did not, even though it is more strongly attracted to graphite than are xenon and argon. So the scientists concluded that a very strong attraction between adsorbate and substrate prevents wetting.

To test this conclusion, physicists at the University of Washington in Seattle and at Luminy measured the wetting behaviors of these same gases on gold, to which the gases are much more strongly attracted than they are to graphite. The scientists found that none of the three gases wet the gold.

The cause of the failure of solid adsorbates to wet substrates to which they are strongly attracted appears to be internal distortion. The atoms in the first few film layers are packed together very tightly because of their strong attraction to the substrate. In layers farther from the substrate, the attraction is weaker and the packing

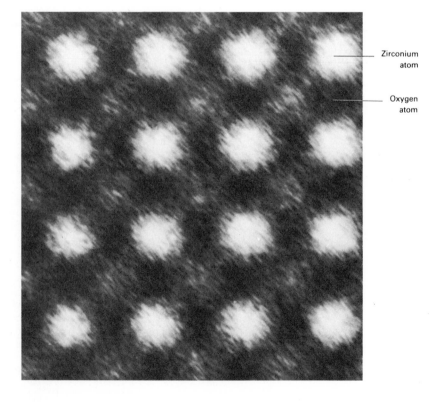

The atomic resolution microscope, an electron microscope installed at Lawrence Berkeley Laboratory in California in the fall of 1983, made it possible for the first time to photograph atoms in a crystal directly, without computer enhancement.

Zirconium atom

Oxygen atom

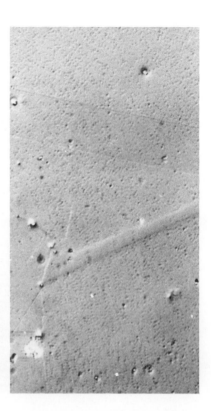

Imperfections in a polished brass surface stand out as wide, dark bands, *right,* when scanned by a microscope that uses sound waves to produce an image with far more contrast than one produced by an optical microscope, *far right.*

Physics

Continued

therefore is looser. But a film made up of both tightly and loosely packed atoms is subject to internal distortion — and the more layers, the greater the distortion. When the distortion becomes sufficiently large, the film can no longer take on more layers. It appears that in order for a film to grow thick enough to wet a substrate, the attraction between the adsorbate and the substrate must be neither too strong nor too weak. A substrate that is just right for a given adsorbate to grow on seems to be one made up of the same material as the adsorbate itself.

Random magnetic fields. In 1984, physicists reported on how random magnetic fields along with heating and cooling affect *ferromagnetic materials.* A ferromagnetic material is a substance, such as iron, that is easy to magnetize by making magnetic atoms line up in the same direction. Heating such a magnet causes the atomic magnets to fluctuate, or move out of alignment. This fluctuation tends to decrease the magnetism. At high enough temperatures, the magnetism disappears.

If the material is cooled, groups of atomic magnets tend to align with one another to form small magnetic regions. Several neighboring regions whose magnets are all in the same direction quickly grow together to form large magnetic *domains,* while regions of different magnetic direction shrink and disappear. Ferromagnets have large magnetic domains.

Researchers have been interested in how magnetic fields originating outside the ferromagnetic substance influence this process. When a magnetic material is cooled in an outside magnetic field of constant direction, the small regions quickly grow into large domains in which the atomic magnets are aligned with the outside field.

However, if the direction of the outside magnetic field is not constant, but varies randomly, the directions of the atomic magnets will also vary, reducing their tendency to form domains. Scientists have disagreed over whether three-dimensional groups of cooling atomic magnets (groups that have length, width, and depth) can form

301

Laser light beamed through the exhaust of a jet engine is used to analyze combustion gases in a study on how to make more efficient engines that will emit fewer pollutants.

Physics

Continued

domains in the presence of random magnetic fields. Unfortunately, it is very difficult to create a magnetic field that acts in random directions on a ferromagnet. Thus, scientists could not settle the disagreement by experiment.

In 1979, however, physicists Shmuel Fishman and Amnon Aharony of Tel Aviv University in Israel showed that it was easy to produce a random magnetic field in an *antiferromagnet*, in which the atomic magnets tend to align in alternate order — up, down, up, down, for example.

In late 1983, scientists attempted to settle the disagreement by experiments on antiferromagnets. They heated orderly antiferromagnets until the fluctuations of the individual atomic magnets caused the magnetism to disappear. Then the researchers applied random magnetic fields to the antiferromagnets in two ways. In the first case, a group at the University of California in Santa Barbara allowed the antiferromagnets to cool until the atomic magnets reordered themselves into large antiferromagnetic domains,

and then applied the field. The domains remained in order. This was evidence for the ability of a three-dimensional magnet to recover its order in the presence of random magnetic fields.

However, when a team of U.S. and Scottish scientists applied the random field at a high temperature, the atomic magnets remained in random, small regions, even when they cooled. This was evidence against a magnet's ability to recover its magnetism.

Early in 1984, this puzzle was resolved by theoreticians in France and the United States. They argued that any three-dimensional antiferromagnet can become orderly, even in the presence of a random field. However, they said that, in such a field, small magnetic regions take much more time than physicists had thought necessary to grow into large magnetic· domains. So the experiments in which the magnetic field was applied at a high temperature did not give the antiferromagnetic material enough time to recover its magnetism. [Michael Schick]

Psychology

Two psychologists at Stanford University in Palo Alto, Calif., reported in January 1984 on experiments that appear to pinpoint the area in brain tissue where a specific memory is stored. Psychologists were never before able to do this, so many had concluded that memories were distributed throughout the brain and not confined to a specific location. But the Stanford researchers, David A. McCormick and Richard F. Thompson, apparently located a memory circuit in the cerebellum, a small area located at the back of the brain.

McCormick and Thompson trained rabbits to blink at the sound of a tone while they monitored the rabbits' brain waves. They found a group of nerve cells in the cerebellum that showed activity during the learning process. Next, they inserted electrodes and found that stimulating these nerve cells electrically caused the animals to blink. Finally, the researchers surgically removed the nerve cells from the rabbits' brains, and the rabbits forgot their learned responses, even though they were still physically able to blink.

The Stanford researchers were careful to point out that this type of learning, which involves *motor programs*, or sequences of learned physical activities, is different from memory involving networks of ideas or facts. Scientists believe it is likely there are at least two distinct memory systems in the brain — one for factual memory and one for motor memory.

Smart young Einstein. Educational and developmental psychologists have long comforted "slow learners" with stories of theoretical physicist Albert Einstein's academic problems. When he was a youngster, Einstein supposedly flunked mathematics, yet he turned out to be one of the world's great mathematicians. The moral of the story was clear: There is hope for anybody.

Unfortunately, the story is incorrect, according to preliminary reports released in 1984. Einstein's personal papers, scheduled to be released in 1985 by Princeton University Press, reveal he was a child prodigy. John Stachel, director of the Institute for Relativity

"I don't get stress. . . . I give stress!"

Studies at Boston University, who edited the papers, points out that the young Einstein was an excellent violinist, received high marks in Latin and Greek, and was dabbling in college physics — all before the age of 11.

Previous biographers were apparently misled by a change in the grading system at the school Einstein attended in Aarau, Switzerland. For many years, the school used a six-point scale in which one was the highest grade and six the lowest. Then, when Einstein was 16, they reversed the system, making six the highest grade. Scholars looking at Einstein's early school record saw a series of ones for mathematics year after year and concluded that Einstein flunked, when actually he always made the highest grade. It may still be true that "slow learners" can overcome their problems by perseverance, but Einstein's life history does not support the idea that genius can blossom out of failure.

Caring babies. A January 1984 report presented new evidence that toddlers as young as 1 year old are socially aware, sympathetic, and *altruistic* (concerned for others). Psychologists Carolyn Zahn-Waxler and Marian Radke-Yarrow of the National Institute of Mental Health (NIMH) in Bethesda, Md., found there is an "explosion" of social behavior around the age of 1½. This contradicts long-held theories that portray children under age 6 or 7 as selfish and self-centered creatures.

The NIMH researchers studied a volunteer group of young children. They divided their study into two phases. First they asked the mothers to observe the children at home and record incidents of social behavior. According to the mothers, the children often showed unselfish sympathy.

The second phase of the study involved laboratory research. Playmates of the children were brought into the NIMH laboratories, and researchers kept detailed records of the children's natural interactions. The researchers also set up artificial situations in which parents and other adults pretended to be distressed. By the age of 2, the children responded to one-third of both the natural and artificial distress situations. Some of the children even responded too much. Children of trou-

bled or depressed parents seemed "preoccupied with distress" in the laboratory. They stayed longer by the side of a distressed adult, and they had trouble with other, positive, social behavior such as sharing and helping their playmates.

General anesthesia — a state of deep "sleep" used during major surgery — apparently does not prevent memories from being formed. This is the conclusion of psychobiologists Norman Weinberger and Debra Sternberg of the University of California at Irvine and Paul Gold of the University of Virginia. In May 1984, they described research showing that rats learned to associate an electric shock with a tone while under anesthesia.

The researchers anesthetized rats, set off a tone, and administered an electric shock. Some of the rats were also given an injection of adrenalin, a chemical produced by the nervous system during stress. The researchers found that learning took place only in the rats given adrenalin. They behaved as though they feared an electric shock when they heard the tone after being awakened. Weinberger, Sternberg, and Gold suggest that adrenalin switches on areas in the brain where learning takes place.

The psychobiologists' work may help clarify earlier research that suggested human beings might be able to remember events that took place under general anesthesia. Anesthesiologist Jacobus W. Mostert of the University of Chicago in 1975 described an experiment in which 10 surgery patients volunteered to participate. While the patients were under anesthesia, the doctors talked about feigned life-threatening situations. For example, the surgeon commented, "The lung looks cancerous . . . it is black from living in the city."

Although the surgeon's comment was not true, the researchers thought it might be shocking enough to penetrate the anesthesia. Later, under hypnosis, 4 of the 10 patients were able to recite the surgeon's exact words. Four others became alarmed and awoke from hypnosis when instructed to remember the surgeon's comment. Only two of the patients showed no effect.

In light of the Weinberger, Stern-

A pigeon who was earlier trained to push and stand on a tiny box applies this training to the problem of how to sample a tasty banana (A) hanging out of reach. The pigeon sees the box (B), pushes it under the banana (C), then climbs on the box (D) to bite the fruit, proving that some lower animals can solve relatively sophisticated problems.

A | B | C | D

Psychology

Continued

berg, and Gold research, the surgeon's comment apparently was shocking enough to stimulate adrenalin levels in the anesthetized patients, producing memories that could be recalled under hypnosis. This also explains occasional reports from doctors about anesthetized patients who later recall events that occurred during surgery. The remembered events are usually startling, such as a tray of instruments being dropped or a surgeon commenting on a mistake in the operating procedure.

Eyewitness testimony may not always be reliable, according to psychologist Elizabeth F. Loftus of the University of Washington in Seattle. Loftus, a leading expert on the subject, summarized more than 10 years of research in February 1984.

Loftus documented several popular misconceptions about eyewitness testimony. One misconception is that witnesses remember details of a violent crime better than those of a nonviolent crime. Research shows the opposite is true: The added stress caused by violence distorts memory.

A second misconception is that witnesses can give accurate time estimates of how long a criminal act lasted. In reality, they almost always overestimate the time. This, too, may be related to the stress of witnessing a crime. During stressful events, time appears to slow down. Consequently, witnesses almost always think a crime took longer than it really did.

A third misconception is that the more confident a witness seems, the more accurate the testimony is likely to be. In reality, confidence bears little relationship to accuracy.

Other reliability problems involve how witnesses are handled. For example, showing a witness a photograph of a suspect before a police line-up can make the suspect seem familiar during the line-up, even though the witness has never seen the suspect before.

Despite all the drawbacks to eyewitness testimony, it is often critically important in solving crimes. Loftus concludes that eyewitness identification is "essential but unreliable" — a true legal dilemma.   [Russell A. Dewey]

During 1983 and 1984, there was both bad news and good news about a major public-health problem — acquired immune deficiency syndrome (AIDS). This devastating disease, which weakens the immune system of its victims and leaves them defenseless against infection, continued to be identified in new areas of the world. But there was cause for hope when three groups of researchers, working independently, announced that they had discovered the probable cause of AIDS.

The spread of AIDS. AIDS continued to occur throughout the year in an increasing number of areas. The disease appeared in the United States in the late 1970's and then was found in Haiti, but some scientists believe the illness originated in central Africa. In early 1984, field estimates put the number of probable AIDS cases in Zaire as high as 7,000.

In February 1984, Belgian physician Nathan Clumeck and his associates reported AIDS among central Africans living in Belgium. The Belgian doctors described 18 African AIDS patients treated in several Belgian hospitals between 1979 and 1983. Most of them were Zairian businessmen, students, or diplomats and their families. There were 12 men and 6 women, all but one of whom were black.

The African patients had illnesses commonly associated with AIDS. All of them had severe infections from a wide variety of bacteria, fungi, and viruses, and three had Kaposi's sarcoma, an otherwise rare cancer. Studies of the patients' blood showed that all 18 had abnormally low levels of *helper T lymphocytes*, white blood cells that play a major role in immunity. Such lymphocyte abnormalities are the hallmark of AIDS.

All the patients reported that they were heterosexual. None had received any blood transfusions for at least five years. Most AIDS cases in the United States involve homosexual males who have had many sexual contacts; *hemophiliacs* (persons suffering from a blood-clotting disorder); and intravenous drug abusers. This has led researchers to believe that AIDS is spread through intimate bodily contact or blood.

Although homosexuality and blood transfusions do not seem to be factors among the African victims, a strong pattern of exposure to certain viruses is common to all groups of AIDS patients — American, Haitian, and African — so far examined. In 1983 and 1984, three groups of researchers — two French, one American — announced that they had found evidence that a virus causes AIDS. In May 1984, the American Red Cross announced that it would begin evaluating a test to detect one suspected AIDS virus in blood donated for transfusions. See IMMUNOLOGY.

Smoking and pregnancy. Investigators from the University of Maryland in Baltimore reported in February 1984 that health professionals can intervene successfully to reduce women's cigarette smoking during pregnancy, and that doing so increases the birth weight of the women's babies. Low birth weight is strongly associated with both infant death and fetal abnormalities, including defects of the heart and digestive tract. Many . studies have shown that women who smoke during pregnancy are more likely to have small babies. Although researchers have consistently found this association, its interpretation has been questioned by other investigators, who have suggested that the relationship between smoking and birth weight merely reflects the fact that women who smoke are destined for other reasons to have smaller offspring.

To clear up this question, epidemiologists Mary Sexton and J. Richard Hebel of the University of Maryland School of Medicine in Baltimore carried out a controlled study in cooperation with 52 obstetricians and local hospitals. Over a period of 2½ years, 935 women who smoked were selected for the study during the first 15 weeks of pregnancy. They agreed to be part of a group that talked frequently with a health worker — in person and by telephone — about the potential value of quitting or cutting down on cigarettes. A control group — matched according to race, education, income, and age — had no such conversations.

The simple encouragement to cut down was sufficient to achieve a significant reduction in smoking among the pregnant women. Women in the

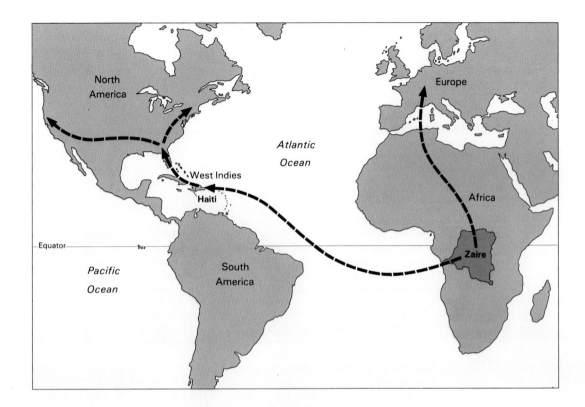

Public Health

Continued

Probable Paths of AIDS
Some scientists believe the AIDS virus appeared first in Zaire, then spread along two separate paths. French and Belgians living in Zaire may have carried the disease back to Europe. The virus also spread to the West Indies, where it may have infected vacationing homosexuals from the United States.

group that received antismoking advice reported that they reduced their smoking to an average of 6.4 cigarettes per day, compared with 12.8 per day in the control group. All the women had smoked at least 10 cigarettes a day before pregnancy.

Of greater importance, however, was the finding that the newborn children of the women who cut down their smoking were significantly bigger — 0.6 centimeter (0.24 inch) longer and 92 grams (3.2 ounces) heavier — than the control group's offspring.

A new bacterium called *Vibrio vulnificus*, found in seawater as well as in marine plants and animals, can cause an unusually deadly disease in human beings. But research reported in 1984 showed the disease can be cured if treated promptly.

First isolated in 1976, *V. vulnificus* is a member of a group of bacteria that resemble bent rods. The organism causes many cases of *septicemia* (blood poisoning), and more than 40 per cent of the victims die.

A *V. vulnificus* infection may take one of two courses. In one, the organisms enter the bloodstream through the intestinal wall. They cause the sudden onset of blood poisoning accompanied by abnormally low blood pressure and shock. Most infections occur after drinking seawater or eating seafood. *V. vulnificus* infections are most common between May and October. The risk of getting the infection from eating shellfish is greatly reduced if the seafood is chilled.

The second type of infection caused by *V. vulnificus* is a localized inflammation that occurs when a wound is contaminated by *V. vulnificus*-infested seawater. Many such infections occur in cuts or scratches incurred while cleaning shellfish or harvesting oysters or clams.

The National Institutes of Health reported in January 1984 that prompt treatment of a *V. vulnificus* infection with penicillin or tetracycline can be lifesaving. But because of the organism's rapid spread and potential deadliness, immediate medical attention is essential. [Michael H. Alderman]

Science Awards

Four American scientists—two of whom were born in other countries—were awarded Nobel Prizes in chemistry, physics, and physiology or medicine in 1983. The awards were presented at ceremonies in Stockholm, Sweden, in December. The cash prize for each award was about $190,000. The physics prize was shared by two astrophysicists.

Chemistry. The Nobel Prize for chemistry was awarded to Henry Taube of Stanford University in California. Taube was recognized "for his work on the mechanisms of electronic transfer reactions, especially in metal complexes."

His research focused on what accounts for differing reaction rates among inorganic compounds. Scientists had thought that such chemical reactions simply involved a transfer of electrons from one atom to another to form the chemical bond. Taube discovered that the motion of atoms or groups of atoms is also involved, and this affects the rate at which electron transfer occurs.

Taube's findings contributed to an understanding of *catalysts*, compounds that affect reaction rates but remain unchanged themselves. His work is especially important to the chemical industries and has helped scientists to understand biological processes in which inorganic elements, such as iron and zinc, might affect the function of enzymes, which act as catalysts for reactions in the body.

Henry Taube was born in Neudorf, Canada, in 1915. He earned his doctorate in chemistry at the University of California, Berkeley, in 1940, and became a citizen of the United States in 1942. He joined the faculty at Stanford in 1961.

Physics. The Nobel Prize for physics was shared by two American astrophysicists—Subrahmanyan Chandrasekhar of the University of Chicago and William A. Fowler of the California Institute of Technology (Caltech).

Chandrasekhar was honored for calculating rules governing the collapse of stars. He began his award-winning work in 1929 on a long voyage from India to England, during which he began to speculate on what happens when a large star *collapses* (begins to condense) at the end of its active life. At that time, astronomers knew that the end products of relatively small stars were extremely dense objects known as white dwarfs.

Chandrasekhar found that if the mass of a star is more than 1.4 times the mass of the sun, the dense matter keeps on shrinking, sometimes to infinite density.

The "Chandrasekhar limit" led to the concept of the neutron star, which is produced by the collapse of a star with two or three times the mass of the sun, accompanied by a *supernova* (stellar explosion). Even more massive stars are thought to collapse into black holes—objects so dense that not even light can escape from them.

Subrahmanyan Chandrasekhar was born in Lahore, India, in 1910 and earned his doctorate in physics at Cambridge University in England in 1933. He moved to the United States in 1936 and became a U.S. citizen in 1953. He has worked since 1936 at the University of Chicago and at Yerkes Observatory in Williams Bay, Wis.

Fowler was recognized for his contribution to the theory of how the heavy elements formed in stars. In the 1950's, in collaboration with three British colleagues—E. Margaret Burbidge, Geoffrey T. Burbidge, and Sir Fred Hoyle—he did much of the theoretical and laboratory work on the origin of the elements, the substances from which stars, planets, and people are made.

Scientists assume that the big bang—the explosive start of the universe—produced only hydrogen and helium. So all other elements had to be synthesized later.

Fowler's work showed the complex succession of steps by which hydrogen and helium atoms that made up the simplest stars in the early universe fused to produce heavier atoms. When these stars aged, they collapsed and exploded. The explosion produced successively heavier elements.

William A. Fowler was born in Pittsburgh, Pa., in 1911. He earned his doctorate in physics in 1936 at Caltech, where he now conducts his research.

Physiology or medicine. The Nobel Prize for physiology or medicine was awarded to botanist Barbara Mc-

Major Awards and Prizes

Winners of the Nobel Prizes and their work are treated more fully in the first portion of this section.

ACS Award in Petroleum Chemistry: Cheves Walling

AIP Prize (physics): Joseph Kilpatrick, Frederick Aronowitz

Amateur Achievement Award (astronomy): Russell Genet

Apker Award (physics): Raymond E. Goldstein

APS Biological Physics Prize: Edward M. Purcell, Howard C. Berg

APS High Polymer Prize: William J. MacKnight, Frank E. Karasz

Arctowski Medal (space science): William E. Gordon

Arthur C. Cope Award (chemistry): Albert Eschenmoser

Arthur L. Day Medal (geology): Allan Cox

Ballantine Medal (communications): Adam Lender

Becton-Dickinson Award (clinical microbiology): Alexander Sonnenwirth

Bonner Prize (nuclear physics): Harald A. Enge

Bowie Medal (geophysics): Marcel Nicolet

Brookdale Award (medicine): Vincent J. Cristofalo, Robert H. Binstock

Bruce Medal (astronomy): Olin C. Wilson

Buckley Solid State Physics Prize: D. C. Tsui

Bueche Award (engineering): Simon Ramo

Carski Award (distinguished teaching): Nancy Harvie

Carty Award (biochemistry): Robert H. Burris

Clamer Medal (metallurgy): S. Stanford Mason, Louis F. Coffin

Collier Trophy (astronautics): U.S. Army/Hughes Helicopter Inc.

Dannie Heineman Prize (physics): Robert B. Griffiths

Davisson-Germer Prize (physics): Manfred A. Biondi, Gordon H. Dunn

Eadie Medal (engineering): Colin K. Campbell

Elliott Cresson Medal (physics): Herbert B. Callen, Elizabeth F. Neufeld

Ewing Medal (geophysics): Xavier LePichon

Fahrney Medal (meteorology): Robert M. White

Fermi Award (physics): Alexander Hollaender, John H. Lawrence

Fisher Award (microbiology): Thomas D. Brock

Founders Award (engineering): Harold E. Edgerton

Franklin Medal (meteorology): Verner E. Suomi

Gairdner Awards (medicine): Bruce N. Ames, Gerald D. Aurbach, John A. Clements, Richard K. Gershon, Donald A. Henderson, Susumu Tonegawa

Garvan Medal (chemistry): Martha L. Ludwig

Goddard Award (astronautics): Krafft Echricke

Hazen Award (medicine): Robert J. Lefkowitz

Horton Medal (geophysics): Charles V. Theis

Horwitz Prize (biology): Viktor Hamburger, Rita Levi-Montalcini, Stanley Cohen

I-R 100 Award (industrial research): Ray Dils, Ared Cezairliyan, Robert Cutkosky, Robert Kaesar, Richard Martinez, John Herron

Kihara Prize (biology): Susumu Ohno

Klumpke-Roberts Award (contributions to public understanding of astronomy): Deborah Byrd

Langer Award (medicine): Janet Rowley

Lasker Awards: basic research, Eric R. Kandel, Vernon B. Mountcastle, Jr.; clinical research, F. Mason Sones, Jr.; public service, Saul Krugman, Maurice R. Hilleman

Lilly Award (microbiology): Linda L. Randall

Macelwane Award (physics): Mary K. Hudson, Raymond Jeanloz, John H. Woodhouse

McLaughlin Medal (medicine): Charles P. LeBlond

Michelson Medal (optics): Hyatt M. Gibbs

Miller Medal (geology): Donald F. Stott

National Medal of Science: Philip W. Anderson, Seymour Benzer, Glenn W. Burton, Mildred Cohn, F. Albert Cotton, Edward F. Heinemann, Donald L. Katz, Yoichiro Nambu, Gilbert Stork, Edward Teller, Charles H. Townes, Marshall Stone

Nobel Prize: chemistry, Henry Taube; physics, Subrahmanyan Chandrasekhar, William A. Fowler; physiology or medicine, Barbara McClintock

Oersted Medal (physics teaching): Frank Oppenheimer

Penrose Medal (geology): G. Arthur Cooper

Peter Debye Award (physical chemistry): B. S. Rabinovitch

Pierce Prize (astronomy): Allan Dressler

Potts Medal (chemistry): Paul C. Lauterbur, George G. Guilbalt

Priestley Medal (chemistry): Linus Pauling

Radiological Society Gold Medal: Alexander R. Margulis

Reed Award (aeronautics): Frederick T. Rall, Jr.

Richtmeyer Memorial Award (lecturing): David M. Schramm

Robert B. Young Award (technical innovation): Robert Quaintance, James Yee, Abe Shrekenhamer, James Coughlin, Norm Mittermaier

Russell Award (astronomy): E. Margaret Burbidge

Rutherford Medal: chemistry, Juan C. Scaiano; physics, David J. Rowe

3M Life Sciences Award (biology): Leroy E. Hood

Trumpler Prize (astronomy): Deirdre Ann Hunter

Tyler Prize (ecology): Roger Revelle, Edward O. Wilson

Vincent Du Vigneaud Awards (peptide research): Lila M. Gierasch, Betty A. Eipper, Richard E. Mains

Waterford Biomedical Science Award: Harry Eagle

Welch Award (chemistry): Henry Taube

Wetherill Medal (systems): Eugene Garfield

Clintock of the Carnegie Institution's 'Cold Spring Harbor Laboratory in Massachusetts. She was only the third woman to win an unshared Nobel Prize. The others were Marie Curie in 1911 and Dorothy C. Hodgkin in 1964, both for chemistry.

McClintock was honored for her discovery of "jumping genes" — certain genes that can move from one spot to another on *chromosomes* and thus produce changes that can alter how cells function. Such changes can be passed on to offspring. (Chromosomes are the threadlike connections of genes inside cells.)

McClintock studied color changes in kernels of *maize* (Indian corn). She concluded that genes could "jump" to new locations on chromosomes and thus alter the appearance of kernels on the cob produced by the genetic instructions.

McClintock's work was belittled or ignored by most of the scientific community when she reported her findings in 1953. However, over the past decade the revolution in microbiology has confirmed McClintock's theories, and other scientists have come to realize the importance of her work to the study of almost all forms of life.

Her findings will aid in understanding human diseases, such as cancer; how viruses work; and how bacteria can become resistant to drugs. Her work also has important implications for genetic engineering.

Barbara McClintock was born in Hartford, Mass., in 1902. In 1919, she enrolled at Cornell University in Ithaca, N.Y., where she intended to major in plant breeding. However, that field's department would not accept a woman, so she majored in botany. She turned to plant genetics as a graduate student and earned her doctorate at Cornell in 1927. She then taught and did research at several universities.

In 1942, she accepted a research post in the Carnegie Institution's Department of Genetics at Cold Spring Harbor where she still works — alone, as she has always worked — in a laboratory building that now bears her name.   [Irene B. Keller]

Space Exploration

The United States National Aeronautics and Space Administration's (NASA) space shuttles flew five missions between June 1983 and May 1984. Among the highlights of those missions were the first flights of a U.S. woman astronaut and a U.S. black astronaut, the first free flight of astronauts in space, and the first repair of a satellite.

The shuttle *Challenger*, on a mission that lasted from June 18 to June 24, 1983, carried the first U.S. woman into space, physicist Sally K. Ride. The other crew members were U.S. Navy Captain Robert L. Crippen, who commanded the flight; U.S. Air Force Colonel John M. Fabian; Navy Captain Frederick H. Hauck; and physician Norman E. Thagard, who tested the body's adaptation to weightlessness.

The shuttle crew deployed two commercial communications satellites and used the shuttle's robot arm — some 15 meters (50 feet) in length — to release and later retrieve the *Shuttle Pallet Satellite* (*SPAS*). SPAS, a West German scientific satellite, carried a system for photographing Earth that may lead to new mineral and oil discoveries.

Crippen and Hauck tested the shuttle's ability to maneuver near another spacecraft, *SPAS*. Ride and Fabian used the mechanical arm to hook onto *SPAS* and return it to the shuttle's cargo bay. This was the first time that a spacecraft was released to fly freely in space and then was recaptured. The crew released and retrieved *SPAS* several times to test the robot arm. The satellite was in orbit photographing Earth for only a few hours before it was retrieved for the last time for return to Earth. The maneuvering exercises and the test of the robot arm set the stage for the later capture and repair of the *Solar Maximum Mission Satellite* (*Solar Max*).

On its next mission, from August 30 to September 5, *Challenger* carried the first U.S. black astronaut to fly in space, Air Force Lieutenant Colonel Guion S. Bluford, Jr. The other crew members were Navy Commodore Richard H. Truly, who commanded the flight; Navy Captain Daniel C.

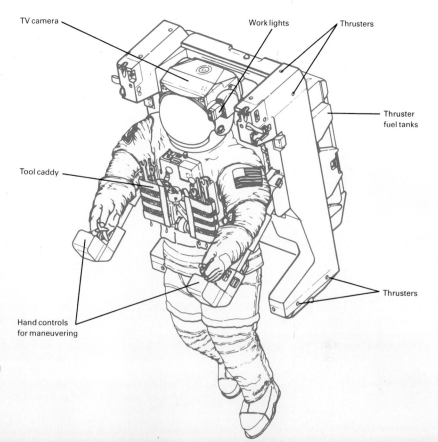

TV camera

Work lights

Thrusters

Thruster
fuel tanks

Tool caddy

Hand controls
for maneuvering

Thrusters

A Human Satellite
In history's first
free-floating space
walk, *below,* some 270
kilometers (170 miles)
above Earth, U.S. Army
Colonel Robert L.
Stewart ventures from the
space shuttle *Challenger*
without any lifelines
attached to the craft.
The manned maneuvering
unit, *right,* that makes
the free flight possible
is equipped with work
lights and powered by
24 individual thrusters.

Spacelab Makes Its Debut

The European-built Spacelab, a laboratory module designed to fit into the cargo bay of the space shuttle, *below,* was launched Nov. 28, 1983, for a 10-day mission. Aboard Spacelab, West German scientist Ulf Merbold, *below center,* performs a physics experiment while astronaut Owen Garriott draws blood from U.S. scientist Byron Lichtenberg, *below, far right,* for a medical experiment.

After 10 years of development, the joint United States and European Spacelab mission was launched on Nov. 28, 1983, from Cape Canaveral, Fla. Spacelab, a European-built research laboratory, is a pressurized cabin, 7 meters (23 feet) long, designed for conducting scientific experiments under the unique conditions of weightlessness in space. The space shuttle *Columbia*, commanded by astronaut John W. Young, carried Spacelab aloft in *Columbia*'s cargo bay.

A joint enterprise of the U.S. National Aeronautics and Space Administration (NASA) and the European Space Agency (ESA), the launching of Spacelab marked the first time that Europeans took a major part in the U.S. space shuttle program. Ten European governments contributed nearly $1 billion to develop Spacelab.

The Spacelab mission lasted longer than any previous shuttle mission — 10 days and 8 hours — and it carried six crew members, the largest crew ever flown into space on a U.S. mission. The Spacelab crew included the first payload specialists to fly on a U.S. space mission. The two payload specialists — so-called because their only mission was to conduct scientific experiments in the shuttle's payload or Spacelab — were German physicist Ulf Merbold of Max Planck Institute in Stuttgart, West Germany, a materials engineer, and U.S. biomedical engineer Byron K. Lichtenberg of Massachusetts Institute of Technology in Cambridge. The other crew members were U.S. Air Force Major Brewster H. Shaw, Jr., and mission specialists Owen K. Garriott and Robert A. R. Parker. The mission ended when *Columbia* landed on December 8 at Edwards Air Force Base in California's Mojave Desert.

Scientists said that the more than 70 experiments conducted on Spacelab during its 10-day flight might one day lead to significant advances in astronomy, solar physics, atmospheric studies, biology, and materials processing — the mixing of metals and formation of crystals under conditions of weightlessness. Scientists from 14 countries de-

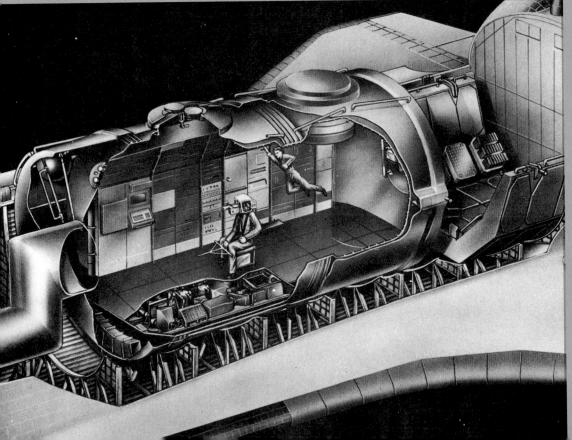

signed the experiments performed aboard Spacelab. Many of those scientists also communicated directly with the payload specialists as the experiments were underway.

One experiment apparently disproved a theory on the function of the inner ear that won the Nobel Prize for physiology or medicine in 1914 for Austrian neurologist Robert Bárány. Physiologist Rudolf von Baumgarten of West Germany said his Spacelab experiment disproved the Austrian scientist's explanation for a relationship between eye movement and sensations in the inner ear.

Spacelab also carried the most sensitive laboratory instruments ever flown in space to study how different metals mix under conditions of weightlessness. The metal mixtures thus created cannot be duplicated on Earth because of gravity.

In addition to experiments conducted aboard Spacelab, scientists also used an instrument pallet, or platform, that carried 38 scientific instruments in *Columbia*'s open cargo bay.

An X-ray telescope provided by the Netherlands collected data that scientists used to determine the presence of specific elements in deep space objects, such as iron on Cygnus X-1, an X-ray star. Some astronomers believe the center of Cygnus X-1 is a *black hole* — an object so dense that not even light can escape from it.

An instrument that was provided by France detected deuterium, a heavy form of hydrogen, in Earth's upper atmosphere. It was the first time that deuterium had ever been found there. This finding may help scientists to predict more accurately the rate at which carbon dioxide is building up in the atmosphere. Such a build-up might cause harmful changes in Earth's climate.

After 10 days, Spacelab had gathered a wealth of scientific information, including 20 million frames of television pictures. NASA officials pronounced the mission a success and predicted that 50 more missions using Spacelab equipment will be flown by the year 2000.   [Craig Covault]

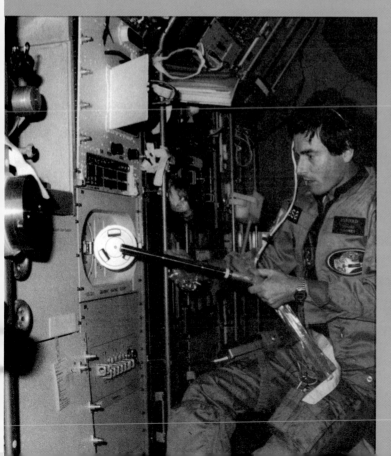

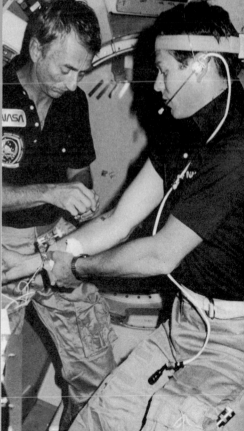

Brandenstein; Navy Lieutenant Commander Dale A. Gardner; and physician William E. Thornton.

Once in orbit, the crew deployed a weather-communications satellite for India. They also used the robot arm to maneuver its heaviest load ever, a dumbbell-shaped test structure that weighed 3,383 kilograms (7,460 pounds). The purpose was to test the mechanical arm's ability to move large, heavy objects.

Spacelab. On November 28, the orbiter *Columbia* returned to space carrying Spacelab, a joint venture of NASA and the European Space Agency (ESA) that required 10 years to develop and an investment of nearly $1 billion by European nations. Spacelab, a self-contained, pressurized laboratory module, rested in *Columbia*'s cargo bay. During the 10-day flight, scientists aboard Spacelab conducted experiments under the conditions of weightlessness over a broad range of scientific areas. See Close-Up.

Human satellites. The 10th space shuttle mission — which lasted from Feb. 3 to Feb. 11, 1984 — made history on February 7, when Navy Captain Bruce McCandless 2nd and Army Colonel Robert L. Stewart left the shuttle and became the first human beings to float freely in space without lifelines attached to the craft. The astronauts used manned maneuvering units (MMU's) — backpacks containing 24 nitrogen-powered thrusters for controlling movement in all directions. The MMU's enabled the astronauts to float up to 90 meters (300 feet) from the shuttle, which was orbiting 270 kilometers (170 miles) above Earth. The astronauts traveled at the same speed as the shuttle, 28,000 kilometers (17,400 miles) per hour, during their free flight, but they sensed nothing of their speed because there is no atmosphere to cause resistance in space.

The mission had some disappointing failures. Two communications satellites valued at $75 million each — the Western Union Corporation's *Westar 6* and Indonesia's *Palapa B-2* — were lost when the rocket motors designed to place them in orbit failed. In addition, a small target balloon intended for shuttle maneuvering tests exploded when it was inflated. However, mission

commander Vance D. Brand, who piloted the *Challenger* along with Navy Commander Robert L. Gibson, was still able to practice maneuvering around the remains of the balloon.

Repairing *Solar Max*. The 11th shuttle mission, which was launched on April 6, rescued the crippled *Solar Max*, a $240-million observatory equipped with several telescopes and sensors for studying the sun. *Solar Max* was launched in February 1980, but within a year, there was a failure in the system that controlled the satellite's ability to point its telescopes at the sun. A crew was sent up in the shuttle *Challenger* to repair *Solar Max*. Astronaut George D. Nelson used an MMU in an attempt to dock with the satellite, but Nelson's docking system could not lock onto the satellite.

Nelson's docking attempt sent *Solar Max* spinning wildly, but ground controllers at NASA's Goddard Space Flight Center in Greenbelt, Md., were able to turn on a system that stopped the spinning. The *Challenger* crew then used the shuttle's robot arm on April 10 to snare the 2,038-kilogram (4,500-pound) satellite and place it in the shuttle's cargo bay. Astronauts Nelson and James D. van Hoften repaired the system that aimed *Solar Max*'s telescopes and also fixed an instrument used to view the solar atmosphere. *Solar Max* was returned to its orbit on April 12, functioning normally.

Soviet efforts. During the year, the Soviet Union had far less success with manned space flight than did the United States. An attempt to place a new cosmonaut crew on board the *Salyut 7* space station failed on April 20, 1983. A small manned transport, the *Soyuz T-8*, used to shuttle crews between Earth and the space station, was unable to dock with the *Salyut 7* when its radar antenna became stuck. The crew returned to Earth on April 22.

On June 27, the Soviets rebounded from that failure by launching cosmonauts Vladimir A. Lyakhov and Aleksandr P. Aleksandrov to the station. On September 9, however, a fuel leak threatened to force their evacuation from the space station. The leak impaired *Salyut 7*'s ability to maneuver.

Then, on September 27, one of the worst known failures in the history of

Physicist Sally K. Ride, aboard the shuttle *Challenger,* in June 1983 became the first U.S. woman in space.

Air Force Lieutenant Colonel Guion S. Bluford, Jr., in August 1983 became the first black astronaut to fly a space mission.

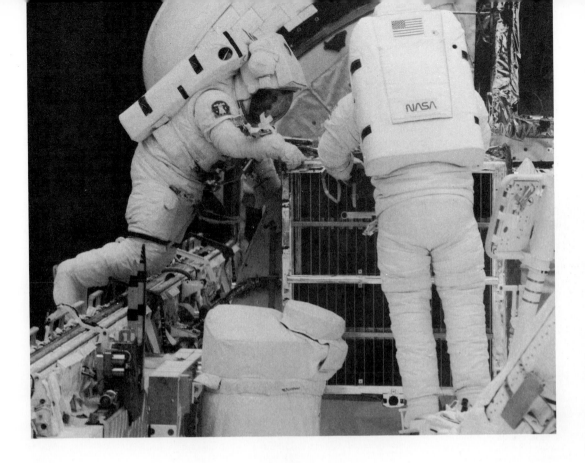

Space Exploration

Continued

Astronauts George D. Nelson, left, and James D. van Hoften repair the *Solar Maximum Mission Satellite* in the cargo bay of the shuttle *Challenger* in April 1984. It was the first repair of a satellite in space, and it salvaged a $240-million observatory that had gone out of control. After the repair, the satellite was returned to orbit.

the Soviet space program occurred at the Tyuratam launch site near the Aral Sea. During an attempt to send two cosmonauts to *Salyut 7* to relieve Lyakhov and Aleksandrov, a booster rocket on the launch vehicle caught fire and exploded. Cosmonauts Vladimir G. Titov and Gennadi Strekalov narrowly escaped death. Launch escape rockets on their *Soyuz* spacecraft fired and pulled them free of the burning booster just seconds before it exploded. The cosmonauts and their spacecraft then parachuted safely to Earth. Lyakhov and Aleksandrov returned to Earth on November 23, after a five-month stay aboard *Salyut 7*.

On April 2, 1984, a *Soyuz T-11* spacecraft carried three cosmonauts, including Rakesh Sharma, the first Indian cosmonaut to fly in space, to the *Salyut 7* space station.

Venus mission. With unmanned space activities, the Soviets were more successful. Two *Venera* spacecraft, launched toward Venus on June 2 and 7, 1983, returned important new data about the planet. Both spacecraft en-

tered into orbit around Venus in October and used radar to penetrate the planet's dense cloud cover and return information about the surface. The radar images revealed rugged volcanoes in the northern polar regions.

Other U.S. developments. The *Landsat 5* satellite, used to monitor crop growth and to gather data for mineral and petroleum exploration, was launched on March 1, 1984. The new satellite replaced *Landsat 4*, which was losing its power.

On Dec. 22, 1983, a new course and a new name was set for NASA's *International Sun Earth Explorer* (*ISEE-3*), first launched in 1978. On its new course, *ISEE-3* — renamed the *International Cometary Explorer* — will approach close to Comet Giacobini-Zinner in September 1985, for the first time enabling astronomers to acquire data directly from a comet.

In his Jan. 25, 1984, State of the Union message, President Ronald Reagan called for the development of an $8-billion, permanently manned U.S. space station by 1994. [Craig Covault]

Zoology

After seven years of trying, Ling-Ling and Hsing-Hsing, the two giant pandas at the National Zoological Park in Washington, D.C., mated for the first time. The birth on July 21, 1983, of a tiny male cub to Ling-Ling brought joy to panda lovers around the world. But the newborn died the same day of pneumonia. Then, in December, Ling-Ling almost died of a kidney infection. By mid-1984, she had recovered and was thought to be pregnant again.

Starving pandas. In January 1984, zoologist George B. Schaller of the New York Zoological Society reported that about 250 of the estimated 1,000 giant pandas in China were threatened with starvation. By mid-1984, at least two pandas had died in a famine caused partly by human activities but mainly by the natural dying away of bamboo, the panda's principal food.

Pandas eat almost nothing but bamboo. Bamboo plants grow for many years without flowering. Then, all at once, groups of bamboo plants flower, form seeds, and die. Therefore, entire forests of bamboo can suddenly disappear. In place of the mature plants, seedlings sprout up, and at least 45 years later, those plants bloom, make seeds and die, completing the cycle.

It takes several years for the seedlings to grow large enough to restore the bamboo forests and provide adequate food for the pandas. Years ago, the panda's habitat was large enough that the animals could find another source of bamboo when one stand of bamboo began dying. But because so much of that habitat has been altered by the clearing of forests, the bamboo's peculiar life cycle could now be fatal to the pandas.

To help the pandas through this crisis, China set up rescue teams to seek out starving animals and, if necessary, bring them to emergency holding stations. The government set up a program for relocating people away from areas where pandas live so that bamboo can be planted on their land to provide food for the pandas.

New phylum. In 1983, a Danish scientist became one of the few persons in this century to name a new animal

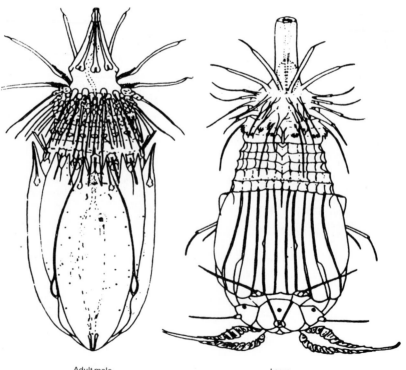

Loricifera, a microscopic animal that lives in sand and gravel on the ocean floor, was identified as a new animal phylum in 1983. The animal gets its name – Loricifera, the Latin word for *girdle wearer* – from the plates on its abdomen.

Adult male

Larva

A spider detaches its leg and moves to the center of its web after the leg is stung by a poisonous insect, at bottom right. Biologists at Cornell University in Ithaca, N.Y., believe this behavior shows that lower animals may have a mechanism for sensing poisons and may feel pain much as higher animals do.

phylum. This is a rare event because a phylum is the second broadest scientific classification after a kingdom. Animals in a phylum are related by descent from a common ancestor. Scientists have classified all living things into more than 30 phyla.

At two international conferences in August and September 1983, zoologist Reinhardt M. Kristensen of the University of Copenhagen announced his discovery of Loricifera, a group of ocean-living, microscopic animals. The new phylum was not discovered until recently because Loricifera live secluded in sand and gravel on the sea floor anywhere from 10 meters (33 feet) to several hundred meters below the ocean's surface.

The Loricifera has a retractable mouth tube that can be pulled back into the animal. The head of its teardrop-shaped body has a collar of spines, and its abdomen is ringed with plates, hence its name, which is Latin for *girdle wearer*.

In April 1982, Kristensen found one Loricifera species off the French coast. A month later, he discovered a different species in western Greenland.

Toad-eating fly. In a bizarre reversal of traditional predator roles, scientists in November 1983 reported the first known case of a fly that eats toads. Photographer Rodger Jackman and biologist Thomas Eisner of Cornell University in Ithaca, N.Y., reported that in 1982 they had observed thousands of spadefoot toads emerging from a pond in Cochise County, Arizona, east of Tucson. The toads were all of adult size, about 2 centimeters (¾ inch) long. Among them, the two observers found dead and dying toads that apparently had been seized by a predator and drawn into the mud until only their heads, or heads and trunks, projected above the surface. By sifting through the mud around the captive toads, the investigators found grublike larvae of a horsefly.

Eisner and two Cornell colleagues re-created the scene in an aquarium, using horsefly larvae buried in mud with just their mouthparts flush with the surface. When toads came to rest upon the mouthparts of the larvae, the larvae caught them and dragged them into the mud. The larvae injected the

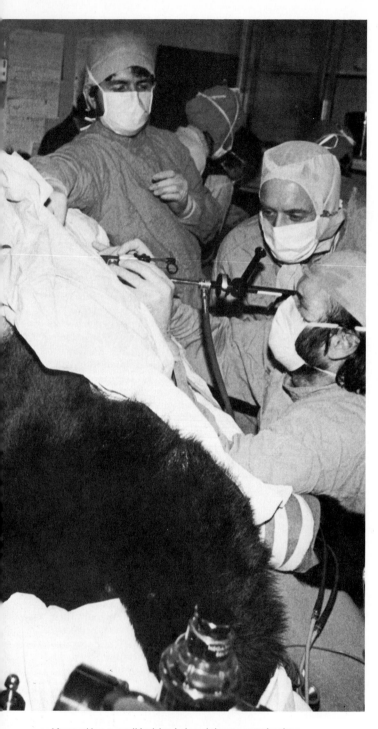

After making a small incision in her abdomen, veterinarians using a sophisticated instrument examine the kidneys of Ling-Ling, the female giant panda at the National Zoological Park in Washington, D.C. Kidney disease brought Ling-Ling close to death in December 1983, but she had fully recovered by mid-1984.

toads with venom and then sucked out the toads' blood and body fluids.

When the scientists tested the strength required by fly larvae to pull down a toad, they found that even though the larvae weighed only 0.57 gram (1/50 of an ounce), they pulled with a force 30 times their own weight and 10 to 16 times the toad's weight.

Sharks may save humans. Biochemists Anne Lee and Robert S. Langer reported in September 1983 that sharks contain an abundant supply of a substance useful in antitumor research.

In the mid-1970's, scientists found an antitumor substance in the cartilage of calves, but the substance exists only in small quantities in mammals, and this limited further study. Sharks, however, have a skeleton composed entirely of cartilage. Consequently, they provide a large supply of the substance, which blocks the growth of new blood vessels to certain tumors.

Working at the Massachusetts Institute of Technology in Cambridge, Mass., and the Children's Hospital Medical Center in Boston, the two biochemists obtained purified samples of the antitumor substance from the tails and fins of basking sharks, a common species of shark. They tested it on cancerous tumors in animals and found it checked tumor growth by reducing the number of blood vessels that feed the tumor.

The antitumor substance appears to act only on blood vessel growth and not directly on the tumor itself. With sharks providing a source, the antitumor substance may prove helpful in cancer research.

Cheetahs in trouble. The cheetah, the world's fastest mammal, has a history of mating among close relatives, and this may spell doom for this species, a team of scientists reported in July 1983.

Scientists from the National Cancer Institute, the National Institute of Mental Health, and the Smithsonian Institution studied 55 cheetahs from South Africa and from two zoos in the United States. To ensure a good mix of animals, the scientists included wild cheetahs from widely separated areas of South Africa and cheetahs born in zoos of parents from different regions.

Zoology

Continued

A naked mole rat, a tiny rodent found in Africa, is dwarfed by a researcher's hand. Colonies of mole rats were set up in laboratories at Cornell University and the University of Michigan so scientists could study the curious insectlike behavior of this hairless, wrinkled creature. The mole rat lives in large underground colonies where one female becomes the queen and the only breeding female. This type of behavior is rare in mammals.

The researchers compared 47 enzymes in blood samples taken from the 55 cheetahs. In similar studies done with animals of other species, scientists have found differences in the enzymes among the individual animals in the study group. But in this study, all the cheetahs had identical enzymes. This meant that the animals have similar genes, the basic units of heredity.

Such genetic similarity, the researchers suggest, comes about when the population of a species falls to low levels and *inbreeding* (mating of close relatives) follows. Such a decline in the cheetah population, resulting in inbreeding, may have occurred as long as 20,000 years ago because of drastic climate changes that killed off many animals. Or, it may have been more recent, caused by overhunting during the early 1900's. Scientists have no way of determining when the inbreeding occurred.

Inbreeding produces animals that are less able to reproduce. When the researchers measured the amount of sperm produced by cheetahs, they found that the animals had 10 times less sperm than related species of wild cats. That may worsen the decline of these animals, which once ranged worldwide but today number fewer than 15,000 in isolated regions of East and South Africa. In the Special Reports section, see HOW SCIENCE IS SAVING WILD ANIMALS.

Inbreeding is not necessarily a death sentence. Other animals, such as the northern elephant seal, have rebounded, though their numbers were drastically reduced in the late 1800's.

Sex change in fish. Some females among the saddle-back wrasse, a colorful coral-reef fish, undergo a sex change and become males. Marine biologists Robert M. Moss and George S. Losey of the Hawaii Institute of Marine Biology in Kaneohe, Hawaii, and biologist Milton Diamond of the University of Hawaii School of Medicine in Honolulu, studied groups of wrasse from coral reefs near Oahu, Hawaii. By August 1983, they had discovered what triggers the sex change.

The scientists first brought the fish

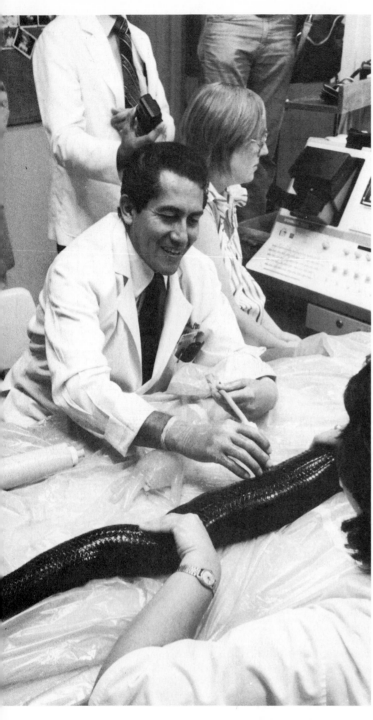

Gynecologist Rigo Santos of the University of Texas Southwestern Medical School in Dallas performs an ultrasound scan on a rare New Guinea black python. Dallas Zoo officials requested the scan, which is often performed on pregnant women, to learn if the snake was pregnant. Unfortunately, test results were inconclusive.

to a laboratory where they determined the sex, weight, and size of each fish. They placed the fish in small square pens in a protected lagoon with one to four adult fish in each pen. Some pens contained barriers restricting movement and preventing the fish from touching. In some experiments, the barriers prevented the fish from both touching and seeing one another.

The researchers found that a female does not change sex simply because there are too few males. Instead, the largest female in a group changes into a male following the loss of the group's largest fish. When a female wrasse was placed with one larger and one smaller fish, it did not change sex. This suggested that sex change is blocked by the presence of a larger individual. Large fish are usually males, and small fish are usually females.

The researchers also found that the largest female in a group needs some kind of cue from other fish before it will change into a male. It does not have to touch other fish, but it must be able to see them.

The researchers concluded that if the number of larger fish is low compared with the number of smaller fish, that would indicate too few males and too many females. A sex change in a large female then would be expected because a new male added to the social group would benefit reproduction.

Lost world. In April 1984, a team of U.S. and Venezuelan scientists reported the discovery of a virtual "lost world" atop a high mesa in Venezuela's tropical rain forest where life has evolved in unique ways. The scientists believe that about 98 per cent of the plant species they found on the mesa exist nowhere else on earth and that many of the animals are new species.

The 650-square-kilometer (250-square-mile) area is known as Neblina or the Mountain of the Mists. The steep-sided mesa rises 1,800 meters (6,000 feet) above the rain forest, and because of its isolation, scientists call it an "island in the clouds." Among the creatures the scientists found there was a bizarre frog that may date from the time, 200 million years ago, when South America and Africa were part of the same continent.
[William J. Bell and Elizabeth Pennisi]

Science You Can Use

In areas selected for their current interest, *Science Year* presents information that the reader as a consumer can use in making decisions — from buying products to caring for personal health and well-being.

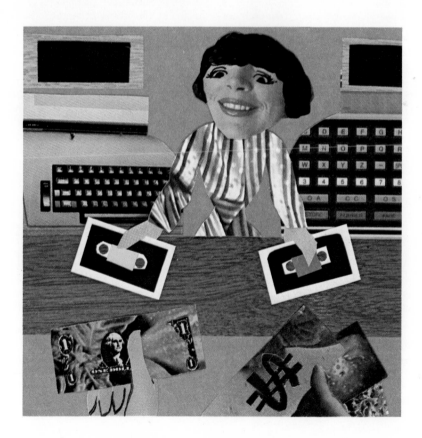

What's New in Telephones?

The year 1984 will long be remembered as one of revolutionary change in the United States telephone industry. The changes began in January, when the American Telephone and Telegraph Company (AT&T) complied with a U.S. Department of Justice ruling and gave up its entire national network of local telephone systems. From the consumer's point of view, one of the most important results of this historic action was that it became cheaper to own a phone than to rent one from the phone company.

The prices of today's telephones range up to several hundred dollars. How much you spend on a phone depends on the number of special features you want. You can buy a telephone that fits into your pocket, one that remembers and dials the phone numbers you use most frequently, or even one that doubles as a smoke detector and burglar alarm.

If you want just a basic telephone, you can buy one for as little as $10 — sometimes less. Some of these inexpensive phones have useful features. For example, most of them are equipped with an automatic dialing feature that will remember and redial the last number you placed, which can be a timesaver when you keep getting a busy signal.

However, as with most products, quality varies with price. You should not expect a $10 phone to be as durable or work as effectively as the one you rented from the telephone company. If you buy a low-cost telephone, consider it the same way you might an inexpensive wristwatch — as something you will use for a few years and throw away when it stops working.

There is another aspect of inexpensive phones you should be aware of: Even though most of them have push buttons, they usually are actually rotary dialers rather than true touch-tone phones. Therefore, unless you spend $25 to $100 for a separate device called an autodialer that produces the genuine touch-tone notes, you will not be able to use discount long-distance services such as Sprint and MCI. And even with an autodialer, a phone without touch-tone dialing cannot be used for certain telephone services, such as call forwarding.

A basic touch-tone phone of good quality costs about $70; a good-quality rotary-dial phone, about $30. Both kinds of phones are made by a number of manufacturers, including AT&T's Western Electric Company, and are available at AT&T Phone Center stores, electronics shops, department stores, and a growing number of "telephone boutiques."

Beyond the basics, there are at least 300 kinds of telephones to choose from — phones shaped like Mickey Mouse or Superman, phones designed to accent the decor of a room, and phones combined with devices such as an AM-FM radio or an alarm clock. These telephones range in price from about $30 to more than $200.

Many of the electronic features offered can save time in placing calls. "On-hook dialing" enables you to place a number without lifting the receiver. One model has a small speaker that allows you to hear the ring on the other end of the line. When you hear the call being answered, you pick up the receiver and talk.

On-hook dialing is often incorporated with other features, such as speed-dialing. A speed-dialing telephone is equipped with an electronic memory, enabling you to program the phone with frequently dialed or emergency numbers for quick one- or two-button dialing. Most phones with this feature cost between $80 and $200. The less-expensive phones store as few as two numbers, while those in the upper price ranges remember anywhere from a dozen to 100 numbers.

Ordinary telephones can be converted to speed-dialing phones by the addition of various accessories. For instance, most autodialers are also

Auto/speed dialer

"Glow" phone with lighted numbers

Telephone headset

Cordless phone with clock radio

Mickey Mouse phone

Portable cordless phone

Smoke/Alert phone

speed-dialers with memories that store as many as 100 numbers. One combination auto/speed-dialer, costing about $100, screws into the mouthpiece of standard handheld receivers and remembers 83 numbers.

Some telephones allow greater freedom of movement than ever before. Telephone headsets, priced at $50 to $150, consist of a pair of lightweight earphones and a wraparound mouthpiece and allow users to converse while leaving their hands free to do other things. The speakerphone, which costs $100 to $400, is a desk-top console containing a speaker and a sensitive microphone. It picks up your voice from anywhere in the room and amplifies the voice of the person you are talking with.

Cordless telephones, however, offer the maximum mobility. These phones, which cost from $70 to $250, consist of a "base station" that plugs into the wall and a portable, battery-powered handset. The base station receives a call from the telephone line and transmits it to the handset over an FM radio frequency.

Because cordless phones operate like a two-way radio, their performance is affected by the surrounding environment. Brick walls or hills, for example, diminish a cordless phone's operating range and sound quality.

Many of the electronic options offered by cord-attached telephones are also available on their cordless cousins. And many models have a speaker-microphone in the base station that acts like an intercom, enabling a person in the room where the base station is located to talk with the person carrying the handset.

Most cordless phones in use today transmit and receive signals within a radio bandwidth permitting only five channels. In areas where many cordless phones are operating, interference caused by channel overcrowding can make conversation difficult. However, channel overcrowding on cordless phones was lessened somewhat in the spring of 1984 when the FCC permitted an additional five channels at higher transmission frequencies. The new frequencies should also make transmissions stronger and clearer.

All cordless phones manufactured after October 1984 will have a 10-channel capacity, and models due to be introduced in 1985 will electronically scan all the channels and transmit over the least congested one. The telephone industry and the FCC are already discussing the possibility of adding an additional 10 channels by 1989.

Telephones have long been used to summon help in an emergency. Combined with electronic sensing devices, they now offer expanded security for the home. Western Electric's Smoke/Alert system, which costs about $200, is both a smoke detector and an automatic-dialing telephone. When it senses smoke, the device relays an emergency message in a computer-synthesized voice to two telephone numbers that you program into the system. Gulf and Western's Sensaphone Security Monitoring System, costing about $250, has sensors that are on the alert for smoke, electrical power failure, excessively high or low temperatures, leaks or flooding in the basement, or forced entry through a door or window. If any of these conditions are detected, the system reports an appropriate taped message to four preprogrammed numbers, such as the police and fire department.

Telephones are emerging as a key link in the home telecommunications center of the future. Already available are services allowing you to bank, shop, and receive preselected stock quotations over telephone lines.

Many experts predict that the familiar dialing system will be expanded to allow telephone users to more easily communicate with computers. They also envision a portable, pocket-sized video telephone, equipped with a small screen that will use radio transmission techniques similar to those used for today's cordless phones and cellular radio telephones (in the Science File section, see ELECTRONICS [Close-Up]).

Many of the functions and appliances of tomorrow's home will be controlled by the family computer working "hand in hand" with your telephone. In the not-so-distant future, you may be able to turn on the air conditioner, start the microwave oven, and open the garage door with the press of a button on your portable communicator. [M. S. Kaplan]

Choosing the Right Adhesive

Glues and other adhesives are among the most useful and versatile materials in everyday life. They are used for everything from mending pottery to laying floor tiles.

Glues are a type of adhesive derived from animal protein. Adhesives other than glues, such as acrylics and epoxies, are made from various synthetic chemicals.

Adhesives work in two basic ways, mechanically and chemically. Mechanical binding is somewhat like nailing materials together on a microscopic level. The adhesive fills in the pores of the two surfaces being joined together and becomes trapped there when it dries. The surfaces are then locked together. An adhesive that works chemically bonds together atoms or molecules of the adhesive with those of the surfaces to which the adhesive has been applied.

The best adhesive to use for a given task depends on several factors, including the materials to be joined and the kind of bond you want. There are at least a dozen types of adhesives, but most of those in everyday use fall into five major categories: glues, epoxies, polyvinyl adhesives, acrylic adhesives, and household cements.

Some Facts About Adhesives

	Glues	Household cement	"Super" adhesives	Polyvinyl adhesives	Epoxies
Brand names	Franklin Hide Glue, Weldwood Casein Glue	Duco Cement, Ambroid Cement, Le Page's Household Cement	Krazy Glue, Super Glue, Elmer's Wonder Bond	Scotch Wood and Paper Glue, Fas 'n-it, Elmer's Glue-All	E-pox-e, Weldwood Epoxy, Foxy Poxy
Used for	wood, furniture veneers	wood, leather, glass, metal, plastics, vinyl tile, ceramic tile	metal, glass, hard plastics, vinyl tile, ceramic tile	wood, cardboard, textiles, paper	glass, wood, hard plastics, metal, pottery, ceramic tile
Setting time	24 hours	10 to 15 minutes	instantly	30 to 60 minutes	fast epoxy— 5 minutes; slow epoxy— 24 hours
Bond resistant to water?	no	somewhat	yes	no	waterproof
Bond strength	very strong	strong	very strong	very strong	fast epoxy— strong; slow— very strong
Flammable?	no	very	yes	no	yes

Glues are the oldest type of wood adhesive. Some glues are made from collagen, a protein found in connective tissue. These glues are strong, inexpensive, and comparatively easy to work with. However, they dry yellow or brown, do not resist moisture well, and become brittle with age. Nevertheless, they are often the best choice for repairing furniture and, traditionally, they are the cabinetmaker's adhesive. Another kind of glue, called casein glue, is made from milk protein. Casein glues are also effective for joining wood.

Epoxies are two-part adhesives, made up of a resin and a hardener that must be mixed just before use. They produce a very strong, waterproof bond and can be either colorless or tinted. They can be used with smooth, hard materials such as metals, tile, and glass, as well as with porous materials such as leather or wood. Epoxies are especially good for bonding two dissimilar materials, such as wood and tile or glass and concrete. Because epoxy adhesives are hard to remove, even before they "set," it is best to apply them with a cheap brush that you can throw away when you are finished.

Polyvinyl adhesives are milky white liquids usually sold in squeeze bottles. These adhesives dry clear and provide a strong, flexible bond. They work best on porous materials such as wood, paper, textiles, and cardboard.

Acrylic adhesives — more commonly known as "superglues" — form extremely strong tan-colored bonds. These adhesives set quickly and are resistant to water, gasoline, and oil. They can be used for almost any job except for binding soft plastics or porous materials such as wood. Superglues are relatively expensive and must be used with extreme care, mainly because they are eye irritants and can instantly bond skin — such as your fingertips — together.

Household cements, also called plastic cements, are colorless or amber-colored adhesives, usually packaged in tubes. Most are made from cellulose, a substance derived from plant fibers. Household cements form strong bonds with a variety of materials. They are popular with hobbyists because with little fuss they can join plastic, glass, fabrics, wood, or china. However, their fumes are toxic and flammable, so be sure to use them in a well-ventilated area away from all flames.

No matter how good an adhesive is, it can bind only if it is in direct contact with the surfaces to be joined. Therefore, before you apply an adhesive, be sure to clean the surfaces. Use alcohol, dry-cleaning solvents, or detergent and water to remove dirt and oil. Paint, rust, and old adhesive must be scraped off or removed with a chemical solvent.

Most metals will be covered with an oxide, formed from reaction with the air. This oxide is often invisible and resists normal cleaning, but you can remove it by rubbing the metal's surface with an abrasive, such as a wire brush or coarse steel wool, until the surface is lightly etched. Then clean off the oxide particles with detergent and water before using the adhesive. In fact, before applying an adhesive to any surface, you should make certain that the surface is completely dry and free of particles that could weaken the bond.

The hardening time of most adhesives varies from a few minutes to several hours but can be as much as a day or more. While a bond is setting, it can be helpful to apply pressure to it to keep the surfaces in contact. Clamps, weights, or tying with string may hold the join until the job is done. A small sandbag is sometimes useful for holding an uneven surface in place.

Many adhesives have a limited shelf life or begin to deteriorate soon after opening, and almost all begin to set fairly quickly, giving you just a short time in which to make adjustments before the bond is fixed. Be sure to read the label before you start so that you can avoid using an adhesive that is not right for your purpose or sets too quickly. And if you have had an adhesive for a long time, it would be better to throw it out and buy a new adhesive than to risk making a faulty bond. Choosing the right adhesive for your purpose — and then following the manufacturer's instructions on the label so that you use it correctly — will assure you of getting the best possible results.   [Peter J. Andrews]

Camping Out with Computers

We all know about summer camp: two weeks at Camp Wannagohoma making moccasins, sleeping in tents, catching poison ivy, and maybe writing home about all the fun you're having (or how bad the food is). But that is not always how it is these days. The growing trend in summer camps for the 1980's — as in so many other fields — is computers.

Instead of spending two weeks at the old kind of camp, more and more youngsters are going off to computer camp. In some cases, the computers are out there among the pine trees and the frogs in traditional camp settings. More often, though, computer camps are held on college or prep school campuses.

Computer camps began in the late 1970's in response to two developments: the sudden, rapid growth of the personal-computer industry and the magnetic attraction between youngsters and computers. Michael Zabinski, a mathematics professor at Fairfield University in Fairfield, Conn., is generally credited with establishing the first such camp in the summer of 1977. Zabinski's organization, National Computer Camps, Incorporated, now runs camps in Simsbury, Conn.; Pepper Pike, Ohio; St. Louis, Mo.; Atlanta, Ga.; and McMinnville, Ore. — all in campus settings.

However, Denison Bollay, president of the Original Computer Camp, Incorporated, claims that he held the first "all-summer-long, overnight, true camp-setting [computer] camp" in 1980. Original Computer Camp has seven locations, five in wilderness settings — at Lake Sequoia, Calif.; Lake Tahoe, Nev.; Winnisquam Lake, N.H.; Steamboat Springs, Colo.; and in the Pocono Mountains of northeastern Pennsylvania. Two others are in campus surroundings, at Santa Barbara, Calif.; and New Milford, Conn.

There are now about 3,000 privately run summer programs offering some sort of computer training. They are located in every part of the United States and in many parts of Canada, but they are particularly numerous in California, New York, North Carolina, Ohio, and Utah. Tom Copley of Yellow Springs Computer Camp in Ohio

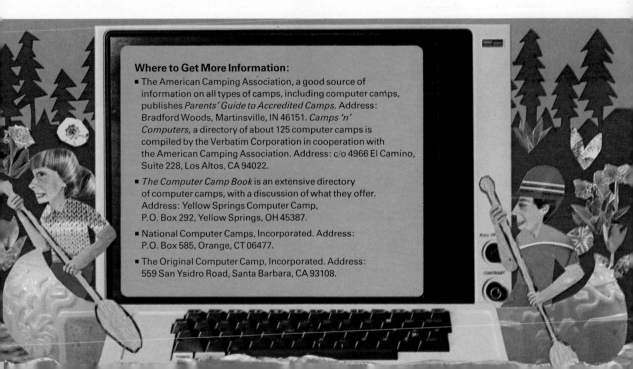

Where to Get More Information:

- The American Camping Association, a good source of information on all types of camps, including computer camps, publishes *Parents' Guide to Accredited Camps.* Address: Bradford Woods, Martinsville, IN 46151. *Camps 'n' Computers,* a directory of about 125 computer camps is compiled by the Verbatim Corporation in cooperation with the American Camping Association. Address: c/o 4966 El Camino, Suite 228, Los Altos, CA 94022.

- *The Computer Camp Book* is an extensive directory of computer camps, with a discussion of what they offer. Address: Yellow Springs Computer Camp, P.O. Box 292, Yellow Springs, OH 45387.

- National Computer Camps, Incorporated. Address: P.O. Box 585, Orange, CT 06477.

- The Original Computer Camp, Incorporated. Address: 559 San Ysidro Road, Santa Barbara, CA 93108.

says, "The number of computer camps is expanding at a geometric rate. This growth rate is tied to the tremendous increase in personal computer sales." Another factor, he says, is the current inability of America's school systems to keep pace with the demand for instruction in computer science.

The public schools, however, are starting to get into the act. In Boulder, Colo., for example, the Boulder Valley School District sponsors a one-week summer computer camp for fifth-through eighth-graders at a ranch in the nearby Rocky Mountains. The Gove Community School in Denver is planning a similar session. Colleges in every state, from Hawaii to Maine, also offer computer camps. There probably is a college or university within 100 miles of where you live that sponsors such a camp.

Not all computer camps are limited to children. At some, such as the Family Computer Camp at Clarkson College of Technology in Potsdam, N.Y., the whole family can take an apartment for a week and enter the Computer Age together.

To learn more about the various offerings or narrow down the choices, you may find it helpful to consult a 1982 directory published by the Yellow Springs Computer Camp or a new listing compiled by the Verbatim Corporation, a maker of memory disks for personal computers. The American Camping Association is another good source of information. (See the resource list accompanying this article for details and addresses.)

Of course, getting the name of a computer camp and a brief description of its programs will not guarantee that you will be satisfied with it. Before settling on a camp, you would be wise to talk with one of the directors, either in person or by phone. You should ask, for example, about the ratios of campers to computers and instructors. More than two campers for each computer or five campers per instructor may indicate that the camp has inadequate staff and facilities.

You might also ask whether the camp has anything to offer advanced students, what the qualifications of the instructors are, and exactly what is taught. Decide what you want from a camp, and then make sure the camp you are considering can "deliver the goods." If you receive evasive answers, look elsewhere.

Also consider the type of recreational activities a camp provides. The typical campus computer camp offers tennis, swimming, and movies, and camps in wilderness areas might also include hiking and horseback riding. The five camps operated by Computer Tutor of Larkspur, Calif., offer what they call a trilogy curriculum. This program provides a balance of three types of activities: mental (computer training); physical (games and sports); and cultural (such activities as visiting museums).

More boys than girls seem to be interested in computers. At most camps, the boy-girl ratio ranges between 2 to 1 and 5 to 1. The Yellow River Station Camp in northeastern Iowa has separate sessions for boys and girls.

Virtually all the camps use Apple II or TRS-80 computers. Costs average $750 to $900 for a two-week session. The age of campers generally ranges from about 8 to 15.

Parents send children to computer camp for a variety of reasons. Some may regard it as a two-week diversion; others may believe children will need to be computer-literate in the future. But the most compelling reason for children wanting to attend computer camp is the incredible magnetism between youngsters and computers. Like ducks and water, kids and computers just seem to go together. "Kids like the instant response computers give," says Tom Copley, "they're definitely habit-forming." Denison Bollay adds, "Computers are a continuous exploration, just like sailing a ship for a new world or climbing a tree. You're exploring new territory."

But some youngsters see beyond the fun of playing with computers at a summer camp. As a 13-year-old camper attending Timber Tech in California put it, "I love computers and what they do, and I feel that their role in the future is going to be extremely important. In about 10 years, there won't be a job that doesn't require computers. If you want to be successful, you will have to know something about them."   [Diane W. Johnson]

Sunscreens: Beach Umbrellas in a Bottle

Many people regard a suntan as a symbol of health. But when you bask in the sun, you are doing more than just darkening your skin; you are damaging it. However, if you are intent on sunbathing, there are ways to protect yourself. One of the most important of these is the use of a good *sunscreen*. These lotions and creams, by blocking the sun's harmful rays, can protect your skin from injury and disease.

If used properly, sunscreens will allow you to tan without getting a painful burn. If used faithfully, they protect against premature aging of the skin — that dry, crinkly look so common to long-time sunbathers — and they may prevent skin cancer, which scientists believe is caused mainly by long-term exposure to strong sunlight. Excessive exposure to the sun is particularly dangerous for fair-skinned persons, whose skin is most easily damaged by the sun.

Skin cancer is the most common type of cancer, with 400,000 cases diagnosed in the United States each year. Men, because they often work outdoors, are at higher risk than women. Fortunately, most skin cancers are rarely fatal. In the Special Reports section, see THE SKIN WE LIVE IN.

The visible rays of sunlight are not dangerous. All sunburn — and most tanning — is caused by invisible ultraviolet (UV) light rays that are transformed into heat as they strike the skin, and so burn it.

The closer to the equator one goes, the more intense the UV rays become. A person who develops a serious sunburn after 80 minutes on a beach outing in June in New Jersey would get an equally bad burn after only 50 minutes on the beach on the same day in the Florida Keys.

The body's natural defense against sunburn is the dark skin pigment *melanin*, which absorbs ultraviolet radiation before it can penetrate and burn the deeper layers of skin. Ultraviolet light stimulates additional melanin production, and as a result the skin gets darker. The problem is that, for most light-skinned persons, producing enough melanin to be visible as a tan takes about two weeks of daily exposure to the sun. But too much sun on any one day can produce a burn. Skin-care experts warn that very fair-skinned persons, particularly blonds and redheads, are 30 times more susceptible to sunburn than dark-skinned persons of African descent.

A fair-skinned person who wants to enjoy the sun without burning must either wear cover-up clothing or try to block ultraviolet rays as they strike the skin. This blocking, in essence, is what sunscreens do. All sunscreen products — lotions, creams, oils, and gels — contain one or more chemicals that in tests absorb from 85 to 95 per cent, and in some cases up to 99 per cent, of the harmful rays before they can burn the skin. Sunscreen chemicals also tend to be quite safe, because they are *inert*. This means that for the most part they do not penetrate or damage the skin, though some may cause allergic reactions and irritation in persons with sensitive skin.

Sunscreen ingredients have jaw-breaking names. Many are designated on labels only by their initials or chemical nicknames. For example, the full name for PABA, which is one of the most effective sun blocks, is para-aminobenzoic acid. The chemically related substance known as padimate A has a technical name that is even longer. Other shorthand names for commonly used sunscreen ingredients include cinoxate, homosolate, and oxybenzone.

You can tell how much protection a sunscreen provides by its SPF (sun protection factor) number. This classification system was recommended by a medical advisory panel of the United States Food and Drug Administration. Each sunscreen is assigned an SPF number on a scale of 2 to 15 or higher. The higher the number, the greater the protection. The SPF number tells you how long you can safely stay out in the sun with a particular sunscreen. But first, you must know how long you can safely stay in the sun without a sunscreen.

The FDA's medical advisers say it is safe to remain in the sun, with or without a sunscreen, until your skin first becomes red. If you then cover up quickly or go indoors, the blush will fade, and you will not feel burned later in the day. However, if you stay exposed to the sun past the time when your skin reddens, you are courting a burn. And if you stay out twice as long as it has taken your skin to redden, you will be badly burned.

Once you have determined how long you can stay in the sun unprotected before you start to burn, the SPF numbers enable you to tell how much sunlight you can safely get using various sunscreens. For example, if you ordinarily begin to turn red after 40 minutes, you can use an SPF 4 sunscreen to safely stay out four times longer, or 160 minutes. If you use an SPF 8 sun block, you can safely expose yourself to the sun eight times longer. Of course, you must remember to

**Skin Types and Recommended
Sun Protection Factor (SPF)**

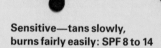

**Sensitive—tans slowly,
burns fairly easily: SPF 8 to 14**

**Very Sensitive—always
burns easily: SPF 15 and over**

reapply the sunscreen each time it is washed away by swimming or sweating, or rubbed off by friction.

You thus can match sunscreens to different kinds of outdoor activities at different times of the year. If you tan slowly and are taking a winter weekend vacation in the tropics, use a sunscreen with a higher SPF than you would use for summer sunbathing. You won't tan — you wouldn't anyway — but you *will* be able to spend much or all of your time at the beach or poolside without burning. If, on the other hand, you have a two-week vacation and want to play *and* tan, then use a product with your regular SPF number. When you begin to get red, switch to a sunscreen with a much higher SPF — or cover up. As the days go by and melanin production begins to darken and protect your skin, you can use a lower SPF or stay out longer.

Keep in mind, though, that any tanning is causing some skin damage. Therefore, doctors urge people to forsake suntanning altogether. But if you can't resist lying in the sun, at least give your skin a chance — use a sunscreen.

[David Zimmerman]

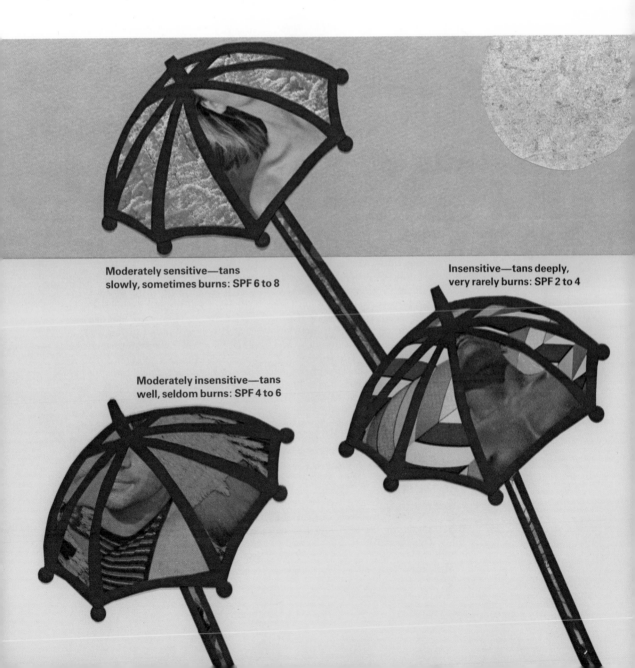

Moderately sensitive—tans slowly, sometimes burns: SPF 6 to 8

Insensitive—tans deeply, very rarely burns: SPF 2 to 4

Moderately insensitive—tans well, seldom burns: SPF 4 to 6

Selecting a Video Recorder

Are you thinking about buying a video cassette recorder (VCR)? Then you may be confused about which model is best for you. Should you buy a model that uses the Beta system, pioneered by the Sony Corporation? Or should you opt for the video home system (VHS), developed by Matsushita Electric Industrial Company? How do the two systems differ, what options do they offer, and what developments are expected in the future?

As with personal computers, stereo systems, and video games, you may want to put off buying a VCR while you wait to see what new developments come along. Or you can buy now and hope that today's system will be able to use the tapes of tomorrow.

All VCR's, whatever their options, perform one basic function: They record and/or play back video programs on videotape. These programs can be recorded at home from either antenna or cable television broadcasts. They can also be commercially prerecorded programs, such as movies, that can be rented or purchased.

Both Beta and VHS have their supporters, but VHS is being adopted by more and more electronics manufacturers, while Beta's sales have not kept pace. The recent success of VHS has been due largely to Matsushita's aggressive marketing techniques and does not mean that VHS is technologically superior to Beta. Except for the fact that VHS can record for a longer time on a given length of tape, both systems are about the same — though some electronics experts claim that Beta produces a clearer picture. However, because VHS has become the more popular format, there are many more prerecorded tapes available in VHS than Beta.

Because each system offers pretty much the same features, one of the important considerations in choosing one system over the other is *compatibility* — the ability of the machine you buy to play tapes recorded on other VCR's.

If you have friends with VCR's who are willing to trade tapes with you, you will want to be sure that their machines are compatible with yours. You cannot play a Beta tape on a VHS machine, nor can you play a VHS tape on a Beta machine. VHS and Beta are incompatible because they use different-sized cartridges and have different ways of creating the video image on the tape.

Most VCR's — both VHS and Beta — now come with fast forward and reverse, a timer that enables you to record programs automatically, a remote control device (either infrared or connected to the set by wire), the ability to record one program while watching another, and a *visual search* ability that lets you run the tape at about 10 times the normal speed without losing the picture in case you want to speed through a commercial. The price rises as you add other features, such as slow motion, a device for the automatic deletion of commercials, or a more versatile timer. Depending on its features, a VCR can cost as little as $400 or as much as $1,500.

One of the most useful functions of a VCR is that it lets you record a program and watch it at a later time. This is called *time shifting* in the slang of VCR owners. With the automatic timer, you can tape shows while you are asleep or away from home. You set the time and channel, and the recorder starts and stops at the correct time.

Nearly all VCR's have timers that enable them to record from the same channel at the same time each day until the tape runs out. But more expensive models can be set to record from different channels at different times for as long as three weeks. This can be a valuable feature if you are going on vacation and do not wish to miss your favorite TV programs. Obviously, though, you cannot set the recorder for more time than is available on the tape. So, if you plan to do a lot of au-

tomatic recording, a VCR's maximum taping time will be an important consideration. And taping time is related to how fast the machine records.

The speed at which you record can be varied. Most new VCR's have three speeds. By setting a VCR's controls for a slow speed, recording time is increased. VHS machines will record for as long as eight hours on a single tape, while Beta machines will record for only five hours on the same length of tape. However, as you gain time you lose quality; a program recorded at a slow speed will have a slightly poorer — and, with some VCR's, significantly poorer — picture and sound when played back than a program recorded at normal speed.

Beyond the basics, there are several optional features you can buy that will enable you to do even more with your VCR. For example, if you want to eliminate commercials when you tape a broadcast automatically, you will need a *commercial killer*. This device, which costs about $250, senses the fade-out of program material just prior to a commercial and stops the tape, starting it again when the commercial is over. Because there is a lag in restarting the tape you might miss a few seconds of the program, but you save several minutes of tape.

Another popular option is the *radio frequency (RF) switcher*, costing $30 to $175, depending on its complexity. The RF switcher links your VCR, video game player, and computer to your television set. It then lets you show a videotape, a computer display, or a video game on the TV with the push of a button, eliminating complicated wiring.

The ability to record stereo sound is now available on many VCR's. Stereo may become an important feature to have because the Federal Communications Commission in March 1984 gave its approval to stereo TV broadcasts. Televisions equipped with stereo speakers have been available since 1983 and will become more common in the future. However, no one is sure when stereo programming will begin; broadcasters are reluctant to invest in the necessary equipment until large numbers of homes have stereo TV sets. In the meantime, owners of stereo VCR's can enjoy stereo TV by playing prerecorded videotapes with stereophonic sound and connecting their TV to high-fidelity speakers.

Perhaps you would like to make home video programs with your own camera and videotape recorder. Most of these *camcorder* systems are VHS and cost from $1,400 to $1,700. A new format, using 8-millimeter tape — about half the width of the ½-inch tape used by VHS — is being developed by a number of electronics manufacturers. These cameras are lighter and simpler to operate than older camcorder systems, but their tape size makes them incompatible with VCR's. Some manufacturers, meanwhile, have been making ½-inch camcorder cameras that are easier to use.

If you are interested only in playing prerecorded programs but want the best possible picture and sound, you might not want a VCR at all. You might be happier with a videodisc player. The most popular of these are *digital* players. These units use a laser beam to read sound and picture signals etched into plastic-coated aluminum discs. Because the metal surface of the disc is never touched by anything but light, it will last virtually forever with no reduction of quality.

The quality of all home video will improve dramatically if the United States adopts high-definition television (HDTV). A TV picture consists of electronic horizontal lines "drawn" across the picture tube. The more lines there are on the screen, the sharper the picture is. The standard for American television has always been 525 lines, while in Europe it is 625 lines. However, the HDTV system, which is still experimental, is based on 1,125 lines. The increased number of lines greatly enhances the sharpness of the picture because finer details can be picked up by the television camera and reproduced on the screen.

HDTV is still a few years in the future, but electronics experts feel certain it will eventually become the worldwide standard. Fortunately, current VCR's will continue to work just fine with 1,125-line television, so don't let worries about HDTV stop you from buying a video recorder if you decide you want one. [E. Joseph Piel]

Making Money Grow Is a Matter of Interest

Someone once asked Henry Ford, the founder of Ford Motor Company, what he considered to be humanity's greatest invention. Ford thought for a second and then replied, "Compound interest." Although he was in the business of making automobiles rather than lending money, Ford realized the power of interest to build wealth.

Everywhere we look these days, we see advertisements for a bewildering variety of bank accounts, each offering a different rate of compound interest. Just what is compound interest, and how can it build wealth?

Interest has been called "the price of money," which is correct if we remember that it is the "rental price" rather than the "purchase price." If we want to own money, we work for it or sell something we possess, so goods and services are the purchase price. If we borrow money and later pay back more than we borrowed, the extra amount of money is the rental price, or interest.

Banks, too, must pay interest for using others' money. When you put money into a savings account, the bank is then able to lend that money to its other customers. In return, the bank pays you interest on your account.

Interest rates are stated in *per cent per year*. *Per cent* is an abbreviation of the Latin words for *out of one hundred*. For example, 8 per cent equals 8/100 or 0.08. If you put $100 into a savings account for one year at an 8 per cent interest rate, at the end of the year you will have your original $100 — called the *principal* — plus $8 of interest ($100 × 0.08) for a total of $108. If at the end of the second year, your account has gone up only by another $8, you have been earning *simple interest*. Simple interest is figured on just the original principal.

However, interest-yielding bank accounts nearly always pay *compound interest*, which is computed from the sum of the principal and the accumulated interest. With compound interest, if you leave the money in your account for a second year, the interest for the second year will not be another $8, but $8.64 ($108 × 0.08), for a total of $116.64. The third year's interest will be $9.33 ($116.64 × 0.08), bringing the total to $125.97.

In determining how much money an account would earn in a given number of years, you need not calculate each year separately. There is a faster way. If, to take the same example, you wish to know how much interest a $100 account earning 8 per cent compound interest will yield in three years, you can multiply $100 × 1.08 × 1.08 × 1.08. Again, the answer is $125.97. For each additional year, you multiply by another 1.08.

On the other hand, what if you want to know how much money you must put into an account at 8 per cent compound interest to have it grow to $100 in three years? In that case, you multiply 1.08 × 1.08 × 1.08 and get an answer of 1.2597. Then you divide $100 by the 1.2597 and get an answer of $79.38.

Compound interest can produce large returns in just a few years. Each dollar left in an account paying 8 per cent interest more than doubles to $2.16 after 10 years. At the end of 20 years, each dollar increases to $4.66, and at the end of 100 years, each dollar has become $2,199.76.

Even at low interest rates, money can grow to a huge amount if it is left in an account long enough. One dollar invested 2,000 years ago at only 1 per cent interest would today be worth $439,290,000, and at 2 per cent it would be $158,610,000,000,000,000.

To get some perspective on this growth, we use the *rule of 70*. Dividing 70 by the compound interest rate gives us the approximate number of years it takes money to double. At 8 per cent, it takes about 8.75 years (70 ÷ 8) for money to double, and it goes on doubling every 8.75 years as long as it is left in the account. [Donald Swanton]

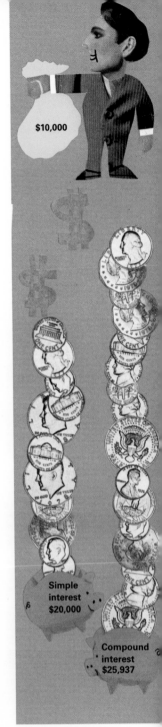

$10,000

Simple interest $20,000

Compound interest $25,937

In 10 years, $10,000 earning 10 per cent simple interest would increase to $20,000. At 10 per cent interest compounded annually, it would total $25,937.

People in Science

Learning about science can be a lifelong process that helps us understand nature and our place in the natural world. This section deals with people engaged in this process. It begins with the teachers whose task is to communicate both the facts and the excitement of science to young students. It continues with the story of a woman who, after being introduced to science, saw the problems it could solve and made a career of learning to solve them.

Science Year profiles four of the outstanding science and math teachers who received the first presidential awards for excellence.

Honoring the Best Teachers

BY THOMAS H. MAUGH II

The crowd in the East Room of the White House grew quiet as the President of the United States stepped to the podium and began to speak. He quickly got to the point. It was evident, said Ronald Reagan, "that the American people are realizing again how important our schools are and how vital and honorable the role of the teacher is in our communities. This is especially so in the area of science and mathematics. . . . With all the demands of educational reform, we must not forget the most important goal of all: to attract the most competent and dedicated people to teach and then to hang on to them."

And that was the object of the ceremony in Washington, D.C., on Oct. 19, 1983 — to honor some of the most competent and dedicated teachers in the United States with the first Presidential Awards for Excellence in Science and Mathematics Teaching. When the President finished his address, a certificate was handed to 104 science and math teachers by other dignitaries — Secretary of Education Terrel H. Bell, Presidential Science Adviser George A. Keyworth II, and National Science Foundation Director Edward A. Knapp.

In addition to certificates and plaques for their school's trophy cases, each winner received a $5,000 grant from the National Science Foundation (NSF) to spend on classroom resources. Each also received a Texas Instruments portable computer and books and magazine subscriptions. Each winner's school received THE WORLD BOOK ENCYCLOPEDIA and an IBM Personal Computer along with accessories and software.

The creation of these presidential awards grew out of the current crisis in science and mathematics education — which includes a critical shortage of qualified teachers at the elementary and high school levels. In the Special Reports section, see CLOSING IN ON THE MATH AND SCIENCE GAP.

The awards, administered by the NSF, were established to recognize teachers for outstanding classroom performance and for encouragement of excellence in all their students, not just the brightest. There were two winning teachers from each of the 50 states plus Puerto Rico and the District of Columbia. The selection process began with four teachers in each state nominated for the award by their peers. The final winners were chosen by the NSF.

In addition to the White House ceremony, the teachers were honored at a reception at the National Air and Space Museum, where they met with senators, congressmen, and other government officials. They also attended an Honors Workshop with the staff of the NSF and the National Academy of Sciences where they shared their experiences, heard about recent developments in their fields, and made recommendations for the improvement of teaching.

The teachers took advantage of their Washington visit to argue passionately for more federal help for education, especially more money. One award winner, Gerald Loomer of Rapid City, S. Dak., stepped to the podium after the President had left the East Room and told Education Secretary Bell that "seven cents of every [tax] dollar is not enough" for education.

Many of the teachers pressed the NSF to restore funding for continuing teacher-education programs conducted during the summer months. The teachers said it is unfair that they must pay for such programs themselves to keep up to date in their field.

The teachers also agreed that more emphasis should be placed on teaching science in elementary schools. "The average time given to science teaching at that level is seven minutes a day," said George Hague of Bernardsville, N.J. "That is unfortunate," he added, "because kids love science at that age."

And finally there was the subject of salaries. Too many potential teachers go into industry, the teachers argued, because the starting salaries are so much higher. "After teaching for 30 years," said Eleanor Milliken of Durham, N.H., "I have finally reached a salary of $24,000.

"I talked last night with a man who said he was paid four times as much for coaching athletics as he was for being head of his

The author:
Thomas H. Maugh II
is senior staff writer
for *Science* magazine.

While in Washington, D.C., the award-winning teachers enjoyed many activities, such as a reception at the National Air and Space Museum, *left,* and a chance to express their concerns about education to the press, *below left.* At the White House, National Science Foundation Director Edward A. Knapp presents the presidential award to Doris B. DeBoe of Washington, D.C., *below.*

school's math department. Until we treat academics like athletics, America will not solve its education problems."

Meanwhile, the effort has begun to recognize and honor the outstanding science and mathematics teachers in the United States today. Four of the teachers who received the first presidential awards are profiled on the following pages. Each of the four embodies the characteristics that President Reagan said "we found in all of you: your dedication to your profession, your breadth of experience and interests, your thorough preparation and continuing education in the subjects you teach, your insistence on hard work by your students, and your recognition that math and science are important for everyone and that everyone can be taught."

George A. Tinker
Marshfield High School, Coos Bay, Ore.

A Lifelong Love of the Sea

George A. Tinker says that his classroom at Marshfield High School in Coos Bay, Ore., looks like a mini-Smithsonian Institution. "There are a lot of sea shells and stuffed and mounted animals hanging around the room, including dried cow lungs hanging from the ceiling. All of this is to grab the students' attention." That is also the way Tinker teaches — by developing many different activities to capture and hold the students' interest.

Tinker teaches four classes in basic biology. But his main personal interest is in marine biology. So, taking advantage of his school's setting on the Pacific Northwest coast, he also set up an oceanography course.

"We go on a lot of local field trips digging up animals and fossils," he says. "The students have a lot of fun stomping around in the mud. In biology, we study marine biology at the coast and plant ecology at the nearby Sand Dunes National Recreation Area. The oceanography class studies such things as rocky tide pool areas and bays where river and ocean waters mix in the South Slough Estuarine Sanctuary only about 15 miles away."

Tinker tries to take the oceanography students out to sea. He started doing this several years ago with a charter boat trip in early April at the time of the gray whale migrations so that the students could see one of the biggest animals on earth. During the boat trip he would assign other activities to the students, such as trawling, dredging the bottom, taking plankton samples, and learning something about navigation. For the past few years the U.S. Coast Guard has taken them out on a 180-foot cutter.

Tinker came by his interest in the sea naturally. He was born in Honolulu, Hawaii, in 1945 to a science-oriented family. His father, a marine biologist, was director of the University of Hawaii's Waikiki Aquarium. After high school, Tinker attended Oregon State University at Corvallis, where he developed an affection for the Pacific Northwest coast that led him to a teaching job at Marshfield High School and has kept him there for 15 years.

He tries to make his classroom activities as interesting as the field trips. "We go through textbook material just like any other biology class. But I like to work in as much laboratory time as possible. We dissect sharks and fish that we get fresh from the local fishermen. We hatch salmon eggs and raise the fish. The biology students watch the salmon to learn about an animal's growth and development; the oceanography students use them as an aid to the study of commercial fisheries and aquaculture."

Tinker thinks that students have recently become more receptive to learning. "There is a little more seriousness," he says. "They look around and see that to be successful they need schooling beyond high school. And to prepare for that, they must follow through with math, science, and English to the limit of their abilities." He believes that even the students who are not going on to college need more exposure to science and math.

Like many of the other award winners, Tinker thinks that more emphasis should be placed on science in elementary schools. "Some elementary-school teachers are doing great, but some slight science, perhaps because they do not understand science very well themselves. I think elementary teachers should get some in-service workshops on science so they would be more comfortable teaching it."

Tinker hopes to use his grant money to help elementary-school teachers and students in the Coos Bay area. First, he wants to create a refrigerated fish-filled aquarium, containing water as cold as that in the ocean. The aquarium would travel from one elementary school to another. "This could add some interest and excitement to some of the other things the students are learning about," he says. "For example, they might observe the fish while they read stories about fish for their language arts classes."

Tinker also wants to stuff and mount some small animals in glass cases. "An elementary teacher could pick out two or three — such as a raccoon and a duck and a hawk — and take these to the classroom," he says. "Like the aquarium, these could add interest to reading or spelling. Or the teacher might want to introduce the students to biology by talking about how the animals live.

"Both of these projects would help enhance science education in our elementary schools. And I think that's an overall concern across the country, not just in the Coos Bay area."

Tinker inspires a feel for the sea and its many life forms by taking his students on daylong ocean cruises.

Doris B. DeBoe
Banneker High School, Washington, D.C.

High Expectations in Math

Doris B. DeBoe was a good student in college. "But I had problems writing papers," she says. "Things that I thought were good the teachers didn't always think were very good. So I decided that most subjects, particularly social studies, were very subjective and you had to think like the teacher. But mathematics is so exacting that once you understand what you are doing, there is no deviation, and the teacher's impression of what you do is not important."

DeBoe, however, did not set out to pursue a career in either mathematics or education. "I wanted to be a nurse," she says. The program called for two years of premedical courses in college, then a transfer to nursing school. "But my mother felt that it was important for me to finish four years of college and not stop after two years," says DeBoe. "At her insistence, I took education courses. When I finished school and needed a job, I took one as a teacher. I guess that's how I got sidetracked from nursing, but I've had no regrets since." That was 29 years ago. Today, DeBoe teaches mathematics at Banneker High School, Washington, D.C.'s only public college-preparatory high school, recruiting the top students throughout the city.

Perhaps the main reason she won the presidential award, her colleagues say, is her concern for her students. "The very first thing that I try to do with all of my students — whether they are slow or advanced in mathematics — is raise their level of expectation for themselves, help them develop confidence in themselves. I don't try to rush my students, but I do set high expectations for them."

DeBoe insists on a great deal of drill and practice. "I try to explain to my students that algebra is a skill like ball playing and piano playing. Once you learn the basics, practice is necessary to ensure mastery."

Her concern for students is not limited to the classroom. "In most of my career, I have tutored children — at school, after school, during the summer, in my home, and at my church. I have done this without compensation, because most of the students who needed help couldn't afford to pay for it anyway."

Nor is her concern limited to students deficient in math. DeBoe also conducts an after-school program for gifted students who are preparing for the citywide mathematics contests, and she is adviser to the math club. In addition, she chairs the math department, heads the school's public relations committee, and is codirector of

Concerned that all of her students have the opportunity to excel, DeBoe stays after class to give a young man special attention.

the school's general knowledge team, which appears on a local television quiz show. She is especially proud of the fact that a former student of hers, another mathematics teacher from the District of Columbia, was nominated for the presidential award.

DeBoe has watched the teaching of mathematics change, perhaps not always for the better. "In the early years of my teaching," she says, "there was a great deal of emphasis placed on computational skills and repetition drills. Then we went through this period of the 'new mathematics.' We started emphasizing concepts, such as set theory and number systems, I think probably at the expense of some computational skills. Students coming out of school could reason fairly well in mathematics, but they didn't have the skills to do the arithmetic well.

"So now we've reverted back somewhat. We're still trying to teach children mathematical concepts, but we're also trying to make sure that they can do computations fairly well. We're also teaching them to use mechanical aids, such as computers and calculators, to acquire more exact answers."

DeBoe believes the main problem with science and math education today is the lack of qualified teachers. "We simply aren't able to recruit science and math teachers, particularly qualified ones. I am in favor of some kind of examination for teachers. I feel that there are certain skills that all teachers should have before they are placed in a classroom."

DeBoe's concern about her students and about the lack of qualified teachers is reflected in her plans for spending her award money. "I would like to hire college math students to work, under my direction, toward helping math-deficient students acquire an additional math credit after school. If the college students could really get in there and feel the excitement and the warmth of an exchange with the high school students, maybe they might consider teaching."

John J. Skrocky, Jr.
Northwest Senior High School, Omaha, Nebr.

A Salesman for Physics

"Talking about physics is exciting. Physics itself is exciting," says John J. Skrocky, Jr., of Northwest Senior High School in Omaha, Nebr. "Physics helps us understand the world around us.

"I think everyone needs some exposure to physics. Some physics teachers will tell you straight out that if the students are not in the top 5 per cent of the school enrollment, then they shouldn't be in the physics class. I disagree with that very strongly. Physics may be the most basic and fundamental science because of its wide scope. Physics helps develop a well-rounded individual."

Skrocky backs his words with action. He does not wait for the students to come to him. Instead, like a good salesman, he goes out and gets the students. Skrocky more than doubled the enrollment in his physics classes at Northwest Senior High by going to other science and math classes in the school and giving 15-minute demonstrations in physics. "There was one that I found in *The Physics Teacher* magazine," he says, "in which you drive a nail through a ¾-inch pine board, holding the nail against a small piece of wood in your hand and taking just one swing. That really catches the student's eye.

"Then I go through all the equations that tie that flashy demonstration down to real honest-to-goodness physics. I spend the remainder of the time talking about the things physics deals with and what experiences a student would have in my physics class. However, I make it very clear that it is a hard course, that they are going to have to do homework. But students seem more willing to do homework now."

Skrocky took a circuitous route to his present teaching position. "I guess I always wanted to be a physics teacher," he says. "Even though I found physics difficult to learn and understand—the mathematical aspects of it were especially difficult—there was a reward in it for me. I wanted to share that with other people. But that was in the 1960's when young men had to face military draft requirements. So after college I joined the Air Force."

The Air Force made him a meteorologist and sent him first to West Germany, then to Omaha. After he left the Air Force, Skrocky worked in the insurance and oil industries before the urge to teach grew strong again. By the time he returned to school to get his teacher's certification, he was married, and he and his wife had to share a house with another couple to minimize expenses. His cur-

Two cans of soup "race" down a ramp as Skrocky explains the laws of physics that govern how fast the cans will roll. It all depends on the density of the soup inside, so broth always beats minestrone.

rent job opened up when a teacher quit just before school started. "They needed somebody right away," he says, "to take over a full load of physics classes."

In the first-year physics course, Skrocky tries to schedule at least one laboratory period for every chapter in the physics textbook. "And I bring in as many demonstrations as I can," he says. "I try to use them in ways that are connected with something very real in the students' lives." For example, he shows them how letting a heavy object hit and bounce off them would cause more *recoil* (a bigger jolt) than catching it would cause. Skrocky also teaches a second-year physics course in which the students do independent research.

Skrocky's teaching methods seem to bring out the best in gifted students. "In the five years that I have been teaching the second-year physics course, we have had 11 students named to the Westinghouse Science Talent Search honors group," he says, and one made it into the top 40 winners group. "At the local and state science fairs, we've usually done very well. Four students have been sent to international science fairs." In 1983, the physics department at Northwest Senior High was chosen by the National Science Teachers Association (NSTA) as one of 10 exemplary programs in America.

Skrocky plans to use his $5,000 grant to buy computers, lasers, and other equipment that will be useful in the students' research projects. Some of the grant will also be used to help other teachers at Northwest High attend an NSTA convention.

Skrocky thinks that the most important thing about his teaching technique is his own excitement about physics, his own belief that everyone should experience physics. "By the time students finish the second semester, they make comments like 'You can't do anything without involving physics!' Of course, that's what I've been telling them week after week. When they start saying it themselves, that's when they've really been sold."

Luz V. Concepcion de Gaspar
University of Puerto Rico Laboratory School, San Juan, P.R.

Seeing Science as Life

In the interest of teaching, Luz V. Concepcion de Gaspar has been known to sell chocolates. "I have to sell things, such as chocolates, to get money to buy material that is used in the labs," says Gaspar. She teaches at the University of Puerto Rico's Laboratory School in San Juan, a high school attended by the children of local residents and university employees. Gaspar has run these fund-raising sales because there is only a minimal budget provided by the Parent-Teacher Association for science and laboratory equipment. "All the science teachers and the students help. One year, we raised $1,200 and bought a whole kit of equipment for the physics course," she says.

Gaspar believes it is important to involve her students in many different ways. "I try to teach them the scientific method and the process of science. But I also try to show them how science affects their lives and how they can use it to try to be better human beings, better Puerto Ricans, and how they can use science in society's decision-making processes when they are old enough to do so.

"I am not especially inclined to teach science to the elite. I think science is vital and important for all students because science, for me, is life."

Like some of the other presidential award winners, Gaspar did not always want to be a teacher. "When I started at the University of Puerto Rico, I wanted to be a pharmacist," she says. "But I had financial problems and could not afford all the training needed. I had another sister who wanted to go to college, too. So I decided to enroll in the college of education. When I graduated I could get a teaching job and help her through school."

One day Gaspar confessed this to a teacher. "She told me, 'You better get out of the college of education, because the worst possible thing is to have a teacher who doesn't want to teach.' Those words were really hard for me, so I started doing my best and I began to like teaching. When I did my practice teaching in an elementary school, I realized that I really loved it. I've been a teacher for 20 years and would never be a druggist or a doctor or anything else."

Through the 13 years that she has been at the University of Puerto Rico's Laboratory School, Gaspar has taught mathematics, environmental studies, health, energy conservation, introduction to physical science, and chemistry. She also is adviser to a science club. Whatever the course, she tries to teach the students how to inquire.

In the laboratory, Gaspar teaches students how to test for acid liquids, such as acid rain, using blue litmus, which turns red in the presence of an acid.

"I give them problems and see how they would solve them. For instance, one day I asked, 'Do you know that some of the rainfall is quite acid?' They said, 'Are you kidding?' So we took some rain samples and tested them with blue litmus paper, which turns red in an acid liquid. They found out firsthand that the rain was acid.

"They decided to start an acid rain survey and set up a number of sampling stations at different spots in the San Juan area. Then they shared their data with some other classes and science clubs. The students became aware of the amount of acid pollution that was coming into San Juan and how it was affecting the quality of our water. That's the type of thing I like to be involved in."

Gaspar thinks the teaching of science has changed during her career. "Twenty years ago, students memorized facts from textbooks. Now, there is more emphasis on getting the students involved in analyzing problems. That's good, because the most important part of science is to teach students how to think so they can use what they learn in other areas of their lives. That's education."

She is also concerned with teaching teachers. "Science teachers, especially in the elementary schools, need a lot of help. If we don't have teachers who can teach science in elementary school, it's going to be hard for the other schools to do a good job.

"I feel that colleges of education and universities have a lot to do with this problem. Teachers who get a bachelor's degree in education and science today know the concepts, but they don't know how to teach them to students in a spectacular and attractive way. Many teachers need to be retrained, even many of those who train new teachers at the colleges of education."

Reflecting her interest in teacher training, Gaspar slated part of her prize money for sending at least two of her fellow teachers to an NSTA convention for some in-service training. The rest of the money will be used for computers and software. "Perhaps this year," she says, "we won't have to sell any chocolates."

349

This remarkable scientist, a leading expert
on the biology of rivers, has greatly influenced
efforts to clean up U.S. waterways.

Ruth Patrick

BY MARION STEINMANN

Ruth Patrick, one of the world's leading biologists, is somewhat of a biological phenomenon herself. In her 70's, she has the look and vigor of a much younger person and keeps a pace that would tire many people half her age. She spends three or four days a week at the Academy of Natural Sciences of Philadelphia, where she is senior curator of *limnology* — the scientific study of freshwater rivers and lakes. There, she directs scientific research, consults with students, and confers with colleagues about the academy's projects.

In a typical week, Patrick also spends two or three days traveling. On these trips, she speaks to university students, environmental groups, and other audiences about a variety of nature topics, and serves as a consultant to industry and government agencies involved with water pollution. Patrick is an expert on the biology of rivers and streams, and particularly on the effects of water pollution on the plants and animals living in them. One of her many environmental concerns is acid rain. Patrick is one of seven scientists on President Ronald Reagan's Acid Rain Peer Review Panel, which is preparing a report on the problem for the White House.

Patrick has served the Academy of Natural Sciences for more than 50 years. In 1947, she founded its Department of Limnology, which she headed for 26 years. From 1973 through 1976, she was chairman of the academy's Board of Trustees. For more than 30 years, she has also taught limnology at the University of Pennsylvania, where she holds the rank of adjunct professor. Patrick has also served on the Board of Directors of the Pennsylvania Power and Light Company, and of E. I. du Pont de Nemours & Company, where she was the first woman on the board. Such is the breadth of activities of one of America's most distinguished scientists.

"To be a good biologist and make contributions," Patrick stresses, "you first have to learn one group of organisms in great depth." The group of organisms that Patrick knows deeply are the microscopic, single-celled algae called *diatoms*. "She is, I suppose, the world's leading expert on diatoms," says biochemist Thomas Peter Bennett, president of the Academy of Natural Sciences.

The study of diatoms may sound like a narrow specialty, but these tiny algae are actually among the most common and most important organisms on our planet. They flourish by the billions in every body of water, if it is not polluted. They are the dominant organisms in plankton — the mass of minute living things that float in the upper levels of the ocean and provide food for many fish. Diatoms also thrive in freshwater lakes, ponds, swamps, rivers, and streams — and even in wet places in gardens. To the eye, they look like brownish scum. Under the microscope, however, one can see that they come in a variety of jewellike shapes including stars, triangles, squares, and wheels. One of Patrick's greatest contributions was developing a way to determine the degree of pollution in a body of water from the number and species of diatoms in it.

Ruth Patrick's interest in diatoms dates back to her childhood in Topeka, Kans., and Kansas City, Mo. Her father, Frank Patrick,

The author:
Marion Steinmann
is a free-lance
science writer.

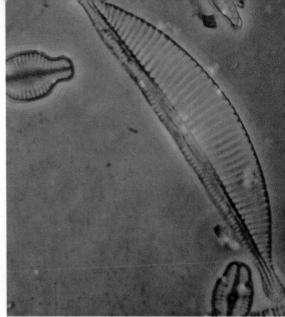

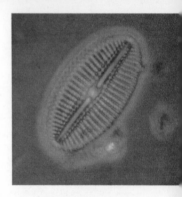

In her laboratory at the Academy of Natural Sciences of Philadelphia, *top left,* Patrick studies diatoms, the tiny single-celled algae that are her specialty. Magnified 670 times under the microscope, *top right* and *above,* diatoms reveal a variety of jewellike shapes.

earned his living as a lawyer and a banker, but his passion was science. He had a degree in botany from Cornell University in Ithaca, N.Y., and he loved to study diatoms through the four microscopes he kept on his roll-top desk. When Ruth was scarcely more than a toddler, he began taking her and her sister on Sunday excursions. Splashing about in streams, they collected diatoms and other specimens. He gave Ruth her first microscope when she was 7 years old.

After Ruth's graduation from high school, where her interests extended to trees and other plants, she took general biology courses at the University of Kansas in Lawrence. Then she was shipped off ("at my mother's insistence," Patrick says) to Coker College in Hartsville, S.C., then a small college for women. Her father, however, felt that Coker could not offer her enough science, so he sent her to summer courses at Woods Hole Oceanographic Institution in Massachusetts and at Cold Spring Harbor Laboratory on Long Island, N.Y. During her junior year, she considered becoming a physician, but by her senior year, she says, "I reverted to my diatoms." At a time when few women got beyond high school, Frank Patrick's daughter never seriously considered *not* going to graduate school.

"Father said I could go anyplace in the country," she recalls. The best professor on algae in the United States was at the University of Virginia in Charlottesville — so Ruth Patrick went there. Her doctoral dissertation dealt with the diatoms of Southeast Asia, and she received her Ph.D. in 1934, when she was 26 years old.

While still a graduate student, Patrick married Charles Hodge IV, whom she had met one summer at Cold Spring Harbor. But she kept her father's name professionally, at his specific request. "When I got married," she explains, "my father said to Charles: 'I always wanted to be a scientist. Would you mind if Ruth kept the name of Patrick in her research? I'd like to see it go on.' "

As a bride, she moved to Philadelphia, where the Hodge family has deep roots in American history. Charles Hodge is a direct descendant of American scientist and statesman Benjamin Franklin. Like his wife, Hodge is a scientist, but his specialty is *entomology* (the study of insects), with a particular interest in beetles and grasshoppers. He taught zoology at Temple University in Philadelphia for more than 30 years. Throughout their careers, Hodge and Patrick have occasionally worked together in the field, she in the water collecting her diatoms, he on land collecting his insects. They have one child, a son named Charles Hodge V, now a pediatrician in Kansas City, Mo., doing research on the digestive tract.

Ruth Patrick arrived in Philadelphia during the Great Depression, and she could not find a job to match her education and skills. Jobs in science were scarce in those lean years, particularly for women. She finally went to work as an unpaid volunteer at the Academy of Natural Sciences, which has the largest collection of diatoms in the United States. For more than 10 years, Patrick served as curator of the Microscopical Society and associate curator of the Microscopy Department without drawing a salary.

Then, when she was nearly 40, a chance meeting at a scientific gathering dramatically changed Patrick's career. In a paper she presented about the diatoms of Pennsylvania's Pocono Mountains, she pointed out that different species of diatoms need different nutrients and therefore different water conditions. By identifying the diatom species in a given body of water, she suggested, scientists might learn much about the condition of that water.

In the audience was an oil company executive named William B. Hart, who was concerned about the growing problem of water pollution. Hart was so intrigued by the possibility of using diatoms to diagnose the health of waterways that he raised money to finance an investigation of it. And he asked that Patrick head the study. "When Mr. Hart first came to the academy," Patrick says, "I think they were very skeptical about a woman having charge of so much money. But he insisted that I was to be in charge. I am sure I never would have had my chance if it had not been for Mr. Hart."

At that time, in the late 1940's, most people were unaware of water pollution. It would be another 20 years before the state of the environment became a subject of widespread public concern. Relatively few scientists had studied the problem, and those who had looked into it tended to seek a single organism or group of organisms that could serve as an indicator of the degree of pollution. Although Patrick began with an interest in diatoms, she quickly recognized that studying only diatoms or any other living thing was not enough. Instead, she planned to investigate a variety of species — a major advance. "My idea," she explains, "was to study all major groups of plants and animals and also look at the overall structure or pattern of the aquatic [water-related] community." Biologists define a *community* as a group of plants and animals living together in the same area and depending on one another.

To apply her idea, Patrick organized two teams of scientists during the summer of 1948. The groups included chemists; entomologists; botanists specializing in algae; bacteriologists; zoologists specializing in one-celled organisms; invertebrate zoologists to study worms, snails, and other creatures without a backbone; and vertebrate zoologists to study fish and higher animals. The scientists chose to examine a 475-square-mile region drained by the Conestoga Creek, which flows into the Susquehanna River near Lancaster, Pa. The creek offered natural, unpolluted lengths of stream as well as stretches contaminated by various pollutants, including sewage, agricultural runoff from pastures and chicken yards, and industrial discharges from chocolate and hat factories. At 171 survey stations, Patrick and her team collected all the aquatic species they could find, from bacteria and diatoms to insects and fish.

Their results showed, for the first time, how the aquatic community of a stream indicates the degree of water pollution. In the healthy stretches of stream, a rich diversity of life flourished, with dozens of different species from each of the major groups of organisms. In the polluted sections, however, the pollution had killed off all the more sensitive species and left only a few hardier ones. In the most polluted places, virtually all life was gone.

This pioneering study of the Conestoga launched Ruth Patrick on her career as an expert on rivers and streams, and on the biological

During water pollution studies in 1977 for a power company, Patrick used dry ice to freeze stream-bed sediment near a power plant, *left,* so the sediment layers could be removed for study. In another study, *above,* she checked how dumping heated water in a stream would affect the stream's life forms.

Patrick dredges the bottom of a stream, *right,* to sample the material there. The kinds of sediment she collects, *far right,* indicate the degree of pollution.

In another test of the stream's cleanliness, *right,* Patrick studies the organisms and other floating matter that she caught by dragging a screen through the water near the surface.

Patrick checks for acid pollution with a chemical indicator that turns different colors depending on the level of acidity.

Using a flask, Patrick mixes stream water with a chemical that turns the water yellow if its oxygen content is low.

effects of water pollution. Since then, she has sloshed about in rivers and streams of all sizes and types in every major river system in the United States and on every continent except Africa. Wearing wading boots and a pith helmet, she often plows into icy water well above her waist to gather specimens.

In the United States, Patrick has done many river studies under grants and contracts from corporations and government agencies. One of the rivers she knows best is the Savannah River, which forms much of the boundary between Georgia and South Carolina. She has been studying the Savannah continuously since the early 1950's for both Du Pont and U.S. government agencies. She also has been supervising an Academy of Natural Sciences survey of the Flint River, which runs southward across Georgia toward the Gulf of Mexico. For the National Science Foundation, she has studied the Delaware River, which flows past Philadelphia between Pennsylvania and New Jersey. In the 1970's, Patrick codirected a survey of the marshland of the Delaware's tidal estuary, a 133-mile stretch between Trenton, N.J., and the Atlantic Ocean where the river water mingles with salt water from the sea.

Once, Patrick even dug herself a new stream. She wanted to learn the succession of species that would invade a completely barren river — that is, which plants and animals would move in first, and which others would eventually follow. Such information is important in restoring a polluted river to health. So, near Paoli, Pa., she had a bulldozer and backhoe excavate a channel 88 feet long and 5 to 10 feet wide off an existing creek. She carefully constructed a stream's typical habitats, including a pool, a riffle of white water, and an area of slow-moving water. To make sure the stream bed was completely sterile — without any seeds or eggs — she dug rocks from deep in the subsoil and scrubbed them with disinfectant.

Patrick confers with Charles W. Reimer, a fellow diatom expert at the Academy of Natural Sciences and her coauthor on *The Diatoms of the United States.*

After Patrick let the water in, the first settlers were microscopic organisms. By the end of the two weeks, the populations of bacteria, algae, and protozoans were up to normal levels. These tiny organisms, she points out, form the base of the *food chain*, a group of animals and plants that depend on one another for food. Each member of the group feeds on the one below it in the food chain and is in turn eaten by the organism above it. The first visible creatures to move in were larvae of the black fly and other insects that filter their food from the water. After six months, there were several insect species as well as worms and one species of snail. Fish swam through the stream occasionally, but none settled there. After two years, most of the species living in the parent, or original, creek — except fish — had established themselves in the new stream. This showed that there were enough space and diversity of habitats to accommodate all the small species. However, the new stream's habitats were not large enough to support fish. The complete recovery of a damaged stream, Patrick points out, is a slow process.

In 1955, Patrick mounted an expedition to study the wildlife of the greatest waterway of all, the 4,000-mile-long Amazon River of South America. Land areas in the tropics support a huge variety of plants and animals, many more species than in the temperate zone. Patrick wondered whether this was also true for tropical waterways. To find out, she led eight scientists, lugging 3,000 pounds of equipment, by plane over the Andes Mountains to the headwaters of the Amazon in eastern Peru. There they examined streams similar in size, *gradient* (slope), and other characteristics to those in the United States, taking inventory of the various plants and animals. They discovered that a habitat in the tropics, such as a pool, had about the same number of species as would a pool in the temperate zone. But the species found in nearby pools would be different, much more

Ruth Patrick examines microscope slides in the Diatom Herbarium, where the academy's enormous collection of diatom specimens is stored.

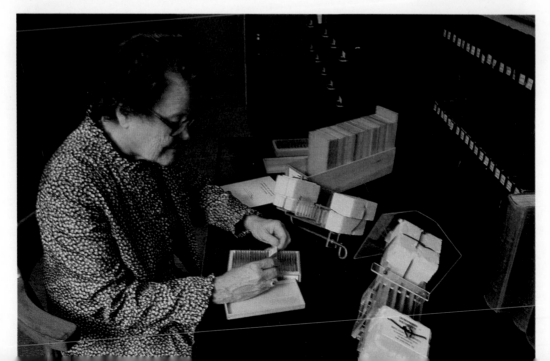

so than in the temperate zone. Thus a collector in the tropics going from pool to pool would find a greater total number of species than on a similar collecting expedition in the temperate zone. This also proved to be true of land habitats.

Throughout her career, Ruth Patrick has continued her research on diatoms, even using these little algae to look back in time. Where diatoms have formed thick *fossil* deposits (preserved plant or animal remains) over the centuries, the oldest fossils are in the bottom layers and the youngest are in the top layers. By identifying the diatom species in *strata* (layers) of different ages, scientists can learn how water conditions have changed over time. The examination of such layers of material is called *stratigraphy*. While Patrick was still a graduate student, she coauthored a paper on the history of the 750-square-mile Dismal Swamp, which straddles the border between Virginia and North Carolina along the Atlantic Coast. Layers of fossil pollen about 6 feet down showed that an ancient forest had mysteriously died off. What had happened? Patrick identified fossil diatoms typical of fresh water in the layers below 6 feet. At the 6-foot level, however, the fossils were of diatoms that live only in saltwater. She concluded that an invasion of seawater apparently had killed the forest.

A similar analysis by Patrick in the 1930's of fossil diatoms underlying Utah's Great Salt Lake added to the growing evidence that the waters there had once been fresh. A study of fossils in Italy from Lake Monterosi, a small lake north of Rome, showed a shift in diatom species from those that thrive in soft water — that is, water with few dissolved minerals — to those that prefer water with more minerals. The change occurred during the 100's B.C., just about the time the ancient Romans disturbed the lake's drainage basin by constructing the Via Cassia, a road between Rome and Arezzo.

Thomas Peter Bennett, president of the Academy of Natural Sciences, applauds Patrick at a dinner and convocation celebrating her 50th anniversary with the academy in November 1983.

"Ruth was the first one in North America to do such stratigraphic work," says G. Evelyn Hutchinson, emeritus professor of zoology at Yale University in New Haven, Conn. "Her papers on stratigraphy are a contribution that, if she had done nothing else, would be a very solid and remarkable piece of work."

At the Academy of Natural Sciences, Ruth Patrick has been a considerable force in shaping what that institution is today. The Department of Limnology that she founded has become the Division of Environmental Research, which now includes more than half the academy's scientific staff. During her long tenure as department chairman, she also established two field laboratories: Stroud Water Research Center, on a creek southwest of Philadelphia, and Benedict Estuarine Research Laboratory, on the Patuxent River in Maryland. As chairman of the academy's Board of Trustees in the mid-1970's, she spearheaded the addition of a modern, eight-story research wing to the academy's building, which dates from 1875.

On Nov. 11, 1983, the Academy of Natural Sciences formally honored this remarkable woman, who has served the academy longer than any other person now on the scientific staff, with a 50th-anniversary dinner and a convocation attended by hundreds of her admirers. "It was a great occasion," Patrick says. The academy presented her with letters of tribute from all over the world and announced that the laboratories of her division would be renamed the Patrick Center for Environmental Research.

Ruth Patrick should be growing accustomed to such accolades. In 1970, she was elected to the National Academy of Sciences, only the 12th woman so honored. She has received honorary doctorates from 18 colleges and universities, including her own Coker College

(1971), Drexel University in Philadelphia (1975), Bucknell University in Lewisburg, Pa. (1976), and Princeton University in Princeton, N.J. (1980). And in 1975, she received the $150,000 John and Alice Tyler Ecology Award—then the world's largest monetary prize for scientific achievement—for her "contribution to mankind in the field of ecology and improvement of the environment."

To accomplish so much, Patrick has given up many things that most people regard as essential. She subscribes to scientific journals but seldom reads a newspaper. "Instead, I listen to the radio on the way to and from work," she explains. "I don't read many novels, and I read very few articles of any kind other than in my field. I enjoy parties, but I do not have the time to attend many of them." She spends evenings catching up on her scientific reading and writing, and her greatest pleasure is wading around in a river or stream. "That is my life," she says. "I just love to explore the natural world."

The size and scope of Ruth Patrick's overall scientific output is impressive. She has produced more than 140 scientific papers and several books. With Charles W. Reimer, a fellow diatom specialist at the academy, she has written two volumes of *The Diatoms of the United States*, a catalog and description of all U.S. freshwater diatoms. Patrick and Reimer are now working on the third and final volume of this definitive treatise.

Patrick's main project these days, however—where she says she is "putting my whole soul"—is her most ambitious book yet. Tentatively called *The Rivers of the United States*, it brings together her own decades of experience and the writings of other scientists.

The book is planned in three parts. The first section will deal with the physical structure of rivers—the force, volume, and depth of the flow; the slope and shape of the channel; and whether the river meanders or has white water. "These all influence the kinds of habitats and the species you will find," Patrick explains.

The second part of the book will cover the chemistry of river waters. "There are only about a half dozen different kinds of rivers, chemically, in this country," Patrick says. There are two types of soft-water rivers—clear ones and those that are brown with decaying organic debris. "Then there are rivers of two or three different degrees of hardness, and also alkaline ones, rich in sodium and potassium," Patrick explains. "And, finally, the saltwater estuaries."

Each of these kinds of rivers has its own characteristic biology, which will be the subject of the third and final section of Patrick's book. She will discuss "not only what plants and animals are found in the rivers, but also where they are and their life histories, and the structure and functioning of the aquatic communities."

This massive book will summarize the knowledge gathered during a lifetime of energetic research. But even with a long career behind her, Ruth Patrick has no plans to retire. She continues to contribute, without slacking, to her scientific field.

World Book Supplement

Revised articles on subjects in science and technology reprinted from the 1984 edition of *The World Book Encyclopedia.*

© Edward S. Ross

A Copper Butterfly stops at a flower and sucks up nectar with its long, tubelike *proboscis*. Most adult butterflies feed only on nectar. The proboscis coils up when not in use.

BUTTERFLY

BUTTERFLY is one of the most beautiful of all insects. People have always been charmed by the delicate, gorgeously colored wings of butterflies. The beauty and grace of these insects have inspired artists and poets. Butterflies have also played a part in religious beliefs. For example, the ancient Greeks believed that the soul left the body after death in the form of a butterfly. Their symbol for the soul was a lovely, butterfly-winged girl named Psyche.

Butterflies live almost everywhere in the world. Tropical rain forests have the most kinds of butterflies. Other kinds of butterflies live in woodlands, fields, and prairies. Some butterflies live on cold mountaintops, and others live in hot deserts. Many butterflies travel great distances to spend the winter in a warm climate.

Lee D. Miller, the contributor of this article, is Curator of the Allyn Museum of Entomology in Sarasota, Fla.

There are about 15,000 to 20,000 *species* (kinds) of butterflies. The largest butterfly, Queen Alexandra's birdwing of Papua New Guinea, has a wingspread of about 11 inches (28 centimeters). One of the smallest butterflies is the western pygmy blue of North America. It has a wingspread of about $\frac{3}{8}$ inch (1 centimeter). Butterflies are every color imaginable. The colors may be bright, pale, or shimmering and arranged in fantastic patterns. The word *butterfly* comes from the Old English word *buterfleoge*, meaning *butter* and *flying creature*. *Buter* probably referred to the butter-yellow color of some European butterflies.

Butterflies and moths together make up an insect group called Lepidoptera. The name comes from two Greek words: *lepis*, which means *scale;* and *pteron*, which means *wing*. The name refers to the powdery scales that cover the two pairs of wings of both butterflies and moths. However, butterflies differ from moths in four important ways. (1) Most butterflies fly during the day. The majority of moths, on the other hand, fly at dusk or at night. (2) Most butterflies have knobs at the ends of their antennae. The antennae of most moths are not

Western Pygmy Blue
Brephidium exilis
3/8-inch (1-centimeter) wingspread
North America

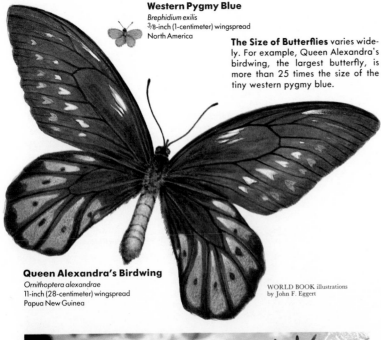

The Size of Butterflies varies widely. For example, Queen Alexandra's birdwing, the largest butterfly, is more than 25 times the size of the tiny western pygmy blue.

Queen Alexandra's Birdwing
Ornithoptera alexandrae
11-inch (28-centimeter) wingspread
Papua New Guinea

WORLD BOOK illustrations
by John F. Eggert

How Butterflies Differ from Moths

Butterflies and moths together make up the insect group Lepidoptera. But butterflies differ from moths in four main ways. (1) Most butterflies fly during the daytime. Most moths fly at night. (2) The majority of butterflies have knobs at the ends of their antennae. The antennae of most moths are not knobbed. (3) Most butterflies have slender, hairless bodies. Most moths have plump, furry bodies. (4) Most butterflies rest with their wings upright over their bodies. Most moths rest with their wings stretched out flat.

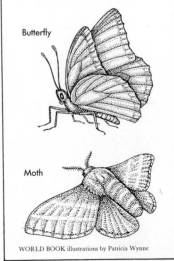

Butterfly

Moth

WORLD BOOK illustrations by Patricia Wynne

© Edward S. Ross

A Caterpillar feeds on plants until it reaches full size, *above*. It then forms a shell, inside which the wormlike caterpillar develops into a beautiful butterfly.

knobbed. (3) Most butterflies have slender, hairless bodies. The majority of moths have plump, furry bodies. (4) Most butterflies rest with their wings held upright over their bodies. Most moths rest with their wings spread out flat.

A butterfly begins its life as a tiny egg, which hatches into a caterpillar. The caterpillar spends most of its time eating and growing. But its skin does not grow, and so the caterpillar sheds it and grows a larger one. It repeats this process several times. After the caterpillar reaches its full size, it forms a protective shell. Inside the shell, an amazing change occurs—the wormlike caterpillar becomes a beautiful butterfly. The shell then breaks open, and the adult butterfly comes out. The insect expands its wings and soon flies off to find a mate and produce another generation of butterflies.

Butterfly caterpillars have chewing mouthparts, which they use to eat leaves and other plant parts. Some kinds of caterpillars are pests because they damage crops. One of the worst pests is the caterpillar of the cabbage butterfly. It feeds on cabbage, cauliflower, and related plants.

Adult butterflies may have sucking mouthparts. The adults feed mainly on nectar and do no harm. In fact, they help pollinate flowers. Many flowers must have pollen from other blossoms of the same kind of flower to produce fruit and seeds. When a butterfly stops at a flower to drink nectar, grains of pollen cling to its body. Some of the pollen grains rub off on the next blossom the butterfly visits.

Kinds of Butterflies

Scientists group the thousands of species of butterflies into families, according to various physical features the insects have in common. The chief families include (1) skippers; (2) blues, coppers, and hairstreaks; (3) brush-footed butterflies; (4) sulphurs and whites; (5) metalmarks; (6) satyrs and wood nymphs; (7) swallowtails; (8) milkweed butterflies; and (9) snout butterflies. Each of these families has representative species in North America.

Skippers differ from all other kinds of butterflies in two major ways, and so scientists classify them separately from *true butterflies*. (1) Skippers have plump,

BUTTERFLY

hairy bodies and therefore look more like moths than butterflies. (2) The antennae of skippers have hooked tips, unlike the rounded tips on the antennae of true butterflies.

There are about 3,500 kinds of skippers. Various species live in all parts of the world, except for the extreme polar regions. Skippers get their name from the way they swiftly skip and dart while flying. They range in color from orangish-brown to dark brown and in many cases have white and yellow markings. Nearly 300 species of skippers can be found in North America. They include the silver-spotted skipper, the roadside skipper, the fiery skipper, the checkered skipper, Juvenal's duskywing, and the least skipperling.

Blues, Coppers, and Hairstreaks account for almost 4,000 species worldwide, and they live in almost every type of environment. They are small butterflies whose names describe their appearance. Blues have a brilliant blue or violet color. Coppers are a fiery orange-red. Most species of hairstreaks have a hairlike "tail" on each of their hind wings. A number of blues and coppers also have such "tails."

About 150 kinds of blues, coppers, and hairstreaks

live in North America. They include the spring azure, the bronze copper, and the great purple hairstreak. The caterpillars of some species produce a sweet liquid known as *honeydew*. Certain ants "milk" the honeydew from the caterpillars and also protect the caterpillars from enemies.

Brush-Footed Butterflies total about 3,500 species. Members of this family live everywhere in the world, except for polar icecaps and the driest deserts. These butterflies have short front legs, called *brush feet*, which contain special organs that help the insects locate food. Most species of brush-footed butterflies have bright colors on the upper wing surface and dark colors on the undersurface. When a brush-footed butterfly closes its wings, the dark undersurface helps the insect blend with its surroundings.

About 150 kinds of brush-footed butterflies live in North America. They include such small butterflies as crescents and checkerspots and such large ones as fritillaries. Some of the best-known butterflies—the viceroy, the red admiral, and the mourning cloak—belong to this family.

Sulphurs and Whites form a family of about 1,000 species. They can be found throughout the world, but most of them live in tropical regions. At least 60 species

Butterflies of the World
Skippers

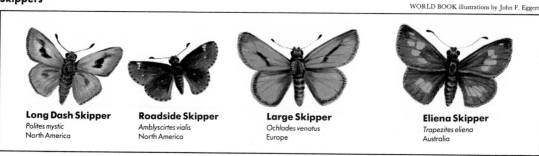

Long Dash Skipper
Polites mystic
North America

Roadside Skipper
Amblyscirtes vialis
North America

Large Skipper
Ochlodes venatus
Europe

Eliena Skipper
Trapezites eliena
Australia

Blues, Coppers, and Hairstreaks

Great Purple Hairstreak
Atlides halesus
North America

Silvery Blue
Glaucopsyche lygdamus
North America

Common Oakblue
Narathura micale amphis
Australia

American Copper
Lycaena phlaeas
North America

Lycaena orus
Africa

Adonis Blue
Lysandra bellargus
Europe

Brush-Footed Butterflies

Painted Lady
Vanessa cardui
North America and Europe

Red Admiral
Vanessa atalanta
North America and Europe

Marpesia marcella
South America

Sulphurs and Whites

Cabbage White
Artogeia rapae
North America and Europe

Orange Sulphur
Colias eurytheme
North America

Northern Jezabel
Delias argenthona argenthona
Australia

Sara Orangetip
Anthocharis sara
North America

Metalmarks

Little Metalmark
Calephelis virginiensis
North America

Ancyluris formosissima
South America

Satyrs and Wood Nymphs

Pearly Eye
Enodia portlandia
North America

Coenonympha dorus
Europe

Tisiphone abeona morrisi
Australia

BUTTERFLY

of sulphurs and whites live in North America. Sulphurs range in color from light yellow to orange and are named after the powdery yellow mineral. The wings of most sulphurs have black edges. One species, the southern dogface, has markings that suggest the face of a dog. In orange-tip butterflies, the tips of the front wings have brilliant orange coloring.

Whites have white wings that may be marked with black, brown, yellow, or red spots. The most common white is the cabbage butterfly. The caterpillar of this butterfly is a major pest.

Metalmarks form a family of about 1,000 species. These butterflies live throughout the world but are especially common in South America. Their name comes from metallic-looking marks on the wings of most species. Tropical metalmarks are of almost every combination of colors and patterns imaginable. Fewer than 25 species of metalmarks live in North America. Most of them, including the northern metalmark and the little metalmark, range in color from dull reddish-brown to dark brown.

Satyrs and Wood Nymphs total about 800 species. Most kinds live in the tropics. However, a few species are found in high mountainous regions and the Arctic. Satyrs and wood nymphs have short front legs and fly close to the ground. Most have brown wings dotted with *eyespots* (markings that look like eyes).

More than 50 species of satyrs and wood nymphs live in North America. The names of several of these species, including the pearly eye and the eyed brown, refer to their beautiful eyespots.

Swallowtails account for about 600 species of butterflies. They are a worldwide family, though most species are found in the tropics. Swallowtails are among the largest and most beautiful butterflies. They include Queen Alexandra's birdwing, the largest of all butterflies, and the African giant swallowtail, which has a wingspan of up to 10 inches (25 centimeters). Most swallowtails have a long extension on each hind wing. The butterflies get their name from these extensions, which resemble the tails of certain swallows.

Most swallowtails are black, brown, and yellow with red and blue spots on their hind wings. One group, the parnassians, has white or creamy wings with red and black spots. Parnassians do not have "tails."

About 35 species of swallowtails live in North America. They include the black swallowtail, the tiger swallowtail, and the zebra swallowtail.

Swallowtails

WORLD BOOK illustrations by John F. Eggert

Clodius Parnassian
Parnassius clodius
North America

Giant Swallowtail
Papilio cresphontes
North America

Tiger Swallowtail
Papilio glaucus
North America

Anise Swallowtail
Papilio zelican
North America

Swallowtails (continued)

Papilio dardonus
Africa

Papilio memnon
Asia

Ulysses or
Mountain Blue
Papilio ulysses joesa
Australia

Common Swallowtail
Papilio machaon
Europe

Milkweed Butterflies

Monarch
Danaus plexippus
North America

Lycorea ceres
South America

Common Australian Crow
Euploea core corinna
Australia

Snout Butterflies

Southern Snout
Libytheana bachmannii
North America

Australian Beak
Libythea geoffroy genia
Australia

BUTTERFLY

Milkweed Butterflies total about 200 species worldwide. They are large, slow-flying butterflies with very short front legs. Most of these butterflies range in color from orange to brown. Their wings have black veins and black margins with white spots. Some species that live in Africa and Asia are blue, violet, or white, with brown markings. The caterpillars of this family feed on milkweed plants.

Only four species of milkweed butterflies live in North America. And only two of these species are common. They are the monarch butterflies, famous for their long flights south each fall, and the queen butterflies, which do not make such journeys.

Snout Butterflies form a small family of 17 species, most of which live in the tropics. The butterflies get their name from their long, beaklike mouthparts. Only two species, the snout butterfly and the southern snout butterfly, live in North America. Both have brown wings with orange and white markings.

The Bodies of Butterflies

Butterflies have certain body features in common with other insects. For example, a butterfly has a hard, shell-like skin called an *exoskeleton* (outer skeleton). The exoskeleton supports the body and protects the internal organs. A butterfly's body, also like that of any other insect, has three main parts: (1) the head, (2) the thorax, and (3) the abdomen.

The Head is the center of sensation. It bears a butterfly's (1) eyes, (2) antennae, and (3) mouthparts.

Eyes. On each side of its head, a butterfly has a large *compound eye*, which consists of thousands of tiny lenses. Each lens provides the insect with an image of part of its surroundings. The brain combines the separate images into a complete view.

Antennae. Two long, slender antennae grow between the eyes. The antennae are organs of smell. A butterfly uses its sense of smell to locate food and to find mates. The antennae probably also serve as hearing and touch organs.

Mouthparts. A butterfly caterpillar has chewing mouthparts that consist of two lips and two pairs of jaws. These structures re-form as the caterpillar changes into an adult butterfly. One pair of jaws nearly disappears. The other pair becomes a long sucking tube, called a *proboscis*, that coils up when not in use. The lips form a sheath for the proboscis.

A butterfly uses its proboscis to suck nectar and other liquids. Muscles in the head help the insect draw fluid up the proboscis and into a cavity in the head. A covering on the end of the proboscis closes and keeps fluid from flowing out. Other muscles force the fluid into the stomach.

The Thorax forms the middle section of a butterfly's body. A short, thin neck connects it to the insect's head. Attached to the thorax are a butterfly's (1) wings and (2) legs.

Wings. A butterfly has a pair of front wings and a pair of back wings. A network of veins runs through the wings. The veins are mainly filled with air and serve as wing supports. The wings are stiff near the front edges and at the bases. The outer margins of the wings, however, are flexible. They bend when flapped in flight.

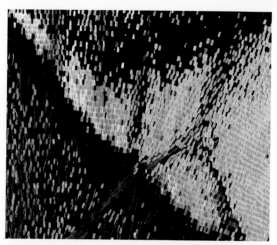

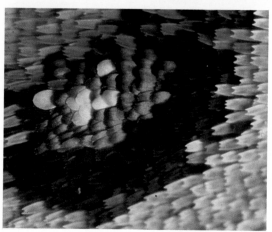

Overlapping Scales cover the wings of butterflies. The scales give the wings their color and pattern. These close-up photographs show how the scales are set in the wings.

This bending pushes the air backward and moves the butterfly forward. The front margins of the wings give the insect "lift" as it flies forward.

Butterflies and moths cannot fly if their body temperature is less than 86° F. (30° C). At air temperatures below this point, they must "warm up" their flight muscles either by sunning their bodies or by shivering their wings. The flight muscles then absorb enough heat to make flight possible.

The size of a butterfly's body and wings determines how the insect flies. For example, milkweed butterflies and swallowtails have small, lightweight bodies and large wings. These butterflies can fly by beating their wings slowly. They are excellent gliders and can fly great distances. On the other hand, skippers have large, heavy bodies and small, pointed wings. They must beat their wings rapidly to stay aloft. Skippers do not soar or glide, but they can fly swiftly for short distances.

A butterfly's wings are covered with tiny, flat scales that overlap. The scales provide color and form beautiful patterns. Some scales contain *pigment* (coloring matter). Colors produced by pigment include black, brown, red, white, and yellow. Other kinds of scales produce color by reflecting light from their surfaces. Shiny, metallic colors—for example, blue and green—are reflected colors.

Legs. Butterflies have three pairs of legs. Each leg has five main segments. Joints between the segments enable a butterfly to move its legs in various directions. Each leg ends in a pair of claws and hairy pads. The insect uses the claws to grip surfaces. The hairs on the pads are taste organs. Butterflies have weak legs and can walk only short distances.

In some species, the front legs are very short. These "brush feet" are useless for walking, but the taste organs on them are highly developed. By brushing or scraping leaves with these feet, brush-footed butterflies can determine whether particular plants are good sources of food or suitable places on which to lay eggs.

The Abdomen chiefly contains a butterfly's reproductive organs. It also has organs for digesting food and for getting rid of waste products.

The Internal Organs of butterflies are grouped into five main systems: (1) circulatory, (2) nervous, (3) respiratory, (4) digestive, and (5) reproductive.

The Circulatory System carries blood throughout the body by means of a long tube that lies just under the exoskeleton of the back. The tube extends from the head to the end of the abdomen. The heart, the pumping part of the tube, lies in the thorax. The blood empties out of the tube into the head. It then floods the entire body. The blood reenters the tube through little openings along the sides. A butterfly's blood is yellowish, greenish, or colorless. It carries food, but not oxygen, to the cells of the body.

The Nervous System of butterflies consists of a brain, which is located in the head, and two nerve cords that run through the thorax and abdomen. Small bundles of nerve cells along the cords branch out to all parts of the butterfly's body.

The Respiratory System carries oxygen to the cells of the body and takes away carbon dioxide. Oxygen enters the body through tiny holes, called *spiracles*, located along the sides of the body. Each spiracle connects to a tube-like structure called a *trachea*. The tracheae branch out to all the cells of the butterfly's body. In this way, the body cells obtain oxygen directly from the air rather than from the blood.

The Digestive System is basically a long tube that extends from the mouth to the *anus*, an opening at the end of the abdomen. After nectar has been sucked up by the proboscis, it passes to the *gut*, where nourishing substances in the food are absorbed. The remaining waste products pass through the *hindgut* and out of the body through the anus.

The Reproductive System. Butterflies reproduce sexually—that is, a new butterfly can be created only after a *sperm* (male sex cell) unites with an *egg* (female sex cell). Female butterflies have two organs, called *ovaries*, in which eggs develop. A tube called an *oviduct* carries the eggs from each ovary to an opening near the end of the abdomen. Male butterflies have a sperm-producing organ, called the *testis*. A tube carries the sperm from the testis to a tube that extends to the outside of the insect's abdomen.

The Life Cycle of Butterflies

The life of an adult butterfly centers on reproduction. The reproductive cycle begins with courtship, in which the butterfly seeks a mate. If the courtship proves successful, mating occurs.

Butterflies use both sight and smell in seeking mates.

The Anatomy of a Butterfly

A butterfly's body has three main parts: (1) the head, (2) the thorax, and (3) the abdomen. The drawings below show the chief external features and internal organs of a typical female butterfly.

WORLD BOOK illustrations by Patricia Wynne

External View

Back wing
Front wing
Veins
Antennae
Compound eye
Proboscis
Spiracles
Front leg   Middle leg   Back leg

Internal View

Circulatory system   Digestive system
Nervous system   Reproductive system

Head   Thorax   Abdomen
Ovary
Brain   Heart   Hindgut   Anus
Gut   Oviduct

BUTTERFLY

Either the male or the female may give signals, called *cues*, of a certain kind or in a particular order. If a butterfly presents the wrong cue, or a series of cues in the wrong sequence, it will be rejected.

In courtship involving visual cues, a butterfly reveals certain color patterns on its wings in a precise order. Many visual cues involve the reflection of ultraviolet light rays from a butterfly's wing scales. The cues are invisible to the human eye, but butterflies see them clearly. The visual cues help the insects distinguish between males and females and between members of different species.

Usually, a butterfly that presents an appropriate scent will be immediately accepted as a mate. The scent comes from chemicals, called *pheromones*, that are released from special wing scales. A pheromone may attract a butterfly a great distance away.

In most cases, the male butterfly dies soon after mating. The female goes off in search of a place to lay her eggs. She usually begins laying the eggs within a few hours after mating.

Every butterfly goes through four stages of development: (1) egg, (2) larva, (3) pupa, and (4) adult. This process of development through several forms is called *metamorphosis*.

The Egg. Butterfly eggs vary greatly in size, shape, and color. Some eggs are almost invisible to the human eye. The largest ones are about $\frac{1}{10}$ inch (2.5 millimeters) in diameter. The eggs may be round, oval, cylindrical, or other shapes. Most are green or yellow. A few species have orange or red eggs. Some eggs are smooth. Others have ridges and grooves.

Most female butterflies lay their eggs on plants that will provide the offspring with food. Before depositing the eggs, the female may "taste" a plant with special organs on the ends of her front legs to make sure the plant is suitable. Some females lay their eggs near a plant or drop them at random while flying. After hatching, the young must find the food themselves.

While laying the eggs, the female fertilizes them with sperm that she had stored in her body after mating. Each egg has a small hole through which sperm can enter. Depending on the species, a female may lay several dozen eggs or clusters of up to hundreds of eggs. A sticky substance deposited with the eggs helps hold them on the plant. The eggs of some butterflies hatch in a few days, but others take months. Eggs laid in fall may not hatch until spring.

The Larva, or caterpillar, emerges from the egg and immediately begins its main activity—eating. A caterpillar's first meal is usually its own eggshell. It then begins to eat the nearest food. The majority of caterpillars

The Life Cycle of a Butterfly

A butterfly goes through four stages of development: (1) egg; (2) larva, or caterpillar; (3) pupa; and (4) adult. This process of development is called *metamorphosis*.

© John Shaw, Bruce Coleman Inc.

The Egg is typically green or yellow. The eggs of some species hatch in a few days, but others take months.

After Emerging from the Egg, a caterpillar immediately begins to eat. This photograph shows a newly hatched caterpillar eating its own eggshell.

The Larval Stage lasts two weeks or more. During this period, a caterpillar eats leaves and grows rapidly. After reaching full size, *above,* it is ready to become a pupa.

Hanging from a Twig, a pupa starts to form a hard shell, *above.* Inside the shell, larval structures will be reformed into those of an adult butterfly.

© David Overcash, Bruce Coleman Inc.

A Newly Formed Monarch Butterfly pulls free of its pupal shell, *above.* About an hour after leaving its shell, a butterfly may be ready to fly.

The Anatomy of a Caterpillar

The body of a caterpillar is made up of 14 segments. The first segment consists of the head. The next three segments form the thorax. The last 10 make up the abdomen.

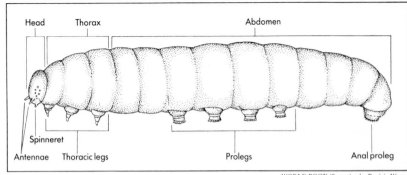

Head   Thorax   Abdomen

Spinneret

Antennae   Thoracic legs   Prolegs   Anal proleg

feed on green plants. In one day, a caterpillar may eat many times its weight in food. Much of this food is stored in the body and used to provide energy in later stages of development.

Most caterpillars are solid green or brown. Many others have patterns of yellow, red, or other bright colors. Some caterpillars have smooth skin. Many others have bristly hair, bumps, fleshy knobs, or eyespots. All these features help protect caterpillars from enemies by making them hard to see or so frightening in appearance that enemies avoid them.

A caterpillar's body is made up of 14 segments. The first segment consists of the head, which includes chewing mouthparts and two short, thick antennae. The head also has six small eyes on each side. The eyes cannot form images, but they help the caterpillar distinguish between light and dark.

The next three segments of the caterpillar's body make up the thorax. Each of these segments has two short, jointed legs with a sharp claw at each tip. The remaining 10 segments form the abdomen. Most caterpillars have a pair of false legs, known as *prolegs*, on the seventh, eighth, ninth, and tenth body segments. At the end of each proleg are tiny hooks. The last segment has a pair of suckerlike legs called *anal prolegs* or *anal claspers*. This variety of legs enables the caterpillar to cling to plants and to move about.

A short structure called a *spinneret* sticks out below the caterpillar's mouth. The spinneret releases a sticky liquid that hardens into a silken thread and gives the caterpillar a foothold wherever it goes. The larva, like the adult butterfly, breathes through spiracles on the sides of the body.

The larval stage lasts at least two weeks. During that time, the caterpillar grows rapidly. Its exoskeleton, however, does not grow. When the skin becomes too tight, it splits lengthwise along the back. But before the exoskeleton splits, the larva forms a new skin under the old one. It then crawls out of the old skin. The new exoskeleton is soft, and the larva stretches it to provide growing room. The larva then lies motionless a few hours as the new exoskeleton hardens. Most caterpillars *molt*—that is, shed their exoskeletons—four or five times.

The Pupa. After a caterpillar reaches its full size, it is ready to become a pupa. In preparation for this stage, most moth larvae spin silken cocoons around themselves. However, only a few butterfly species spin cocoons. Instead, the typical butterfly caterpillar finds a sheltered spot, usually high on a twig or leaf, and deposits sticky liquid from its spinneret. The liquid quickly hardens into a silklike pad. The exoskeleton then begins to split near the head, and the pupa starts to emerge. As the exoskeleton falls from the tail, the pupa thrusts its *cremaster*—a many-clawed structure at the end of the abdomen—into the pad. This procedure is dangerous. If it does not grasp at the pad fast enough, the pupa may fall to the ground and die.

Many pupae hang head downward, supported only by the cremaster hooked into the silken pad. Other pupae are positioned head upward. Such a pupa has an additional support of silken thread spun around the thorax and the twig or leaf to which it is anchored.

The pupa is soft at first, but a hard shell immediately begins to form over it. Some shells have unusual shapes and colorful patterns. In some cases, the shell has a golden shimmer, and so scientists call the pupa a *chrysalis*. This word comes from the Greek word *chrysos*, which means *gold*.

The pupa is motionless and is often called a "resting stage." However, much activity occurs within the shell. Larval structures are being broken down and re-formed into those of an adult butterfly. Only the internal organs remain basically the same.

The pupal period ranges from a few days to more than a year, according to the species and the time the pupal stage begins. Many species spend the winter as pupae and emerge as adults in the spring.

The Adult. After the adult butterfly has formed, its body gives off a fluid that loosens it from the pupal shell. The thorax swells and cracks the shell. The head and thorax then emerge. Next, the butterfly pushes its legs out and pulls the rest of its body free. The entire process may take only a few minutes.

The exoskeleton of the newly emerged butterfly is soft. The wings are damp and crumpled. The proboscis is split in half lengthwise. The butterfly uses its muscles to pump air and blood through its body and wings. The butterfly's exoskeleton hardens, and the legs and other body parts become firm. The wings flatten and expand. Using its front legs, the butterfly joins the halves of its proboscis together. About an hour after leaving the pupal shell, the adult butterfly may be ready to fly.

Most adult butterflies live only a week or two, but some species may live up to 18 months. Most butterflies feed only on nectar, which provides quick energy but does not contain life-prolonging proteins. Certain species of butterflies obtain proteins by feeding on moist, decaying animal matter. Some other species obtain proteins from pollen, which they pick up while feeding on nectar. A number of butterflies do not feed on anything.

Instead, these butterflies live on food stored during the larval stage.

How Butterflies Protect Themselves

Butterflies have many enemies, including other insects and birds. To escape their enemies, butterflies have developed various means of self-defense.

Many butterflies and caterpillars escape harm because they blend with their surroundings. This form of defense is known as *protective coloration*. Butterflies may look like bark or other vegetation. Most caterpillars are green or brown. Green ones blend with the plants they eat. Brown ones look like dead leaves or twigs.

Many butterflies have chemical defenses. Among certain swallowtails, the caterpillar has an organ just behind the head that gives off an unpleasant odor when the caterpillar is disturbed. Some butterflies are protected as both larvae and adults because they taste bad to enemies. During the larval stage, many of these butterflies eat plants that have bitter or poisonous juices. The juices are stored in the tissues, making the insects distasteful to enemies. Most such butterflies have bright colors and so advertise that they taste unpleasant. This form of protection is called *warning coloration*. An animal that has eaten one of these butterflies will probably avoid eating another butterfly with that coloration.

Some nonprotected butterflies resemble, or *mimic*, distasteful species. Enemies cannot tell them apart and so leave both alone. The most familiar mimic in North America is the viceroy butterfly, which looks like the monarch butterfly. Enemies avoid the viceroy because the monarch tastes unpleasant. Some protected butterflies even resemble other protected ones. By mimicking each other, these insects gain extra protection.

Hibernation and Migration

Butterflies cannot live actively in cold weather. They must either hibernate through the winter or migrate to warmer areas in the fall.

Hibernation. Many species of butterflies survive the winter by hibernating in a sheltered place. Butterflies may hibernate in the egg, larval, pupal, or adult stage. But each species usually hibernates in only one stage, and it is as pupae in most cases.

Just before hibernation, the blood of a larva, pupa, or adult produces substances called *glycols*. These substances are related to the antifreeze used in automobiles. Scientists believe the production of glycols may be triggered by the decreasing daylight that occurs as winter approaches. The presence of glycols enables the insect to survive even the severest cold. After warm weather returns, the glycols are gradually replaced by normal blood substances.

Migration. A few kinds of butterflies escape the winter by migrating to a warmer region. One species, the monarch, is a long-distance champion. Dense clouds of monarchs may travel up to 2,000 miles (3,200 kilometers) from Canada and the Northern United States to California, Florida, and Mexico. The butterflies spend the winter resting and conserving energy for their return flight in the spring. Few of the adults live long enough to complete the return trip. Female monarchs lay eggs along the way. The offspring, after maturing, continue the northward journey. Other migrating butterflies include the painted lady, the cabbage butterfly, the red admiral, and the clouded yellow.

How to Collect Butterflies

Collecting butterflies can be a fascinating hobby. Some large, elaborate collections include rare and valuable specimens and are worth much money. But even a small, inexpensive collection can be interesting and attractive.

The equipment you need to collect butterflies includes a long-handled net, a poisoning jar with an airtight lid, and a poison called *ethyl acetate*. You also need cotton, a tweezers, mounting pins, mounting boards, and display boxes. All the equipment can be purchased at a hobby or craft store. But many of the items can be made from materials at home.

Capture the butterflies with the net and place them in the poisoning jar, which contains cotton soaked with ethyl acetate. Fumes from the poison will kill the butterflies. Use the tweezers to remove the dead butterflies from the jar. Place the body of each insect in the groove in the mounting board and insert a pin through the thorax. Spread the wings fully and pin threads or thin strips of paper over the wings to hold them in place. After the specimens have dried, remove them from the board and mount them on cardboard or some other material. Label each butterfly specimen with its name and where and when it was captured. Then put the butterflies in a glass-covered box to protect them from moisture and other damage.

To obtain perfect butterfly specimens, some collectors capture caterpillars and raise them to maturity. Such a collector must determine the species so that the caterpillars can be fed the proper food. The collector can watch the larvae become pupae and then adult butterflies.

You can learn more about collecting butterflies by reading books on butterflies available in libraries and by viewing museum collections. Some butterfly collectors join clubs in which the members exchange information and trade specimens.

Scientific Classification. Butterflies belong to the order Lepidoptera, which also includes moths. Skippers make up the superfamily Hesperioidea, as well as the family Hesperiidae. All other butterflies are *true butterflies* and belong to the superfamily Papilionoidea. True butterflies include the following families: blues, coppers, and hairstreaks (Lycaenidae); brush-footed butterflies (Nymphalidae); sulphurs and whites (Pieridae); metalmarks (Riodinidae); satyrs and wood nymphs (Satyridae); swallowtails (Papilionidae); milkweed butterflies (Danaidae); and snout butterflies (Libytheidae).   LEE D. MILLER

Related Articles in WORLD BOOK include:

Caterpillar	Insect
Chrysalis	Larva
Compound Eye	Metamorphosis
Entomology	Molting
Flower (picture: Pollination	Moth
by Butterflies)	Pheromone
Hibernation	Pupa

MARSUPIAL is a mammal whose young are born in an extremely immature state. The newborn undergoes most of its development attached to one of its mother's nipples and nourished by her milk. In most species, the nipples are located in a pouch called the *marsupium*.

There are over 200 species of marsupials, all of which live in either the Americas or Australasia. They include kangaroos, koalas, and opossums. Marsupials inhabit many environments, including forests, plains, and deserts. Kangaroos are the biggest marsupials. Some large male red kangaroos stand up to 7 feet (2.1 meters) tall. The smallest marsupials are the marsupial mice, some of which measure less than 3¾ inches (9.5 centimeters) long, including their tail.

Characteristics of Marsupials. Marsupials differ from other mammals by giving birth to extremely undeveloped young. Most mammals give birth to relatively well-developed offspring. Such mammals are called *placentals*. At the other extreme are the mammals called *monotremes*, which lay eggs. See MAMMAL (Reproduction).

At birth, a marsupial is expelled from the birth canal onto the base of its mother's tail. It wiggles along the mother's fur until it reaches the nipples. The young attaches itself to a nipple and begins to nurse. The nipple expands in the youngster's mouth, so there is little danger of separation. A young marsupial stays attached to its mother's nipples for several months. Then it separates itself from its mother but continues to stay close to her. If it is frightened, it returns to her, hopping into her pouch, or clinging to her teats.

Marsupials also differ from most other mammals in the details of their skeleton. Marsupials have two bones, called the *marsupial bones* or *epipubic bones*, that extend forward from the pelvis. The only other mammals that share this skeletal feature are the monotremes.

Kinds of Marsupials. There are six major groups of marsupials. Two are found only in the Americas. One American group, the *didelphids*, contains the opossums. The common opossum is the only marsupial found north of Mexico. Other opossum species live in Central and South America. Most didelphids eat almost any plant and animal food. The rat opossums make up the other American group, the *caenolestids*. Rat opposums live in western South America. They eat insects and other invertebrates.

The remaining four major groups of marsupials are found only in Australia, New Guinea, and neighboring islands. The *macropods* include kangaroos and wallabies. Macropods have hind legs that are larger than their front legs. They eat mainly grasses.

The *phalangers* often nest in hollow places in trees. They eat mainly fruits, flowers, and nectar. Many Phalanger species are commonly called *possums*, but should not be confused with the opossums of the Americas.

The *dasyurids* include meat-eaters. Most are small insect-eating animals, often called *marsupial mice*. The group also includes the native cat and Tasmanian devil.

Bandicoots make up the *peramelids*. Most bandicoots are about the size of a large rat and have long pointed noses, which they use to root in the soil for insects.

Koalas and wombats do not fit easily into any of these six major groups. Koalas eat eucalyptus leaves. Wombats are burrowers that eat mainly grasses.

History of Marsupials. Scientists think marsupials originated on a large continent that later split to become present-day South America, Antarctica, and Australia. Many of the American marsupials eventually became extinct as a result of competition with placental mammals. But the Australian marsupials were isolated from most placentals. They flourished and developed into the unique animals found in Australia today.

Many Australian marsupials face extinction. They are threatened chiefly by placental mammals, such as foxes, rabbits, and *dingoes* (wild dogs), which have been introduced to Australia by human beings.

Scientific Classification. Marsupials make up the order Marsupialia.   MICHAEL L. AUGEE

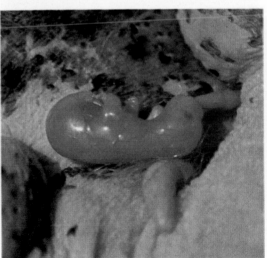

© Ray Williams   © Tom McHugh, Photo Researchers

Marsupials are born at an extremely immature stage of development. The photograph on the left shows a newborn wallaby attached to a nipple in its mother's pouch. An adult female wallaby with a much older offspring in her pouch is shown in the photograph on the right.

Jerry Herman, FPG

A Male Frog Sounding a Mating Call

Dennis Hallinan, FPG

Ken Sexton

A Tone-Producing Tuning Fork

Trombonists in a Marching Band

All Sounds Are Produced by Vibrations. When a tuning fork is struck, the vibration of its prongs generates a specific tone. A frog croaks by forcing air over its vocal cords, making them vibrate. A trombone produces sound when the player causes the air column inside the instrument to vibrate.

SOUND

SOUND surrounds us all the time. The buzzing of an alarm clock or the chirping of birds may awaken us in the morning. Throughout the day, we hear many kinds of sounds, such as the clatter of pots and pans, the roar of traffic, and the voices of people. As we fall asleep at night, we may listen to the croaking of frogs or the whistle of the wind.

All the sounds we hear have one thing in common. Every sound is produced by vibrations of an object. When an object vibrates, it makes the surrounding air vibrate. The vibrations in the air travel outward in all directions from the object. When the vibrations enter our ears, the brain interprets them as sounds (see EAR [The Sense of Hearing]). Although many of the sounds we hear travel through the air, sound can move through any material. For example, sound travels well through solid earth. You may have read that American Indians used to put their ears to the ground to listen for distant hoofbeats.

Sound has great importance in our lives. First of all, sound makes it possible for us to communicate with one another through speech. Many sounds, such as music and the singing of birds, provide pleasure. The sounds

Alan B. Coppens and James V. Sanders, the contributors of this article, are Associate Professors of Physics at the Naval Postgraduate School.

of radio and television broadcasts bring us entertainment and information. We are warned of danger by such sounds as automobile horns and fire alarms.

How Some Familiar Sounds Are Produced

The Human Voice is produced in the *larynx*, a section of the throat. Two small bands of tissue stretch across the larynx. These bands, called *vocal cords*, have a slitlike opening between them. When we speak, muscles in the larynx tighten the vocal cords, narrowing the opening. Air from the lungs rushes past the tightened cords, causing them to vibrate. The vibrations produce the sound of the voice. The tighter the vocal cords are, the more rapidly they vibrate and the higher are the sounds produced. See LARYNX; VOICE.

Animal Sounds. Birds, frogs, and almost all mammals have vocal cords or similar structures and make sounds the same way that people do. A dolphin produces clicks and whistles in air-filled pouches connected to the *blowhole*, a nostril in the top of its head. The buzzing of bees and flies results from the vibrations of their wings beating against the air. Many other insects produce sounds by rubbing one part of the body against another part. For example, a cricket "sings" by scraping parts of its front wings together.

Some kinds of fishes cluck, croak, grunt, or make other sounds by vibrating a baglike organ, known as a *swim bladder* or *air bladder*, that is located below the backbone. Certain kinds of shellfish produce clicking sounds by striking their claws together. The pistol shrimp makes a sound much like a gunshot by snapping one of its claws.

Musical Sounds are usually pleasing or interesting sounds. Different kinds of musical instruments produce sounds in different ways.

Certain instruments produce sounds when struck. When the membrane of a drum is hit, for example, it vibrates and produces sound. Such instruments as chimes and xylophones have a series of bars or tubes, each of which sounds a particular note when struck.

The sounds of the cello, violin, harp, and piano are produced when a player makes one or more of their strings vibrate. The vibrating strings in turn cause parts of the body of the instrument to vibrate, setting the surrounding air in motion. The strings of cellos and violins are usually stroked with a bow. A musician plucks the strings of a harp. When the keys of a piano are struck, padded hammers hit strings inside the piano, making them vibrate.

Wind instruments, such as the clarinet, flute, and trumpet, generate sounds by the vibration of columns of air inside the instruments. A clarinet has a flat, thin part called a *reed* attached to the mouthpiece. The reed vibrates when a player blows on it, which makes the air column inside the clarinet vibrate. The column of air in a flute vibrates when a musician blows across a hole in the flute's mouthpiece. In a trumpet, the vibrating lips of the player make the air column vibrate.

Noises are unpleasant, annoying, and distracting sounds. Most kinds of noises are produced by vibrating objects that send out irregular vibrations at irregular

Terms Used in the Study of Sound

Acoustics is the science of sound and of its effects on people.

Beats are periodic variations in the loudness of a sound. Beats are heard when two tones of slightly different frequencies are sounded at the same time.

Condensation is a region of compression in a sound wave.

Decibel is the unit used to measure the intensity level of a sound. A 3,000-hertz tone of zero decibels is the weakest sound that the normal human ear can hear.

Frequency of sound waves refers to the number of condensations or rarefactions produced by a vibrating object each second.

Hertz is the unit used to measure frequency. One hertz equals one *cycle* (vibration) per second.

Infrasound is sound with frequencies below the range of human hearing.

Intensity of a sound is related to the amount of energy flowing in the sound waves.

Phon is a unit often used to measure the loudness level of tones. The loudness level in phons of any tone is the intensity level in decibels of a 1,000-hertz tone that seems equally loud.

Pitch is the degree of highness or lowness of a sound as perceived by a listener.

Rarefaction is a region of expansion in a sound wave.

Resonance Frequency is approximately the frequency at which an object would vibrate naturally if disturbed in some way.

Sound Quality, also called *timbre*, is a characteristic of musical sounds. Sound quality distinguishes between notes of the same frequency and intensity produced by different musical instruments.

Ultrasound is sound with frequencies above the range of human hearing.

intervals. Such noises include the banging of garbage cans, the barking of a dog, and the roar of a crowd. Many machines and devices, such as air conditioners, vacuum cleaners, and the engines of motor vehicles, produce noise. Natural events also create noise. The shaking of the earth generates the rumble of earthquakes. The crash of thunder is produced by violent vibrations of air that has been heated by lightning.

Some noises consist of *impulsive sounds*—that is, vibrations which start suddenly and quickly die. Impulsive sounds include the crack of a gunshot and the pop of a firecracker. A power lawn mower produces a series of impulsive sounds. Such noises as the screech of chalk or a fingernail on a blackboard and the wail of a siren consist of a collection of rapid vibrations that do not blend well. See NOISE.

The Nature of Sound

If you drop a pebble into a still pond, you will see a series of waves travel outward from the point where the pebble struck the surface. Sound also travels in waves as it moves through the air or some other *medium* (substance). The waves are produced by a vibrating object. As a vibrating object moves outward, it compresses the surrounding medium, producing a region of compression called a *condensation*. As the vibrating object then moves inward, the medium expands into the space formerly occupied by the object. This region of expansion is called a *rarefaction*. As the object continues to move outward and inward, a series of condensations and rarefactions travels away from the object. *Sound waves* consist of these condensations and rarefactions.

Sound waves must travel through a medium. Thus,

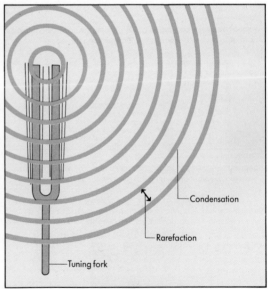

WORLD BOOK diagram by Bill and Judic Anderson

Sound Waves form when a vibrating object causes the surrounding *medium* (substance) to vibrate. As the object moves outward, it produces a region of compression called a *condensation*. As the object then moves inward, a region of expansion known as a *rarefaction* forms. Sound waves consist of the series of condensations and rarefactions generated by the vibrating object.

SOUND

sound is absent in the vacuum of outer space, which contains no material for a vibrating object to compress and expand.

The nature of a particular sound can be described in terms of (1) frequency and pitch, (2) intensity and loudness, and (3) quality.

Frequency and Pitch. The number of condensations or rarefactions produced by a vibrating object each second is called the *frequency* of the sound waves. The more rapidly an object vibrates, the higher will be the frequency. Scientists use a unit called the *hertz* to measure frequency. One hertz equals one *cycle* (vibration) per second (see HERTZ). As the frequency of sound waves increases, the *wavelength* decreases. Wavelength is the distance between any point on one wave and the corresponding point on the next one.

Most people can hear sounds with frequencies from about 20 to 20,000 hertz. Bats, dogs, and many other kinds of animals can hear sounds with frequencies far above 20,000 hertz. Different sounds have different frequencies. For example, the sound of jingling keys ranges from 700 to 15,000 hertz. A person's voice can produce frequencies from 85 to 1,100 hertz. The tones of a piano have frequencies ranging from about 30 to 15,000 hertz.

The frequency of a sound determines its *pitch*—the degree of highness or lowness of the sound as perceived by a listener (see PITCH). High-pitched sounds have higher frequencies than low-pitched sounds. Musical instruments can produce a wide range of pitches. For example, a trumpet has valves that can shorten or lengthen

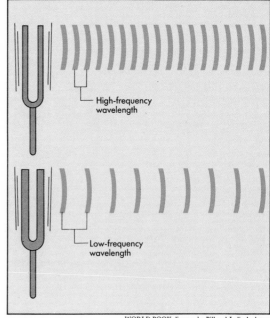

High-frequency wavelength

Low-frequency wavelength

WORLD BOOK diagram by Bill and Judie Anderson

Frequency of sound waves is the number of condensations or rarefactions produced by a vibrating object each second. The more rapidly an object vibrates, the higher will be the frequency. As the frequency increases, the *wavelength*—the distance between any point on one wave and the corresponding point on the next one—decreases. The frequency of a sound determines its pitch. High-pitched sounds have higher frequencies than low-pitched sounds.

Some Common Frequency Ranges

Scientists use a unit called the *hertz* to measure frequency. One hertz equals one *cycle* (vibration) per second. This graph shows the range of frequencies, in hertz, that human beings and some animals can *emit* (give off) and receive. Many animals hear frequencies far above those heard by people.

WORLD BOOK graph

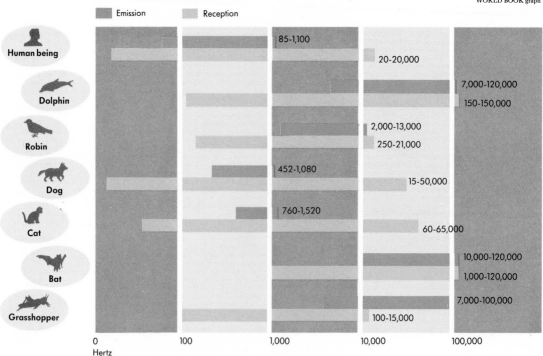

■ Emission   ■ Reception

Human being — 85-1,100 / 20-20,000
Dolphin — 7,000-120,000 / 150-150,000
Robin — 2,000-13,000 / 250-21,000
Dog — 452-1,080 / 15-50,000
Cat — 760-1,520 / 60-65,000
Bat — 10,000-120,000 / 1,000-120,000
Grasshopper — 7,000-100,000 / 100-15,000

0   100   1,000   10,000   100,000
Hertz

the vibrating column of air inside the instrument. A short column produces a high-frequency, high-pitched sound. A long column results in a note of low frequency and low pitch.

Intensity and Loudness. The *intensity* of a sound is related to the amount of energy flowing in the sound waves. Intensity depends on the *amplitude* of the vibrations producing the waves. Amplitude is the distance that a vibrating object moves from its position of rest as it vibrates. The larger the amplitude of vibration is, the more intense will be the sound.

The *loudness* of a sound refers to how strong the sound seems to us when it strikes our ears. At a given frequency, the more intense a sound is, the louder it seems. But equally intense sounds of different frequencies are not equally loud. The ear has low sensitivity to sounds near the upper and lower limits of the range of frequencies we can hear. Thus, a high-frequency or low-frequency sound does not seem as loud as a sound of the same intensity in the middle of the frequency range.

Water waves in a pond get weaker as they travel away from their source. In the same way, sound waves lose intensity as they spread outward in all directions from their source. Thus, the loudness of a sound decreases as the distance increases between a person and the source of the sound. You can observe this effect in a large field by walking away from a friend who is talking at a constant level. As you move farther and farther away, the voice of your friend gets fainter and fainter.

Sound Quality, also called *timbre*, is a characteristic of musical sounds. Quality distinguishes between sounds of the same frequency and intensity produced by different musical instruments.

Almost every musical sound consists of a combination of the actual note sounded and a number of higher tones related to it. The actual note played is the *fundamental*. The higher tones are *overtones* of the fundamental. For example, when a note is produced by a violin string, the string vibrates as a whole and produces the fundamental. But the string also vibrates in separate sections at the same time. It may vibrate in two, three, four, or more parts. Each of these separate vibrations produces an overtone of higher frequency and pitch than the fundamental. The greater the number of vibrating parts is, the higher will be the frequency of the overtone.

The number and strength of the overtones help determine the characteristic sound quality of a musical instrument. For instance, a note on the flute sounds soft and sweet because it has only a few, weak overtones. The same note played on the trumpet has many, strong overtones and thus seems powerful and bright.

How Sound Behaves

The Speed of Sound depends on the medium through which the sound waves travel. The properties of a medium that determine the speed of sound are *density* and *compressibility*. Density is the amount of material in a unit volume of a substance. Compressibility measures how easily a substance can be crushed into a smaller volume. The denser a medium is and the more compressible it is, the slower the speed of sound will be.

In general, liquids and solids are denser than air. But they are also far less compressible. Therefore, sound travels faster through liquids and solids than through air. Compared with its speed through air, sound travels

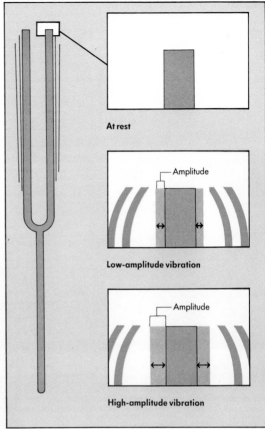

At rest

Amplitude

Low-amplitude vibration

Amplitude

High-amplitude vibration

WORLD BOOK diagram by Bill and Judie Anderson

Amplitude is the distance that a vibrating object moves from its position of rest as it vibrates. The larger the amplitude of vibration is, the more intense will be the sound.

about 4 times faster through water and about 15 times faster through steel. The speed of sound through air increases as the air temperature rises. For instance, sound travels 1,085 feet (331 meters) per second through air at 32° F. (0° C) and 1,268 feet (386 meters) per second through air at 212° F. (100° C).

The speed of sound is much slower than the speed of light. In a vacuum, light travels 186,282 miles (299,792 kilometers) per second—almost a million times faster than sound. As a result, we see the flash of lightning during a storm before we hear the thunder. If you watch a

The Speed of Sound in Various Mediums

Medium	Speed	
	In feet per second	In meters per second
Air at 32° F. (0° C)	1,085	331
Aluminum	16,000	5,000
Brick	11,980	3,650
Distilled water at 77° F. (25° C)	4,908	1,496
Glass	14,900	4,540
Seawater at 77° F. (25° C)	5,023	1,531
Steel	17,100	5,200
Wood (maple)	13,480	4,110

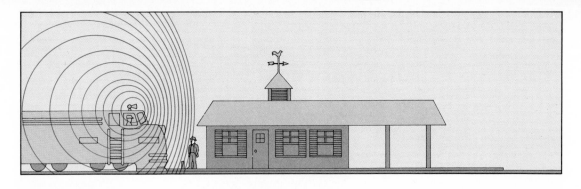

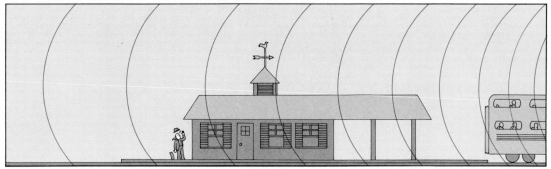

WORLD BOOK diagrams by Bill and Judie Anderson

The Doppler Effect is an apparent change in pitch produced by moving objects. For example, the pitch of a train whistle appears higher as the train approaches and lower as the train moves away. As the train approaches, *top,* sound waves from the whistle are crowded together, producing a higher apparent pitch to the listener on the platform. As the train moves away, *bottom,* the waves are spread out, producing a lower apparent pitch. The people on the train hear a uniform pitch.

carpenter hammering on a distant building, you will see the hammer strike before you hear the sound of the blow.

You may have noticed that the pitch of a train whistle seems higher as the train approaches and lower after the train passes and moves away. The sound waves produced by the whistle travel through the air at a constant speed, regardless of the speed of the train. But as the train approaches, each successive wave produced by the whistle travels a shorter distance to your ears. The waves arrive more frequently, and the pitch of the whistle appears higher. As the train moves away, each successive wave travels a longer distance to your ears. The waves arrive less frequently, producing a lower apparent pitch. This apparent change in pitch produced by moving objects is called the *Doppler effect.* To a listener on the train, the pitch of the whistle does not change.

Jet airplanes sometimes fly at supersonic speeds. A plane flying faster than the speed of sound creates *shock waves,* strong pressure disturbances that build up around the aircraft. People on the ground hear a loud noise, known as a *sonic boom,* when the shock waves from the plane sweep over them. See AERODYNAMICS (Shock Waves and Sonic Booms).

Reflection. If you shout toward a large brick wall at least 30 feet (9 meters) away, you will hear an echo. The echo is produced when the sound waves are reflected from the wall to your ears. Generally, when sound waves in one medium strike a large object of another medium—such as the waves in air hitting the

brick wall—some of the sound is reflected. The remainder is sent into the new medium. The speed of sound in the two mediums and the densities of the mediums help determine the amount of reflection. If sound travels at about the same speed in both materials and both have about the same density, little sound will be reflected. Instead, most of the sound will be transmitted into the new medium. If the speed differs greatly in the two mediums and their densities are greatly different, most of the sound will be reflected. Sound waves travel much more slowly through air than through brick, and brick is much denser than air. Thus when you shout at the brick wall, most of the sound is reflected. See ECHO.

Refraction. When sound waves leave one medium and enter another in which the speed of sound differs, the direction of the waves is altered. This change in direction results from a change in the speed of the waves and is called *refraction.* If sound waves travel slower in the second medium, the waves will be refracted toward the *normal.* The normal is an imaginary line perpendicular to the boundary between the mediums. If sound travels faster in the second medium, the waves will be refracted away from the normal.

Sound waves can also be refracted if the speed of sound changes according to their position in a medium. The waves bend toward the region of slower speed. You may have noticed that sounds carry farther at night than during a sunny day. During the day, air near the ground is warmer than the air above. Sound waves in the air are bent away from the ground into the cooler air above, where their speed is slower. This bending of the waves results in weaker sound near the ground. At night, air near the ground becomes cooler than the air above. Sound waves are bent toward the ground, enabling sound near the ground to be heard over longer distances.

Diffraction. Sound waves traveling along the side of a building spread out around the corner of the building. When sound waves pass through a doorway, they spread out around its edges. This spreading out of waves as they pass by the edge of an obstacle or through an opening is called *diffraction*. Diffraction occurs whenever a sound wave encounters an obstacle or opening. But it is most evident when the wavelength of the sound wave is long compared with the size of the obstacle or opening. Diffraction enables you to hear a sound from around a corner, even though no straight path exists from the source of the sound to your ears. See DIFFRACTION.

Resonance is the reinforcing of sound. It occurs when a small repeated force produces larger and larger vibrations in an object. To produce resonance, the repeated force must be applied with the same frequency as the *resonance frequency* of the object. Resonance frequency is approximately the frequency at which an object would vibrate naturally if disturbed in some way. It is said that some opera singers can shatter a wineglass by singing a note with a frequency equal to the resonance frequency of the glass. The vibrations produced in the glass get larger and larger until it breaks apart.

You can demonstrate resonance by holding a vibrating tuning fork over a tube that is open at one end and

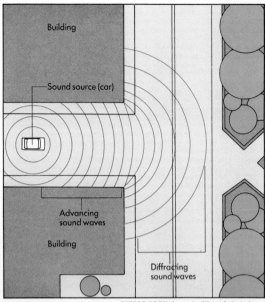

WORLD BOOK diagram by Bill and Judie Anderson

Diffraction is the spreading out of waves as they pass by the edge of an obstacle or through an opening. Diffraction enables the sound produced by the approaching car above to be heard around the corners of the buildings at the intersection.

Refraction of Sound Waves

When sound waves leave one medium and enter another in which the speed of sound differs, the waves are *refracted*—that is, their direction is altered. Sound waves can be refracted either away from or toward the *normal,* an imaginary line perpendicular to the boundary between the mediums.

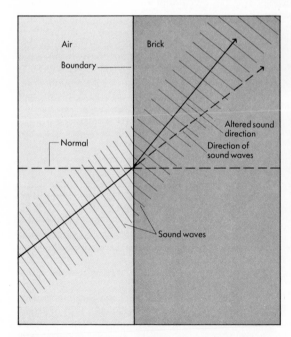

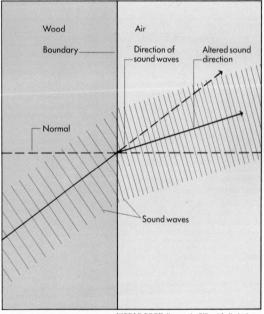

WORLD BOOK diagrams by Bill and Judie Anderson

Refraction Away from the Normal. If sound waves in one medium enter another medium in which the speed of sound is faster, the waves will be refracted away from the normal. For example, sound waves passing from air into brick are refracted away from the normal because sound travels faster in brick than in air.

Refraction Toward the Normal. If sound waves traveling in one medium enter another medium in which the speed of sound is slower, the waves will be refracted toward the normal. For example, sound waves passing from wood into air are refracted toward the normal because sound travels slower in air than in wood.

closed at the other end. If the tube is almost exactly one-fourth as long as the wavelength of the sound waves from the fork, the waves will travel down the column of air inside the tube and be reflected from the bottom. The original waves and the reflected waves combine and form wave patterns that appear to stand still. Such patterns are called *standing waves*. When standing waves form in the tube, the air column and the tuning fork are in resonance. The standing waves in the tube cause the surrounding air to vibrate with a larger amplitude, resulting in a louder sound.

Resonance increases the loudness of the sounds produced by many musical instruments. For example, a wind instrument produces resonance in the same way as the tuning fork and the tube. Standing waves are set up in the column of air inside the instrument. The air column resonates with the vibrations at the mouthpiece, amplifying the sound of the instrument.

Beats. When two tones of slightly different frequencies are sounded together, you hear a single sound that gets louder and softer at regular intervals. These periodic variations of loudness are *beats*. Beats are produced because the sound waves of the two tones overlap and interfere with each other.

The interference of the combined waves is called *constructive* if condensations coincide with condensations and rarefactions meet rarefactions. The waves reinforce each other, producing a louder sound. The interference between the waves is *destructive* if condensations coincide with rarefactions. A weaker sound or silence results. If the periods of constructive and destructive interference alternate, the loudness of the sound increases and decreases, producing beats. See INTERFERENCE.

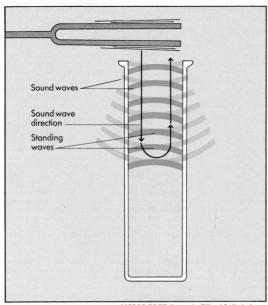

WORLD BOOK diagram by Bill and Judie Anderson

Resonance is the reinforcing of sound. The tuning fork above is in resonance with the air column inside the beaker. Sound waves from the fork travel down the column and are reflected from the water. The original waves and the reflected waves combine and form patterns called *standing waves* that result in a louder sound.

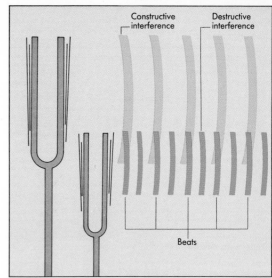

WORLD BOOK diagram by Bill and Judie Anderson

Beats are periodic variations in loudness that occur when the sound waves of two tones overlap and interfere with each other. In *constructive* interference, condensations coincide with condensations, producing a louder sound. In *destructive* interference, condensations meet rarefactions, resulting in a weaker sound.

The number of beats per second, called the *beat frequency*, equals the difference between the frequencies of the two tones. For example, if a 256-hertz tone and a 257-hertz tone are sounded together, one beat will be heard each second.

Working with Sound

Measuring Sound. Scientists use a unit called the *decibel* to measure the intensity level of a sound. A 3,000-hertz tone of zero decibels marks the *threshold of audibility*—the weakest sound that the normal human ear can hear. A sound intensity level of 140 decibels is the *threshold of pain*. Sounds of 140 decibels or more produce pain in the ear, rather than hearing. A whisper amounts to about 20 decibels. Ordinary conversation has an intensity level of about 60 decibels. Loud rock music can produce up to 120 decibels of sound. See DECIBEL.

A unit called the *phon* is often used to measure the loudness level of tones. The loudness level in phons of any tone is the intensity level in decibels of a 1,000-hertz tone that seems equally loud. For example, a tone of 20 decibels with a frequency of 1,000 hertz has a loudness level of 20 phons. A tone of any frequency and intensity that seems equally loud is also assigned a loudness level of 20 phons. For instance, a tone of 80 decibels with a frequency of 20 hertz seems as loud as the 20-decibel tone at 1,000 hertz. Thus, the 80-decibel tone has a loudness level of 20 phons.

Controlling Sound. The science of *acoustics* deals with sound and its effects on people. A major field of acoustics is *environmental acoustics*, which involves control of noise pollution.

We are continually exposed to noise from a variety of sources, such as airplanes, construction projects, industries, motor vehicles, and even household appliances. People exposed to loud noise for long periods may suffer temporary or permanent loss of hearing. Loud sounds of short duration, such as the noise of a gunshot or a firecracker, can also damage the ear. Constant noise—even if it is not extremely loud—can cause fatigue, headaches, hearing loss, irritability, nausea, and tension.

Noise pollution can be controlled in a number of ways. Acoustical engineers have quieted the noise made by many devices. For example, mufflers help reduce the noise from automobile engines. In buildings, thick, heavy walls, well-sealed doors and windows, and various other means may be used to block noise (see INSULATION [Insulation Against Sound]). Industrial workers and other people exposed to intense noise should wear some form of ear protectors to help prevent hearing loss.

Acoustics also involves providing good conditions for producing and listening to speech and music in such places as auditoriums and concert halls. For example, acoustical engineers work to control *reverberation*—the bouncing back and forth of sound against the ceiling, walls, floor, and other surfaces of an auditorium or hall. Some reverberation is necessary to produce pleasing sounds. But too much reverberation can blur the voice of a speaker or the sound of a musical instrument. Engineers use such sound-absorbing items as acoustical tiles, carpets, draperies, and upholstered furniture to control reverberation. See ACOUSTICS.

Using Sound. Sound has many uses in science and industry. Geophysicists often use sound in exploring for minerals and petroleum. In one technique, they set off a

Intensity of Some Common Sounds

The unit used to measure the intensity level of a sound is called the *decibel*. A 3,000-hertz tone of zero decibels is the weakest sound that the human ear can hear. Sounds of 140 decibels or more produce pain in the ear and may damage the delicate tissues.

WORLD BOOK chart

Decibels

	160 — Threshold of pain
	150
Jet take-off at close range	140
	130
	120 — Amplified rock band
	110
Circular saw	100
	90
	80 — Vacuum cleaner
	70
Telephone bell	60
	50
	40 — Conversation
	30
	20
Whispering	10 — Threshold of audibility
	0

small explosion on or just below the earth's surface. The resulting sound waves bounce off underground layers of rock. The nature of each echo and the time it takes for the waves to reach the surface indicate the type and thickness of each rock layer present. Geophysicists can thus locate possible mineral- or oil-bearing rock formations. A device called *sonar* uses sound waves to detect underwater objects (see SONAR). Warships can locate enemy submarines with sonar. Fishing boats use sonar systems to detect schools of fish.

Sound with frequencies above the range of human hearing is called *ultrasound*. It is used to clean watches and other delicate instruments. Manufacturers also use ultrasonic waves to test metals, plastics, and other materials. Physicians can diagnose brain tumors, gallstones, liver diseases, and other disorders with ultrasound. Ultrasonic waves also provide a relatively safe means to check the development of unborn children. See ULTRASOUND.

Scientists and engineers have developed several devices for recording and reproducing sound. These devices include the microphone, the speaker, and the amplifier. A *microphone* changes sound waves into electric signals that correspond to the pattern of the waves. A *speaker* changes electric signals, such as those produced by a microphone, back into sound. An *amplifier* is used in most sound-reproduction systems to strengthen the electric signals and make them powerful enough to operate the speaker. Every phonograph, public address system, radio, tape recorder, and television set has at least one amplifier. See MICROPHONE; SPEAKER; ELECTRONICS (Amplification).

In recording music, engineers sometimes make two or more separate recordings from microphones placed at various points around the source. If these recordings are played back together correctly, they produce *stereophonic sound*. Stereophonic sound has qualities of depth and direction similar to those of the original sound. To reproduce stereophonic sound, a sound system must have an amplifier and a speaker for each of the recordings. See HIGH FIDELITY (Stereophonic Hi-Fi).

The Study of Sound

Early Thought. The study of sound began in ancient times. As early as the 500's B.C., Pythagoras, a Greek philosopher and mathematician, conducted experiments on the sounds produced by vibrating strings. Pythagoras is said to have invented the *sonometer*, an instrument used to study musical sounds (see SONOMETER). About 400 B.C., a Greek scholar named Archytas stated that sound is produced by the motion of one object striking another. About 50 years later, the Greek philosopher Aristotle suggested that sound is carried to our ears by the movement of air. From then until about A.D. 1300, little scientific investigation took place in Europe. But scientists in the Middle East and India developed some new ideas about sound by studying music and working out systems of music theory.

The Wave Theory. The understanding that sound travels in the form of waves may have originated with the Italian artist Leonardo da Vinci about 1500. But European scientists did not begin extensive experiments on the nature of sound until the early 1600's. About that 'time, the Italian astronomer and physicist Galileo demonstrated that the frequency of sound waves determines pitch. Galileo scraped a chisel across a brass plate, producing a screech. He then related the spacing of the grooves made by the chisel to the pitch of the screech.

About 1640, Marin Mersenne, a French mathematician, obtained the first measurement of the speed of sound in air. About 20 years later, the Irish chemist and physicist Robert Boyle demonstrated that sound waves must travel in a medium. Boyle showed that a ringing bell could not be heard if placed in a jar from which as much air had been removed as possible. During the late 1600's, the English scientist Sir Isaac Newton formulated an almost correct relationship between the speed of sound in a medium and the density and compressibility of the medium.

In the mid-1700's, Daniel Bernoulli, a Swiss mathematician and physicist, explained that a string could vibrate at more than one frequency at the same time. In the early 1800's, a French mathematician named Jean Baptiste Fourier developed a mathematical technique that could be used to break down complex sound waves into the pure tones that make them up. During the 1860's, Hermann von Helmholtz, a German physicist, investigated the interference of sound waves, the production of beats, and the relationship of both to the ear's perception of sound.

Recent Developments. Much of modern acoustics is based on the principles of sound described in *The Theory of Sound*, a book published by the British physicist Lord Rayleigh in 1878. Although many of the properties of sound have thus been long established, the science of acoustics has continued to expand into new areas. In the 1940's, Georg von Békésy, an American physicist, showed how the ear distinguishes between various sounds. During the 1960's, the field of environmental acoustics expanded in response to growing concern over physical and psychological effects of noise pollution.

Acoustical research of the 1970's included the study of new uses of ultrasound, and the development of better ultrasonic equipment. During the early 1980's, research included the design of better sound-reproducing equipment and the development of computers that can understand and reproduce speech. Acoustical engineers also studied possible uses of *infrasound*—that is, sound with frequencies below the range of human hearing.

ALAN B. COPPENS and JAMES V. SANDERS

Additional Resources

Level I

BRANLEY, FRANKLYN M. *High Sounds, Low Sounds.* Crowell, 1967.
HEUER, KENNETH. *Thunder, Singing Sounds, and Other Wonders: Sound in the Atmosphere.* Dodd, 1981.
KETTLEKAMP, LARRY. *The Magic of Sound.* Rev. ed. Morrow, 1982.
KNIGHT, DAVID C. *Silent Sound: The World of Ultrasonics.* Morrow, 1980.

Level II

CHEDD, GRAHAM. *Sound: From Communication to Noise Pollution.* Doubleday, 1971.
HUNT, FREDERICK V. *Origins in Acoustics: The Science of Sound from Antiquity to the Age of Newton.* Yale, 1978.
KOCK, WINSTON E. *Seeing Sound.* Wiley, 1971.
TANNENBAUM, BEULAH, and STILLMAN, MYRA. *Understanding Sound.* McGraw, 1973.

ULTRASOUND is sound with *frequencies* above the range of human hearing. Frequency refers to the number of sound waves a vibrating object produces per second. It is measured in terms of *hertz*. One hertz equals one *cycle* (vibration) per second. Most people can hear sounds with frequencies between 20 and 20,000 hertz. However, ultrasound has frequencies above 20,000 hertz.

In addition to its high frequency, ultrasound has other qualities that distinguish it from the sound that is audible to human beings. For example, ultrasonic waves are shorter than the waves of audible sound. When the short waves of ultrasound encounter small obstacles, they are easily reflected, forming echoes. The longer waves of audible sound, however, flow around small obstacles, with very little reflection.

Bats, porpoises, and certain other animals that can hear frequencies above 20,000 hertz make important use of ultrasound. For example, some bats give off short, ultrasonic cries that bounce off nearby objects, making echoes. They use these echoes to find insects or other food and to avoid obstacles.

Producing Ultrasound. Scientists have invented whistles and other devices that produce ultrasound. One commonly used device, called an *ultrasonic transducer*, converts electric energy into ultrasonic waves. Some ultrasonic transducers include a special disk made of quartz or of a ceramic material. When charged with electricity, the disk vibrates so rapidly that ultrasonic waves are created.

Many transducers can also convert ultrasonic waves into electric energy. These transducers give off ultrasonic waves at the same time that they change the returning echoes back to electricity. Strong echoes create stronger electric pulses than weak ones do. A computer registers such data as the intensity of the electric pulses and the direction of the returning echoes. The computer can then provide information on the substances that reflected the ultrasonic waves. Some computers transform the data they receive into images on a screen.

Uses. Ultrasound has a wide variety of uses. They can be divided into two basic groups—(1) passive uses and (2) active uses.

Passive Uses of Ultrasound include those in which it is used only to obtain information. For example, doctors use ultrasound to check the development of unborn babies. Special ultrasonic equipment can produce an image of an unborn baby on a screen. Ultrasound can also aid in the diagnosis of tumors, gallstones, heart disease, and other disorders. Most doctors believe that ultrasonic examinations have no dangerous side effects.

Manufacturers use ultrasound to measure the wall thickness of metal or plastic pipes and to test the concentration of particles in inks and paints. Sonar devices locate enemy ships, schools of fish, and underwater obstacles through the use of ultrasound (see SONAR).

Active Uses of Ultrasound include those in which it is used to produce certain effects in materials. For example, brain tumors and kidney stones can be destroyed by ultrasound. Ultrasonic waves can also be used to clean watches and other delicate instruments and to mix chemicals. At certain frequencies, ultrasound can produce enough energy to weld certain metals.   LASZLO ADLER

See also REMOTE CONTROL (diagram); MACHINE TOOL (Other Advanced Machining Operations).

Index

This index covers the contents of the 1983, 1984, and 1985 editions of SCIENCE YEAR, The World Book Science Annual.

Each index entry gives the edition year and a page number, for example, 85-123. The first number, 85, indicates the edition year, and the second number, 123, is the page number on which the desired information begins.

There are two types of entries in the index.

In the first type, the index entry (in **boldface**) is followed immediately by numbers:
   Botany, 85-233, 84-235, 83-234
This means that SCIENCE YEAR has an article titled Botany and that in the 1985 edition, the article begins on page 233. In the 1984 edition, the article begins on page 235, and in the 1983 edition, it is on page 234.

In the second type of entry, the boldface title is followed by a clue word instead of by numbers:
   Chemotherapy: bone marrow, Special Report, 85-31; drugs, 83-243
This means there is no SCIENCE YEAR article titled chemotherapy, but that information about chemotherapy as it relates to bone marrow can be found in a Special Report in the 1985 edition, on page 31. There is also information about chemotherapy and drugs in the 1983 edition, on page 243.

When the clue word is "il.," the reference is to an illustration only:
   Flamingo tongue snail: il., 85-21
This means there is an illustration of this snail in the 1985 SCIENCE YEAR, on page 21.

The various "See" and "See also" cross-references in the index direct the reader to other entries within the index:
   Horticulture: See **Agriculture; Botany; Plant.**
This means that for the location of information on horticulture — look under the boldface index entries
   Agriculture, Botany, and **Plant.**

Index

Index

Index

Index

Index

Index

Index

Acknowledgments

The publishers of *Science Year* gratefully acknowledge the courtesy of the following artists, photographers, publishers, institutions, agencies, and corporations for the illustrations in this volume. Credits should be read from top to bottom, left to right, on their respective pages. All entries marked with an asterisk (*) denote illustrations created exclusively for *Science Year*. All maps, charts, and diagrams were prepared by the *Science Year* staff unless otherwise noted.

	Advanced Information & Decision Systems, Mountain View, Calif.	264	Hochtemperatur-Reaktorbau
196	David Povilaitis*	265	Atlantic Richfield Company
198	William Cigliano*	267	Argonne National Laboratory
202	The College Board; William Cigliano*	269	Herman H. Torres, NYT Pictures
205	National Science Foundation; William Cigliano*	270	Rockwell International
207	National Science Board. Data from *A Challenge for American Precollege Education: Scientific Literacy in Japan, China, The Germanies and the Soviet Union.* Edited by Margarete Klein and F. James Rutherford; Macmillan. Embassy of France and The British Embassy, Washington, D.C. National Center of Educational Statistics, *High School and Beyond;* William Cigliano*	272	Institute of Animal Physiology, Agricultural Research Council, Cambridge, England

196 David Povilaitis*
198 William Cigliano*
202 The College Board; William Cigliano*
205 National Science Foundation; William Cigliano*
207 National Science Board. Data from *A Challenge for American Precollege Education: Scientific Literacy in Japan, China, The Germanies and the Soviet Union.* Edited by Margarete Klein and F. James Rutherford; Macmillan. Embassy of France and The British Embassy, Washington, D.C. National Center of Educational Statistics, *High School and Beyond;* William Cigliano*
210 Atlantic Richfield Company; U.S. Department of Agriculture; Ed L. Nowak, State University of New York at Buffalo
211 NASA; George E. Stuart, © National Geographic Society; © Michael Gamer
212 U.S. Department of Agriculture
213 Gerald R. Carner, Clemson University; U.S. Department of Agriculture
214 Australian Information Service
216 Jim Wallace
217 © Jodie Cobb, National Geographic Society
218 © National Geographic Society
219 © Wilbur E. Garrett, National Geographic Society; George E. Stuart, © National Geographic Society
220 Smithsonian Institution
221 AP/Wide World
222 Sovfoto; NASA
223 Drawing by Chas. Addams; © 1983 The New Yorker Magazine, Inc.
225 California Institute of Technology
226 Royal Greenwich Observatory
228 C. R. Lawrence, D. P. Schneider and M. Schmidt, California Institute of Technology, C. L. Bennett, J. N. Hewitt and B. F. Burke, Massachusetts Institute of Technology and E. L. Turner and J. E. Gunn, Princeton University Observatory
230 Hale Observatory
231 Sierra Club Books; Cambridge University Press
232 W. W. Norton & Company Inc.; Charles Scribner's Sons
233 U.S. Department of Agriculture
235 David W. Harbaugh
236 Glasgow College of Technology
237 Gene Dzaman, Rensselaer Polytechnic Institute
238 International Business Machines
239 CERN; Stanford University; University of Arizona
240 Brad Bower, Picture Group; AP/Wide World; Black Star
241 U.S. Department of Agriculture
242 Lederle Laboratories
243 The Australian National University Research School of Earth Sciences
244 Peter Webb, Ohio State University
245 © L. Burr, Gamma/Liaison
247 Michael W. Nickell
249 U.S. Air Force
253 Ed L. Nowak, State University of New York at Buffalo
256 U.S. Department of Agriculture
257 Mitsubishi
258 Drawing by Stevenson; © 1983 The New Yorker Magazine, Inc.
259 Buick Motor Division
260 © Michael Gamer; University of Bristol, England
261 Suncom
263 © Thomas Pfundel, *Bild der Wissenschaft*

264 Hochtemperatur-Reaktorbau
265 Atlantic Richfield Company
267 Argonne National Laboratory
269 Herman H. Torres, NYT Pictures
270 Rockwell International
272 Institute of Animal Physiology, Agricultural Research Council, Cambridge, England
273 Baylor College of Medicine
275 K. William Mopper, D.D.S.
276 Tribune Media Services, Inc.
277 Hank Morgan © 1984 *Discover* Magazine, Time Inc.
278 Stuart Houston, M.D., University of Saskatchewan
279 Ken Sexton*
280 Ronald H. Williams
281 Charles A. Engh, M.D.
283 Robert London Moore, Jr.
284 Frederick A. Leighton, New York State College of Veterinary Medicine
285 Sidney Harris
286 Russell C. Schnell, University of Colorado; Michael R. Brown, Gamma/Liaison
288 Imperial Chemical Industries
291 Pat Smith, College of Agriculture, University of Georgia
292 Larry McCann*
295 Oak Ridge National Laboratory
296 CERN
297 University of Chicago
300 Lawrence Berkeley Laboratory, University of California
301 Stanford University
302 United Technologies Research Center
303 Tribune Media Services, Inc.
305 R. Epstein
311 NASA
312 NASA/ESA
313–315 NASA
316 Reinhardt Kristensen, Smithsonian Institution
317 Thomas Eisner
318 Jessie Cohen, National Zoological Park
319 Christopher Springman, © National Geographic Society
320 Health Science Center, University of Texas
321 George Suyeoka*
323 AT&T Information Systems; Radio Shack, a Division of Tandy Corporation; George Suyeoka*
325 George Suyeoka*
327 Larry McCann*; George Suyeoka*
330 Adapted from U.S. Department of Health and Human Services data; George Suyeoka*
333–335 George Suyeoka*
336 Dick Weisgrau*
337 Terry Arthur*; Jim Crictenden
338–342 Terry Arthur*
343 Jim Crictenden
344 Terry Arthur*
345 Gwendolyn R. Morgan
346 Terry Arthur*
347 Doug Dornacker
348 Terry Arthur*
349 Lourdes M. Morales
350 Dick Weisgrau*
353 Dick Weisgrau*; A. Podzorski from Ruth Patrick; A. Podzorski from Ruth Patrick
355 Pennsylvania Power & Light Company; Du Pont Company
356–359 Dick Weisgrau*
360 Academy of Natural Sciences of Philadelphia
361 Dick Weisgrau*
363 © Edward S. Ross